ODDITIES and CURIOSITIES
of WORDS and LITERATURE

(Gleanings for the Curious)

BY

C. C. BOMBAUGH

EDITED AND ANNOTATED

BY

MARTIN GARDNER

DOVER PUBLICATIONS, INC.
NEW YORK

Published in Canada by General Publishing Company, Ltd., 30 Lesmill Road, Don Mills, Toronto, Ontario.

Published in the United Kingdom by Constable and Company, Ltd., 10 Orange Street, London W. C. 2.

This new Dover edition, first published in 1961, is an unabridged and unaltered republication of the first 310 pages and the chapters on Refractory Rhyming and Conformity of Sense to Sound of *Gleanings for the Curious from the Harvest-Fields of Literature,* third edition, published in 1890 by J. B. Lippincott Company.

This new Dover edition also contains a new Introduction and Notes by Martin Gardner.

Standard Book Number: 486-20759-5
Library of Congress Catalog Card Number *61-2008*

Manufactured in the United States of America
Dover Publications, Inc.
180 Varick Street
New York, N. Y. 10014

INTRODUCTION

Charles Carroll Bombaugh (1828–1906) surely must have been, to those who knew him, a more whimsical fellow than one would gather from the few dull facts that are known about him. He graduated from Harvard in 1850, obtained a degree from Jefferson Medical College, Philadelphia, in 1853, and served during the Civil War as a medical officer for a Philadelphia brigade. After the war he settled in Baltimore where, because of bad health, he gave up general practice to become a journalist and author. A dozen insurance companies kept him on their payroll as a doctor, and for 33 years he edited *The Baltimore Underwriter*, an insurance journal that he founded.

Bombaugh's principal works are: *The Book of Blunders*, 1871 (a collection of funny typographical errors); *Gleanings for the Curious from the Harvest Fields of Literature*, 1874; and *The Literature of Kissing*, 1876 (382 pages of history, anecdote, and literary allusion). In 1896 he co-authored a lengthy treatise on *Stratagems and Conspiracies to Defraud Life Insurance Companies*. Three years later a fire wrecked the plant of J. B. Lippincott Company, publisher of *Gleanings*, and the book's plates were destroyed. Rather than reset a fat book of 864 pages, the firm asked Bombaugh to write a smaller one on similar topics. The result was *Facts and Fancies for the Curious*. It was published in 1905, a year before Bombaugh's death.

The chapters reprinted here are from the third and last revision (in 1890) of *Gleanings for the Curious*, Bombaugh's most popular book. They were chosen because they deal with language "curiosities" in the stricter sense of the term. This can be explained by listing the topics of some chapters not included here: proverbs and other lore about the weather, origins of familiar things, historical anecdotes, quaint customs, epigrams, sources of familiar quotations, valentines, epitaphs, curious inscriptions, and so on. These chapters are interesting, but they have only a slim connection with the language oddities that are the subject matter of chapters selected for this book.

Many readers will shake their heads sadly at the thought of how much talent and energy has been wasted on such trivialities. Very clever indeed, I can hear them say, but of course these linguistic puzzles have nothing whatever to do with serious literature. Perhaps so, but one of the curiosities of twentieth century letters is the appearance of precisely these puzzle elements in the work of writers who wish very much to be taken seriously. It all began, I suppose, with the experimental poetry of such movements as Dadaism and Italian futurism, and reached a crescendo of obscurity in the writings of Gertrude Stein, E. E. Cummings, and James Joyce. Is *Finnegans Wake* a great work of literature, not yet appreciated outside a small circle of discerning readers? Or is it simply, to borrow two of its own phrases, a huge "Jabberwocky joke" of "pure chingchong idiotism with any way words all in one soluble"?

Edmund Wilson has called *Finnegans Wake* "... a very great poem, one of the top works of literature of our time ... exhibiting Joyce's musical genius as perhaps none of his other books does." On the other hand we find Paul Elmer More writing in 1935 that he cannot comprehend how any man capable of writing the last scene of "The Dead" (that magnificent final story in *Dubliners*) could "posture through the linguistic impertinences" of *Finnegans Wake*. H. G. Wells wrote to Joyce: "You have in your composition a mighty genius for expression which has escaped discipline. . . . So I ask: Who the hell is this Joyce who demands so many waking hours of the few thousands I have still to live for a proper appreciation of his quirks and fancies?" And Joyce's friend Oliver St. John Gogarty, the Buck Mulligan of *Ulysses*, has recorded his honest belief that the worshippers of Joyce are "the victims of a gigantic hoax, of one of the most enormous leg-pulls in history."

I raise the question here because it is one of the most fascinating problems in contemporary criticism, and one that is closely tied to the subject matter of Bombaugh's book. No one who has seriously studied *Finnegans Wake* can doubt the genius behind it. It is filled with poetry, humor, gigantic myth and intricate symbolism. Joyce worked eighteen years on the book and it is not hard to believe that every syllable was put there with careful attention to its place in the vast architecture of the whole. On the other hand, in what sense is there an aesthetic gain in having to spend hours on every page, solving curious and complicated and sometimes very private little word puzzles in order to unearth some of the meanings that Joyce intended his words on that page to have? It will not do to argue that only in this way could Joyce convey the dark mysterious atmosphere of Earwicker's dream, for no man ever dreamed in endless verbal conundrums of the sort that make every page of *Finnegans Wake* such an exasperating challenge.

No one has expressed the critics' dilemma better than Thornton Wilder. In a little essay on Joyce in *Poetry* magazine, March, 1941, he pictures Joyce as a man torn with unresolved love and hate towards his youth, the Catholic Church, the role of the artist, Dublin, and language itself. "We cannot know yet," Wilder writes, "whether hate has buried this conception under the debris of language analyzed to dust or whether love through identification with human history, through the laughter of the comic genius, and through the incomparable musicality of its style, has won the greatest triumph of all."

Truth sometimes has a way of being dull. There are all sorts of alternatives between the horns in Wilder's statement; and I, not being a critic, dare to suspect that posterity will find *Finnegans Wake* an eccentric mixture of good and bad, of literary values and banal word play such as Bombaugh collated in this volume. "You pays your money," as Clifton Fadiman was the first to say, "and you takes your Joyce."

I am much indebted to two outstanding creators of word puzzles, Dmitri Borgmann of Oak Park, Illinois, and Leigh Mercer of London, for invaluable help in preparing my notes on Bombaugh's text. Aside from their files and my own, the references that I found most useful are the following books: *Handy-Book of Literary Curiosities*, William S. Walsh, 1892; *Curiosities of the English Language*, Little Blue Book No. 1350, and *Fascinating Pastimes with Words*, Little Blue Book No. 1433, both by Lloyd E. Smith, both undated; *Words: Tricks and Traditions*, J. Newton Friend, 1957; *Naming Day in Eden*, Noah J. Jacobs, 1958; and *The Little Book of Word Tricks*, Frank Mittler, 1958. Other references will be cited in the notes.

The Enigma, official organ of the National Puzzlers' League, is a monthly periodical devoted exclusively to word puzzles. It has been published interruptedly since 1912. Complete *Enigma* files are available in the library of the Franklin Institute, Philadelphia. Members of the League contribute to *The Enigma* under various pseudonyms (Mr. Mercer's, for example, is the palindromic name *Roger G. M'Gregor*) and it is by these names that members address each other at local meetings and national conventions. Mr. Bryan was kind enough to look over my notes and offer valuable corrections.

Among many friends who have suggested appropriate material for the notes I wish particularly to thank Stephen Barr, Everett Bleiler, and Gershon Legman. My wife has done her usual chore of helpful editing and proofing.

MARTIN GARDNER

Dobbs Ferry, N.Y.
February, 1960

Contents.

Alphabetical Whims.

Palindromes.

Equivoque.

The Cento.

Macaronic Verse.

Chain Verse.

Bouts Rimes.

Emblematic Poetry.

Monosyllables.

The Bible.

The Name of God.

I. H. S.

The Lord's Prayer.

Ecclesiasticæ.

Puritan Peculiarities.

Paronomasia.

English Words and Forms of Expression.

Tall Writing.

Metric Prose.

The Humors of Versification.

Echo Verse.

Puzzles.

Refractory Rhyming.

Conformity of Sense to Sound.

Notes.

Alphabetical Whims.

LIPOGRAMMATA AND PANGRAMMATA.

IN No. 59 of the Spectator, Addison, descanting on the different species of false wit, observes, "The first I shall produce are the Lipogrammatists, or letter droppers of antiquity, that would take an exception, without any reason, against some particular letter in the alphabet, so as not to admit it once in a whole poem. One Tryphiodorus was a great master in this kind of writing. He composed an Odyssey, or Epic Poem, on the adventures of Ulysses, consisting of four-and-twenty-books, having entirely banished the letter A from his first book, which was called *Alpha*, (as *lucus a non lucendo*,) because there was not an alpha in it. His second book was inscribed *Beta*, for the same reason. In short, the poet excluded the whole four-and-twenty letters in their turns, and showed them that he could do his business without them. It must have been very pleasant to have seen this Poet avoiding the reprobate letter as much as another would a false quantity, and making his escape from it, through the different Greek dialects, when he was presented with it in any particular syllable; for the most apt and elegant word in the whole language was rejected, like a diamond with a flaw in it, if it appeared blemished with the wrong letter."

In No. 63, Addison has again introduced Tryphiodorus, in his Vision of the Region of False Wit, where he sees the phantom of this poet pursued through the intricacies of a dance by four-and-twenty persons, (representatives of the alphabet,) who are unable to overtake him.

Addison should, however, have mentioned that Tryphiodorus is kept in countenance by no less an authority than Pindar, who, according to Athenæus, wrote an ode from which the letter *sigma* was carefully excluded.

This caprice of Tryphiodorus has not been without its imitators. Peter de Riga, a canon of Rheims, wrote a summary of the Bible in twenty-three sections, and throughout each section omitted, successively, some particular letter.

Gordianus Fulgentius, who wrote " De Ætatibus Mundi et Hominis," has styled his book a wonderful work, chiefly, it may be presumed, from a similar reason; as from the chapter on Adam he has excluded the letter A; from that on Abel, the B; from that on Cain, the C; and so on through twenty-three chapters.

Gregorio Letti presented a discourse to the Academy of Humorists at Rome, throughout which he had purposely omitted the letter R, and he entitled it *the exiled R.* A friend having requested a copy as a literary curiosity, (for so he considered this idle performance,) Letti, to show it was not so difficult a matter, replied by a copious answer of seven pages, in which he observed the same severe ostracism against the letter R.

Du Chat, in the "Ducatiana," says "there are five novels in prose, of Lope de Vega, similarly avoiding the vowels; the first without A, the second without E, the third without I, the fourth without O, and the fifth without U."

The Orientalists are not without this literary folly. A Persian poet read to the celebrated Jami a ghazel of his own composition, which Jami did not like; but the writer replied it was, notwithstanding, a very curious sonnet, for the letter *Aliff* was not to be found in any of the words! Jami sarcastically answered, "You can do a better thing yet; take away *all the letters* from every word you have written."

This alphabetical whim has assumed other shapes, sometimes taking the form of a fondness for a particular letter. In the *Ecloga de Calvis* of Hugbald the Monk, all the words begin with a C. In the Nugæ Venales there is a Poem by Petrus Placentius, entitled Pugna Porcorum, in which every word begins with a P. In another performance in the same work, entitled *Canum cum cattis certamen*, in which "apt alliteration's artful aid" is similarly summoned, every word begins with a C.

Lord North, one of the finest gentlemen in the Court of James I., has written a set of sonnets, each of which begins with a successive letter of the alphabet. The Earl of Rivers, in the reign of Edward IV., translated the Moral Proverbs of Christiana of Pisa, a poem of about two hundred lines, almost all the words of which he contrived to conclude with the letter E.

The Pangrammatists contrive to crowd all the letters of the alphabet into every single verse. The prophet Ezra may be regarded as the father of them, as may be seen by reference to ch. vii., v. 21, of his Book of Prophecies. Ausonius, a Roman poet of the fourth century, whose verses are characterized by great mechanical ingenuity, is fullest of these fancies.

The following sentence of only 48 letters, contains every letter of the alphabet:—*John P. Brady, give me a black walnut box of quite a small size.*

The stanza subjoined is a specimen of both lipogrammatic and pangrammatic ingenuity, containing every letter of the alphabet except *e*. Those who remember that *e* is the most indispensable letter, being much more frequently used than any other,* will perceive the difficulty of such composition.

---

* The relative proportions of the letters, in the formation of words, have been pretty accurately determined, as follows:—

A 85	E 120	I 80	M 30	Q 5	U 34	Y 20
B 16	F 25	J 4	N 80	R 62	V 12	Z 2
C 30	G 17	K 8	O 80	S 80	W 20	
D 44	H 64	L 40	P 17	T 90	X 4	

> A jovial swain may rack his brain,
>   And tax his fancy's might,
> To quiz in vain, for 'tis most plain,
>   That what I say is right.

The *Fate of Nassan* affords another example, each stanza containing the entire alphabet except *e*, and composed, as the writer says, with *ease* without *e's*.

> Bold Nassan quits his caravan,
> A hazy mountain-grot to scan;
> Climbs jaggy rocks to spy his way,
> Doth tax his sight, but far doth stray.

> Not work of man, nor sport of child,
> Finds Nassan in that mazy wild;
> Lax grow his joints, limbs toil in vain—
> Poor wight! why didst thou quit that plain?

> Vainly for succor Nassan calls.
> Know, Zillah, that thy Nassan falls:
> But prowling wolf and fox may joy
> To quarry on thy Arab boy.

LORD HOLLAND, after reading the five Spanish novels already alluded to, in 1824, composed the following curious example, in which all the vowels except E are omitted:—

EVE'S LEGEND.

Men were never perfect; yet the three brethren Veres were ever esteemed, respected, revered, even when the rest, whether the select few, whether the mere herd, were left neglected.

The eldest's vessels seek the deep, stem the element, get pence; the keen Peter, when free, wedded Hester Green,—the slender, stern, severe, erect Hester Green. The next, clever Ned, less dependent, wedded sweet Ellen Heber. Stephen, ere he met the gentle Eve, never felt tenderness: he kept kennels, bred steeds, rested where the deer fed, went where green trees, where fresh breezes, greeted sleep. There he met the meek, the gentle Eve: she tended her sheep, she ever neglected self: she never heeded pelf, yet she heeded the shepherds even less. Nevertheless, her cheek reddened when she met Stephen; yet decent reserve, meek respect, tempered her speech, even when she shewed tenderness. Stephen felt the sweet effect: he felt he erred when he fled the sex, yet felt he defenceless when Eve seemed tender. She, he reflects, never deserved neglect; she never vented spleen; he esteems her gentleness, her endless deserts; he reverences her steps; he greets her :—

"Tell me whence these meek, these gentle sheep,—whence the yet meeker, the gentler shepherdess?"

"Well bred, we were eke better fed, ere we went where reckless men seek fleeces. There we were fleeced. Need then rendered me shepherdess, need renders me sempstress. See me tend the sheep; see me sew the wretched shreds. Eve's need preserves the steers, preserves the sheep; Eve's needle mends her dresses, hems her sheets; Eve feeds the geese; Eve preserves the cheese."

Her speech melted Stephen, yet he nevertheless esteems, reveres her. He bent the knee where her feet pressed the green; he blessed, he begged, he pressed her.

"Sweet, sweet Eve, let me wed thee; be led where Hester Green, where Ellen Heber, where the brethren Vere dwell. Free cheer greets thee there; Ellen's glees sweeten the refreshment; there severer Hester's decent reserve checks heedless jests. Be led there, sweet Eve!"

"Never! we well remember the Seer. We went where he dwells—we entered the cell—we begged the decree,—

' Where, whenever, when, 'twere well
Eve be wedded? Eld Seer, tell.'

"He rendered the decree; see here the sentence decreed!" Then she presented Stephen the Seer's decree. The verses were these:—

" *Ere the green reed be red,*
Sweet Eve, be never wed ;
Ere be green the red cheek,
Never wed thee, Eve meek."

The terms perplexed Stephen, yet he jeered the terms; he resented the senseless credence, " Seers never err." Then he repented, knelt, wheedled, wept. Eve sees Stephen kneel; she relents, yet frets when she remembers the Seer's decree. Her dress redeems her. These were the events:—

Her well-kempt tresses fell; sedges, reeds, bedecked them. The reeds fell, the edges met her cheeks; her cheeks bled. She presses the green sedge where her cheek bleeds. Red then bedewed the green reed, the green reed then speckled her red cheek. The red cheek seems green, the green reed seems red. These were e'en the terms the Eld Seer decreed Stephen Vere.

HERE ENDETH THE LEGEND.

ALPHABETICAL ADVERTISEMENT.

TO WIDOWERS AND SINGLE GENTLEMEN.—
WANTED by a lady, a SITUATION to superintend the household and preside at table. She is Agreeable, Becoming, Careful, Desirable, English, Facetious, Generous, Honest, In-

dustrious, Judicious, Keen, Lively, Merry, Natty, Obedient, Philosophic, Quiet, Regular, Sociable, Tasteful, Useful, Vivacious, Womanish, Xantippish, Youthful, Zealous, &c. Address X. Y. Z., Simmond's Library, Edgeware-road.—*London Times*, 1842.

JACOBITE TOAST.

THE following remarkable toast is ascribed to Lord Duff, and was presented on some public occasion in the year 1745.

A. B. C. . . .	A Blessed Change.
D. E. F. . . .	Down Every Foreigner.
G. H. J. . . .	God Help James.
K. L. M. . . .	Keep Lord Marr.
N. O. P. . . .	Noble Ormond Preserve.
Q. R. S. . . .	Quickly Resolve Stewart.
T. U. V. W. . .	Truss Up Vile Whigs.
X. Y. Z. . . .	'Xert Your Zeal.

THE THREE INITIALS.

THE following couplet, in which initials are so aptly used, was written on the alleged intended marriage of the Duke of Wellington, at a very advanced age, with Miss Angelina Burdett Coutts, the rich heiress :—

> The Duke must in his second childhood be,
> Since in his doting age he turns to A. B. C.

ENIGMAS.

THE letter E is thus enigmatically described :—

> The beginning of eternity,
>   The end of time and space,
> The beginning of every end,
>   The end of every place.

The letter M is concealed in the following Latin enigma by an unknown author of very ancient date :

> Ego sum principium mundi et finis seculorum:
> Ego sum trinus et unus, et tamen non sum Deus.

THE LETTER H.

THE celebrated enigma on the letter H, commonly attributed to Lord Byron,* is well known. The following amusing petition is addressed by this letter to the inhabitants of Kidderminster, England—*Protesting*:

> Whereas by you I have been driven
> From 'ouse, from 'ome, from 'ope, from 'eaven,
> And placed by your most learned society
> In Hexile, Hanguish, and Hanxiety;
> Nay, charged without one just pretence,
> With Harrogance and Himpudence—
> I here demand full restitution,
> And beg you'll mend your Helocution.

Rowland Hill, when at college, was remarkable for the frequent wittiness of his observations. In a conversation on the powers of the letter H, in which it was contended that it was no letter, but a simple aspiration or breathing, Rowland took the opposite side of the question, and insisted on its being, to all intents and purposes, a *letter;* and concluded by observing that, if it were not, it was a very serious affair to him, as it would occasion his being ILL all the days of his life.

When Kohl, the traveller, visited the Church of St. Alexander Nevskoi, at St. Petersburg, his guide, pointing to a corner of the building, said, " *There lies a Cannibal.* " Attracted to the tomb by this strange announcement, Kohl found from the inscription that it was the Russian general Hannibal; but as the Russians have no H,† they change the letter into K; and hence the strange misnomer given to the deceased warrior.

---

* Now known to have been written by Miss Catherine Fanshawe.

† The Sandwich Island alphabet has twelve letters; the Burmese, nineteen; the Italian, twenty; the Bengalese, twenty-one; the Hebrew, Syriac, Chaldee, and Samaritan, twenty-two each; the French, twenty-three; the Greek, twenty-four; the Latin, twenty-five; the German, Dutch, and English, twenty-six each; the Spanish and Sclavonic, twenty-seven each; the Arabic, twenty-eight; the Persian and Coptic, thirty-two; the Georgian, thirty-five; the Armenian, thirty-eight; the Russian, forty-one; the Muscovite, forty-three; the Sanscrit and Japanese, fifty; the Ethiopic and Tartarian, two hundred and two each.

A city knight, who was unable to aspirate the H, on being deputed to give King William III. an address of welcome, uttered the following equivocal compliment :—

"Future ages, recording your Majesty's exploits, will pronounce you to have been *a Nero!*"

Mrs. Crawford says she wrote one line in her song, *Kathleen Mavourneen,* for the express purpose of confounding the cockney warblers, who sing it thus :—

The 'orn of the 'unter is 'eard on the 'ill.

Moore has laid the same trap in the *Woodpecker:*—

A 'eart that is 'umble might 'ope for it 'ere.

And the elephant *confounds* them the other way :—

A helephant heasily heats at his hease,
Hunder humbrageous humbrella trees.

ON THE MARRIAGE OF A LADY TO A GENTLEMAN NAMED GEE.

Sure, madam, by your choice a taste we see :
What's good or great or grand without a G ?
A godly glow must sure on G depend,
Or oddly low our righteous thoughts must end :
The want of G all gratitude effaces ;
And without G, the Graces would run races.

ON SENDING A PAIR OF GLOVES.

From this small token take the letter G,
And then 'tis love, and that I send to thee.

UNIVOCALIC VERSES.

A.—THE RUSSO-TURKISH WAR.

Wars harm all ranks, all arts, all crafts appall :
At Mars' harsh blast, arch, rampart, altar, fall !
Ah ! hard as adamant, a braggart Czar
Arms vassal swarms, and fans a fatal war !
Rampant at that bad call, a Vandal band
Harass, and harm, and ransack Wallach-land.
A Tartar phalanx Balkan's scarp hath past,
And Allah's standard falls, alas ! at last.

E.—THE FALL OF EVE.

Eve, Eden's Empress, needs defended be;
The Serpent greets her when she seeks the tree.
Serene, she sees the speckled tempter creep;
Gentle he seems,—perversest schemer deep,—
Yet endless pretexts ever fresh prefers,
Perverts her senses, revels when she errs,
Sneers when she weeps, regrets, repents she fell;
Then, deep revenged, reseeks the nether hell!

I.—THE APPROACH OF EVENING.

Idling, I sit in this mild twilight dim,
Whilst birds, in wild, swift vigils, circling skim.
Light winds in sighing sink, till, rising bright,
Night's Virgin Pilgrim swims in vivid light!

O.—INCONTROVERTIBLE FACTS.

No monk too good to rob, or cog, or plot.
No fool so gross to bolt Scotch collops hot.
From Donjon tops no Oronoko rolls.
Logwood, not Lotos, floods Oporto's bowls.
Troops of old tosspots oft, to sot, consort.
Box tops, not bottoms, school-boys flog for sport.
No cool monsoons blow soft on Oxford dons,
Orthodox, jog-trot, book-worm Solomons!
Bold Ostrogoths, of ghosts no horror show.
On London shop-fronts no hop-blossoms grow.
To crocks of gold no dodo looks for food.
On soft cloth footstools no old fox doth brood.
Long storm-tost sloops forlorn, work on to port.
Rooks do not roost on spoons, nor woodcocks snort,
Nor dog on snow-drop or on coltsfoot rolls,
Nor common frogs concoct long protocols.

U.—THE SAME SUBJECT, CONTINUED.

Dull humdrum murmurs lull, but hubbub stuns.
Lucullus snuffs up musk, mundungus shuns.
Puss purrs, buds burst, bucks butt, luck turns up trumps;
But full cups, hurtful, spur up unjust thumps.

———

A young English lady, on observing a gentleman's lane newly
planted with lilacs, made this neat impromptu :—

Let lovely lilacs line Lee's lonely lane.

5

6

ALPHABETICAL ALLITERATION.

THE SIEGE OF BELGRADE.

An Austrian army, awfully arrayed,
Boldly, by battery, besieged Belgrade;
Cossack commanders cannonading come—
Dealing destruction's devastating doom;
Every endeavor, engineers essay,
For fame, for fortune—fighting furious fray :—
Generals 'gainst generals grapple—gracious God!
How honors Heaven, heroic hardihood!
Infuriate,—indiscriminate in ill,
Kindred kill kinsmen,—kinsmen kindred kill!
Labor low levels loftiest longest lines—
Men march 'mid mounds, 'mid moles, 'mid murderous mines :
Now noisy, noxious, noticed nought
Of outward obstacles opposing ought :
Poor patriots, partly purchased, partly pressed :
Quite quaking, quickly quarter, quarter quest,
Reason returns, religious right redounds,
Suwarrow stops such sanguinary sounds.
Truce to thee, Turkey—triumph to thy train!
Unjust, unwise, unmerciful Ukraine!
Vanish vain victory, vanish victory vain!
Why wish ye warfare? Wherefore welcome were
Xerxes, Ximenes, Xanthus, Xaviere?
Yield! ye youths! ye yeomen, yield your yell!
Zeno's, Zapater's, Zoroaster's zeal,
And all attracting—arms against acts appeal.

THE BUNKER HILL MONUMENT CELEBRATION.

Americans arrayed and armed attend;
Beside battalions bold, bright beauties blend.
Chiefs, clergy, citizens conglomerate,—
Detesting despots,—daring deeds debate;
Each eye emblazoned ensigns entertain,—
Flourishing from far,—fan freedom's flame.
Guards greeting guards grown grey,—guest greeting guest.
High-minded heroes, hither, homeward, haste.
Ingenuous juniors join in jubilee,
Kith kenning kin,—kind knowing kindred key.
Lo, lengthened lines lend Liberty liege love,
Mixed masses, marshaled, *Monumentward* move.

Note noble navies near,—no novel notion,—
Oft our oppressors overawed old Ocean;
Presumptuous princes, pristine patriots paled,
Queens' quarrel questing quotas, quondam quailed.
Rebellion roused, revolting ramparts rose.
Stout spirits, smiting servile soldiers, strove.
These thrilling themes, to thousands truly told,
Usurpers' unjust usages unfold.
Victorious vassals, vauntings vainly veiled,
Where, whilesince, Webster, warlike Warren wailed.
'Xcuse 'xpletives 'xtra-queer 'xpressed,
Yielding Yankee yeomen zest.

PRINCE CHARLES PROTECTED BY FLORA MACDONALD.

All ardent acts affright an Age abased
By brutal broils, by braggart bravery braced.
Craft's cankered courage changed Culloden's cry;
"Deal deep" deposed "deal death"—"decoy," "defy:"
Enough. Ere envy enters England's eyes,
Fancy's false future fades, for Fortune flies.
Gaunt, gloomy, guarded, grappling giant griefs,
Here, hunted hard, his harassed heart he heaves;
In impious ire incessant ills invests,
Judging Jove's jealous judgments, jaundiced jests!
Kneel, kirtled knight! keep keener kingcraft known,
Let larger lore life's levelling lessons loan:
Marauders must meet malefactors' meeds;
No nation noisy non-conformists needs.
O oracles of old! our orb ordain
Peace's possession—Plenty's palmy plain!
Quiet Quixotic quests; quell quarrelling;
Rebuke red riot's resonant rifle ring.
Slumber seems strangely sweet since silence smote
The threatening thunders throbbing through their throat.
Usurper! under uniform unwont
Vail valor's vaguest venture, vainest vaunt.
Well wot we which were wise. War's wildfire won
Ximenes, Xerxes, Xavier, Xenophon:
Yet you, ye yearning youth, *your* young years yield
Zuinglius' zealot zest—Zinzendorf zion-zealed.

CACOPHONOUS COUPLET ON CARDINAL WOLSEY.

Begot by butchers, but by bishops bred,
How high his honor holds his haughty head!

ADDRESS TO THE AURORA, WRITTEN IN MID-OCEAN.

Awake Aurora! and across all airs
By brilliant blazon banish boreal bears.
Crossing cold Canope's celestial crown,
Deep darts descending dive delusive down.
Entranced each eve Europa's every eye
Firm fixed forever fastens faithfully,
Greets golden guerdon gloriously grand;
How Holy Heaven holds high his hollow hand!
Ignoble ignorance, inapt indeed—
Jeers jestingly just Jupiter's jereed:
Knavish Kamschatkans, knightly Kurdsmen know,
Long Labrador's light lustre looming low;
Midst myriad multitudes majestic might
No nature nobler numbers Neptune's night.
Opal of Oxus or old Ophir's ores
Pale pyrrhic pyres prismatic purple pours,—
Quiescent quivering, quickly, quaintly queer,
Rich, rosy, regal rays resplendent rear;
Strange shooting streamers streaking starry skies
Trail their triumphant tresses—trembling ties.
Unseen, unhonored Ursa,—underneath
Veiled, vanquished—vainly vying—vanisheth:
Wild Woden, warning, watchful—whispers wan
Xanthitic Xeres, Xerxes, Xenophon,
Yet yielding yesternight yule's yell yawns
Zenith's zebraic zigzag, zodiac zones.

Pulci, in his *Morgante Maggiore*, xxiii. 47, gives the following remarkable double alliterations, two of them in every line:—

La *casa cosa* parea *bretta* e *brutta,*
Vinta dal *vento,* e la *natta* e la *notte,*
Stilla le *stelle,* ch'a *tetto* era *tutta,*
Del *pane* appena ne *dette* ta' *dotte;*
Pere avea *pure* e qualche *fratta frutta,*
E *svina* e *svena* di *botto* una *botte;*
Poscia per *pesci lasche* prese all'*esca,*
Ma il *letto* al*lotta* alla *frasca* fu*fresca.*

In the imitation of Laura Matilda, in the *Rejected Addresses* occurs this stanza:—

Pan beheld Patroclus dying,
Nox to Niobe was turned;
From Busiris Bacchus flying,
Saw his Semele inurned.

TITLE-PAGE FOR A BOOK OF EXTRACTS FROM MANY AUTHORS.

Astonishing Anthology from Attractive Authors.
Broken Bits from Bulky Brains
Choice Chunks from Chaucer to Channing.
Dainty Devices from Diverse Directions.
Echoes of Eloquence from Eminent Essayists.
Fragrant Flowers from Fields of Fancy.
Gems of Genius Gloriously Garnished.
Handy Helps from Head and Heart.
Illustrious Intellects Intelligently Interpreted.
Jewels of Judgment and Jets of Jocularity.
Kindlings to Keep from the King to the Kitchen.
Loosened Leaves from Literary Laurels.
Magnificent Morsels from Mighty Minds.
Numerous Nuggets from Notable Noodles.
Oracular Opinions Officiously Offered.
Prodigious Points from Powerful Pens.
Quirks and Quibbles from Queer Quarters.
Rare Remarks Ridiculously Repeated.
Suggestive Squibs from Sundry Sources.
Tremendous Thoughts on Thundering Topics.
Utterances from Uppermost for Use and Unction.
Valuable Views in Various Voices.
Wisps of Wit in a Wilderness of Words.
Xcellent Xtracts Xactly Xpressed.
Yawnings and Yearnings for Youthful Yankees.
Zeal and Zest from Zoroaster to Zimmerman.

COMPLIMENTARY CONSIDERATIONS CONCERNING CHESS.

Cherished chess! The charms of thy checkered chambers chain me changelessly. Chaplains have chanted thy charming choiceness; chieftains have changed the chariot and the chase for the chaster chivalry of the chess-board, and the cheerier charge of the chess-knights. Chaste-eyed Caissa! For thee are the chaplets of chainless charity and the chalice of childlike cheerfulness. No chilling churl, no cheating chafferer, no chattering changeling, no chanting charlatan can be thy champion; the chivalrous, the charitable, and the cheerful are the chosen ones thou cherishest. Chance cannot change thee: from the cradle of childhood to the charnel-house, from our first childish chirpings to the chills of the church-yard, thou art our cheery, changeless chieftainess. Chastener of the churlish, chider of the changeable, cherisher of the chagrined, the chapter of thy chiliad of charms should be chanted in cherubic chimes by choicest choristers, and chiselled on chalcedon in cherubic chirography.

Hood, in describing the sensations of a dramatist awaiting his debut, thus uses the letter F in his Ode to Perry:—

> All Fume and Fret,
> Fuss, Fidget, Fancy, Fever, Funking, Fright,
> Ferment, Fault-fearing, Faintness—more F's yet:
> Flushed, Frigid, Flurried, Flinching, Fitful, Flat,
> Add Famished, Fuddled, and Fatigued to that;
> Funeral, Fate-Foreboding.

The repetition of the same letter in the following is very ingenious:—

FELICITOUS FLIGHT OF FANCY.

"A famous fish-factor found himself father of five flirting females—Fanny, Florence, Fernanda, Francesca, and Fenella. The first four were flat-featured, ill-favored, forbidding-faced, freckled frumps, fretful, flippant, foolish, and flaunting. Fenella was a fine-featured, fresh, fleet-footed fairy, frank, free, and full of fun. The fisher failed, and was forced by fickle fortune to forego his footman, forfeit his forefathers' fine fields, and find a forlorn farm-house in a forsaken forest. The four fretful females, fond of figuring at feasts in feathers and fashionable finery, fumed at their fugitive father. Forsaken by fulsome, flattering fortune-hunters, who followed them when first they flourished, Fenella fondled her father, flavored their food, forgot her flattering followers, and frolicked in a frieze without flounces. The father, finding himself forced to forage in foreign parts for a fortune, found he could afford a faring to his five fondlings. The first four were fain to foster their frivolity with fine frills and fans, fit to finish their father's finances; Fenella, fearful of flooring him, formed a fancy for a full fresh flower. Fate favored the fish-factor for a few days, when he fell in with a fog; his faithful Filley's footsteps faltered, and food failed. He found himself in front of a fortified fortress. Finding it forsaken, and feeling himself feeble, and forlorn with fasting, he fed on the fish, flesh, and fowl he found, fricasseed, and when full fell flat on the floor. Fresh in the forenoon, he forthwith flew to the fruitful fields, and not forgetting Fenella, he filched a fair flower; when a foul, frightful, fiendish figure flashed forth: 'Felonious fellow, fingering my flowers, I'll finish you! Fly; say farewell to your fine felicitous family, and face me in a fortnight!' The faint-hearted fisher fumed and faltered, and fast and far was his flight. His five daughters flew to fall at his feet and fervently felicitate him. Frantically and fluently he unfolded his fate. Fenella, forthwith fortified by filial fondness, followed her father's footsteps, and flung her faultless form at the foot of the frightful figure, who forgave the father, and fell flat on his face, for he had fervently fallen in a fiery fit of love for the fair Fenella. He feasted her till, fascinated by his faithfulness, she forgot the ferocity of his face, form, and features, and frankly and fondly fixed Friday, fifth of February, for the affair to come off. There was festivity, fragrance, finery, fireworks, fricasseed frogs, fritters, fish, flesh, fowl, and frumentry, frontignac, flip, and fare fit for the fastidious; fruit, fuss, flambeaux, four fat fiddlers and fifers; and the frightful form of the fortunate and frumpish fiend fell from him, and he fell at Fenella's feet a fair-favored, fine, frank, freeman of the forest. Behold the fruits of filial affection.

A BEVY OF BELLES.

The following lines are said to have been admirably descriptive of the five daughters of an English gentleman, formerly of Liverpool:—

Minerva-like majestic Mary moves.
Law, Latin, Liberty, learned Lucy loves.
Eliza's elegance each eye espies.
Serenely silent Susan's smiles surprise.
From fops, fools, flattery, fairest Fanny flies.

MOTIVES TO GRATITUDE.

A remarkable example of the old fondness for antithesis and alliteration in composition, is presented in the following extract from one of Watts' sermons :—

The last great help to thankfulness is to compare various circumstances and things together. Compare, then, your sorrows with you sins; compare your mercies with your merits; compare your comforts with your calamities; compare your own troubles with the troubles of others; com pare your sufferings with the sufferings of Christ Jesus, your Lord; compare the pain of your afflictions with the profit of them; compare your chastisements on earth with condemnation in hell; compare the present hardships you bear with the happiness you expect hereafter, and try whether all these will not awaken thankfulness.

ACROSTICS. 7

THE acrostic, though an old and favorite form of verse, in our own language has been almost wholly an exercise of ingenuity, and has been considered fit only for trivial subjects, to be classed among *nugæ literariæ*. The word in its derivation includes various artificial arrangements of lines, and many fantastic conceits have been indulged in. Generally the acrostic has been formed of the first letters of each line; sometimes of the last; sometimes of both; sometimes it is to be read downward, sometimes upward. An ingenious variety called the Telestich, is that in which the letters beginning the lines spell a word, while the letters ending the lines, when taken together, form a word of an opposite meaning, as in this instance :—

U nite and untie are the same—so say yo U.
N ot in wedlock, I ween, has this unity bee N.
I n the drama of marriage each wandering *gou T*
T o a new face would fly—all except you and I—
E ach seeking to alter the *spell* in their scen E.

In these lines, on the death of Lord Hatherton, (1863), the initial and final letters are doubled :—

H ard was his final fight with ghastly Deat *h,*
H e bravely yielded his expiring breat *h.*
A s in the Senate fighting freedom's ple *a,*
A nd boundless in his wisdom as the se *a.*
T he p u b l i c welfare seeking to direc *t,*
T he weak and undefended to protec *t.*
H is steady course in noble life from birt *h,*
H as shown his public and his private wort *h.*
E vincing mind both lofty and sedat *e,*
E ndowments great and fitted for the Stat *e,*
R eceiving high and low with open doo *r,*
R ich in his bounty to the rude and poo *r.*
T he crown reposed in him the highest trus *t,*
T o show the world that he was wise and jus *t.*
O n his a n c e s t r a l banners long ag *o,*
O urs willingly relied, and will do s *o.*
N or yet extinct is noble H a t h e r t o *n,*
N ow still he lives in gracious Littleto *n.*

Although the fanciful and trifling tricks of poetasters have been carried to excess, and acrostics have come in for their share of satire, the origin of such artificial poetry was of a higher dignity. When written documents, were yet rare, every artifice was employed to enforce on the attention or fix on the memory the verses sung by bards or teachers. Alphabetic associations formed obvious and convenient aids for this purpose. In the Hebrew Psalms of David, and in other parts of Scripture, striking specimens occur. The peculiarity is not retained in the translations, but is indicated in the common version of the 119th Psalm by the initial letters prefixed to its divisions. The Greek Anthology also presents examples of acrostics, and they were often used in the old Latin language. Cicero, in his treatise " De Divinatione," has this remarkable passage :—"The verses of the Sybils (said he) are distinguished by that arrangement which the Greeks call Acrostic; where, from the first letters of each verse in order, words are formed which express some particular meaning; as is the case with some of Ennius's verses, the initial letters of which make ' which Ennius wrote !' "

Among the modern examples of acrostic writing, the most remarkable may be found in the works of Boccaccio. It is a poem of fifty cantos, of which Guinguenè has preserved a specimen in his Literary History of Italy.

A successful attempt has recently been made to use this form of verse for conveying useful information and expressing agreeable reflections, in a volume containing a series of acrostics on eminent names, commencing with Homer, and descending chronologically to our own time. The alphabetic necessity of the choice of words and epithets has not hindered the writer from giving distinct and generally correct character to the biographical subjects, as may be seen in the following selections, which are as remarkable for the truth and discrimination of the descriptions as for the ingenuity of the diction :

GEORGE HERBERT.

G ood Country Parson, cheerful, quaint,
E ver in thy life a saint,
O 'er thy memory sweetly rise
R are old Izaak's eulogies,
G iving us, in life-drawn hue,
E ach loved feature to our view.

H oly Herbert, humble, mild,
E 'en as simple as a child,
R eady thy bounty to dispense,
B eaming with benevolence,
E ver blessing, ever blest,
R escuing the most distrest ;
T hy "Temple" now is Heaven's bright rest.

DRYDEN.

D eep rolls on deep in thy majestic line.
R ich music and the stateliest march combine;
Y et, who that hears its high harmonious strain
D eems not thy genius thou didst half profane?
E xhausting thy great power of song on themes
N ot worthy of its strong, effulgent beams.

REYNOLDS.

R are Painter! whose unequall'd skill could trace
E ach light and shadow of the changeful face;
Y oung "Samuel's," now, beaming with piety,
N ow the proud "Banished Lord's" dark misery,
O r "Ugolino's" ghastly visage, wild,
L ooking stern horror on each starving child;
D elights not less of social sort were thine,
S uch as with Burke, or e'en with Johnson shine.

BURKE.

B rilliant thy genius 'mongst a brilliant throng;
U nique thy eloquence of pen and tongue;
R ome's Tully loftier flights could scarce command,
K indling thy soul to thoughts that matchless stand
E ver sublime and beautiful and grand.

HUBER.

H ow keen thy vision, e'en though reft of sight!
U sing with double power the mind's clear light:
B ees, and their hives, thy curious ken has scanned.
E ach cell, with geometric wisdom planned,
R ich stores of honeyed knowledge thus at thy command.

CRABBE.

C opyist of Nature—simply, sternly true,—
R eal the scenes that in thy page we view.
"A mid the huts where poor men lie" unknown,
B right humor or deep pathos thou hast thrown.
B ard of the "Borough" and the "Village," see—
E 'en haughty Byron owns he's charm'd by thee.

WALTER SCOTT.

W ondrous Wizard of the North,
A rmed with spells of potent worth!
L ike to that greatest Bard of ours
T he mighty magic of thy powers:
E 'en thy bright fancy's offspring find
R esemblance to his myriad mind.

S uch the creations that we see—
C haracter, manners, life in thee—
O f Scotia's deeds, a proud display,
T he glories of a bygone day;
T hy genius foremost stands in all her long array.

WORDSWORTH.

W andering, through many a year, 'mongst Cumbria's hills,
O 'er her wild fells, sweet vales, and sunny lakes,
R ich stores of thought thy musing mind distils,
D ay-dreams of poesy thy soul awakes:—
S uch was thy life—a poet's life, I ween;
W orshipper thou of Nature! every scene
O f beauty stirred thy fancy's deeper mood,
R eflection calmed the current of thy blood:
T hus in the wide "Excursion" of thy mind,
H igh thoughts in *words* of *worth* we still may find.

IRVING.

I n easy, natural, graceful charm of style,
R esembling Goldy's "Vicar,"—free from guile:
V ein of rich humor through thy "Sketch-Book" flows.
I magination her bright colors shows.
N o equal hast thou 'mongst thy brother band,
G enial thy soul, worthy our own loved land.

MACREADY.

M aster Tragedian! worthy all our praise.
A ction and utterance such as bygone days
C ould oftener boast, were thine. Need we but name
R oman Virginius? while our Shakspeare's fame
E ver 'twas thy chief joy and pride to uprear,
A nd give us back Macbeth, Othello, Lear.
D elight to thousands oft thou gav'st, and now
Y ears of calm lettered ease 'tis thine to know.

LONGFELLOW.

L ays like thine have many a charm;
O ft thy themes the heart must warm.
N ow o'er Slavery's guilt and woes,
G rief and shame's deep hues it throws;
F ar up Alpine heights is heard
"E xcelsior," now the stirring word;
"L ife's Psalm," now, onward is inviting,
   L ongings for nobler deeds exciting;
   O 'er Britain now resounds thy name,
   W hile States unborn shall swell thy fame.

SOUTHEY.

S erenely bright thy life's pure stream did glide,
O n sweet romantic Derwentwater's side.
U nder great Skiddaw—there, in Epic lays,
T hou dream'dst a poet's dreams of olden days,
H ow Madoc wandered o'er the Atlantic wave,
E astern Kehama, Roderic the brave,
Y ears cannot from our fondest memory lave.

MACAULAY.

M asterly critic! in whose brilliant style
A nd rich historic coloring breathes again—
C lothed in most picturesque costume the while—
A ll the dim past, with all its bustling train.
U nder this vivid, eloquent painting, see
L ife given anew to our old history's page;
A nd in thy stirring ballad poetry,
Y outh's dreams of ancient Rome once more our minds engage.

OLIVER'S IMPROMPTU.

OLIVER, a sailor and patriot, with a merited reputation for extempore rhyming, while on a visit to his cousin Benedict Arnold, after the war, was asked by the latter to amuse a party of English officers with some extemporaneous effusion, whereupon he stood up and repeated the following Ernulphus curse, which would have satisfied Dr. Slop* himself:—

B orn for a curse to virtue and mankind,
E arth's broadest realm ne'er knew so black a mind.
N ight's sable veil your crimes can never hide,
E ach one so great, 'twould glut historic tide.
D efunct, your cursed memory will live
I n all the glare that infamy can give.
C urses of ages will attend your name,
T raitors alone will glory in your shame.

A lmighty vengeance sternly waits to roll
R ivers of sulphur on your treacherous soul:
N ature looks shuddering back with conscious dread
O n such a tarnished blot as she has made.
L et hell receive you, riveted in chains,
D oomed to the hottest focus of its flames.

---

* Tristram Shandy.

ALLITERATIVE ACROSTIC.

THE following alliterative acrostic is a gem in its way. Miss Kitty Stephens was the celebrated London vocalist, and is now the Dowager Countess of Essex :—

S he sings so soft, so sweet, so soothing still
T hat to the tone ten thousand thoughts there thrill ;
E lysian ecstasies enchant each ear—
P leasure's pure pinions poise—prince, peasant, peer,
H ushing high hymns, Heaven hears her harmony,—
E arth's envy ends ; enthralled each ear, each eye ;
N umbers need ninefold nerve, or nearly name,
S oul-stirring STEPHENS' skill, sure seraphs sing the same.

CHRONOGRAMMATIC PASQUINADE.

ON the election of Pope Leo X., in 1440, the following satirical acrostic appeared, to mark the date

M C C C C X L.

Multi Cœci Cardinales Creaverunt Cœcum Decimum (X) Leonem.

MONASTIC VERSE.

THE merit of this fine specimen will be found in its being at the same time *acrostic, mesostic,* and *telestic.*

Inter cuncta micans   Igniti   sidera   cœlI
Expellit tenebras   E toto Phœbus ut orbE ;
Sic cæcas removet   JESUS caliginis umbraS,
Vivificansque simul   Vero præcordia motV,
Solem justitiæ   Sese probat esse beatiS.

The following translation preserves the acrostic and mesostic, though not the telestic form of the original :—

In glory see the rising sun,   Illustrious orb of day,
Enlightening heaven's wide expanse,   Expel night's gloom away.
So light into the darkest soul,   JESUS, Thou dost impart,
Uplifting Thy life-giving smiles   Upon the deadened heart :
Sun Thou of Righteousness Divine,   Sole King of Saints Thou art.

THE figure of a FISH carved on many of the monuments in the Roman Catacombs, is an emblematic acrostic, intended formerly to point out the burial-place of a Christian, without revealing the fact to the pagan persecutors. The Greek word for *fish* is *ἰχθὺς*, which the Christians understood to mean *Jesus Christ, the Son of God, the Saviour,*—the letters forming the initials of the following Greek words:—

> *Ιησους*— Jesus
> *Χριστος*—Christ,
> *Θεου*— of God,
> *Υιος*— Son,
> *Σωτηρ*— Saviour.

NAPOLEON FAMILY.

THE names of the male crowned heads of the extinct Napoleon dynasty form a remarkable acrostic:—

> N apoleon, Emperor of the French.
> I oseph, King of Spain.
> H ieronymus, King of Westphalia.
> I oachim, King of Naples.
> L ouis, King of Holland.

RACHEL.

RACHEL, on one occasion, received a most remarkable present. It was a diadem, in antique style, adorned with six jewels. The stones were so set as to spell, in acrostic style, the name of the great *artiste*, and also to signify six of her principal *rôles*, thus:

R uby,	R oxana,
A methyst,	A menaide,
C ornelian,	C amille,
H ematite,	H ermione,
E merald,	E milie,
L apis Lazuli,	L aodice.

This mode of constructing a name or motto by the initial letters of gems was formerly fashionable on wedding rings.

MASONIC MEMENTO.

THE following curious memento was written in the early part of last century :—

M—Magnitude, Moderation, Magnanimity.
A—Affability, Affection, Attention.
S—Silence, Secrecy, Security.
O—Obedience, Order, Œconomy.
N—Noble, Natural, Neighborly.
R—Rational, Reciprocative, Receptive.
Y—Yielding, Ypight (fixed), Yare (ready).

Which is explained thus :—

Masonry, of things, teaches how to attain their just	Magnitude.
To inordinate affections the art of - - -	Moderation.
It inspires the soul with true - - -	Magnanimity.
It also teaches us - - - - -	Affability.
To love each other with true - - -	Affection,
And to pay to things sacred a just - - -	Attention.
It instructs us how to keep - - -	Silence,
To maintain - - - - - -	Secrecy,
And preserve - - - - - -	Security ;
Also, to whom it is due, - - - -	Obedience,
To observe good - - - - -	Order,
And a commendable - - - -	Œconomy.
It likewise teaches us how to be worthily -	Noble,
Truly - - - - - - -	Natural,
And without reserve - - - -	Neighborly.
It instils principles indisputably - -	Rational,
And forms in us a disposition - - -	Reciprocative,
And - - - - - - -	Receptive.
It makes us, to things indifferent, - -	Yielding,
To what is absolutely necessary, perfectly -	Ypight,
And to do all that is truly good, most willingly	Yare.

HEMPE.

BACON says, " The trivial prophecy which I heard when I was a child and Queen Elizabeth was in the flower of her years was—

When Hempe is spun
England's done;

whereby it was generally conceived that after the sovereigns had reigned which had the letters of that word HEMPE, (which were Henry, Edward, Mary, Philip, Elizabeth,) England should come to utter confusion; which, thanks be to God, is verified in the change of the name, for that the King's style is now no more of *England*, but of *Britain*."

THE BREVITY OF HUMAN LIFE.

Behold, alas! our days we spend:
How vain they be, how soon they end!

BEHOLD

How short a span
Was long enough of old
To measure out the life of man;
In those well-tempered days his time was then
Surveyed, cast up, and found but threescore years and ten.

ALAS!

What is all that?
They come and slide and pass
Before my tongue can tell thee what.
The posts of time are swift, which having run
Their seven short stages o'er, their short-lived task is done.

OUR DAYS

Begun, we bend
To sleep, to antic plays
And toys, until the first stage end;
12 waning moons, twice 5 times told, we give
To unrecovered loss: we rather breathe than live.

WE SPEND

A ten years' breath
Before we apprehend
What 'tis to live in fear of death;
Our childish dreams are filled with painted joys
Which please our sense, and waking prove but toys.

HOW VAIN,

How wretched is
Poor man, that doth remain
A slave to such a state as this!
His days are short at longest; few at most;
They are but bad at best, yet lavished out, or lost.

THEY BE

The secret springs
That make our minutes flee
On wings more swift than eagles' wings!
Our life's a clock, and every gasp of breath
Breathes forth a warning grief, till time shall strike a death.

HOW SOON

Our new-born light
Attains to full-aged noon!
And this, how soon to gray-haired night;
We spring, we bud, we blossom, and we blast,
Ere we can count our days, our days they flee so fast.

THEY END
When scarce begun,
And ere we apprehend
That we begin to live, our life is done.
Man, count thy days; and if they fly too fast
For thy dull thoughts to count, count every day the last.

A VALENTINE.

THE reader, by taking the first letter of the first of the following lines, the second letter of the second line, the third of the third, and so on to the end, can spell the name of the lady to whom they were addressed by Edgar A. Poe.

For her this rhyme is penned whose luminous eyes,
BRightly expressive as the twins of Lœda,
ShAll find her own sweet name, that nestling lies
UpoN the page, enwrapped from every reader.
SearCh narrowly the lines!—they hold a treasure
DivinE—a talisman—an amulet
That muSt be worn *at heart.* Search well the measure—
The wordS—the syllables! Do not forget
The triviAlest point, or you may lose your labor!
And yet theRe is in this no Gordian knot
Which one miGht not undo without a sabre,
If one could mErely comprehend the plot.
Enwritten upoN the leaf where now are peering
Eyes scintillaTing soul, there lie *perdus*
Three eloquent wOrds, oft uttered in the hearing
Of poets, by poets—aS the name's a poet's, too.
Its letters, althouGh naturally lying
Like the knight PintO—Mendez Ferdinando—
Still form a synonym fOr Truth. Cease trying!
You will not read the riDdle, though you do the best you *can do.*

ANAGRAMS. 8

But with still more disordered march advance
(Nor march it seemed, but wild fantastic dance)
The uncouth Anagrams, distorted train,
Shifting in double mazes o'er the plain.—*Scribleriad.*

CAMDEN, in a chapter in his *Remains,* on this frivolous and now almost obsolete intellectual exercise, defines Anagrams to be a dissolution of a name into its letters, as its elements; and a new connection into words is formed by their transposition, if possible, without addition, subtraction, or change of the letters: and the words should make a sentence applicable to the person or thing named. The anagram is complimentary or satirical; it may contain some allusion to an event, or describe some personal characteristic. Thus, Sir Thomas Wiat bore his own designation in his name:—

Wiat—A Wit.

Astronomer may be made *Moon-starer*, and *Telegraph*, *Great Help*. *Funeral* may be converted into *Real Fun*, and *Presbyterian* may be made *Best in prayer*. In *stone* may be found *tones*, *notes*, or *seton*; and (taking *j* and *v* as duplicates of *i* and *u*) the letters of the alphabet may be arranged so as to form the words *back*, *frown'd*, *phlegm*, *quiz*, and *Styx*. *Roma* may be transposed into *amor*, *armo*, *Maro*, *mora*, *oram*, or *ramo*. The following epigram occurs in a book printed in 1660:

Hate and debate Rome through the world has spread;
Yet Roma *amor* is, if backward read:
Then is it strange Rome hate should foster? No;
For out of backward *love* all hate doth grow.

It is said that the cabalists among the Jews were professed anagrammatists, the third part of their art called *themuru* (changing) being nothing more than finding the hidden and mystical meaning in names, by transposing and differently combining the letters of those names. Thus, of the letters of *Noah's* name in Hebrew, they made *grace*; and of the *Messiah* they made *he shall rejoice*.

Lycophron, a Greek writer who lived three centuries before the Christian era, records two anagrams in his poem on the siege of Troy entitled *Cassandra*. One is on the name of Ptolemy Philadelphus, in whose reign Lycophron lived:—

ΠΤΟΛΕΜΑΙΣ. ΑΠΟ ΜΕΛΙΤΟΣ—Made of honey.

The other is on Ptolemy's queen, Arsinoë:—

ΑΡΣΙΝΟΕ. ΕΡΑΣ ΙΟΝ—Juno's violet.

Eustachius informs us that this practice was common among the Greeks, and gives numerous examples ; such, for instance, as the transposition of the word *Αρετη*, virtue, into *Ερατη*, lovely.

Owen, the Welsh epigrammatist, sometimes called the British Martial, lived in the golden age of anagrammatism. The following are fair specimens of his ingenuity :—

GALENUS—ANGELUS.

Angelus es bonus anne malus; *Galene !* salutis
Humana custos, *angelus* ergo bonus,

DE FIDE—ANAGRAMMA QUINCUPLEX.

Recta fides, *certa* est, *arcet* mala schismata, non est,
Sicut *Creta*, fides fictilis, arte *caret.*

BREVITAS—ANAGRAMMA TRIPLEX.

Perspicua brevitate nihil magis afficit aures
In *verbis, ubi res* postulat, esto *brevis.*

In a *New Help to Discourse,* 12mo, London, 1684, occurs an anagram with a very quaint epigrammatic "exposition :"—

TOAST—A SOTT.

A toast is like a sot; or, what is most
Comparative, a sot is like a toast;
For when their substances in liquor sink,
Both properly are said to be in drink.

Cotton Mather was once described as distinguished for—

" Care to guide his flock and feed his lambs
By words, works, prayers, psalms, alms, *and anagrams.*"

Sylvester, in dedicating to his sovereign his translation of Du Bartas, rings the following loyal change on the name of his liege :—

James Stuart—A just master.

Of the poet Waller, the old anagrammatist said :—

His brows need not with *Lawrel* to be bound,
Since in his name with *Lawrel* he is crowned.

The author of an extraordinary work on heraldry was thus expressively complimented :—

Randle Holmes.
Lo, Men's Herald !

The following on the name of the mistress of Charles IX. of France is historically true :—

Marie Touchet,
Je charme tout.

In the assassin of Henry III.,

Frère Jacques Clement,

they discovered

C'est l'enfer qui m'a créé.

The French appear to have practised this art with peculiar facility. A French poet, deeply in love, in one day sent his mistress, whose name was *Magdelaine,* three dozen of anagrams on her single name.

The father Pierre de St. Louis became a Carmelite monk on discovering that his lay name—

Ludovicus Bartelcmi—

yielded the anagram—

Carmelo se devovet.

Of all the extravagances occasioned by the anagrammatic fever when at its height, none equals what is recorded of an infatuated Frenchman in the seventeenth century, named André Pujom, who, finding in his name the anagram *Pendu à Riom,* (the seat of criminal justice in the province of Auvergne,) felt impelled to fulfill his destiny, committed a capital offence in Auvergne, and was actually hung in the place to which the omen pointed.

The anagram on General Monk, afterwards Duke of Albemarle, on the restoration of Charles II., is also a chronogram, including the date of that important event :—

Georgius Monke, Dux de Aumarle,
Ego Regem reduxi Ano. Sa. MDCLVV.

The mildness of the government of Elizabeth, contrasted with her intrepidity against the Iberians, is thus picked out of her title : she is made the English lamb and the Spanish lioness.

Elizabetha Regina Angliæ,
Anglis Agna, Hiberiæ Lea.

The unhappy history of Mary Queen of Scots, the depriva-
tion of her kingdom, and her violent death, are expressed in
the following Latin anagram :—

> Maria Steuarda Scotorum Regina.
> Trusa vi Regnis, morte amara cado.

In Taylor's *Suddaine Turne of Fortune's Wheele,* occurs the
following very singular example :—

> But, holie father, I am certifyed
> That they your power and policye deride;
> And how of you they make an anagram,
> The best and bitterest that the wits could frame.

> As thus :
> *Supremus Pontifex Romanus.*
> Annagramma :
> *O non sum super petram fixus.*

The anagram on the well-known bibliographer, William
Oldys, may claim a place among the first productions of this
class. It was by Oldys himself, and was found by his execu-
tors among his MSS.

> In word and WILL I AM a friend to you;
> And one friend OLD IS worth a hundred new.

The following anagram, preserved in the files of the First
Church in Roxbury, was sent to Thomas Dudley, a governor
and major-general of the colony of Massachusetts, in 1645.
He died in 1653, aged 77.

> THOMAS DUDLEY.
> Ah ! old must dye.
> A death's head on your hand you neede not weare,
> A dying head you on your shoulders beare.
> You need not one to mind you, you must dye,
> You in your name may spell mortalitye.
> Younge men may dye, but old men, these dye must;
> 'Twill not be long before you turne to dust.
> Before you turne to dust! ah! must! old! dye!
> What shall younge doe when old in dust doe lye?
> When old in dust lye, what N. England doe?
> When old in dust doe lye, it's best dye too.

In an Elegy written by Rev. John Cotton on the death of John Alden, a magistrate of the old Plymouth Colony, who died in 1687, the following *phonetic* anagram occurs :—

John Alden—End al on hi.

The Calvinistic opponents of Arminius made of his name a not very creditable Latin anagram:—

Jacobus Arminius,
Vani orbis amicus;
(The friend of a false world.)

while his friends, taking advantage of the Dutch mode of writing it, *H*arminius, hurled back the conclusive argument,

Habui curam Sionis.
(I have had charge of Zion.)

Perhaps the most extraordinary anagram to be met with, is that on the Latin of Pilate's question to the Saviour, " What is truth ?"—St. John, xviii. 38.

Quid est veritas?
Est vir qui adest.
(It is the man who is before you.)

Live, vile, and evil, have the self-same letters;
He lives but vile, whom evil holds in fetters.

If you transpose what ladies wear—VEIL,
'Twill plainly show what bad folks are—VILE.
Again if you transpose the same,
You'll see an ancient Hebrew name—LEVI.
Change it again, and it will show
What all on earth desire to do—LIVE.
Transpose the letters yet once more,
What bad men do you'll then explore—EVIL.

9

PERSIST.

A lady, being asked by a gentleman to join in the bonds of matrimony with him, wrote the word " STRIPES," stating at the time that the letters making up the word stripes could be changed so as to make an answer to his question. The result proved satisfactory.

When *I cry that I sin* is transposed, it is clear,
My resource *Christianity* soon will appear.

The two which follow are peculiarly appropriate :—

Florence Nightingale,	John Abernethy,
Flit on, cheering angel.	Johnny the bear.

TIME
ITEM
METI
EMIT

This word, Time, is the only word in the English language
which can be thus arranged, and the different transpositions
thereof are all at the same time Latin words. These words, in
English as well as in Latin, may be read either upward or
downward. Their signification as Latin words is as follows :—
Time—fear thou; Item—likewise; Meti—to be measured;
Emit—he buys.

Some striking German and Latin anagrams have been made
of Luther's name, of which the following are specimens.
Doctor Martinus Lutherus transposed, gives *O Rom, Luther
ist der schwan.* In D. Martinus Lutherus may be found *ut
turris das lumen* (like a tower you give light). In Martinus
Lutherus we have *vir multa struens* (the man who builds up
much), and *ter matris vulnus* (he gave three wounds to the
mother church). Martin Luther will make *lehrt in Armuth*
(he teaches in poverty).

Jablonski welcomed the visit of Stanislaus, King of Poland,
with his noble relatives of the house of Lescinski, to the annual examination of the students under his care, at the gymna-
sium of Lissa, with a number of anagrams, all composed of the
letters in the words *Domus Lescinia.* The recitations closed
with a heroic dance, in which each youth carried a shield inscribed with a legend of the letters. After a new evolution, the
boys exhibited the words *Ades incolumis;* next, *Omnis es
lucida;* next, *Omne sis lucida;* fifthly, *Mane sidus loci;*
sixthly, *Sis columna Dei;* and at the conclusion, *I scande
solium.*

A TELEGRAM ANAGRAMMATISED.

Though but a *late germ*, with a wondrous elation,
Yet like a *great elm* it o'ershadows each station.
Et malgré the office is still a large fee mart,
So joyous the crowd was, you'd thought it a *glee mart;*
But they raged at no news from the nation's belligerent,
And I said *let'm rage*, since the air is refrigerant.
I then *met large* numbers, whose drink was not sherbet,
Who scarce could look up when their eyes the gas-*glare met;*
So when I had learned from commercial adviser
That *mere galt* for sand was the great fertilizer,
I bade *Mr. Eaglet*, although 'twas ideal,
Get some from the clay-pit, and so *get'm real;*
Then, just as my footstep was leaving the portal,
I met an *elm targe* on a great Highland mortal,
With the maid he had woo'd by the loch's flowery *margelet*,
And row'd in his boat, which for rhyme's sake call *bargelet*,
And blithe to the breeze would have set the sail daily,
But it blew at that rate which the sailors *term gale*, aye;
I stumbled against the fair bride he had married,
When a *merle gat* at large from a cage that she carried;
She gave a loud screech! and I could not well blame her,
But lame as I was, I'd no wish to *get lamer;*
So I made my escape—ne'er an antelope fleeter,
Lest my verse, like the poet, should limp through *lag metre.*

Anagrams are sometimes found in old epitaphial inscriptions.
For example, at St. Andrews :—

> Catharine Carstairs,
> *Casta rara Christiana.*
> *Chaste, rare Christian.*

At Newenham church, Northampton :—

> William Thorneton.
> *O little worth in man.*

At Keynsham :—

> Mrs. Joane Flover.
> *Love for anie.*

At Mannington, 1631 :—

> Katherine Lougher,
> *Lower taken higher.*

Maitland has the following curious specimen :—

How much there is in a word—*monastery*, says I : why, that makes *nasty Rome;* and when I looked at it again, it was evidently *more nasty*—a very vile place *or mean sty. Ay, monster,* says I, you are found out. What monster ? said the Pope. What monster ? said I. Why, your own image there, *stone Mary.* That, he replied, is *my one star,* my Stella Maris, my treasure, my guide ! No, said I, you should rather say, *my treason. Yet no arms,* said he. No, quoth I, quiet may suit best, as long as you have *no mastery,* I mean *money arts.* No, said he again, those are *Tory means;* and Dan, *my senator,* will baffle them. I don't know that, said I, but I think one might make no *mean story* out of this one word—*monastery.*

CHRONOGRAMS.

ADDISON, in his remarks on the different species of false wit, (Spect. No. 60,) thus notices the chronogram. "This kind of wit appears very often on modern medals, especially those of Germany, when they represent in the inscription the year in which they were coined. Thus we see on a medal of Gustavus Adolphus the following words :—

CHRISTVs DuX ergo trIVMPhVs.

If you take the pains to pick the figures out of the several words, and range them in their proper order, you will find they amount to MDCXVVVII, or 1627, the year in which the medal was stamped; for as some of the letters distinguish themselves from the rest and overtop their fellows, they are to be considered in a double capacity, both as letters and as figures. Your laborious German wits will turn over a whole dictionary for one of these ingenious devices. A man would think they were searching after an apt classical term; but instead of that they are looking out a word that has an L, an M, or a D, in it. When therefore we meet with any of these in-

scriptions, we are not so much to look in them for the thought
as for the year of the Lord."

Apropos of this humorous allusion to the *Germanesque*
character of the chronogram, it is worthy of notice that Euro-
pean tourists find far more numerous examples of it in the inscriptions on the churches on the banks of the Rhine than in
any other part of the continent.

On the title-page of " *Hugo Grotius his Sophompaneas*,"
the date, 1652, is not given in the usual form, but is included
in the name of the author, thus :—

fraNCIs goLDsMIth.

Howell, in his *German Diet*, after narrating the death of
Charles, son of Philip II. of Spain, says :—

If you desire to know the year, this chronogram will tell you:

fILIVs ante DIeM patrIos InqVIrIt In annos.
MDLVVIIIIIIII, or 1568.

The following commemorates the death of Queen Elizabeth :—

My Day Is Closed In Immortality.   (1603.)

A German book was issued in 1706, containing fac-similes
and descriptions of more than two hundred medals coined in
honor of Martin Luther. An inscription on one of them expresses the date of his death, 1546, as follows :—

ECCe nVnc MorItVs IVstVs In paCe ChrIstI exItV tVto et beato.

The most extraordinary attempt of this kind that has yet
been made, bears the following title :—

*Chronographica Gratulatio in Felicissimum adventum Se-
renissimi Cardinalis Ferdinandi, Hispaniarum Infantis, a
Collegio Soc. Jesu.*

A dedication to St. Michael and an address to Ferdinand are
followed by one hundred hexameters, *every one of which is a
chronogram*, and each gives the same result, 1634. The first
and last verses are subjoined as a specimen.

AngeLe CæLIVogI MIChaëL LUX UnICa CætUs.
VersICULIs InCLUsa, fLUent In sæCULa CentUM.

𝔓alíndromes.   11

RECURRENT, RECIPROCAL, OR REVERSIBLE WORDS AND VERSES.

THE only fair specimen we can find of reciprocal words, or those which, read backwards or forwards, are the same, is the following couplet, which, according to an old book, cost the author a world of foolish labor:—

> Odo tenet mulum, madidam mulum tenet Odo.
> Anna tenet mappam, madidam mappam tenet Anna.

The following admired reciprocal lines, addressed to St. Martin by Satan, according to the legend, the reader will find on perusal, either backwards or forwards, precisely the same:—

> Signa te signa; temere me tangis et angis;
> Roma tibi subito motibus ibit amor.

[St. Martin having given up the profession of a soldier, and having been made Bishop of Tours, when prelates neither kept carriages nor servants, had occasion to go to Rome, in order to consult the Pope upon ecclesiastical matters. As he was walking along the road he met the devil, who politely accosted him, and ventured to observe how fatiguing and indecorous it was for him to perform so long a journey on foot, like the commonest pilgrim. The Saint understood the drift of Old Nick's address, and commanded him immediately to become a beast of burden, or *jumentum;* which the devil did in a twinkling by assuming the shape of a mule. The Saint jumped upon the fiend's back, who at first trotted cheerfully along, but soon slackened his pace. The bishop of course had neither whip nor spurs, but was possessed of a much more powerful stimulus, for, says the legend, he made the sign of the cross, and the smarting devil instantly galloped away. Soon however, and naturally euough, the father of sin returned to sloth and obstinacy, and Martin hurried him again with repeated signs of the cross, till, twitched and stung to the quick by those crossings so hateful to him, the vexed and tired reprobate uttered the foregoing distich in a rage, meaning, *Cross, cross yourself; you annoy and vex me without necessity; for owing to my exertions, Rome, the object of your wishes, will soon be near.*]

The Palindrome changes the sense in the backward reading; the *Versus Cancrinus* retains the sense in both instances unchanged, as in this instance:—

> Bei Leid lieh stets Heil die Lieb.
> (In trouble comfort is lent by love.)

Similarly recurrent is the lawyer's motto,—

Si nummi immunis,

translated by Camden, " Give me my fee, I warrant you free."

The Greek inscription on the mosque of St. Sophia, in Constantinople,

Νίψον ἀνομήματα μὴ μόναν ὄψιν,*

presents the same words, whether read from left to right, or from right to left. So also the expressions in English,—

Madam, I'm Adam. (*Adam to Eve.*)

Name no one man.

Able was I ere I saw Elba. (*Napoleon loq.*)

Snug & raw was I ere I saw war & guns.

Red rum did emit revel ere Lever time did murder.

Red root put up to order.

Trash? even interpret Nineveh's art.

Lewd did I live, evil I did dwel.

Draw pupil's lip upward.

This enigmatical line surrounds a figure of the sun in the mosaic pavement of Sa. Maria del Fiori, at Florence:—

En giro torte sol ciclos et rotor igne.

These lines are supposed to be addressed to a young man detained at Rome by a love affair :—

Roma ibi tibi sedes—ibi tibi Amor;

Româ etsi te terret et iste Amor,

Ibi etsi vis te non esse—sed es ibi,

Roma te tenet et Amor.

At Rome you live—at Rome you love;

From Rome that love may you affright,

Although you'd leave, you never move,

For love and Rome both bar your flight.

Dean Swift wrote a letter to Dr. Sheridan, composed of Latin words strung together as mere gibberish but each word, when

---

* Meaning in substance, *Purify the mind as well as the body.*

read backwards, makes passable English. Take for example the following short sentences :—

Mi sana. Odioso ni mus rem. Moto ima os illud dama nam ?
(I'm an ass. O so I do in summer. O Tom, am I so dull, I a mad man ?)

Inscription for a hospital, paraphrased from the Psalms :—

Acide me malo, sed non desola me, medica.

The ingenious Latin verses subjoined are reversible verbally only, not literally, and will be found to embody opposite meanings by commencing with the last word and reading backwards :—

Prospicimus modo, quod durabunt tempore longo,
Fœdera, nec patriæ pax cito diffugiet.

Diffugiet cito pax patriæ, nec fœdera longo,
Tempore durabunt, quod modo prospicimus.

The following hexameter from Santa Marca Novella, Florence, refers to the sacrifice of Abel (Gen. iv. 4). Reversed, it is a pentameter, and refers to the sacrifice of Cain (iv. 3).

Sacrum pingue dabo non macrum sacrificabo,
Sacrificabo macrum non dabo pingue sacrum.

The subjoined distich arose from the following circumstance. A tutor, after having explained to his class one of the odes of Horace, undertook to dictate the same in hexameter verses, as an exercise (as he said). It cost him considerable trouble : he hesitated several times, and occasionally substituted other words, but finally succeeded. Some of his scholars thought he would not accomplish his task ; others maintained that, having begun, it was a point of honor to complete it.

Retro mente labo, non metro continuabo ;
Continuabo metro ; non labo mente retro.

Addison mentions an epigram called the *Witches' Prayer*, that "fell into verse when it was read either backward or forward, excepting only that it cursed one way, and blessed the other."

One of the most remarkable palindromes on record is the following. Its distinguishing peculiarity is that the first letter of each successive word unites to spell the first word; the second letter of each, the second word; and so on throughout; and the same will be found precisely true on reversal.

12   SATOR AREPO TENET OPERA ROTAS.

But the neatest and prettiest specimen that has yet appeared comes from a highly cultivated lady who was attached to the court of Queen Elizabeth. Having been banished from the court on suspicion of too great familiarity with a nobleman then high in favor, the lady adopted this device,—*the moon covered by a cloud*,—and the following palindrome for a motto :—

ABLATA AT ALBA.

(Banished, but blameless.)

The merit of this kind of composition was never in any example so heightened by appropriateness and delicacy of sentiment.

Paschasius composed the recurrent epitaph on Henry IV. :—

Arca serenum me gere regem, munere sacra,
Solem, arcas, animos, omina sacra, melos.

A very curious continuous series of palindromes was printed in Vienna in 1802. It was written in ancient Greek by a modern Greek named Ambrosius, who called it Ποίημα χαρχινιχὸν. It contains 455 lines, every one of which is a literal palindrome. A few are selected at random, as examples :—

Ἴσα πασι Ση τε γη, Συ ὁ Μουσηγετης ις απασι.
Νεαν ασω μελιφωνον, ὦ φιλε, Νωσαν αεν.
Ὦ λακωνικε, σε μονω τω Νομε, σε κινω καλω.
Ἀρετα πηγασε σε σα γη πατερα.
Σωτηρ συ εσο, ὦ ελεε Θεε λεω ος ευς ρητως.

The following line is expressive of the sentiments of a Roman Catholic; read backwards, of those of a Huguenot :—

Patrum dicta probo, nec sacris belligerabo.
Belligerabo sacris, nec probo dicta patrum.

These lines, written to please a group of youthful folk, serve to show that our English tongue is as capable of being twisted into uncouth shapes as is the Latin, if any one will take the trouble:—

One winter's eve, around the fire, a cozy group we sat,
Engaged, as was our custom old, in after-dinner chat;
Small-talk it was, no doubt, because the smaller folk were there,
And they, the young monpolists! absorbed the lion's share.
Conundrums, riddles, rebuses, cross-questions, puns atrocious,
Taxed all their ingenuity, till Peter the precocious—
Old head on shoulders juvenile—cried, "Now for a new task:
Let's try our hand at *Palindromes!*" "Agreed! But first," we ask,
"Pray, Peter, what *are* Palindromes?" The forward imp replied,
"A *Palindrome* 's a string of words of sense or meaning void,
Which reads both ways the same: and here, with your permission,
I'll cite some half a score of samples, lacking all precision
(But held together by loose rhymes, to test my definition):—

"A milksop, jilted by his lass, or wandering in his wits,
Might murmur, '*Stiff, O dairy-man, in a myriad of fits!*'

"A limner by photography dead-beat in competition,
Thus grumbled, '*No, it is opposed ; art sees trade's opposition!*'

"A nonsense-loving nephew might his soldier-uncle dun
With '*Now stop, major-general, are negro jam-pots won?*'

"A supercilious grocer, if inclined that way, might snub
A child with '*But regusa store, babe, rots a sugar-tub.*'

"Thy spectre, Alexander, is a fortress, cried Hephaestion.
Great A. said, '*No, it's a bar of gold, a bad log for a bastion!*'

"A timid creature, fearing rodents—mice and such small fry—
'*Stop, Syrian, I start at rats in airy spots,*' might cry.

"A simple soul, whose wants are few, might say, with hearty zest,
'*Desserts I desire not, so long no lost one rise distressed.*'

"A stern Canadian parent might in earnest, not in fun,
Exclaim, '*No sot nor Ottawa law at Toronto, son!*'

"A crazy dentist might declare, as something strange or new,
That '*Paget saw an Irish tooth, sir, in a waste gap!*' True!

"A surly student, hating sweets, might answer with *elan,*
'*Name tarts? no, medieval slave, I demonstrate man!*'

"He who in Nature's bitters findeth sweet food every day,
'*Eureka! till I pull up ill I take rue,*' well might say."

Equivoque.

COPY OF A LETTER WRITTEN BY CARDINAL RICHELIEU TO THE
FRENCH AMBASSADOR AT ROME.

First read the letter across, then double it in the middle, and read the first column.

Sir,—Mons. Compigne, a Savoyard by birth, | a Friar of the order of Saint Benedict,
is the man who will present to you | as his passport to your protection,
this letter. He is one of the most | discreet, the wisest and the least
meddling persons that I have ever known | or have had the pleasure to converse with.
He has long earnestly solicited me | to write to you in his favor, and
to give him a suitable character, | together with a letter of credence;
which I have accordingly granted to | his real merit, rather I must say, than to
his importunity; for, believe me, Sir, | his modesty is only exceeded by his worth,
I should be sorry that you should be | wanting in serving him on account of being
misinformed of his real character; | I should be afflicted if you were
as some other gentlemen have been, | misled on that score, who now esteem him,
and those among the best of my friends; | wherefore, and from no other motive
I think it my duty to advertise you | that you are most particularly desired,
to have especial attention to all he does, | to show him all the respect imaginable,
nor venture to say any thing before him, | that may either offend or displease him
in any sort; for I may truly say, there is | no man I love so much as M. Compigne,
none whom I should more regret to see | neglected, as no one can be more worthy to be
received and trusted in decent society. | Base, therefore, would it be to injure him.
And I well know, that as soon as you | are made sensible of his virtues, and
shall become acquainted with him | you will love him as I do; and then
you will thank me for this my advice. | The assurance I entertain of your
Courtesy obliges me to desist from | urging this matter to you further, or
saying any thing more on this subject. | Believe me, Sir, &c.

RICHELIEU.

A LOVE-LETTER.

13

The reader, after perusing it, will please read it again, commencing on the first line, then the third and fifth, and so on, reading each alternate line to the end.

To Miss M———.

—The great love I have hitherto expressed for you
is false and I find my indifference towards you
—increases daily. The more I see of you, the more
you appear in my eyes an object of contempt.
—I feel myself every way disposed and determined
to hate you. Believe me, I never had an intention
—to offer you my hand. Our last conversation has
left a tedious insipidity, which has by no means
—given me the most exalted idea of your character.
Your temper would make me extremely unhappy
—and were we united, I should experience nothing but
the hatred of my parents added to the anything but
—pleasure in living with you. I have indeed a heart
to bestow, but I do not wish you to imagine it
—at your service. I could not give it to any one more
inconsistent and capricious than yourself, and less
—capable to do honor to my choice and to my family.
Yes, Miss, I hope you will be persuaded that
—I speak sincerely, and you will do me a favor
to avoid me. I shall excuse you taking the trouble
—to answer this. Your letters are always full of
impertinence, and you have not a shadow of
—wit and good sense. Adieu! adieu! believe me
so averse to you, that it is impossible for me even
—to be your most affectionate friend and humble
servant.   L———.

INGENIOUS SUBTERFUGE.

A young lady newly married, being obliged to show to her husband all the letters she wrote, sent the following to an intimate friend. The key is, to read the first and then every alternate line only.

—I cannot be satisfied, my dearest friend!
blest as I am in the matrimonial state,
—unless I pour into your friendly bosom,
which has ever been in unison with mine,
—the various sensations which swell

with the liveliest emotion of pleasure,
—my almost bursting heart. I tell you my dear
husband is the most amiable of men,
—I have now been married seven weeks, and
never have found the least reason to
—repent the day that joined us. My husband is
both in person and manners far from resembling
—ugly, cross, old, disagreeable, and jealous
monsters, who think by confining to secure—
—a wife, it is his maxim to treat as a
bosom friend and confidant, and not as a
—plaything, or menial slave, the woman
chosen to be his companion. Neither party
—he says, should always obey implicitly;
but each yield to the other by turns.
—An ancient maiden aunt, near seventy,
a cheerful, venerable, and pleasant old lady,
—lives in the house with us; she is the delight of both young and old; she is ci-
—vil to all the neighborhood round,
generous and charitable to the poor.
—I am convinced my husband loves nothing more
than he does me; he flatters me more
—than a glass; and his intoxication
(for so I must call the excess of his love)
—often makes me blush for the unworthiness
of its object, and wish I could be more deserving
—of the man whose name I bear. To
say all in one word, my dear, and to
—crown the whole—my former gallant lover
is now my indulgent husband; my husband
—is returned, and I might have had
a prince without the felicity I find in
—him. Adieu! may you be blest as I am unable to wish that I could be more
—happy.

DOUBLE-FACED CREED.

The following cross-reading from a history of Popery, published in 1679, and formerly called in New England *The
Jesuits' Creed*, will suit either Catholic or Protestant accordingly as the lines are read downward in single columns or
across the double columns :—

Pro fide teneo sana
Affirmat quæ Romana
Supremus quando rex est
Erraticus tum Grex est
Altari cum ornatur
Populus tum beatur
Asini nomen meruit
Missam qui deseruit

Quæ docet Anglicana,
Videntur mihi vana.
Tum plebs est fortunata,
Cum caput fiat papa.
Communio fit inanis,
Cum mensa vina panis.
Hunc morem qui non capit,
Catholicus est et sapit.

I hold for faith
What Rome's church saith,
Where the king is head
The flock's misled,
Where the altar's drest
The people's blest,
He's but an ass
Who shuns the mass,

What England's church allows,
My conscience disavows.
The flock can take no shame,
Who hold the pope supreme.
The worship's scarce divine,
Whose table's bread and wine.
Who their communion flies,
Is Catholic and wise.

REVOLUTIONARY VERSES.

The author of the following Revolutionary double entendre, which originally appeared in a Philadelphia newspaper, is unknown. It may be read in three different ways,—1st. Let the whole be read in the order in which it is written; 2d. Then the lines downward on the left of each comma in every line; and 3d. In the same manner on the right of each comma. By the first reading it will be observed that the Revolutionary cause is condemned, and by the others, it is encouraged and lauded :—

Hark! hark! the trumpet sounds, the din of war's alarms,
O'er seas and solid grounds, doth call us all to arms;
Who for King George doth stand, their honors soon shall shine;
Their ruin is at hand, who with the Congress join.
The acts of Parliament, in them I much delight,
I hate their cursed intent, who for the Congress fight,
The Tories of the day, they are my daily toast,
They soon will sneak away, who Independence boast;
Who non-resistance hold, they have my hand and heart.
May they for slaves be sold, who act a Whiggish part;
On Mansfield, North, and Bute, may daily blessings pour,
Confusion and dispute, on Congress evermore;
To North and British lord, may honors still be done,
I wish a block or cord, to General Washington.

THE HOUSES OF STUART AND HANOVER.

I love with all my heart	The Tory party here
The Hanoverian part	Most hateful do appear
And for that settlement	I ever have denied
My conscience gives consent	To be on James's side
Most righteous is the cause	To fight for such a king
To fight for George's laws	Will England's ruin bring
It is my mind and heart	In this opinion I
Though none will take my part	Resolve to live and die.

Lansdowne MSS. 852

THE NEW REGIME.

The following equivoque was addressed to a republican at the commencement of the French Revolution, in reply to the question, "What do you think of the new constitution?"

A la nouvelle loi	Je veux être fidèle
Je renonce dans l'âme	Au régime ancien,
Comme épreuve de ma foi	Je crois la loi nouvelle
Je crois celle qu'on blâme	Opposée à tout bien ;
Dieu vous donne la paix	Messieurs les démocrats
Noblesse desolée	Au diable allez-vous en ;
Qu'il confonde à jamais	Tous les Aristocrats
Messieurs de l'Assemblée	Ont eux seuls le bon sens.

The newly made law	'Tis my wish to esteem
From my soul I abhor	The ancient regime
My faith to prove good,	I maintain the new code
I maintain the old code	Is opposed to all good.
May God give you peace,	Messieurs Democrats,
Forsaken Noblesse,	To the devil go hence.
May He ever confound	All the Aristocrats
The Assembly all round	Are the sole men of sense.

FATAL DOUBLE MEANING.

Count Valavoir, a general in the French service under Turenne, while encamped before the enemy, attempted one night to pass a sentinel. The sentinel challenged him, and the count answered "*Va-la-voir*," which literally signifies "Go and see." The soldier, who took the words in this sense, indignantly repeated the challenge, and was answered in the same manner, when he fired; and the unfortunate Count fell dead upon the spot,—a victim to the whimsicality of his surname.

A TRIPLE PLATFORM.

Among the memorials of the sectional conflict of 1861–5, is an American platform arranged to suit all parties. The first column is the *Secession ;* the second, the *Abolition* platform ; and the whole, read together, is the Democratic platform :—

Hurrah for	The Old Union
Secession	Is a curse
We fight for	The Constitution
The Confederacy	Is a league with hell
We love	Free speech
The rebellion	Is treason
We glory in	A Free Press
Separation	Will not be tolerated
We fight not for	The negro's freedom
Reconstruction	Must be obtained
We must succeed	At every hazard
The Union	We love
We love not	The negro
We never said	Let the Union slide
We want	The Union as it was
Foreign intervention	Is played out
We cherish	The old flag
The stars and bars	Is a flaunting lie
We venerate	The *heabus corpus*
Southern chivalry	Is hateful
Death to	Jeff Davis
Abe Lincoln	Isn't the Government
Down with	Mob law
Law and order	Shall triumph.

LOYALTY, OR JACOBINISM ?

This piece of amphibology was circulated among the United Irishmen, previous to the Rebellion of 1798. First, read the lines as they stand, then according to the numerals prefixed :—

1. I love my country—but the king,
3. Above all men his praise I sing,
2. Destruction to his odious reign,
4. That plague of princes, Thomas Paine;
5. The royal banners are displayed,
7. And may success the standard aid
6. Defeat and ruin seize the cause
8. Of France her liberty and laws.

NON COMMITTAL.

NEAT EVASION.

Bishop Egerton, of Durham, avoided three impertinent questions by replying as follows:—

1. What inheritance he received from his father?
   "Not so much as he expected."
2. What was his lady's fortune?
   "Less than was reported."
3. What was the value of his living of Ross?
   "More than he made of it."

A PATRIOTIC TOAST.

Most readers will remember the story of a non-committal editor who, during the Presidential canvass of 1872, desiring to propitiate subscribers of both parties, hoisted the ticket of "Gr—— and ——n" at the top of his column, thus giving those who took the paper their choice of interpretations between "Grant and Wilson" and "Greeley and Brown." A story turning on the same style of point—and probably quite as apocryphal—though the author labels it "*historique*"—is told of an army officers' mess in France. A brother-soldier from a neighboring detachment having come in, and a *champenoise* having been uncorked in his honor, "Gentlemen," said the guest, raising his glass, "I am about to propose a toast at once patriotic and political." A chorus of hasty ejaculations and of murmurs at once greeted him. "Yes, gentlemen," coolly proceeded the orator, "I drink to a thing which—an object that—Bah! I will out with it at once. It begins with an *R* and ends with an *e*."

"Capital!" whispers a young lieutenant of Bordeaux promotion. "He proposes the *République*, without offending the old fogies by saying the word."

"Nonsense! He means the *Radicale*," replies the other, an old Captain Cassel.

"Upon my word," says a third, as he lifts his glass, "our friend must mean *la Royauté*."

"I see!" cries a one-legged veteran of Froschweiler: "we drink to *la Revanche*."

In fact the whole party drank the toast heartily, each interpreting it to his liking.

In the hands of a Swift, even so trivial an instance might be made to point a moral on the facility with which, alike in theology and politics—from Athanasian creed to Cincinnati or Philadelphia platform—men comfortably interpret to their own diverse likings some doctrine that "begins with an *R* and ends with an *e*," and swallow it with great unanimity and enthusiasm.

THE HANDWRITING ON THE WALL.

During the war of the Rebellion, a merchant of Milwaukee, who is an excellent hand at sketching, drew most admirably on the wall of his store a negro's head, and underneath it wrote, in a manner worthy of the Delphic oracle, "Dis-Union for eber." Whether the sentence meant loyalty to the Union or not, was the puzzling question which the gentleman himself never answered, invariably stating to the inquirers, "Read it for yourselves, gentlemen." So from that day to this, as the saying goes, "no one knows how dat darkey stood on de war question."

Another question is puzzling the young ladies who attend a Western Female College. It seems that one of them discovered that some person had written on the outer wall of the college, "Young women should set good examples; for young men *will* follow them." The question that is now perplexing the heads of several of the young ladies of the college is, whether the writer meant what he or she (the handwriting was rather masculine) wrote, in a moral sense or in an ironical one.

HOW FRENCH ACTRESSES AVOID GIVING THEIR AGE.

A servant robbed Mlle. Mars of her diamonds one evening while she was at the theatre. Arrested, he was put upon trial, and witnesses were summoned to bear testimony to his guilt. Among these was Mlle. Mars. She was greatly annoyed at this, as, according to the rules of French practice, the witness, after being sworn, gives his age. Now the age of Mlle. Mars was an impenetrable mystery, for it was a theme she never alluded to, and she possessed the art of arresting time's flight, or at least of repairing its ravages so effectually that her face never revealed acquaintance with more than twenty years. She was for some days evidently depressed; then, all at once, her spirits rose as buoyant as ever. This puzzled the court—for people in her eminent position always have a court; parasites are plenty in Paris— they did not know whether she had determined frankly to confess her age, or whether she had hit upon some means of eluding this thorny point of practice.

The day of trial came, and she was at her place. The court-room was filled, and when she was put in the witness-box every ear was bent towards her to catch the age she would give as her own. "Your name?" said the presiding judge. "Anne Francoise Hippolyte Mars." "What is your profession?" "An actress of the French Comedy." "What is your age?" "——ty years." "What?" inquired the presiding judge, leaning forward. "I have just told your honor!" replied the actress, giving one of those irresistible smiles which won the most hostile pit. The judge smiled in turn, and when he asked, as he did immediately, "Where do you live?" hearty applause long prevented Mlle. Mars from replying.

Mlle. Cico was summoned before a court to bear witness in favor of some cosmetic assailed as a poison by victims and their physicians. All the youngest actresses of Paris were there, and they reckoned upon a good deal of merriment and profit when Mlle. Cico came to disclose her age. She was called to the stand—sworn—gave her name and profession. When the judge said "How old are you?" she quitted the stand, went up to the bench, stood on tip-toe, and whispered in the judge's ear the malicious mystery. The bench smiled, and kept her secret.

The Cento.

14

A CENTO primarily signifies a cloak made of patches. In poetry it denotes a work wholly composed of verses, or passages promiscuously taken from other authors and disposed in a new form or order, so as to compose a new work and a new meaning. According to the rules laid down by Ausonius, the author of the celebrated *Nuptial Cento*, the pieces may be taken from the same poet, or from several; and the verses may be either taken entire, or divided into two, one half to be connected with another half taken elsewhere; but two verses are never to be taken together.

The Empress Eudoxia wrote the life of Jesus Christ in centos taken from Homer. Proba Falconia, and, long after him, Alexander Ross, both composed a life of the Saviour, in the same manner, from Virgil. The title of Ross' work, which was republished in 1769, was *Virgilius Evangelizans, sive historia Domini et Salvatoris nostri Jesu Christi Virgilianis verbis et versibus descripta.*

Subjoined are some modern specimens of this literary confectionery, called in modern parlance

MOSAIC POETRY.

I only knew she came and went   *Lowell.*
    Like troutlets in a pool;   *Hood.*
She was a phantom of delight,   *Wordsworth.*
    And I was like a fool.   *Eastman.*

"One kiss, dear maid," I said and sighed,   *Coleridge.*
    "Out of those lips unshorn."   *Longfellow.*
She shook her ringlets round her head,   *Stoddard.*
    And laughed in merry scorn.   *Tennyson.*

Ring out, wild bells, to the wild sky!   *Tennyson.*
    You hear them, oh my heart?   *Alice Cary.*
'Tis twelve at night by the castle clock,   *Coleridge.*
    Beloved, we must part!   *Alice Cary.*

"Come back! come back!" she cried in grief,   *Campbell.*
    "My eyes are dim with tears—   *Bayard Taylor.*
How shall I live through all the days,   *Mrs. Osgood.*
    All through a hundred years?"   *T. S. Perry*

'Twas in the prime of summer time,   *Hood.*
  She blessed me with her hand;   *Hoyt.*
We strayed together, deeply blest,   *Mrs. Edwards.*
  Into the Dreaming Land.   *Cornwall.*

The laughing bridal roses blow,   *Patmore.*
  To dress her dark brown hair;   *Bayard Taylor.*
No maiden may with her compare,   *Brailsford.*
  Most beautiful, most rare!   *Read.*

I clasped it on her sweet cold hand,   *Browning.*
  The precious golden link;   *Smith.*
I calmed her fears, and she was calm,   *Coleridge.*
  "Drink, pretty creature, drink!"   *Wordsworth.*

And so I won my Genevieve,   *Coleridge.*
  And walked in Paradise;   *Hervey.*
The fairest thing that ever grew   *Wordsworth.*
  Atween me and the skies.   *Osgood.*

———

Breathes there a man with soul so dead,
Who never to himself hath said,
    Shoot folly as it flies?
Ah, more than tears of blood can tell,
Are in that word farewell, farewell;
    'Tis folly to be wise.

And what is Friendship but a name
That burns on Etna's breast of flame?
    Thus runs the world away.
Sweet is the ship that's under sail
To where yon taper points the vale
    With hospitable ray.

Drink to me only with thine eyes
Through cloudless climes and starry skies,
    My native land, good-night.
Adieu, adieu, my native shore;
'Tis Greece, but living Greece no more.
    Whatever is is right.

Oh, ever thus from childhood's hour,
Daughter of Jove, relentless power,
    In russet mantle clad.

The rocks and hollow mountains rung
While yet in early Greece she sung,
   I'm pleased, and yet I'm sad.

In sceptred pall come sweeping by,
O, thou, the nymph with placid eye,
   By Philip's warlike son;
And on the light fantastic toe
Thus hand-in-hand through life we'll go;
   Good-night to Marmion.

LIFE.

1.—Why all this toil for triumphs of an hour?
2.—Life's a short summer, man a flower.

3.—By turns we catch the vital breath and die—
4.—The cradle and the tomb, alas! so nigh.

5.—To be is better far than not to be,
6.—Though all man's life may seem a tragedy.

7.—But light cares speak when mighty griefs are dumb;
8.—The bottom is but shallow whence they come.

9.—Your fate is but the common fate of all,
10.—Unmingled joys, here, to no man befall.

11.—Nature to each allots his proper sphere,
12.—Fortune makes folly her peculiar care.

13.—Custom does not often reason overrule
14.—And throw a cruel sunshine on a fool.

15.—Live well, how long or short permit, to heaven;
16.—They who forgive most, shall be most forgiven.

17.—Sin may be clasped so close we cannot see its face—
18.—Vile intercourse where virtue has not place.

19.—Then keep each passion down, however dear,
20.—Thou pendulum, betwixt a smile and tear;

21.—Her sensual snares let faithless pleasure lay,
22.—With craft and skill, to ruin and betray.

23.—Soar not too high to fall, but stop to rise;
24.—We masters grow of all that we despise.

25.—Oh then renounce that impious self-esteem;
26.—Riches have wings and grandeur is a dream.

27.—Think not ambition wise, because 'tis brave,
28.—The paths of glory lead but to the grave.

29.—What is ambition? 'Tis a glorious cheat,
30.—Only destructive to the brave and great.

31.—What's all the gaudy glitter of a crown?
32.—The way to bliss lies not on beds of down.

33.—How long we live, not years but actions tell;
34.—That man lives twice who lives the first life well.

35.—Make then, while yet ye may, your God your friend,
36.—Whom Christians worship, yet not comprehend.

37.—The trust that's given guard, and to yourself be just;
38.—For, live we how we can, yet die we must.

---

1. Young. 2. Dr. Johnson. 3. Pope. 4. Prior. 5. Sewell. 6. Spenser. 7. Daniel.
8. Sir Walter Raleigh. 9. Longfellow. 10. Southwell. 11. Congreve. 12. Churchill.
13. Rochester. 14. Armstrong. 15. Milton. 16. Baily. 17. Trench. 18. Somerville.
19. Thompson. 20. Byron. 21. Smollet. 22. Crabbe. 23. Massinger. 24. Crowley.
25. Beattie. 26. Cowper. 27. Sir Walter Davenant. 28. Grey. 29. Willis. 30. Addison. 31. Dryden. 32. Francis Quarles. 33. Watkins. 34. Herrick. 35. William Mason. 36. Hill. 37. Dana. 38. Shakespeare.

CENTO FROM POPE.

'Tis education forms the common mind;	*Moral Essays.*
A mighty maze! but not without a plan.	*Essay on Man.*
Ask of the learned the way? The learned are blind;	" "
The proper study of mankind is man.	" "

A little learning is a dangerous thing;	*Essay on Criticism.*
Some have at first for wits, then poets passed—	" "
See from each clime the learned their incense bring,	" "
For rising merit will buoy up at last.	" "

Tell (for you can) what is it to be wise.—	*Essay on Man.*
Virtue alone is happiness below;	" "
Honor and shame from no condition rise,	" "
And all our knowledge is ourselves to know.	" "

Who shall decide when doctors disagree?	*Moral Essay.*
One truth is clear, whatever is, is right.	*Essay on Man.*
Since men interpret texts, why should not we	*January and May.*
Read them by day and meditate by night?	*Essay on Criticism.*

BIBLICAL CENTO.

Cling to the Mighty One,	Ps. lxxxix. 19.
Cling in thy grief;	Heb. xii. 11.
Cling to the Holy One,	Ps. xxxix. 18.
He gives relief;	Ps. lxxxvi. 7.

Cling to the Gracious One,	Ps. cxvi. 5.
Cling in thy pain;	Ps. lv. 4.
Cling to the Faithful One,	1 Thess. v. 24.
He will sustain.	Ps. xxviii. 8.

Cling to the Living One,	Heb. vii. 25.
Cling in thy woe;	Ps. lxxxvi. 7.
Cling to the Loving One,	1 John iv. 16.
Through all below:	Rom. viii. 38, 39.
Cling to the Pardoning One,	Isa. lv. 7.
He speaketh peace;	John xiv. 27.
Cling to the Healing One,	Exod. xv. 26.
Anguish shall cease.	Ps. cxlvii. 3.

Cling to the Bleeding One,	1 John i. 7.
Cling to His side;	John xx. 27.
Cling to the Risen One,	Rom. vi. 9.
In Him abide;	John xv. 4.
Cling to the Coming One,	Rev. xxii. 20.
Hope shall arise;	Titus ii. 13.
Cling to the Reigning One,	Ps. xcvii. 1.
Joy lights thine eyes.	Ps. xvi. 11.

THE RETURN OF ISRAEL.

I will surely gather the remnant of Israel.—MICAH ii. 12.

And the Temple again shall be built,
    And filled as it was of yore;
And the burden be lift from the heart of the world,
    And the nations all adore;
Prayers to the throne of Heaven,
    Morning and eve shall rise,
And unto and not of the Lamb
    Shall be the sacrifice.—FESTUS.

In many strange and Gentile lands	Micah v. 8.
Where Jacob's scattered sons are driven,	Jer. xxiii. 8.
With longing eyes and lifted hands,	Lam. i. 17.
They wait Messiah's sign from heaven.	Matth. xxiv. 30.

The cup of fury they have quaffed,	Isa. li. 17.
Till fainted like a weary flock;	Isa. li. 20.
But Heaven will soon withdraw the draught,	Isa. li. 22.
And give them waters from the rock.	Exod. xvii. 6.

What though their bodies, as the ground,	Isa. li. 23.
Th' Assyrian long has trodden o'er!	Isa. lii. 4.
Zion, a captive daughter bound,	Isa. lii. 2.
Shall rise to know her wrong no more.	Isa. liv. 3, 4.

The veil is passing from her eyes,	2 Cor. iii. 16.
The King of Nations she shall see;	Zech. xiv. 9.
Judea! from the dust arise!	Isa. lii. 2.
Thy ransomed sons return to thee!	Jer. xxxi. 17.
How gorgeous shall thy land appear,	Isa. liv. 12.
When, like the jewels of a bride,	Isa. xlix. 18.
Thy broken bands, all gathered there,	Zech. xi. 14.
Shall clothe thy hills on every side!	Isa. xlix. 18.
When on thy mount, as prophets taught,	Isa. xxiv. 23.
Shall shine the throne of David's Son;	Ezek. xxxvii. 22.
The Gospel's latest triumphs brought	Micah iv. 2.
Where first its glorious course begun.	Luke xxiv. 47.
Gentiles and Kings, who thee oppressed,	Isa. lx. 14.
Shall to thy gates with praise repair;	Isa. lx. 11.
A fold of flocks shall Sharon rest,	Isa. lxv. 10.
And clustered fruits its vineyard bear.	Joel ii. 22.
Then shall an Eden morn illume	Isa. li. 3.
Earth's fruitful vales, without a thorn:	Isa. lv. 13.
The wilderness rejoice and bloom,	Isa. xxxv. 1.
And nations in a day be born.	Zech. ii. 11.
The LORD his holy arm makes bare;	Isa. lii. 10.
Zion! thy cheerful songs employ!	Zeph. iii. 14.
Thy robes of bridal beauty wear,	Isa. lii. 1.
And shout, ye ransomed race, for joy!	Isa. lii. 9.

Macaronic Verse.

"A TREATISE OF WINE."

THE following specimen of macaronic verse, from the commonplace book of Richard Hilles, who died in 1535, is probably the best of its kind extant. The scriptural allusions and the large intermixture of Latin evidently point to the refectory of some genial monastery as its source:—

> The best tree if ye take intent,
> Inter ligna fructifera,
> Is the vine tree by good argument,
> Dulcia ferens pondera.

Saint Luke saith in his Gospel,
  Arbor fructu noscitur,
The vine beareth wine as I you tell,
  Hinc aliis præponitur.

The first that planted the vineyard,
  Manet in cœli gaudio,
His name was Noe, as I am learned,
  Genesis testimonio.

God gave unto him knowledge and wit,
  A quo procedunt omnia,
First of the grape wine for to get,
  Propter magna mysteria.

The first miracle that Jesus did,
  Erat in vino rubeo,
In Cana of Galilee it betide,
  Testante Evangelio.

He changed water into wine,
  Aquæ rubescunt hydriæ,
And bade give it to Archetcline,
  Ut gustet tunc primarie.

Like as the rose exceedeth all flowers,
  Inter cuncta florigera,
So doth wine all other liquors,
  Dans multa salutifera.

David, the prophet, saith that wine
  Lætificat cor hominis,
It maketh men merry if it be fine,
  Est ergo digni nominis.

It nourisheth age if it be good,
  Facit ut esset juvenis,
It gendereth in us gentle blood,
  Nam venas purgat sanguinis.

By all these causes ye should think
  Quæ sunt rationabiles,
That good wine should be best of all drink
  Inter potus potabiles.

Wine drinkers all, with great honor,
  Semper laudate Dominum,
The which sendeth the good liquor
  Propter salutem hominum.

Plenty to all that love good wine,
  Donet Deus largius,
And bring them some when they go hence,
  Ubi non sitient amplius.

THE SUITOR WITH NINE TONGUES.

Τι σοι λεγω, μειρακιον,
Now that this fickle heart is won?
Me semper amaturam te
And never, never, never stray?
Herzschätzchen, Du verlangst zu viel
When you demand so strict a seal.
N'est-ce pas assez que je t'aime
Without remaining still the same?
Gij daarom geeft u liefde niet
If others may not have a treat.
Muy largo es mi corazon,
And fifty holds as well as one.
Non far nell' acqua buco che
I am resolved to have my way;
Im lo boteach atta bi,
I'm willing quite to set you free:
Be you content with half my time,
As half in English is my rhyme.

MAGINN'S ALTERNATIONS—HORACE, EPODE II.

Blest man, who far from busy hum,
Ut prisca gens mortalium,
Whistles his team afield with glee
Solutus omni fenore:
He lives in peace, from battles free,
Nec horret iratum mare;
And shuns the forum, and the gay
Potentiorum limina.
Therefore to vines of purple gloss
Altas maritat populos,
Or pruning off the boughs unfit
Feliciores inserit.

  *   *   *   *

Alphius the usurer, babbled thus,
Jam jam futurus rusticus,
Called in his cast on th'Ides—but he
Quærit Kalendis ponere.

CONTENTI ABEAMUS.

Come, jocund friends, a bottle bring,
  And push around the jorum;
We'll talk and laugh, and quaff and sing,
  Nunc suavium amorum.

While we are in a merry mood,
  Come, sit down ad bibendum;
And if dull care should dare intrude,
  We'll to the devil send him.

A moping elf I can't endure
  While I have ready rhino;
And all life's pleasures centre still
  In venere ac vino.

Be merry then, my friends, I pray,
  And pass your time in joco,
For it is pleasant, as they say,
  Desipere in loco.

He that loves not a young lass
  Is sure an arrant stultus,
And he that will not take a glass
  Deserves to be sepultus.

Pleasure, music, love and wine
  Res valde sunt jucundæ,
And pretty maidens look divine,
  Provided ut sunt mundæ.

I hate a snarling, surly fool,
  Qui latrat sicut canis,
Who mopes and ever eats by rule,
  Drinks water and eats panis.

Give me the man that's always free,
  Qui finit molli more,
The cares of life, what'er they be;
  Whose motto still is " Spero."

Death will turn us soon from hence,
  Nigerrimas ad sedes;
And all our lands and all our pence
  Ditabunt tunc heredes.

Why should we then forbear to sport?
  Dum vivamus, vivamus,
And when the Fates shall cut us down
  Contenti abeamus.

FLY-LEAF SCRIBBLING.

Iste liber pertinet,
And bear it well in mind,
    Ad me, Johannem Rixbrum,
So courteous and so kind.
    Quem si ego perdam,
And by you it shall be found,
    Redde mihi iterum,
Your fame I then will sound.
    Sed si mihi redeas,
Then blessed thou shalt be,
    Et ago tibi gratias
Whenever I thee see.

THE CAT AND THE RATS.

Felis sedit by a hole,
Intentus he, cum omni soul,
        Prendere rats
Mice cucurrerunt trans the floor,
In numero duo, tres, or more—
        Obliti cats.

Felis saw them, oculis;
"I'll have them," inquit he, "I guess,
        Dum ludunt."
Tunc ille crept toward the group,
"Habeam," dixit, "good rat soup—
        Pingues sunt."

Mice continued all ludere,
Intenti they in ludum vere,
        Gaudenter.
Tunc rushed the felis into them,
Et tore them omnes limb from limb,
        Violenter.

MORAL.

Mures omnes, nunc be shy,
Et aurem præbe mihi,
        Benigne.
Sit hoc satis—"verbum sat,"
Avoid a whopping big tom-cat
        Studiose.

POLYGLOT INSCRIPTION.

The following advertisement in five languages, is inscribed on the window of a public house in Germany:—

> In questa casa trovarete
> Toutes les choses que vous souhaitez;
> Vinum bonum, costas, carnes,
> Neat post-chaise, and horse and harness.
> Βους, ὀρνιϑές, ἰχϑυς, ἄρνες.

PARTING ADDRESS TO A FRIEND,

Written by a German gentleman on the termination of a very agreeable, but brief acquaintance.

> I often wished I had a friend,
> Dem ich mich anvertrauen könnt',
> A friend in whom I could confide,
> Der mit mir theilte Freud und Leid;
> Had I the riches of Girard—
> Ich theilte mit ihm Haus und Heerd;
> For what is gold? 'tis but a passing metal,
> Der Henker hol' für mich den ganzen Bettel.
> Could I purchase the world to live in it alone,
> Ich gäb' dafür nicht eine hohle Bohn';
> I thought one time in you I'd find that friend,
> Und glaubte schon mein Sehnen hät ein End;
> Alas! your friendship lasted but in sight,
> Doch meine grenzet an die Ewigkeit.

AM RHEIN.

> Oh, the Rhine—the Rhine—the Rhine—
> Comme c'est beau! wie schön! che bello!
> He who quaffs thy Luft und Wein,
> Morbleu! is a lucky fellow.

> How I love thy rushing streams,
> Groves of ash and birch and hazel,
> From Schaffhausen's rainbow beams
> Jusqu'à l'écho d'Oberwesel!

> Oh, que j'aime thy Brüchen when
> The crammed Dampfschiff gayly passes!—

Love the bronzed pipes of thy men,
  And the bronzed cheeks of thy lasses!

Oh, que j'aime the "oui," the "bah,"
  From thy motley crowds that flow,
With the universal "ja,'
  And the allgemeine "so"!

THE DEATH OF THE SEA SERPENT.

Arma virumque cano, qui first in Monongahela
Tarnally squampushed the sarpent, mittens horrentia tella.
Musa, look sharp with your Banjo! I guess to relate this event, I
Shall need all the aid you can give; so nunc aspirate canenti.
Mighty slick were the vessels progressing, Jactata per æquora ventis,
But the brow of the skipper was sad, cum solicitudine mentis;
For whales had been scarce in those parts, and the skipper, so long as
    he'd known her,
Ne'er had gathered less oil in a cruise to gladden the heart of her owner.
"Darn the whales," cries the skipper at length, "with a telescope forte
    videbo
Aut pisces, aut terras." While speaking, just two or three points on the
    lea bow,
He saw coming towards them as fast as though to a combat 'twould
    tempt 'em,
A monstrum horrendum informe (qui lumen was shortly ademptum).
On the taffrail up jumps in a hurry, dux fortis, and seizing a trumpet,
Blows a blast that would waken the dead, mare turbat et aera rumpit—
"Tumble up all you lubbers," he cries, "tumble up, for careering be-
    fore us
Is the real old sea sarpent himself, cristis maculisque decorus."
"Consarn it," cried one of the sailors, "if e'er we provoke him he'll kill us,
He'll certainly chaw up hos morsu, et longis, implexibus illos."
Loud laughs the bold skipper, and quick premit alto corde dolorem ;
(If he does feel like running, he knows it won't do to betray it before 'em).
"O socii", inquit. "I'm sartin you're not the fellers to funk, or
Shrink from the durem certamen, whose fathers fit bravely at Bunker
You, who have waged with the bears, and the buffalo, prœlia dura,
Down to the freshets, and licks of our own free enlightened Missourer;
You could whip your own weight, catulus sævis sine telo,
Get your eyes skinned in a twinkling, et ponite tela phæsello !"
Talia voce refert, curisque ingentibus æger,
Marshals his cute little band, now panting their foes to beleaguer
Swiftly they lower the boats, and swiftly each man at the oar is,
Excipe Britanni timidi duo, virque coloris.

(Blackskin, you know, never feels, how sweet, 'tis pro patria mori;
Ovid had him in view when he said, " Nimium ne crede colori.")
Now swiftly they pull towards the monster, who seeing the cutter and
    gig nigh,
Glares at them with terrible eyes, suffectis sanguine et igni,
And, never conceiving their chief will so quickly deal him a floorer,
Opens wide to receive them at once, his linguis vibrantibis ora;
But just as he's licking his lips, and gladly preparing to taste 'em,
Straight into his eyeball the skipper stridentem conjicit hastam.
Straight as he feels in his eyeball the lance, growing mightly sulky,
At 'em he comes in a rage, ora minax, lingua trusulca.
"Starn all," cry the sailors at once, for they think he has certainly
    caught 'em,
Præsentemque viris intentant omnia mortem.
But the bold skipper exclaims, " O terque quaterque beati!
Now with a will dare viam, when I want you, be only parati;
This hoss feels like raising his hair, and in spite of his scaly old cortex,
Full soon you shall see that his corpse rapidus vorat æquore vortex."
Hoc ait, and choosing a lance: " With this one I think I shall hit it,
He cries, and straight into his mouth, ad intima viscera mittit.
Screeches the creature in pain, and writhes till the sea is commotum,
As if all its waves had been lashed in a tempest per Eurum et Notum.
Interea terrible shindy Neptunus sensit, et alto
Prospiciens sadly around, wiped his eye with the cuff of his paletôt;
And, mad at his favorite's fate, of oaths uttered one or two thousand,
Such as " Corpo di Bacco! Mehercle! Sacre! Mille Tonnerres! Potz-
    tausend!"
But the skipper, who thought it was time to this terrible fight dare finem,
With a scalping-knife jumps on the neck of the snake secat et dextrâ
    crinem,
And hurling the scalp in the air, half mad with delight to possess it,
Shouts " Darn it—I've fixed up his flint, for in ventos vita recessit!"

Concatenation or Chain Verse.

LASPHRISE'S NOVELTIES.

LASPHRISE, a French poet of considerable merit, claims the
invention of several singularities in verse, and among them the
following, in which it will be found that the last word of every
line is the first word of the following line:—

Falloit-it que le ciel me rendit amoureux,
Amoureaux, jouissant d'une beauté craintive,
Craintive à recevoir douceur excessive,
Excessive au plaisir qui rend l'amant heureux?
Heureux si nous avions quelques paisibles lieux,
Lieux où plus surement l'ami fidèle arrive,
Arrive sans soupçon de quelque ami attentive,
Attentive à vouloir nous surprendre tous deux.

Subjoined are examples in our own vernacular:—

TO DEATH.

The longer life, the more offence;
　The more offence, the greater pain;
The greater pain, the less defence;
　The less defence, the lesser gain—
The loss of gain long ill doth try,
Wherefore, come, death, and let me die.

The shorter life, less count I find;
　The less account, the sooner made;
The count soon made, the merrier mind;
　The merrier mind doth thought invade—
Short life, in truth, this thing doth try,
Wherefore, come, death, and let me die.

Come, gentle death, the ebb of care;
　The ebb of care the flood of life;
The flood of life, the joyful fare;
　The joyful fare, the end of strife—
The end of strife that thing wish I,
Wherefore, come, death and let me die.

TRUTH.

Nerve thy soul with doctrines noble,
　Noble in the walks of Time,
Time that leads to an eternal,
　An eternal life sublime;
Life sublime in moral beauty,
　Beauty that shall ever be,
Ever be to lure thee onward,
　Onward to the fountain free;
Free to every earnest seeker,
　Seeker at the Fount of Youth,
Youth exultant in its beauty,
　Beauty found in the quest of Truth.

TRYING SKYING.

Long I looked into the sky,
　　Sky aglow with gleaming stars,
Stars that stream their courses high,
　　High and grand, those golden cars,
Cars that ever keep their track,
　　Track untraced by human ray,
Ray that zones the zodiac,
　　Zodiac with milky-way,
Milky-way where worlds are sown,
　　Sown like sands along the sea,
Sea whose tide and tone e'er own,
　　Own a feeling to be free,
Free to leave its lowly place,
　　Place to prove with yonder spheres,
Spheres that trace athrough all space,
　　Space and years—unspoken years.

A RINGING SONG.

The following gem is from an old play of Shakspeare's time, called *The True Trojans :*—

The sky is glad that stars above
　　Do give a brighter splendor;
The stars unfold their flaming gold,
　　To make the ground more tender:
The ground doth send a fragrant smell,
　　That air may be the sweeter;
The air doth charm the swelling seas
　　With pretty chirping metre;
The sea with rivers' water doth
　　Feed plants and flowers so dainty;
The plants do yield their fruitful seed,
　　That beasts may live in plenty;
The beasts do give both food and cloth,
　　That men high Jove may honor;
And so the World runs merrily round,
　　When Peace doth smile upon her!
Oh, then, then oh! oh then, then oh!
　　This jubilee last forever;
That foreign spite, or civil fight,
　　Our quiet trouble never!

Bouts Rimés.

BOUTS RIMÉS, or Rhyming Ends, afford considerable amusement. They are said by Goujet to have been invented by Dulot, a French poet, who had a custom of preparing the rhymes of sonnets, leaving them to be filled up at leisure. Having been robbed of his papers, he was regretting the loss of three hundred sonnets. His friends were astonished that he had written so many of which they had never heard. "They were blank sonnets," said he, and then explained the mystery by describing his "Bouts Rimés." The idea appeared ridiculously amusing, and it soon became a fashionable pastime to collect some of the most difficult rhymes, and fill up the lines. An example is appended :—

> nettle,
> pains.
> mettle.
> remains.
> natures.
> rebel.
> graters.
> well.

The rhymes may be thus completed :—

> Tender-handed stroke a nettle,
>   And it stings you for your pains;
> Grasp it like a man of mettle,
>   And it soft as silk remains.
> 'Tis the same with common natures,
>   Use them kindly, they rebel;
> But be rough as nutmeg-graters,
>   And the rogues obey you well.

A sprightly young belle, who was an admirer of poetry, would often tease her beau, who had made some acquaintance with the muses, to write verses for her. One day, becoming quite importunate, she would take no denial. "Come, pray, do now write some poetry for me—won't you? I'll help you out. I'll

furnish you with rhymes if you will make lines for them.
Here now :—

please,	moan,
tease,	bone."

He at length good-humoredly complied, and filled up the
measure as follows :—

> To a form that is faultless, a face that must—please,
> Is added a restless desire to—tease ;
> O, how my hard fate I should ever be—moan,
> Could I but believe she'd be bone of my—bone!

Mr. Bogart, a young man of Albany, who died in 1826, at
the age of twenty-one, displayed astonishing facility in impromptu writing.

It was good-naturedly hinted on one occasion that his "im-
promptus" were prepared beforehand, and he was asked if he
would submit to the application of a test of his poetic abilities.
He promptly acceded, and a most difficult one was immediately
proposed.

Among his intimate friends were Col. J. B. Van Schaick
and Charles Fenno Hoffman, both of whom were present.   Said
Van Schaick, taking up a copy of Byron, "The name of Lydia
Kane" (a lady distinguished for her beauty and cleverness,
who died a few years ago, but who was then just blushing into
womanhood) "has in it the same number of letters as a stanza
of Childe Harold has lines : write them down in a column."
They were so written by Bogart, Hoffman, and himself.
"Now," he continued, "I will open the poem at random ; and
for the ends of the lines in Miss Lydia's *Acrostic* shall be used
the words ending those of the verse on which my finger may
rest."   The stanza thus selected was this :—

> And must they fall, the young, the proud, the brave,
> To swell one bloated chief's unwholesome reign?
> No step between submission and a grave?
> The rise of rapine and the fall of Spain?
> And doth the Power that man adores ordain
> Their doom, nor heed the suppliant's appeal?
> Is all that desperate valor acts in vain?
> And counsel sage, and patriotic zeal,
> The veteran's skill, youth's fire, and manhood's heart of steel?

The following stanza was composed by Bogart within the succeeding ten minutes,—the period fixed in a wager,—finished before his companions had reached a fourth line, and read to them as here presented :*—

L ovely and loved, o'er the unconquered   brave
Y our charms resistless, matchless girl, shall   reign!
D ear as the mother holds her infant's   grave
I n Love's own region, warm, romantic   Spain!
A nd should your fate to court your steps   ordain,
K ings would in vain to regal pomp   appeal,
A nd lordly bishops kneel to you in   vain,
N or valor's fire, law's power, nor churchman's   zeal
E ndure 'gainst love's (time's up!) untarnished   steel.

The French also amuse themselves with *bouts rimés retournés*, in which the rhymes are taken from some piece of poetry, but the order in which they occur is reversed. The following example is from the album of a Parisian lady of literary celebrity, the widow of one of the Crimean heroes. The original poem is by Alfred de Musset, the *retournés* by Marshal Pelissier, who improvised it at the lady's request. In the translation which ensues, the reversed rhymes are carefully preserved.

BY DE MUSSET.

Quand la fugitive espérance
Nous pousse le coude en passant,
Puis à tire d'ailes s'élance
Et se retourne en souriant,
Où va l'homme? où son cœur l'appelle;
L'hirondelle suit le zéphir,
Et moins légère est l'hirondelle
Que l'homme qui suit son désir.
Ah! fugitive enchanteresse,
Sais-tu seulement ton chemin?
Faut-il donc que le vieux destin
Ait une si jeune maîtresse!

BY PELISSIER, DUC DE MALAKOFF.

Pour chanter la jeune maîtresse
Que Musset donne au vieux destin,

---

* The truth of this circumstance was confirmed by Mr. Hoffman in the course of a conversation upon that and similar topics several years afterward.

J'ai trop parcouru de chemin
Sans atteindre l'enchanteresse ;
Toujours vers cet ancien désir
J'ai tendu comme l'hirondelle,
Mais sans le secours du zéphir
Qui la porte où son cœur l'appelle.
Adieu, fantôme souriant,
Vers qui la jeunesse s'élance,
La raison me crie en passant ;
Le souvenir vaut l'espérance.

TRANSLATION.

When Hope, a fugitive, retreating
Elbows us, as away she flies,
Then swift returns, another greeting
To offer us with laughing eyes.
Man goeth when his heart is speaking,
The swallows through the zephyrs dart,
And man, who's every fancy seeking,
Hath yet a more inconstant heart.
Enchantress, fugitive, coquetting !
Know'st thou then true, alone, thy way ?
Hath then stern Fate, so old and gray,
So young a mistress never fretting ?

REVERSED RHYMES.

To sing the mistress, never fretting,
Musset gives Fate, so old and gray,
Too long I've travelled on my way,
And ne'er attained her dear coquetting.
To find that longing of the heart,
I've been, like yonder swallow, seeking,
Yet could not through the zephyrs dart,
Nor reach the wish the heart is speaking.
Adieu then, shade, with laughing eyes,
Towards whom youth ever sends its greeting ;
Better, cries Reason, as she flies,
Remembrance now, than Hope retreating.

Among the eccentricities of literature may be classed *Rhopalic verses*, which begin with a monosyllable and gradually increase the length of each successive word. The name was suggested by the shape of Hercules' club, ῥόπαλον. Sometimes they run from the butt to the handle of the club. Take as an example of each,—

16

Rem tibi confeci, doctissime, dulcisonoram.
Vectigalibus armamenta referre jubet Rex.

17

Emblematic Poetry.

A pair of scissors and a comb in verse.—BEN JONSON.

On their fair standards by the wind displayed,
Eggs, altars, wings, pipes, axes, were portrayed.—*Scribleriad.*

THE quaint conceit of making verses assume grotesque shapes and devices, expressive of the theme selected by the writer, appears to have been most fashionable during the seventeenth century. Writers tortured their brains in order to torture their verses into all sorts of fantastic forms, from a flowerpot to an obelisk, from a pin to a pyramid. Hearts and fans and knots were chosen for love-songs; wineglasses, bottles, and casks for Bacchanalian songs; pulpits, altars, and monuments for religious verses and epitaphs. Tom Nash, according to Disraeli, says of Gabriel Harvey, that "he had writ verses in all kinds: in form of a pair of gloves, a pair of spectacles, a pair of pot-hooks, &c." Puttenham, in his *Art of Poesie,* gives several odd specimens of poems in the form of lozenges, pillars, triangles, &c. Butler says of Benlowes, "the excellently learned," who was much renowned for his literary freaks, "As for temples and pyramids in poetry, he has outdone all men that way; for he has made a *grid-iron* and a *frying-pan* in verse, that, besides the likeness in shape, the very tone and sound of the words did perfectly represent the noise made by these utensils! When he was a captain, he made all the furniture of his horse, from the bit to the crupper, the beaten poetry, every verse being fitted to the proportion of the thing, with a moral allusion to the sense of the thing: as the *bridle of moderation,* the *saddle of content,* and the *crupper of constancy;* so that the same thing was the epigram and emblem, even as a mule is both horse and ass." Mr. Alger tells us that the Oriental poets are fond of arranging their poems in the form of drums, swords, circles, crescents, trees, &c., and that the Alexandrian rhetoricians used to amuse themselves by writing their satires and invectives in the shape of an axe or a spear. He gives the following erotic triplet, composed by a Hindu poet, the first line representing a bow, the second its string, the third an arrow aimed at the heart of the object of his passion :—

One kiss I send, to pierce, like fire, thy too reluctant heart.

O lovely maid, thou art the fairest slave in all God's mart!

Those charms to win, with all my empire I would gladly part

THE WINE GLASS.

Who hath woe? Who hath sorrow?
Who hath contentions? Who
hath wounds without cause?
Who hath redness of eyes?
They that tarry long at the
wine! They that go to
seek mixed wine. Look
not thou upon the
wine when it is red,
when it giveth its
color in the
CUP;
when it
moveth itself
aright.
At
the last
it biteth like a
serpent, and stingeth like an adder

The following specimen of this affectation was written by George Wither, who lived from 1588 to 1677. It is called by Mr. Ellis a

RHOMBOIDAL DIRGE.

Farewell,
Sweet groves, to you!
You hills that highest dwell,
And all you humble vales, adieu!
You wanton brooks and solitary rocks,
My dear companions all, and you my tender flocks!
Farewell, my pipe! and all those pleasing songs whose moving strains
Delighted once the fairest nymphs that dance upon the plains.
You discontents, whose deep and over-deadly smart
Have without pity broke the truest heart,
Sighs, tears, and every sad annoy,
That erst did with me dwell,
And others joy,
Farewell!

The Christian monks of the Middle Ages, who amused them-selves similarly, preferred for their hymns the form of

THE CROSS.

Blest they who seek,
While in their youth,
With spirit meek,
The way of truth.
To them the Sacred Scriptures now display,
Christ as the only true and living way:
His precious blood on Calvary was given
To make them heirs of endless bliss in heaven.
And e'en on earth the child of God can trace
The glorious blessings of his Saviour's face.
For them He bore
His Father's frown,
For them He wore
The thorny crown;
Nailed to the cross,
Endured its pain,
That his life's loss
Might be their gain.
Then haste to choose
That better part—
Nor dare refuse
The Lord your heart,
Lest He declare,—
"I know you not;"
And deep despair
Shall be your lot.
Now look to Jesus who on Calvary died,
And trust on Him alone who there was crucified.

A CURIOUS PIECE OF ANTIQUITY, ON THE CRUCIFIXION OF OUR SAVIOUR AND THE TWO THIEVES.

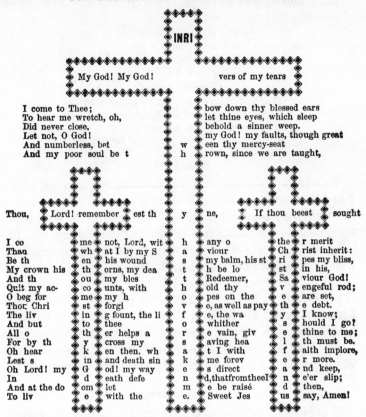

INRI

My God! My God!   vers of my tears

I come to Thee;   bow down thy blessed ears
To hear me wretch, oh,   let thine eyes, which sleep
Did never close,   behold a sinner weep.
Let not, O God!   my God! my faults, though great
And numberless, bet   w   een thy mercy-seat
And my poor soul be t   h   rown, since we are taught,

Thou,   Lord! remember   est th   y   ne,   If thou beest   sought

I co	me	not, Lord, wit	h	any o	the	r merit	
Than	wh	at I by my S	a	viour	Ch	rist inherit:	
Be th	en	his wound	s	my balm, his st	ri	pes my bliss,	
My crown his	th	orns, my dea	t	h be lo	st	in his,	
And th	ou	my bles	t	Redeemer,	Sa	viour God!	
Quit my ac-	co	unts, with	h	old thy	v	engeful rod;	
O beg for	me	my h	o	pes on the	e	are set,	
Thou Chri	st	forgi	v	e, as well as pay	th	e debt.	
The liv	in	g fount, the li	f	e, the wa	y	I know;	
And but	to	thee	o	whither	s	hould I go?	
All o	th	er helps a	r	e vain, giv	e	thine to me;	
For by th	y	cross my	s	aving hea	l	th must be.	
Oh hear	k	en then, wh	a	t I with	f	aith implore,	
Lest s	in	and death sin	k	me forev	e	r more.	
Oh Lord! my	G	od! my way	e	s direct	a	nd keep,	
In	d	eath defe	n	d,thatfromtheeI	n	e'er slip;	
And at the do	om	let	m	e be raisé	d	then,	
To liv	e	with the	e.	Sweet Jes	us	say, Amen!	

EXPLANATION.

The middle cross represents our Saviour; those on either side, the two thieves. On the top and down the middle cross are our Saviour's expression, "My God! My God! why hast thou forsaken me?" and on the top of the cross is the Latin inscription, "INRI"—Jesus Nazarenus Rex Judæorum, i.e. Jesus of Nazareth, King of the Jews. Upon the cross on the right hand is the prayer of one of the thieves:—"Lord! remember me when thou comest into thy kingdom." On the left-hand cross is the saying, or reproach, of the other:—"If thou beest the Christ, save thyself and us." The whole, comprised together, makes a piece of excellent poetry, which is to be read across all the columns, and makes as many lines as there are letters in the alphabet. It is perhaps one of the most curious pieces of composition to be found on record.

INGENIOUS CYPHER

The following was written by Prof. Whewell at the request of a young lady:—

> U 0 a 0 but I 0 U,
> O O no O but O O me;
> O let not my 0 a 0 go,
> But give 0 0 I 0 U so.

Thus de-cyphered :

> (You *sigh for a cypher*, but I *sigh for* you;
> O *sigh for* no *cypher*, but O *sigh for* me:
> O let not my *sigh for a cypher* go,
> But give *sigh for sigh*, for I *sigh for* you so.)

TYPOGRAPHICAL.

We once saw a young man gazing at the *ry heavens, with a † in 1 ☞ and a ⌒ of pistols in the other. We endeavored to attract his attention by .ing to a ¶ in a paper we held in our ☞, relating 2 a young man in that § of the country, who had left home in a state of mental derangement. He dropped the † and pistols from his ☞☜ with the !

"It is I of whom U read. I left home be4 my friends knew of my design. I had s0 the ☞ of a girl who refused 2 lis10 2 me, but smiled b9nly on another. I ——ed madly from the house, uttering a wild ' 2 the god of love, and without replying 2 the ??? of my friends, came here with this † & ⌒ of pistols, 2 put a . 2 my existence. My case has no ‖ in this §."

OXFORD JOKE.

A gentleman entered the room of Dr. Barton, Warden of Merton College, and told him that Dr. Vowel was dead. "What!" said he, "Dr. Vowel dead! well, thank heaven it was neither U nor I."

In an old church in Westchester county, N. Y., the following consonants are written beside the altar, under the Ten Commandments. What vowel is to be placed between them, to make sense and rhyme of the couplet?

P. R. S. V. R. Y. P. R. F. C. T. M. N.
V. R. K. P. T. H. S. P. R. C. P. T. S. T. N.

ESSAY TO MISS CATHARINE JAY.   18

An S A now I mean 2 write
  2 U sweet K T J,
The girl without a ‖,
  The belle of U T K.

I 1 der if U got that 1
  I wrote 2 U B 4
I sailed in the R K D A,
  And sent by L N Moore.

My M T head will scarce contain
  A calm I D A bright
But A T miles from U I must
  M⌣ this chance 2 write.

And 1st, should N E N V U,
  B E Z, mind it not,
Should N E friendship show, B true;
  They should not B forgot.

From virt U nev R D V 8;
  Her influence B 9
A like induces 10 dern S,
  Or 40 tude D vine.

And if U cannot cut a ——
  Or cut an !
I hope U'll put a .
  2 1 ?.

R U for an X ation 2,
  My cous N ?—heart and 🖛
He off R's in a ¶
  A ⅔ 2 of land.

He says he loves U 2 X S,
  U R virtuous and Y's,
In X L N C U X L
  All others in his i's.

This S A, until U I C,
  I pray U 2 X Q's,
And do not burn in F E G
  My young and wayward muse.

Now fare U well, dear K T J,
  I trust that U R true—
When this U C, then you can say,
  An S A I O U.

Monosyllables.

"And ten low words oft creep in one dull line."

SOME of our best writers have very properly taken exception to the above line in Pope's Essay on Criticism, and have shown, by reference to abundant examples, that many of the finest passages in our language are nearly, if not altogether, monosyllabic. Indeed, it could not well be otherwise, if it be true that, as Dean Swift has remarked, the English language is "overstocked with monosyllables." It contains more than five hundred formed by the vowel *a* alone; four hundred and fifty by the vowel *e;* nearly four hundred by the vowel *i;* more than four hundred by the vowel *o;* and two hundred and sixty by the vowel *u;* besides a large number formed by diphthongs. Floy has written a lengthy and very ingenious article, entirely in monosyllables, in which he undertakes, as he says, to "prove that short words, in spite of the sneer in the text, need not creep, nor be dull, but that they give strength, and life, and fire to the verse of those who know how to use them."

Pope himself, however, has confuted his own words by his admirable writings more effectively than could be done by labored argument. Many of the best lines in the Essay above referred to, as well as in the Essay on Man,—and there are few "dull" or "creeping" verses to be found in either,—are made up entirely of monosyllables, or contain but one word of greater length, or a contracted word pronounced as one syllable. The Universal Prayer—one of the most beautiful and elaborate pieces, both in sentiment and versification, ever produced in any language—contains three hundred and four words, of which there are two hundred and forty-nine monosyllables to fifty-five polysyllables, thus averaging but one of the latter to every line. A single stanza is appended as a specimen :—

> If I am right, thy grace impart
> Still in the right to stay;
> If I am wrong, oh, teach my heart
> To find that better way !

Rogers, conversing on this subject, cited two lines from *Eloisa to Abelard*, which he declared could not possibly be improved :—

> Pant on thy lip, and to thy heart be press'd ;
> Give all thou canst—and let me dream the rest.

Among the illustrations employed by Floy, are numerous selections from the hymnology in common congregational use, such as the following :—

> Sweet is the work, my God, my King,
> To praise thy name, give thanks, and sing ;
> To show thy love by morning light,
> And talk of all thy truth at night.—WATTS.

> Are there no foes for me to face ?
>   Must I not stem the flood ?
> Is this vile world a friend to grace
>   To help me on to God ?—WATTS.

> Save me from death ; from hell set free ;
> Death, hell, are but the want of thee :
> My life, my only heav'n thou art,—
> O might I feel thee in my heart !—C. WESLEY.

The same writer, to show Shakspeare's fondness for small words, and their frequent subservience to some of his most masterly efforts, enters upon a monosyllabic analysis of King Lear, quoting from it freely throughout. Those who read the play with reference to this point will be struck with the remarkable number of forcible passages made up of words of one syllable :—

> Thou know'st the first time that we smell the air,
> We wawl and cry : I will preach to thee ; mark me.
> When we are born, we cry that we are come
> To this great stage of fools.—*This a good block ?—Act IV. Sc.* 6.

The following occurs in the play of King John, where the King is pausing in his wish to incite Hubert to murder Arthur :—

> Good friend, thou hast no cause to say so yet ;
> But thou shalt have ; and creep time ne'er so slow,
> Yet it shall come, for me to do thee good.
> I had a thing to say.—But let it go.—*Act III. Sc.* 3.

But who I was, or where, or from what cause,
Knew not; to speak I tried, and forthwith spake
      ——Thou sun, said I, fair light,
And thou enlightened earth, so fresh and gay,
Ye hills, and dales, ye rivers, woods, and plains,
And ye that live and move, fair creatures, tell,
Tell, if ye saw how I came thus, how here?—
Tell me, how may I know Him, how adore,
From whom I have that thus I move and live?—*Paradise Lost, B. VIII.*

Herrick says, in his address to the daffodils :—

        We have short time to stay as you,
          We have as short a spring;
        As quick a growth to meet decay
          As you or any thing.
            We die
        As your hours do, and dry
          Like to the rain,
          Or as the pearls of dew.

Now I am here, what thou wilt do for me,
   None of my books will show;
I read, and sigh, and wish I were a tree,
   For sure I then should grow
To fruit or shade: at least some bird might trust
Her household to me, and I should be just.— GEORGE HERBERT.

Thou who hast given me eyes to see
   And love this sight so fair,
Give me a heart to find out Thee,
   And read Thee everywhere.—KEBLE.

The bell strikes one.　We take no note of time
Save by its loss; to give it then a tongue
Were wise in man.—YOUNG.

Ah, yes! the hour is come
When thou must haste thee home,
   Pure soul! to Him who calls.
The God who gave thee breath
Walks by the side of death,
   And naught that step appalls.—LANDOR.

New light new love, new love new life hath bred;
   A life that lives by love, and loves by light;
A love to Him to whom all loves are wed;
   A light to whom the sun is darkest night:

Eye's light, heart's love, soul's only life, He is;
Life, soul, love, heart, light, eyes, and all are His;
He eye, light, heart, love, soul; He all my joy and bliss.—
FLETCHER'S *Purple Island.*

Bailey's *Festus,* that extraordinary poem the perusal of which makes the reader feel as if he had "eaten of the insane root that takes the reason prisoner," abounds with examples:—

Night brings out stars as sorrow shows us truths:
Though many, yet they help not; bright, they light not.
They are too late to serve us; and sad things
Are aye too true. We never see the stars
Till we can see naught but them. So with truth.
And yet if one would look down a deep well,
Even at noon, we might see those same stars——

Life's more than breath, and the quick round of blood—
We live in deeds, not years; in thoughts, not breaths—
We should count time by heart-throbs. He most lives
Who thinks most—feels the noblest—acts the best.
Life's but a means unto an end—

HELEN (*sings.*) Oh! love is like the rose,
And a month it may not see,
Ere it withers where it grows—
Rosalie!

I loved thee from afar;
Oh! my heart was lift to thee
Like a glass up to a star—
Rosalie!

Thine eye was glassed in mine
As the moon is in the sea,
And its shine is on the brine—
Rosalie!

The rose hath lost its red,
And the star is in the sea,
And the briny tear is shed—
Rosalie!

FESTUS. What the stars are to the night, my love,
What its pearls are to the sea,
What the dew is to the day, my love,
Thy beauty is to me.

We may say that the sun is dead, and gone
Forever; and may swear he will rise no more;

The skies may put on mourning for their God,
And earth heap ashes on her head; but who
Shall keep the sun back when he thinks to rise?
Where is the chain shall bind him? Where the cell
Shall hold him? Hell he would burn down to embers,
And would lift up the world with a lever of light
Out of his way: yet, know ye, 'twere thrice less
To do thrice this, than keep the soul from God.

Many of the most expressive sentences in the Bible are monosyllabic. A few are subjoined, selected at random:—

And God said, Let there be light: and there was light. And God saw the light, that it was good.—*Gen. I.*

At her feet he bowed, he fell, he lay down: at her feet he bowed, he fell: where he bowed, there he fell down dead.—*Judges V.*

O Lord my God, I cried unto thee, and thou hast healed me. O Lord, thou hast brought up my soul from the grave: thou hast kept me alive, that I should not go down to the pit. Sing unto the Lord, O ye saints of his, and give thanks.—*Psalm XXX.*

And he said unto me, Son of man, can these bones live?—*Ezek. XXXVII.*

Prove all things; hold fast that which is good.—1 *Thess. V.*

For if we be dead with him, we shall also live with him.—2 *Tim. II.*

For the great day of his wrath is come; and who shall be able to stand? —*Rev. VI.*

And the gates of it shall not be shut at all by day; for there shall be no night there.—*Rev. XXI.*

THE POWER OF SHORT WORDS.

Think not that strength lies in the big round word,
   Or that the brief and plain must needs be weak.
To whom can this be true who once has heard
   The cry for help, the tongue that all men speak,
When want or woe or fear is in the throat,
   So that each word gasped out is like a shriek
Pressed from the sore heart, or a strange wild note,
   Sung by some fay or fiend? There is a strength
Which dies if stretched too far or spun too fine,
   Which has more height than breadth, more depth than length.
Let but this force of thought and speech be mine,
   And he that will may take the sleek fat phrase
Which glows and burns not, though it gleam and shine—
   Light, but no heat—a flash, but not a blaze!

Nor is it mere strength that the short word boasts :
　It serves of more than fight or storm to tell,
The roar of waves that clash on rock-bound coasts,
　The crash of tall trees when the wild winds swell,
The roar of guns, the groans of men that die
　On blood-stained fields.　It has a voice as well
For them that far off on their sick-beds lie ;
　For them that weep, for them that mourn the dead ;
For them that laugh and dance and clap the hand ;
　To joy's quick step, as well as grief's slow tread,
The sweet, plain words we learnt at first keep time,
　And though the theme be sad, or gay, or grand,
With each, with all, these may be made to chime,
　In thought, or speech, or song, in prose or rhyme.
DR. ALEXANDER, *Princeton Magazine.*

The Bible.

God's cabinet of revealed counsel 'tis,
Where weal and woe are ordered so
That every man may know which shall be his ;
Unless his own mistake false application make.

It is the index to eternity.
He cannot miss of endless bliss,
That takes this chart to steer by,
Nor can he be mistook, that speaketh by this book.

It is the book of God.　What if I should
Say, God of books, let him that looks
Angry at that expression, as too bold,
His thoughts in silence smother, till he find such another.

ACCURACY OF THE BIBLE.

ONE of the most remarkable results of modern research is
the confirmation of the accuracy of the historical books of the
Old Testament.　The ruins of Babylon and Nineveh shed a
light on those books which no skepticism can invalidate.　What
surprises us most is their marvellous accuracy in minute details,
which are now substantiated by recent discoveries.　The fact
seems to be that when writing was laboriously performed on

stone, men had an almost superstitious conscientiousness in making their records true, and had not learned the modern indifference to truth which our facile modes of communicating thought have encouraged. A statement to be chiselled on rock must be correct; a statement which can be written in five minutes is likely to embody only first impressions, which may be amended in five minutes thereafter. Hence it comes to pass that we know more exactly many things which took place in the wars between Sennacherib and Hezekiah, than we know what is the precise truth with regard to some of the occurrences in the battle of Bunker's Hill. Sir Henry Rawlinson, speaking of his researches in Babylon, states that the name and situation of every town of note in ancient Assyria, mentioned in the Bible, can be substantiated by the ruins of that city. The visit of the Queen of Sheba to Solomon is perfectly verified. The prosecution of the researches will be regarded with great interest as corroborating the truth of Scripture.

An astonishing feature of the word of God is, notwithstanding the time at which its compositions were written, and the multitude of the topics to which it alludes, there is not one physical error,—not one assertion or allusion disproved by the progress of modern science. None of those mistakes which the science of each succeeding age discovered in the books preceding; above all, none of those absurdities which modern astronomy indicates in such great numbers in the writings of the ancients,—in their sacred codes, in their philosophy, and even in the finest pages of the fathers of the Church,—not one of these errors is to be found in any of our sacred books. Nothing there will ever contradict that which, after so many ages, the investigations of the learned world have been able to reveal to us on the state of our globe, or on that of the heavens. Peruse with care the Scriptures from one end to the other, to find such blemishes, and, whilst you apply yourselves to this examination, remember that it is a book which speaks of every thing, which describes nature, which recites its creation, which tells us of the water, of the atmosphere, of the mountains, of the animals, and of the plants. It is a book which teaches us the first revolutions of the world, and which also foretells its last. It recounts them in the circumstantial language of history, it extols them in the sublimest strains of poetry, and it chants them in the charms of glowing song. It is a book which is full of Oriental rapture, elevation, variety, and boldness. It is a book which speaks of the heavenly and invisible world, whilst it also speaks of the earth and things visible. It is a book which nearly fifty writers, of every degree of cultivation, of every state, of every condition, and living through the course of fifteen hundred years, have concurred to make. It is a book which was written in the centre of Asia, in the sands of Arabia, in the deserts of Judea, in the court of the Temple of the Jews, in the music-schools of the prophets of Bethel and Jericho, in the sumptuous palaces of Babylon, and on the idolatrous banks of Chebar; and finally, in the centre of Western civilization, in the midst of the Jews and of their ignorance, in the midst of polytheism and its sad philosophy. It is a book whose first writer had been forty years a pupil of the magicians of Egypt, in whose opinion the sun, the stars, and elements were endowed with intelligence, reacted on the elements, and governed the world by a perpetual illuvium. It is a book whose first writer preceded, by more than nine hundred years, the most ancient philosophers of ancient Greece and Asia,—the Thaleses, and the Pythagorases, the Zaleucuses, the Xenophons, and the Confuciuses. It is a book which carries its narrations even to the hierarchies of angels—even to the most distant epochs of the future, and the glorious scenes of the last day. Well: search among its fifty authors, search among its sixty-six books, its eleven hundred and eighty-nine chapters, and its thirty-one thousand one hundred and seventy-three verses; search for only one of those thousand errors which the ancients and moderns have committed in speaking of the heavens or of the earth—of their revolutions, of their elements; search —but you will find none.

THE TESTIMONY OF LEARNED MEN.

SIR WILLIAM JONES' opinion of the Bible was written on the last leaf of one belonging to him, in these terms :—"I have regularly and attentively read these Holy Scriptures, and am of opinion that this volume, independently of its Divine origin, contains more sublimity and beauty, more pure morality, more important history and finer strains of poetry and eloquence, than can be collected from all other books, in whatever age or language they may have been composed."

ROUSSEAU says, "This Divine Book, the only one which is indispensable to the Christian, need only be read with reflection to inspire love for its author, and the most ardent desire to obey its precepts. Never did virtue speak so sweet a language; never was the most profound wisdom expressed with so much energy and simplicity. No one can arise from its perusal without feeling himself better than he was before."

WILBERFORCE, in his dying hour, said to a friend, "Read the Bible. Let no religious book take its place. Through all my perplexities and distresses, I never read any other book, and I never knew the want of any other. It has been my hourly study; and all my knowledge of the doctrines, and all my acquaintance with the experience and realities, of religion, have been derived from the Bible only. I think religious people do not read the Bible enough. Books about religion may be useful enough, but they will not do instead of the simple truth of the Bible."

LORD BOLINGBROKE declared that "the Gospel is, in all cases, one continued lesson of the strictest morality, of justice, of benevolence, and of universal charity."

Similar testimony has been accorded in the strongest terms by LOCKE, NEWTON, BOYLE, SELDEN, SALMASIUS, SIR WALTER SCOTT, and numberless others.

DANIEL WEBSTER, having been commended for his eloquence on a memorable occasion, replied, "If any thing I have ever said or written deserves the feeblest encomiums of my fellow-countrymen, I have no hesitation in declaring that for their partiality I am indebted, solely indebted, to the daily and attentive perusal of the Holy Scriptures, the source of all true poetry and eloquence, as well as of all good and all comfort."

JOHN QUINCY ADAMS, in a letter to his son in 1811, says, "I have for many years made it a practice to read through the Bible once every year. My custom is to read four or five chapters every morning, immediately after rising from my bed. It employs about an hour of my time, and seems to me the most suitable manner of beginning the day. In whatsoever light we regard the Bible, whether with reference to revelation, to history, or to morality, it is an invaluable and inexhaustible mine of knowledge and virtue."

ADDISON says, in relation to the poetry of the Bible, "After perusing the Book of Psalms, let a judge of the beauties of poetry read a literal translation of Horace or Pindar, and he will find in these two last such an absurdity and confusion of style, with such a comparative poverty of imagination, as will make him sensible of the vast superiority of Scripture style."

LORD BYRON, in a letter to Mrs. Sheppard, said, in reference to the truth of Christianity, " Indisputably, the firm believers in the Gospel have a great advantage over all others, for this simple reason:—that, if true, they will have their reward hereafter; and if there be no hereafter, they can be but with the infidel in his eternal sleep, having had the assistance of an exalted hope through life, without subsequent disappointment, since (at the worst, for them) out of nothing nothing can arise,—not even sorrow." The following lines of Walter Scott are said to have been copied in his Bible :—

> Within this awful volume lies
> The mystery of mysteries.
> Oh! happiest they of human race,
> To whom our God has given grace
> To hear, to read, to fear, to pray,
> To lift the latch, and force the way;
> But better had they ne'er been born,
> Who read to doubt, or read to scorn.—*Monastery.*

ENGLISH BIBLE TRANSLATIONS.

Our version of the Bible is to be loved and prized for this, as for a thousand other things,—that it has preserved a purity of meaning to many terms of natural objects. Without this holdfast, our vitiated imaginations would refine away language to mere abstractions. Hence the French have lost their poetical language; and Blanco White says the same thing has happened to the Spanish.—COLERIDGE.

Wickliffe's Bible.—This was the first translation made into the language. It was translated by John Wickliffe, about the year 1384, but never printed, though there are manuscript copies of it in several public libraries.

Tyndale's Bible.—The translation of William Tyndale, assisted by Miles Coverdale, was the first printed Bible in the English language. The New Testament was published in 1526. It was revised and republished in 1530. In 1532, Tyndale and his associates finished the whole Bible, except the Apocrypha, and printed it abroad.

Matthews' Bible.—While Tyndale was preparing a second edition of the Bible, he was taken up and burned for heresy in Flanders. On his death, Coverdale and John Rogers revised it, and added a translation of the Apocrypha. It was dedicated to Henry VIII., in 1537, and was printed at Hamburg, under the borrowed name of Thomas Matthews, whence it was called Matthews' Bible.

Cranmer's Bible.—This was the first Bible printed by authority in England, and publicly set up in the churches. It was Tyndale's version, revised by Coverdale, and examined by Cranmer, who added a preface to it, whence it was called Cranmer's Bible. It was printed by Grafton, in large folio, in 1539. After being adopted, suppressed, and restored under successive reigns, a new edition was brought out in 1562.

The Geneva Bible.—In 1557, the whole Bible in quarto was printed at Geneva by Rowland Harte, some of the English refugees continuing in that city solely for that purpose. The translators were Bishop Coverdale, Anthony Gilby, William Whittingham, Christopher Woodman, Thomas Sampson, and Thomas Cole—to whom some add John Knox, John Bodleigh, and John Pullain, all zealous Calvinists, both in doctrine and discipline. But the chief and most learned of them were the first three. Of this translation there were about thirty editions, mostly printed by the King's and Queen's printers, from 1560 to 1616. In this version, the first distinction in verses was made. The following is a copy of the title-page of the edition of 1559, omitting two quotations from the Scriptures :—

THE BIBLE.
THAT IS. THE HO-
LY SCRIPTURES CONTEI-
NED IN THE OLDE AND NEWE
TESTAMENT.
Translated According
to the Ebrew and Greeke, and conferred with the
best translations in divers languages.
With most profitable Annotations vpon all the hard
places,
and other things of Great importance.
IMPRINTED AT LONDON
by the Deputies of Christopher Barker, Printer to the
Queenes most excellent Maiestie,
1599.
Cum priuilegio.

To some editions of the Geneva Bible, one of which is this of 1599, is subjoined Beza's translation of the new text into English by L. Tomson, who was under-secretary to Sir Francis Walsingham. But, though he pretends to translate from Beza, he has seldom varied a word from the Geneva translation. Dr. Geddes gives honorable testimony to the last Geneva version, as he does not hesitate to declare that he thinks it in general better than that of the King James translators. Our readers will hardly agree with him when they read some extracts from it appended in a succeeding paragraph.

The typographical appearance of this work is quite a curiosity. Like most of the old books, it is well printed, and is ornamented with the pen. The head and foot rules, as well as the division of the columns, are made with the pen in red ink. The title-page is quite profusely ornamented with red lines.

This translation of the Bible is known as "the breeches Bible," from the following rendering of Genesis iii. 7 :—

Then the eyes of them both were opened, and they knew that they were naked; and they sewed fig tree leaves together, and made themselves *breeches.*

A peculiarity in this Bible is the substitution of the letter *v* for *u,* and, *vice versa, u* for *v.* The name of Eve is printed Heuah (Hevah); Cain is printed Kain; Abel, Habel; Enoch, Henock; Isaac, Ishak; Hebrew, Ebrew, &c. The translations of many of the passages differ materially from our received version. The following will serve as illustrations :—

Thus he cast out man; and at the East side of the garden of Eden ne set the cherubims, and the blade of a sword shaken, to keep the way of the tree of life.—Genesis iii. 24.

Then it repented the Lorde that he had made man in the earth, and he was sorie in his heart.—Gen. vi. 6.

Make thee an Arkee of pine trees; thou shalt make cabins in the Arkee, and shalt pitch it within and without with pitch. Thou shalt make it with the lower, second and third roome.—Gen. vi. 14, 16.

And he said, Hagar, Sarais maide, whence comest thou? & whether wilt thou go? and she said, I flee from my dame Sarai.—Gen. xvi. 8.

When Abram was ninetie years old & nine, the Lord appeared to Abram, and said unto him, I am God all sufficient, walke before me, and be thou upright.—Gen. xvii. 1.

Then Abraham rose vp from the sight of his corps, and talked with the Hittites, saying, I am a stranger and a forreiner among you, &c.—Gen. xxiii. 3, 4.

Then Abraham yielded the spirit and died in a good age, an olde man, and of great yeeres, and was gathered to his people.—Gen. xxv. 8.

As many were astonied at thee (his visage was so deformed of men, and his forme of the sonnes of men) so shall hee spunckle many nations.—Isa. lii. 14. This chapter has but fourteen verses in it.

Can the blacke Moore change his skinne? or the leopard his spots?—Jer. xiii. 23.

And after those days we trussed up our fardles, and went up to Jerusalem.—Acts xxi. 15.

But Jesus sayde vnto her, Let the children first bee fed; for it is not good to take the childrens bread, and to cast it unto whelps. Then shee answered, and said unto him, Truthe, Lorde; yet in deede the whelps eate under the table of the childrens crummes.—Mark vii. 27, 28.

And she broght forth her fyrst begotten sonne, and wrapped him in swadlyng clothes, and layd him in a cretche, because there was no rowme for them with in the ynne.—Luke ii. 7.

The Bishops' Bible.—Archbishop Parker engaged bishops and other learned men to bring out a new translation. They did so in 1568, in large folio. It made what was afterwards called the great English Bible, and commonly the Bishops' Bible. In 1589 it was published in octavo, in small, but fine black letter. In it the chapters were divided into verses, but without any breaks for them.

Matthew Parker's Bible.—The Bishops' Bible underwent some corrections, and was printed in large folio in 1572, and called Matthew Parker's Bible. The version was used in the churches for forty years.

The Douay Bible.—The New Testament was brought out by the Roman Catholics in 1582, and called the Rhemish New Testament. It was condemned by the Queen of England, and copies were seized by her authority and destroyed. In 1609 and 1610, the Old Testament was added, and the whole published at Douay, hence called the Douay Bible.

King James's Bible.—The version now in use was brought out by King James's authority in 1611. Fifty-four learned men were employed to accomplish the work of revising it. From death or other cause, seven of them failed to enter upon it. The remaining forty-seven were ranged under six divisions, and had different portions of the Bible assigned to those divisions. They commenced their task in 1607. After some three or four years of diligent labor, the whole was completed. This version was generally adopted, and the other translations fell into disuse. It has continued in use until the present time.

DISSECTION OF THE OLD AND NEW TESTAMENTS.

Books in the Old Testament	...39	In the New..............27	Total.......................66
Chapters................929		" " 260	" 1,189
Verses..... 23,214		" " 7,959	" 31,173
Words...............592,439		" " 181,253	" 773,692
Letters........... 2,728,100		" " 838,380	" 3,566,480

APOCRYPHA.

Chapters................ 183 | Verses................6,081 | Words...............152,185

The middle chapter and the least in the Bible is Psalm cxvii.

The middle verse is the eighth of Psalm cxviii.

The middle line is in 2d Chronicles, 4th chapter, 16th verse.

The word *and* occurs in the Old Testament 35,543 times.

The same in the New Testament, 10,684.

The word *Jehovah* occurs 6,855 times.

OLD TESTAMENT.

The middle book is Proverbs.

The middle chapter is Job xxix.

The middle verse is in 2d Chronicles, 20th chapter, between the 17th and 18th verses.

The least verse is in 1st Chronicles, 1st chapter, and 25th verse.

NEW TESTAMENT.

The middle book is the 2d epistle to Thessalonians.

The middle chapter is between the 13th and 14th of Romans.

The middle verse is the 17th chapter of Acts, and 17th verse.

The least verse is the 11th chapter of John, verse 35.

The 21st verse of the 7th chapter of Ezra has all the letters of the alphabet in it.

The 19th chapter of the 2d book of Kings, and the 37th of Isaiah, are alike.

N.B.—Three years are said to have been spent in this curious but idle calculation.

DISTINCTIONS IN THE GOSPELS.

1. In regard to their external features and characteristics:.

The point of view of the first gospel is mainly Israelitic; of the second, Gentile; of the third, universal; of the fourth, Christian.

The general aspect, and so to speak, physiognomy of the first, mainly, is oriental; of the second, Roman; of the third, Greek; of the fourth, spiritual.

The style of the first is stately and rhythmical; of the second, terse and precise; of the third, calm and copious; of the fourth, artless and colloquial.

The striking characteristic of the first is symmetry; of the second compression; of the third, order; of the fourth, system.

The thought and language of the first are both Hebraistic; of the third, both Hellenistic; while in the second, thought is often accidental though the language is Hebraistic; and in the fourth, the language is Hellenistic, but the thought Hebraistic.

2. In respect to their subject-matter and contents:

In the first gospel, narrative; in the second, memoirs; in the third, history; in the fourth, dramatic portraiture.

In the first we often have the record of events in their accomplishment; in the second, events in detail; in the third, events in their connection; in the fourth, events in relation to the teaching springing from them.

Thus in the first we often meet with the notice of impressions; in the second, of facts; in the third, of motives; in the fourth, of words spoken.

And, lastly, the record of the first is mainly collective, and often antithetical; of the second, graphic and circumstantial; of the third, didactic and reflective; of the fourth, selective and supplemental.

3. In respect to their portraiture of our Lord:

The first presents him to us mainly as the Messiah; the second, mainly as the God-man; the third, as the Redeemer; the fourth, as the only begotten Son of God.

BOOKS MENTIONED IN THE BIBLE NOW LOST OR UNKNOWN.

1. The Prophecy of Enoch. See Epistle to Jude, 14.

2. The Book of the Wars of the Lord. See Numb. xxi. 14.

3. The Prophetical Gospel of Eve, which relates to the Amours of the Sons of God with the Daughters of Men. See Origen cont. Celsum, Tertul. &c.

4. The Book of Jasher. See Joshua x. 13; and 2 Samuel i. 18.

5. The Book of Iddo the Seer. See 2 Chronicles ix. 29, and xii. 15.

6. The Book of Nathan the Prophet. See as above.

7. The Prophecies of Ahijah, the Shilonite. See as above.

8. The acts of Rehoboam, in Book of Shemaiah. See 2 Chronicles xii. 15.

9. The Book of Jehu the Son of Hanani. See 2 Chronicles xx. 34.

10. The Five Books of Solomon, treating on the nature of trees, beasts, fowl, serpents, and fishes. See 1 Kings iv. 33.

11. The 151st Psalm.

THE WORD "SELAH."

The translators of the Bible have left the Hebrew word Selah, which occurs so often in the Psalms, as they found it, and of course the English reader often asks his minister, or some learned friend, what it means. And the minister or learned friend has most often been obliged to confess ignorance, because it is a matter in regard to which the most learned have by no means been of one mind. The Targums, and most of the Jewish commentators, give to the word the meaning of *eternally forever*. Rabbi Kimchi regards it as a sign to elevate the voice. The authors of the Septuagint translation appear to have considered it a musical or rhythmical note. Herder inclines to the opinion that it indicates a change of tone, which is expressed either by increase of force, or by a transition into another time and mode. Matheson thinks it is a musical note, equivalent, perhaps, to the word *repeat*. According to Luther and others, it means *silence*. Gesenius explains it to mean, "Let the instruments play and the singers stop." Wocher regards it as equivalent to *sursum corda*,—up, my soul! Sommer, after examining all the seventy-four passages in which the word occurs, recognizes in every case "an actual appeal or summons to Jehovah." They are calls for aid, and prayers to be heard, expressed either with entire directness, or if not in the imperative, Hear, Jehovah! or Awake, Jehovah, and the like, still, earnest addresses to God that he would remember and hear, &c. The word itself he considers indicative of a blast of trumpets by the priests, Selah being an abridged expression for Higgaion Selah,—Higgaion indicating the sound of the stringed instruments, and Selah a vigorous blast of trumpets.

HEXAMETERS IN THE BIBLE.

In the Psalms.

Gŏd cāme | ŭp wĭth ă | shŏut: ŏur | Lŏrd wĭth thĕ | sŏund ŏf ă | trŭmpĕt.‖
Thēre ĭs ă | rīvĕr thĕ | flŏwĭng whēre- | ŏf shăll | glăddĕn thĕ | cĭtў.‖
Hăllĕ- | lūjăh thĕ | cĭtў ŏf | Gŏd! Jē- | hŏvăh hăth | blēst hēr.‖

In the New Testament.

Art thŏu hĕ | thăt shŏuld ! cŏme, ŏr | dŏ wē | lŏŏk fŏr ă- | nŏthēr?‖
Hūsbănds, | lŏve yŏur | wīves, ănd | bē nŏt | bĭttĕr ă- | gāinst thĕm.‖
Blēss'd ăre thĕ | pŏŏr ĭn | spĭrĭt, fŏr | thĕirs ĭs thĕ | kĭngdŏm ŏf | hēavĕn.‖

Mr. Coleridge, whose enthusiastic and reverential admiration of the rhetorical beauty and poetic grandeur with which the Bible abounds,—all the more beautiful and the more sublime because casual and unsought by the sacred writers,—took great delight in pointing out the *hexametrical rhythm* of numerous passages, particularly in the book of Isaiah :—

Hear, O heavens, and give ear, | O earth : for the Lord hath spoken.
I have nourished and brought up children, | and they have rebelled against me.
The ox knoweth his owner, | and the ass his master's crib :
But Israel doth not know, | my people doth not consider.

Winer points out the following hexameters in the original Greek version of the New Testament :—

Κρῆτες ἀ | εὶ ψεῦ | σται, κακὰ | Θηρία | γαστέρες | ἀργαί.—Titus i. 12.

Πᾶσα δό | σις ἀγα | Θὴ καὶ | πᾶν δώ | ρημα τέ | λειον,—James i. 17.

Καὶ τροχι | ὰς ὀρ | Θὰς ποι | ήσατε | τοῖς ποσὶν | ὑμῶν,—Heb. xii. 13.

PARALLELISM OF THE HEBREW POETRY.

The prominent characteristic of the Hebrew poetry is what Bishop Lowth entitles *Parallelism*, that is, a certain equality, resemblance, or relationship, between the members of each period; so that in two lines, or members of the same period, things shall answer to things, and words to words, as if fitted to each other by a kind of rule or measure. The Psalms, Proverbs, Solomon's Song, Job, and all the Prophets, except Daniel and Jonah, abound with instances.

It is in a great measure owing to this form of composition that our admirable authorized version, though executed in prose, retains so much of a poetical cast; for, being strictly word for word after the original, the form and order of the original sentences are preserved; which, by this artificial structure, this regular alternation and correspondence of parts, makes the ear sensible of a departure from the common style and tone of prose.

The different kinds of parallels are illustrated in the following examples :—

Parallels Antithetic.—Prov. x. 1, 7.

A wise son maketh a glad father;
But a foolish son is the heaviness of his mother.
The memory of the just is blessed;
But the name of the wicked shall rot.

Parallels Synthetic.—Prov. vi. 16–19.

These six things doth the Lord hate;
Yea, seven are an abomination unto him:
A proud look, a lying tongue,
And hands that shed innocent blood,
A heart that deviseth wicked imaginations,
Feet that be swift in running to mischief,
A false witness that speaketh lies,
And he that soweth discord among brethren.

Constructive.—Psalm xix. 7–9.

The law of the Lord is perfect, converting the soul;
The testimony of the Lord is sure, making wise the simple;
The statutes of the Lord are right, rejoicing the heart;
The commandment of the Lord is pure, enlightening the eyes;
The fear of the Lord is clean, enduring forever;
The judgments of the Lord are true, and righteous altogether.

Parallels Synonymous.—Psalm xx. 1–4.

The Lord hear thee in the day of trouble;
The name of the God of Jacob defend thee;
Send thee help from the sanctuary,
And strengthen thee out of Zion;
Remember all thine offerings,
And accept thy burnt sacrifice;
Grant thee according to thine own heart,
And fulfil all thy counsel.

Gradational.—Psalm i. 1.

Blessed is the man
That walketh not in the counsel of the ungodly,
Nor standeth in the way of sinners,
Nor sitteth in the seat of the scornful.

Parallels Introverted.—Prov. xxiii. 15, 16.

My son, if thy heart be wise,
My heart shall rejoice, even mine;
Yea, my reins shall rejoice
When thy lips speak right things.

It may be objected to Hebrew poetry, says Gilfillan, that it has no regular rhythm except a rude parallelism. What then? Must it be, therefore, altogether destitute of music? Has not the rain a rhythm of its own, as it patters on the pane, or sinks on the bosom of its kindred pool? Has not the wind a harmony, as it bows the groaning woods, or howls over the mansions of the dead? Have not the waves of ocean their wild bass? Has not the thunder its own deep and dreadful organ-pipe? Do they speak in rhyme? Do they murmur in blank verse? Who taught them to begin in Iambics, or to close in Alexandrines? And shall not God's own speech have a peculiar note, no more barbarous than is the voice of the old woods or the older cataracts?

Besides, to call parallelism a coarse or uncouth rhythm, betrays an ignorance of its nature. Without entering at large on the subject of Hebrew versification, we may ask any one who has paid even a slight attention to the subject, if the effect of parallels such as the foregoing examples, perpetually intermingled as they are, be not to enliven the composition, often to give distinctness and precision to the train of thought, to impress the sentiments upon the memory, and to give out a harmony which, if inferior to rhyme in the compression produced by the difficulty (surmounted) of uniting varied sense with recurring sound, and in the pleasure of surprise; and to blank verse, in freedom, in the effects produced by the variety of pause, and in the force of long and linked passages, as well as of insulated lines, is less slavish than the one, and less arbitrary than the other? Unlike rhyme, its point is more that of thought than of language; unlike blank verse, it never can, however managed, degenerate into heavy prose. Such is parallelism, which generally forms the differential quality of the poetry of Scripture, although there are many passages in it destitute of this aid, and which yet, in the spirit they breathe, and the metaphors by which they are garnished, are genuine and high poetry. And there can be little question that in the parallelism of the Hebrew tongue we can trace many of the peculiarities of modern writing, and in it find the fountain of the rhythm, the pomp and antithesis, which lend often such grace, and always such energy, to the style of Johnson, of Junius, of Burke, of Hall, of Chalmers,—indeed, of most writers who rise to the grand swells of prose-poetry.

SIMILARITY OF SOUND.

There is a remarkable similarity of sound in a passage in the Second Book of Kings, ch. iii. v. 4, to the metrical rhythm of Campbell's *Battle of the Baltic :—*

A hundred thousand lambs,
And a hundred thousand rams,
With the wool.

By each gun the lighted brand,
In a bold determined hand,
And the Prince of all the land
Led them on.

PARALLEL PASSAGES BETWEEN SHAKSPEARE AND THE BIBLE.

20

An English minister, Rev. T. R. Eaton, has written a work entitled *Shakspeare and the Bible,* for the purpose of showing how much Shakspeare was indebted to the Bible for many of his illustrations, rhythms, and even modes of feeling. The author affirms that, in storing his mind, the immortal bard went first to the word, and then to the works, of God. In shaping the truths derived from these sources, he obeyed the instinct implanted by Him who had formed him Shakspeare. Hence his power of inspiring us with sublime affection for that which is properly good, and of chilling us with horror by his fearful delineations of evil. Shakspeare perpetually reminds us of the Bible, not by direct quotations, indirect allusion, borrowed idioms, or palpable imitation of phrase or style, but by an elevation of thought and simplicity of diction which are not to be found elsewhere. A passage, for instance, rises in our thoughts, unaccompanied by a clear recollection of its origin. Our first impression is that it must belong either to the Bible or Shakspeare. No other author excites the same feeling in an equal degree. In Shakspeare's plays religion is a vital and active principle, sustaining the good, tormenting the wicked, and influencing the hearts and lives of all.

Although the writer carries his leading idea too far, by straining passages to multiply the instances in which Shakspeare has imitated scriptural sentences in thought and construction, and by leading his readers to infer that it was from the Bible Shakspeare drew not only his best thoughts, but in fact his whole power of inspiring us with affection for good and horror for evil, it is certainly true that some hundreds of Biblical allusions, however brief and simple, show Shakspeare's conversance with the Bible, his fondness for it, and the almost unconscious recurrence of it in his mind. The following examples of his parallelisms will be found interesting :—

Othello.—Rude am I in my speech.—i. 3.
But though I be rude in speech.—2 Cor. xi. 6.

Witches.—Show his eyes and grieve his heart.—*Macbeth*, iv. 1.
Consume thine eyes and grieve thine heart.—1 Sam. ii. 33.

Macbeth.—Lighted fools the way to dusty death.—v. 5.
Thou hast brought me into the dust of death.—Ps. xxii. 15.

Dusty death alludes to the sentence pronounced against Adam :—

Dust thou art, and unto dust shalt thou return.—Gen. iii. 19.

Macbeth.—Life's but a walking shadow.—v. 5.
Man walketh in a vain show.—Ps. xxxix. 6.

Prince of Morocco.—Mislike me not for my complexion,
The shadow'd livery of the burnished sun.—*Merch. Ven.* ii. 1.

Look not upon me, because I am black, because the sun hath looked upon me.—Sol. Song, i. 6.

Othello.—I took by the throat, the circumcised dog, and smote him.—v. 2.
I smote him, I caught him by his beard and smote him, and slew him.—1 Sam. xvii. 35.

Macbeth.—Let this pernicious hour stand aye accursed in the calendar.—iv. 1.

Opened Job his mouth and cursed his day; let it not be joined unto the days of the year, let it not come into the number of the months.—Job iii. 1, 6.

Hamlet.—What a piece of work is man! How noble in reason, how infinite in faculties! In form and moving, how express and admirable! In action, how like an angel! In apprehension, how like a God! The beauty of the world, the paragon of animals!—ii. 2.

What is man, that thou art mindful of him? For thou hast made him a little lower than the angels, and hast crowned him with glory and honor. Thou madest him to have dominion over the works of thy hands.—Ps. viii. 4, 5, 6.

Macbeth.—We will die with harness on our back.—v. 5.
Nicanor lay dead in his harness.—2 Maccabees xv. 28.

Banquo.—Woe to the land that's governed by a child.
Woe to thee, O land, when thy king is a child.—Eccles. x. 16.

Banquo.—In the great hand of God I stand.—*Macbeth* ii. 3.
Thy right hand hath holden me up.—Ps. xviii. 35.

Man the image of his Maker.—*Henry VIII.*, iii. 2.—*Gen. I.* 27.
Blessed are the peacemakers.—2 *Henry VI.*, ii. 1.—*Matt. V.* 29.

And when he falls he falls like Lucifer.—*Henry VIII.*, iii. 2.

How art thou fallen from heaven, O Lucifer, son of the morning!—Isaiah xiv. 12.

No, Bolingbroke, if ever I were traitor,
My name be blotted from the book of life.—*Richard II.*, i. 3.

Whose names were not written in the book of life.—Rev. xx., xxi.

Swear by thy gracious self.—*Romeo and Juliet*, ii. 2.

He could swear by no greater, he sware by himself.—Heb. vi. 13.

My stay, my guide, and lantern to my feet.—2 *Henry VI.*, ii. 3.

Thy word is a lamp unto my feet, and a light unto my path.—Ps. cxix. 105.

Who can call him his friend that dips in the same dish?—*Timon of Athens*, iii. 2.

He that dippeth his hand with me in the dish, the same shall betray me.—Matt. xxvi. 23.

You shall see him a palm in Athens again, and flourish with the highest.
—*Timon of Athens*, v. 1.

The righteous shall flourish like the palm-tree.—Ps. xcii. 12.

It is written, they appear to men like angels of light.—*Com. of Errors*, iv. 3

Satan himself is transformed into an angel of light.—2 Cor. xi. 14.

> And lose my way
Among the thorns and dangers of this world.—*King John*, iv. 3.

Thorns and snares are in the way of the froward.—Prov. xxii. 5.

When we first put this dangerous stone a rolling,
'Twould fall upon ourselves.—*Henry VIII.*, v. 2.

He that rolleth a stone, it will return upon him.—Prov. xxvi. 27.

The speech of Ulysses, in "Troilus and Cressida," i. 3, is almost a paraphrase of St. Luke xxi. 25, 26 :—

> But when the planets
> In evil mixture to disorder wander,
> What plagues, and what portents! What mutiny!
> What raging of the sea! Shaking of earth!
> Commotion in the winds! frights, changes, horrors,
> Divert and crack, rend and deracinate
> The unity and married calm of states
> Quite from their fixture.

And there shall be signs in the sun, and in the moon, and in the stars; and upon the earth distress of nations, with perplexity; the sea and the waves roaring; men's hearts failing them for fear, and for looking after those things which are coming on the earth; for the powers of heaven shall be shaken.

Hermia and *Lear* both use an expression derived from the same source :—

Hermia.—An adder did it; for with doubler tongue
Than thine, thou serpent, never adder stung.—*Mid. N. Dream*, iii. 2.

Lear.—Struck me with her tongue,
Most serpent-like, upon the very heart.—ii. 4.

They have sharpened their tongues like a serpent; adders' poison is under their lips.—Ps. cxl. 3.

Lear.—All the stored vengeances of heaven fall on her ingrateful top.—ii. 4.

As for the head of those that compass me about, let the mischief of their own lips cover them.—Ps. cxl. 9.

Fool to King Lear.—We'll set thee to school to an ant, to teach thee there's no laboring in the winter.—ii. 4.

The ants are a people not strong, yet they prepare their meat in the summer.—Prov. xxx. 25.   See also Prov. vi. 6.

WHO IS THE TRUE GENTLEMAN?

The answer to this question will afford one of numberless instances that can be adduced to show the superiority of inspired composition.   Compare Bishop Doane's admired definition with that of the Psalmist :—

A gentleman is but a *gentle* man—no more, no less; a diamond polished that was a diamond in the rough: a gentleman is gentle; a gentleman is modest; a gentleman is courteous; a gentleman is generous; a gentleman is slow to take offence, as being one that never gives it; a gentleman is slow to surmise evil, as being one that never thinks it; a gentleman goes armed only in consciousness of right; a gentleman subjects his appetites; a gentleman refines his tastes; a gentleman subdues his feelings; a gentleman controls his speech; and finally, a gentleman deems every other better than himself.

In the paraphrase of Psalm xv. it is thus answered :—

'Tis he whose every thought and deed
    By rules of virtue moves;
Whose generous tongue disdains to speak
    The thing his heart disproves.
Who never did a slander forge,
    His neighbor's fame to wound,
Nor hearken to a false report,
    By malice whispered round.
Who vice, in all its pomp and power,
    Can treat with just neglect,

And piety, though clothed in rags,
  Religiously respect.
Who to his plighted vows and trust
  Has ever firmly stood ;
And though he promise to his loss,
  He makes his promise good.
Whose soul in usury disdains
  His treasure to employ ;
Whom no rewards can ever bribe
  The guiltless to destroy.

MISQUOTATIONS FROM SCRIPTURE.

"God tempers the wind to the shorn lamb."* From Sterne's *Sentimental Journey to Italy.* Compare Isaiah xxvii. 8.

"In the midst of life we are in death." From the Burial Service ; and this, originally, from a hymn of Luther.

"Bread and wine which the Lord hath commanded to be received." From the English Catechism.

"Not to be wise above what is written." Not in Scripture.

"That the Spirit would go from heart to heart as oil from vessel to vessel." Not in Scripture.

"The merciful man is merciful to his beast." The scriptural form is, "A righteous man regardeth the life of his beast."—Prov. xii. 10.

"A nation shall be born in a day." In Isaiah it reads, "Shall a nation be born at once?"—lxvi. 8.

"As iron sharpeneth iron, so doth a man the countenance of his friend." "Iron sharpeneth iron ; so a man sharpeneth the countenance of his friend." Prov. xxvii. 17.

"That he who runs may read." "That he may run that readeth."—Hab. ii. 2.

"Owe no man any thing but love." "Owe no man any thing, but to love one another."—Rom. xiii. 8.

"Prone to sin as the sparks fly upward." "Born unto trouble, as the sparks fly upward."—Job v. 7.

"Exalted to heaven in point of privilege." Not in the Bible.

Eve was not Adam's *helpmate,* but merely a help meet for him ; nor was Absalom's long hair, of which he was so proud, the instrument of his destruction ;† his head, and not the hair upon it, having been caught in the boughs of the tree. (2 Samuel xviii. 9.)

---

* In a collection of proverbs published in 1594, we find, "*Dieu mesure le vent à la brebis tondue,*" and Herbert has in his Jacula Prudentum, "To a close shorn sheep God gives wind by measure."

† A London periwig-maker once had a sign upon which was painted Absalom suspended from the branches of the oak by his hair, and underneath the following couplet :—

    If Absalom hadn't worn his own hair,
    He'd ne'er been found a hanging there.

"Money is the root of evil." Paul said, I. Timothy, vi. 10, "The love of money is the root of all evil."

"In the sweat of thy face shalt thou eat bread," Gen. iii. 19. Commonly quoted "brow."

"Cleanliness akin to godliness." Not in the Bible.

Our Lord's hearing the doctors in the Temple, and asking them questions, is frequently called his disputing with the doctors.

A SCRIPTURAL BULL.

In the book of Isaiah. chapter xxxvii. verse 36, is the following confusion of ideas:—

Then the angel of the Lord went forth, and smote in the camp of the Assyrians a hundred and fourscore and five thousand : and *when they arose early in the morning, behold, they were all dead corpses.*

WIT AND HUMOR IN THE BIBLE.

"Shocking!" many a good old saint will cry, at the very thought of it. "The Bible a jest-book! What godless folly shall we have up next?" No, the Bible is not a jest-book. But there is wit in it of the first quality; and a good reason why it should be there. Take a few specimens.

Job, in his thirtieth chapter, is telling how he scorned the low-lived fellows, who pretend to look down on him in his adversities. They are fools. They belong to the long-eared fraternity. Anybody, with less wit, might come out bluntly and call them asses. But Job puts it more deftly (xxx. 7): "Among the bushes they *brayed;* under the *nettles* they were gathered together." If that is not wit, there is no such thing as wit. And yet the commentators don't see it, or won't see it. They are perfectly wooden when they come to any such gleam of humor.

Take another instance—Elijah's ridicule of the prophets of Baal. They are clamoring to their god, to help them out of a very awkward predicament. And, while they are at it, the prophet shows them up in a way that must have made the people roar with laughter. The stiff, antiquated style of our English Bible tames down his sallies. Take them in modern phrase. These quack prophets have worked themselves into a perfect desperation, and are capering about on the altar as if they had the St. Vitus's dance. The scene (I. Kings xviii. 26, 27) wakes up all Elijah's sense of the ridiculous. "Shout louder! He is a god, you know. Make him hear! Perhaps he is chatting with somebody, or he is off on a hunt, or gone traveling. Or maybe he is taking a nap. Shout away! Wake him up!" Imagine the priests going through their antics on the altar, while Elijah bombards them in this style, at his leisure.

Paul shows a dry humor more than once, as in II. Cor. xii. 13: "Why haven't you fared as well as the other churches? Ah! there is one grievance—that you haven't had *me to support*. Pray do not lay it up against me!"

These instances might be multiplied from the Old and New Testaments both. What do they show? That the Bible is, on the whole, a humorous book? Far from it. That religion is a humorous subject—that we are to throw all the wit we can into the treatment of it? No. But they show that the sense of the ludicrous is put into a man by his Maker; that it has its uses, and that we are not to be ashamed of it, or to roll up our eyes in a holy horror of it.

THE OLD AND THE NEW TESTAMENT.

The name Old Testament was applied to the books of Moses by St. Paul (II. Cor. iii. 14), inasmuch as the former covenant comprised the whole scheme of the Mosaic revelation, and the history of this is contained in them. The phrase " book of the covenant," taken from Exod. xxiv. 7, was transferred in the course of time by metonymy to signify the writings themselves. The term New Testament has been in common use since the third century, and was employed by Eusebius in the sense in which it is now applied.

A SCRIPTURAL SUM.

Add to your faith, virtue;
And to virtue, knowledge;
And to knowledge, temperance;
And to temperance, patience;
And to patience, godliness;
And to godliness, brotherly kindness;
And to brotherly kindness, charity.

The Answer:—For if these things be in you and abound, they make you that ye shall neither be barren nor unfruitful in the knowledge of our Lord Jesus Christ.—2 Peter i. 5, 8.

BIBLIOMANCY.

Bibliomancy, or divination by the Bible, had become so common in the fifth century, that several councils were obliged expressly to forbid it, as injurious to religion, and savoring of idolatry.

This kind of divination was named *Sortes Sanctorum,* or *Sortes Sacræ,* Lots of the Saints, or Sacred Lots, and consisted in suddenly opening, or dipping into, the Bible, and regarding the passage that first presented itself to the eye as predicting the future lot of the inquirer. The *Sortes Sanctorum* had succeeded the *Sortes Homericæ* and *Sortes Virgilianæ* of the Pagans; among whom it was customary to take the work of some famous poet, as Homer or Virgil, and write out different verses on separate scrolls, and afterwards draw one of them, or else, opening the book suddenly, consider the first verse that presented itself as a prognostication of future events. Even the vagrant fortune-tellers, like some of the gypsies of our own times, adopted this method of imposing upon the credulity of the ignorant. The nations of the East retain the practice to the present day. The famous usurper, Nadir Shah, twice decided upon besieging cities, by opening at random upon verses of the celebrated poet Hafiz.

This abuse, which was first introduced into the church about the third century, by the superstition of the people, afterwards gained ground through the ignorance of some of the clergy, who permitted prayers to be read in the churches for this very purpose. It was therefore found necessary to ordain in the Council of Vannes, held A.D. 465, "That whoever of the clergy or laity should be detected in the practice of this art should be cast out of the communion of the church." In 506, the Council of Agde renewed the decree; and in 578, the Council of Auxerre, amongst other kinds of divination, forbade the Lots of the Saints, as they were called, adding, "Let all things be done in the name of the Lord;" but these ordinances did not effectually suppress them, for we find them again noticed and condemned in a capitulary or edict of Charlemagne, in 793. Indeed, all endeavors to banish them from the Christian church appear to have been in vain for ages.

The Name of God.

Tell them I AM, JEHOVAH said
To Moses, while earth heard in dread;
   And, smitten to the heart,
At once, above, beneath, around,
All nature, without voice or sound,
   Replied, O LORD! THOU ART!
      Christopher Smart, an English Lunatic.

IT is singular that the *name of God* should be spelled with *four letters* in almost every known language. It is in Latin, Deus; Greek, Zeus; Hebrew, Adon; Syrian, Adad; Arabian, Alla; Persian, Syra; Tartarian, Idga; Egyptian, Aumn, or Zeut; East Indian, Esgi, or Zenl; Japanese, Zain; Turkish, Addi; Scandinavian, Odin; Wallachian, Zenc; Croatian, Doga; Dalmatian, Rogt; Tyrrhenian, Eher; Etrurian, Chur; Margarian, Oese; Swedish, Codd; Irish, Dich; German, Gott; French, Dieu; Spanish, Dios; Peruvian, Lian.

The name *God* in the Anglo-Saxon language means *good*, and this signification affords singular testimony of the Anglo-Saxon conception of the essence of the Divine Being. He is goodness itself, and the Author of all goodness. Yet the idea of denoting the Deity by a term equivalent to abstract and absolute perfection, striking as it may appear, is perhaps less remarkable than the fact that the word *Man*, used to designate a human being, formerly signified *wickedness;* showing how well aware were its originators that our fallen nature had become indentified with sin.

JEHOVAH.

The word *Elohim*, as an appellation of Deity, appears to have been in use before the Hebrews had attained a national existence. That *Jehovah* is specifically the God of the Hebrews is clear, from the fact that the heathen deities never receive this name; they are always spoken of as *Elohim*. Both the pronunciation and the etymological derivation of the word *Jehovah* are matters of critical controversy. The Jews of later periods from religious awe abstained from pronouncing it, and whenever it occurred in reading, substituted the word *Adonai* (my Lord); and it is now generally believed that the sublinear vowel signs attached to the Hebrew tetragrammaton *Jhvh* belong to the substituted word. Many believe Jahveh to be the original pronunciation. The Hebrew root of the word is believed to be the verb *havah* or *hayah*, to be; hence its meaning throughout the Scriptures, "the Being," or "the Everlasting."

GOD IN SHAKSPEARE.

Michelet (*Jeanne d'Arc*,) speaking of English literature, says that it is " *Sceptique, judaique, satanique.* " In a note he says, "I do not recollect to have seen the word GOD in Shakspeare. If it is there at all, it is there very rarely, by chance, and without a shadow of religious sentiment." Mrs. Cowden Clarke, by means of her admirable *Concordance to Shakspeare*, enables us to weigh the truth of this eminent French writer's remark. The word GOD occurs in Shakspeare upwards of *one thousand times*, and the word heaven, which is so frequently substituted for the word GOD—more especially in the historical plays—occurs about *eight hundred times*. In the Holy Scriptures, according to Cruden, it occurs about eight hundred times. It is true that the word often occurs in Shakspeare without a reverential sentiment; but M. Michelet says it never occurs with a religious feeling (*un sentiment religieux.*) This statement is almost as erroneous as that regarding the absence of the word. It would be easy for an English scholar to produce from Shakspeare more passages indicative of deep religious feeling than are to be found in any French writer whatever.

THE PARSEE, JEW, AND CHRISTIAN.

A Jew entered a Parsee temple, and beheld the sacred fire. "What!" said he to the priest, "do you worship the fire?"

"Not the fire," answered the priest: "it is to us an emblem of the sun, and of his genial heat."

"Do you then worship the sun as your god?" asked the Jew. "Know ye not that this luminary also is but a work of that Almighty Creator?"

"We know it," replied the priest: "but the uncultivated man requires a sensible sign, in order to form a conception of the Most High. And is not the sun the incomprehensible source of light, an image of that invisible being who blesses and preserves all things?"

"Do your people, then," rejoined the Israelite, "distinguish the type from the original? They call the sun their god, and, descending even from this to a baser object, they kneel before an earthly flame! Ye amuse the outward but blind the inward eye; and while ye hold to them the earthly, ye draw from them the heavenly light! 'Thou shalt not make unto thyself any image or any likeness.'"

"How do you name the Supreme Being?" asked the Parsee.

"We call him Jehovah Adonai, that is, the Lord who is, who was, and who will be," answered the Jew.

"Your appellation is grand and sublime," said the Parsee; "but it is awful too."

A Christian then drew nigh, and said,—

"We call him FATHER."

The Pagan and the Jew looked at each other, and said,—

" Here is at once an image and a reality : it is a word of the heart."

Therefore they all raised their eyes to heaven, and said, with reverence and love, "OUR FATHER !" and they took each by the hand, and all three called one another *brothers!*

DE NOMINE JESU.

I n rebus tantis trina conjunctio mund **I**
E rigit humanum sensum, laudare venust **E**
S ola salus nobis, et mundi summa, potesta **S**
V enit peccati nodum   dissolvere   fruct **V**
S umma salus cunctas nituit per secula terra **S.****

The letters I. H. S. so conspicuously appended to different portions of Catholic churches, are said to have been designed by St. Bernardine of Sienna, to denote the name and mission of the Saviour.   They are to be found in a circle above the principal door of the Franciscan Church of the Holy Cross, (*Santa Croce*,) in Florence, and are said to have been put there by the saint on the termination of the plague of 1347, after which they were commonly introduced into churches.   The letters have assigned to them the following signification :—

Jesus hominum Salvator—Jesus, the Saviour of men.
In hoc salus—In him is salvation.

---

* I n times momentous appeared the world's triple conjunction,
E ncouraging human hearts to shout melodious praises.
S ole salvation for us, that power exalted 'bove measure,
U nloosed the bonds of sin through the precious atonement.
S alvation illumines all earth through ages unceasing.

A maker of playing-cards, which, like missels, were illuminated in those times, was one day remonstrated with by St. Bernardine, upon the sinfulness of his business. The card-maker pleaded the needs of his family. "Well, I will help you," said the saint, and wrote the letters I. H. S., which he advised the card-maker to paint and gild. The new card "took," and the saint himself travelled about the country as a poster of these little sacred handbills of the Church.

THE FLOWER OF JESSE.
1520.

There is a flower sprung of a tree,
The root of it is called Jesse,
A flower of price,—
There is none such in Paradise.

Of Lily white and Rose of Ryse,
Of Primrose and of Flower-de-Lyse,
Of all flowers in my devyce,
The flower of Jesse beareth the prize,
    For most of all
To help our souls both great and small.

I praise the flower of good Jesse,
Of all the flowers that ever shall be,
Uphold the flower of good Jesse,
And worship it for aye beautee;
    For best of all
That ever was or ever be shall.

BEAUTIFUL LEGEND.

One day Rabbi Judah and his brethren, the seven pillars of Wisdom, sat in the Court of the Temple, on feast-day, disputing about REST. One said that it was to have attained sufficient wealth, yet without sin. The second, that it was fame and praise of all men. The third, that it was the possession of power to rule the State. The fourth, that it consisted only in a happy home. The fifth, that it must be in the old age of one who is rich, powerful, famous, surrounded by children and children's children. The sixth said that all that were vain, unless a man keep all the ritual law of Moses. And Rabbi

Judah, the venerable, the tallest of the brothers, said, "Ye have spoken wisely; but one thing more is necessary. He only can find rest, who to all things addeth this, that he keepeth the tradition of the elders."

There sat in the Court a fair-haired boy, playing with some lilies in his lap, and, hearing the talk, he dropped them with astonishment from his hands, and looked up—that boy of twelve—and said, "Nay, nay, fathers: he only findeth rest, who loveth his brother as himself, and God with his whole heart and soul. He is greater than fame, and wealth, and power, happier than a happy home, happy without it, better than honored age; he is a law to himself, and above all tradition." The doctors were astonished. They said, "When Christ cometh, shall He tell us greater things?" And they thanked God, for they said, "The old men are not always wise, yet God be praised, that out of the mouth of this young suckling has His praise become perfect."

PERSIAN APOLOGUE.

In Sir William Jones's Persian Grammar may be found the following beautiful story from NISAMI. Mr. Alger gives a metrical translation in his *Poetry of the East*.

One evening Jesus arrived at the gates of a certain city, and sent his disciples forward to prepare supper, while he himself, intent on doing good, walked through the streets into the market-place.

And he saw at the corner of the market some people gathered together, looking at an object on the ground; and he drew near to see what it might be. It was a dead dog, with a halter around his neck, by which he appeared to have been dragged through the dirt; and a viler, a more abject, a more unclean thing never met the eyes of man.

And those who stood by looked on with abhorrence.

"Faugh!" said one, stopping his nose: "it pollutes the air." "How long," said another, "shall this foul beast offend our sight?" "Look at his torn hide," said a third: "one could not even cut a shoe out of it." "And his ears," said a fourth, "all draggled and bleeding." "No doubt," said a fifth, "he has been hanged for thieving."

And Jesus heard them, and looking down compassionately on the dead creature, he said, "Pearls are not equal to the whiteness of his teeth!"

Then the people turned towards him with amazement, and said among themselves, "Who is this? It must be Jesus of Nazareth, for only HE could find something to pity and approve even in a dead dog." And being ashamed, they bowed their heads before him and went each on his way.

DESCRIPTION OF THE PERSON OF JESUS CHRIST.

The following description is alleged to be derived from an ancient manuscript sent by Publius Lentulus, President of Judea, to the Senate of Rome:—

"There lives at this time in Judea, a man of singular character, whose name is Jesus Christ. The barbarians esteem him as their prophet; but his followers adore him as the immediate offspring of the immortal God. He is endowed with such unparalleled virtue as to call back the dead from their graves and to heal every kind of disease with a word or a touch. His person is tall and elegantly shaped; his aspect, amiable and reverend; his hair flows in those beauteous shades which no united colors can match, falling in graceful curls below his ears, agreeably couching on his shoulders, and parting on the crown of his head; his dress, that of the sect of Nazarites; his forehead is smooth and large; his cheeks without blemish, and of roseate hue; his nose and mouth are formed with exquisite symmetry; his beard is thick and suitable to the hair of his head, reaching a little below his chin, and parting in the middle below; his eyes are clear, bright, and serene.

"He rebukes with mildness, and invokes with the most tender and persuasive language,—his whole address, whether in word or deed, being elegantly grave, and strictly characteristic of so exalted a being. No man has seen him laugh, but the whole world beholds him weep frequently, and so persuasive are his tears that the whole multitude cannot withhold their tears from joining in sympathy with him.   He is moderate, temperate, and wise : in short, whatever the phenomenon may turn out in the end, he seems at present to be a man of excellent beauty and divine perfection, every way surpassing man."

DEATH-WARRANT OF JESUS CHRIST.

Of the many interesting relics and fragments brought to light by the persevering researches of antiquarians, none could be more interesting to the philanthropist and believer than the following,—to Christians, the most imposing judicial document ever recorded in human annals.   It has been thus faithfully transcribed :—

Sentence rendered by Pontius Pilate, acting Governor of Lower Galilee, stating that Jesus of Nazareth shall suffer death on the cross.

In the year seventeen of the Emperor Tiberius Cæsar, and the 27th day of March, the city of the holy Jerusalem—Annas and Caiaphas being priests, sacrificators of the people of God—Pontius Pilate, Governor of Lower Galilee, sitting in the presidential chair of the prætory, condemns Jesus of Nazareth to die on the cross between two thieves, the great and notorious evidence of the people saying :

1. Jesus is a seducer.
2. He is seditious.
3. He is the enemy of the law.
4. He calls himself falsely the Son of God.
5. He calls himself falsely the King of Israel.
6. He entered into the temple followed by a multitude bearing palm branches in their hands.

Orders the first centurion, Quilius Cornelius, to lead him to the place of execution.

Forbids any person whomsoever, either poor or rich, to oppose the death of Jesus Christ.

The witnesses who signed the condemnation of Jesus are—

1. Daniel Robani, a Pharisee.
2. Joannus Robani.

3. Raphael Robani.
4. Capet, a citizen.
   Jesus shall go out of the city of Jerusalem by the gate of
   Struenus.

The foregoing is engraved on a copper plate, on the reverse
of which is written, "A similar plate is sent to each tribe."
It was found in an antique marble vase, while excavating in
the ancient city of Aquilla, in the kingdom of Naples, in the
year 1810, and was discovered by the Commissioners of Arts
of the French army. At the expedition of Naples, it was enclosed in a box of ebony and preserved in the sacristy of the
Carthusians. The French translation was made by the Commissioners of Arts. The original is in the Hebrew language.

DOUBLE HEXAMETER.

$$\text{Si Christum} \begin{Bmatrix} \text{nescis} \\ \text{discis} \end{Bmatrix} \text{nihil est si cætera} \begin{Bmatrix} \text{discis;} \\ \text{nescis.} \end{Bmatrix}$$

ANTICIPATORY USE OF THE CROSS.

Madame Calderon de la Barca, in her *Life in Mexico* (*pub.
1843*), says that the symbol of the Cross was known to the
Indians before the arrival of Cortez. In the island of Cozumel,
near Yucatan, there were several; and in Yucatan* itself there
was a stone cross. And there an Indian, considered a prophet
among his countrymen, had declared that a nation bearing the
same as a symbol should arrive from a distant country. More
extraordinary still was a temple dedicated to the Holy Cross by
the Toltec nation in the city of Cholula. Near Tulansingo there
is also a cross engraved on a rock with various characters. In
Oajaca there was a cross which the Indians from time immemorial had been accustomed to consider as a divine symbol. By
order of Bishop Cervantes it was placed in a chapel in the
cathedral. Information concerning its discovery, together with
a small cup, cut out of its wood, was sent to Rome to Paul V.,
who received it on his knees, singing the hymn *Vexilla regis, etc.*

See also Prescott's *Conquest of Mexico*, Vol. I. Bk. II. Chap. 4; and
Stephens' *Incidents of Travel in Yucatan*, Vol. II. Chap. 20.

The Lord's Prayer.

The Lord's Prayer alone is an evidence of the truth of Christianity,—so admirably is that prayer accommodated to all our wants.—LORD WELLINGTON.

THY AND US.

The two divisions of the Lord's Prayer—the former relating to the glory of God, the latter to the wants of man—appear very evident on a slight transposition of the personal pronouns:—

Thy name be hallowed.
Thy kingdom come.
Thy will be done, &c.
Us give this day our daily bread.
Us forgive our debts, &c.
Us lead not into temptation.
Us deliver from evil.

SPIRIT OF THE LORD'S PRAYER.

The spirit of the Lord's Prayer is beautiful. This form of petition breathes:—

A *filial* spirit—Father.
A *catholic* spirit—Our Father.
A *reverential* spirit—Hallowed be Thy name.
A *missionary* spirit—Thy kingdom come.
An *obedient* spirit—Thy will be done on earth as it is in heaven.
A *dependent* spirit—Give us this day our daily bread.
A *forgiving* spirit—And forgive our debts as we forgive our debtors.
A *cautious* spirit—And lead us not into temptation, but deliver us from evil.
A *confidential* and *adoring* spirit—For thine is the kingdom, and the power, and the glory, forever. Amen.

GOTHIC VERSION.

Ulphilas, who lived between the years 310 and 388, was bishop of the Western Goths, and translated the greater part of the Scriptures into the Gothic language. The following is his rendering of the Lord's Prayer:—

Atta unsar thu in himinam. Weihnai namo thein. Quimai thiudinassus sijaima, swaswe jah weis afletam thaim skulam unsaraim. Jah ni briggais uns in fraistubujai. Ak lausei uns af thamma ubilin, unte theina ist thiu-dangardi, jah maths, jah wulthus in aiwins. Amen.

METRICAL VERSIONS.

Father in heaven, hallowed be thy name;
Thy kingdom come: thy will be done the same
In earth and heaven. Give us daily bread;
Forgive our sins as others we forgive.
Into temptation let us not be led;
Deliver us from evil while we live.
For kingdom, power, and glory must remain
For ever and for ever thine: Amen.

Here the sixty-six words of the original, according to the authorized translation of St. Matthew's version, are reduced to fifty-nine, though the latter is fully implied in all points except two. "This day" is omitted; but, if anything, the Greek is slightly approached, for ἐπιούσιον refers rather to *to-morrow* than to *to-day*. The antithesis in *"But* deliver us" does not appear: if the word deliver be sacrificed, we may read, "But keep us safe."

The subjoined metrical version of the Prayer is at least two and a half centuries old, and was written for adaptation to music in public worship:—

Our Father which in heaven art,
All hallowed be thy name;
Thy kingdom come,
On earth thy will be done,
Even as the same in heaven is.
Give us, O Lord, our daily bread this day:
As we forgive our debtors,
So forgive our debts, we pray.
Into temptation lead us not,
From evil make us free:
The kingdom, power, and glory thine,
Both now and ever be.

The Prayer is commended for its authorship, its efficacy, its perfection, the order of its parts, its brevity, and its necessity.

The following paraphrase, which has been set to music as a duett, is of more recent origin :—

Our Heavenly Father, hear our prayer:
Thy name be hallowed everywhere;
Thy kingdom come; on earth, thy will,
E'en as in heaven, let all fulfill ;
Give this day's bread, that we may live ;
Forgive our sins as we forgive ;
Help us temptation to withstand ;
From evil shield us by Thy hand ;
Now and forever, unto Thee,
The kingdom, power, and glory be.   Amen.

THE PRAYER ILLUSTRATED.

Our Father.—Isaiah lxiii. 16.

1. By right of creation.	Malachi ii. 10.
2. By bountiful provision.	Psalm cxlv. 16.
3. By gracious adoption.	Ephesians i. 5.

Who art in Heaven.—1 Kings viii. 43.

1. The throne of thy glory.	Isaiah lxvi. 1.
2. The portion of thy children	1 Peter i. 4.
3. The temple of thy angels.	Isaiah vi. 1.

Hallowed be thy Name.—Psalm cxv. 1.

1. By the thoughts of our hearts.	Psalm lxxxvi. 11.
2. By the words of our lips.	Psalm li. 15.
3. By the works of our hands.	1 Corinthians x. 31.

Thy Kingdom come.—Psalm cx. 2.

1. Of Providence to defend us.	Psalm xvii. 8.
2. Of grace to refine us.	1 Thessalonians v. 23.
3. Of glory to crown us.	Colossians iii. 4.

Thy will be done on Earth as it is in Heaven.—Acts xxxi. 14.

1. Towards us, without resistance.	1 Samuel iii. 18.
2. By us, without compulsion.	Psalm cxix. 36.
3. Universally, without exception.	Luke i. 6.
4. Eternally, without declension.	Psalm cxix. 93.

Give us this day our daily bread.

1. Of necessity, for our bodies.	Proverbs xxx. 8.
2. Of eternal life, for our souls.	John vi. 34.

And forgive us our trespasses.—Psalm xxv. 11.

1. Against the commands of thy law.	1 John iii. 4.
2. Against the grace of thy gospel.	1 Timothy i. 13.

As we forgive them that trespass against us.—Matthew vi. 15.

    1. By defaming our characters.   Matthew v. 11.
    2. By embezzling our property.   Philemon 18.
    3. By abusing our persons.   Acts vii. 60.

And lead us not into temptation, but deliver us from evil.—Matthew xxvi. 41.

    1. Of overwhelming afflictions.   Psalm cxxx. 1.
    2. Of worldly enticements.   1 John ii. 16.
    3. Of Satan's devices.   1 Timothy iii. 7.
    4. Of error's seduction.   1 Timothy vi. 10.
    5. Of sinful affections.   Romans i. 26.

For thine is the kingdom, and the power, and the glory, forever.—Jude 25.

    1. Thy kingdom governs all.   Psalm ciii. 19.
    2. Thy power subdues all.   Philippians iii. 20, 21.
    3. Thy glory is above all.   Psalm cxlviii. 13.

Amen.—Ephesians i. 11.

    1. As it is in thy purposes.   Isaiah xiv. 27.
    2. So is it in thy promises.   2 Corinthians i. 20.
    3. So be it in our prayers.   Revelation xxii. 20.
    4. So shall it be to thy praise.   Revelation xix. 4.

ACROSTICAL PARAPHRASE.

OUR Lord and King, Who reign'st enthroned on high,
FATHER of Light! mysterious Deity!
WHO art the great I AM, the last, the first,
ART righteous, holy, merciful, and just.
IN realms of glory, scenes where angels sing,
HEAVEN is the dwelling-place of God our King.
HALLOWED Thy name, which doth all names transcend,
BE Thou adored, our great Almighty Friend;
THY glory shines beyond creation's bound;
NAME us 'mong those Thy choicest gifts surround.
THY kingdom towers beyond Thy starry skies;
KINGDOM Satanic falls, but Thine shall rise.
COME let Thine empire, O Thou Holy One,
THY great and everlasting will be done.
WILL God make known his will, his power display?
BE it the work of mortals to obey.
DONE is the great, the wondrous work of love;
ON Calvary's cross he died, but reigns above;
EARTH bears the record in Thy holy word.
As heaven adores Thy love, let earth, O Lord;
IT shines transcendent in the eternal skies,
Is praised in heaven—for man, the Saviour dies.

IN songs immortal, angels laud his name;
HEAVEN shouts with joy, and saints his love proclaim
GIVE us, O Lord, our food, nor cease to give
Us needful food on which our souls may live!
THIS be our boon to-day and days to come,
DAY without end in our eternal home.
OUR needy souls supply from day to day;
DAILY assist and aid us when we pray;
BREAD though we ask, yet, Lord, Thy blessings lend.
AND make us grateful when Thy gifts descend.
FORGIVE our sins, which in destruction place
Us, the vile rebels of a rebel race;
OUR follies, faults, and trespasses forgive,
DEBTS which we ne'er can pay, nor Thou receive.
AS we, O Lord, our neighbor's faults o'erlook,
WE beg Thou 'd'st blot ours from Thy memory's book.
FORGIVE our enemies, extend Thy grace
OUR souls to save, e'en Adam's guilty race.
DEBTORS to Thee in gratitude and love,
AND in that duty paid by saints above,
LEAD us from sin, and in thy mercy raise
Us from the tempter and his hellish ways.
NOT in our own, but in His name who bled,
INTO Thine ear we pour our every need.
TEMPTATION'S fatal charm help us to shun,
BUT may we conquer through Thy conquering Son;
DELIVER us from all that can annoy
Us in this world, and may our souls destroy.
FROM all calamities that man betide,
EVIL and death, O turn our feet aside,—
FOR we are mortal worms, and cleave to clay,—
THINE 'tis to rule, and mortals to obey.
IS not thy mercy, Lord, forever free?
THE whole creation knows no God but Thee.
KINGDOM and empire in Thy presence fall;
THE King eternal reigns the King of all.
POWER is Thine—to Thee be glory given,
AND be thy name adored by earth and heaven.
THE praise of saints and angels is Thy own;
GLORY to Thee, the Everlasting One.
FOREVER be Thy holy name adored.
AMEN! Hosannah! blessed be the Lord

TRIFLING OF BIBLE COMMENTATORS.

Dr. Gill, in his Expository, seriously tells us that the word **ABBA** read backwards or forwards being the same, may teach us that God is the father of his people in adversity as well as in prosperity.

THE PRAYER ECHOED.

If any be distressed, and fain would gather
Some comfort, let him haste unto
            Our Father.

For we of hope and help are quite bereaven
Except Thou succor us
            Who art in heaven.

Thou showest mercy, therefore for the same
We praise Thee, singing,
            Hallowed be Thy name.

Of all our miseries cast up the sum;
Show us thy joys, and let
            Thy kingdom come.

We mortal are, and alter from our birth;
Thou constant art;
            Thy will be done on earth.

Thou madest the earth, as well as planets seven,
Thy name be blessed here
            As 'tis in heaven.

Nothing we have to use, or debts to pay,
Except Thou give it us.
            Give us this day

Wherewith to clothe us, wherewith to be fed,
For without Thee we want
            Our daily bread.

We want, but want no faults, for no day passes
But we do sin.
            Forgive us our trespasses.

No man from sinning ever free did live
Forgive us, Lord, our sins,
            As we forgive.

If we repent our faults, Thou ne'er disdain'st us;
We pardon them
            That trespass against us;

Forgive us that is past, a new path tread us;
Direct us always in Thy faith,
            And lead us—

Us, Thine own people and Thy chosen nation,
Into all truth, but
            Not into temptation.

Thou that of all good graces art the Giver,
Suffer us not to wander,
            But deliver

Us from the fierce assaults of world and devil
And flesh; so shalt Thou free us
            From all evil.

To these petitions let both church and laymen
With one consent of heart and voice, say,
            Amen.

THE PRAYER IN AN ACROSTIC.

In the following curious composition the initial capitals spell, "My boast is in the glorious Cross of Christ." The words in *italics*, when read from top to bottom and bottom to top, form the Lord's Prayer complete:—

Make known the Gospel truths, *Our* Father King;
   Yield up thy grace, dear *Father* from above;
Bless us with hearts *which* feelingly can sing,
   " Our life thou *art* for *ever*, God of Love!"
Assuage our grief *in* love *for* Christ, we pray,
   Since the bright prince of *Heaven* and *glory* died,
Took all our sins and *hallowed* the display,
   Infinite *be*-ing—first man, *and* then the crucified.
Stupendous God! *thy* grace and *power* make known;
   In Jesus' *name* let all *the* world rejoice.
Now all the world *thy* heavenly *kingdom* own,
   The blessed *kingdom* for thy saints *the* choice.
How vile to *come* to thee *is* all our cry,
   Enemies to *thy* self and all that's *thine*,
Graceless our *will*, we live *for* vanity,
   Lending to sin our *be*-ing, *evil* in our design.
O God, thy will be *done from* earth to Heaven;
   Reclining *on* the Gospel let *us* live,
In *earth* from sin *deliver*-ed and forgiven,
   Oh! *as* thyself *but* teach us to forgive.
Unless *it*'s power *temptation* doth destroy,
   Sure *is* our fall *into* the depths of woe,
Carnal *in* mind, we've *not* a glimpse of joy
   Raised against *Heaven;* in *us* no hope can flow.
O *give* us grace and *lead* us on thy way;
   Shine on *us* with thy love and give *us* peace;
Self and *this* sin that rise *against* us slay;
   Oh! grant each *day* our *trespass*-es may cease.
Forgive *our* evil deeds *that* oft we do;
   Convince us *daily* of *them* to our shame;
Help us with heavenly *bread, forgive* us, too,
   Recurrent lusts, *and we*'ll adore thy name.
In thy *forgive*-ness we *as* saints can die,
   Since for *us* and our *trespasses* so high,
Thy son, *our* Saviour, bled on Calvary.

Ecclesiasticæ.

EXCESSIVE CIVILITY.

TOM BROWN, in his *Laconics*, says that in the reign of
Charles II. a certain worthy divine at Whitehall thus addressed himself to the auditory at the conclusion of his sermon:
" In short, if you don't live up to the precepts of the gospel,
but abandon yourselves to your irregular appetites, you must
expect to receive your reward in a certain place, which 'tis
not good manners to mention here." This suggested to Pope
the couplet,

> " To rest, the cushion and soft dean invite,
> Who never mentions hell to ears polite."

SHORT SERMONS.

DEAN SWIFT, having been solicited to preach a charity sermon, mounted the pulpit, and after announcing his text, " He
that giveth to the poor lendeth to the Lord," simply said,
" Now, my brethren, if you are satisfied with the security,
down with the dust." He then took his seat, and there was an
unusually large collection.

The following abridgment contains the pith and marrow,
sum and substance, of a sermon which occupied an hour in
delivery :—

> " Man is born to trouble."
>
> This subject, my hearers, is naturally divisible into **four heads :—**
>
> 1. Man's entrance into the world ;
> 2. His progress through the world ;
> 3. His exit from the world ; and
> 4. Practical reflections from what may be said.
>
> First, then :—
>
> 1. Man's ingress in life is naked and bare,
> 2. His progress through life is trouble and care,
> 3. His egress from it, none can tell where.
> 4. But doing well here, he will be well there.
>
> Now, on this subject, my brethren dear,
> I could not tell more by preaching a year.

A SERMON ON MALT.

The Rev. Dr. Dodd lived within a few miles of Cambridge, (England,) and had offended several students by preaching a sermon on temperance. One day some of them met him. They said one to another,—

"Here's Father Dodd: he shall preach us a sermon." Accosting him with,—

"Your servants."

"Sirs! yours, gentlemen!" replied the Doctor.

They said, "We have a favor to ask of you, which *must* be granted." The divine asked what it was.

"To preach a sermon," was the reply.

"Well," said he, "appoint the time and place, and I will."

"The time, the present; the place, that hollow tree," (pointing to it,) said the students.

"'Tis an imposition!" said the Doctor: "there ought to be consideration before preaching."

"If you refuse," responded they, "we will put you into the tree!" Whereupon the Doctor acquiesced, and asked them for a text.

"Malt!" said they.

The reverend gentleman commenced:—

"Let me crave your attention, my beloved!

"I am a little man, come at a short warning, to preach a short sermon, upon a short subject, to a thin congregation, in an unworthy pulpit. Beloved! my text is 'MALT.' I cannot divide it into syllables, it being but a monosyllable: therefore I must divide it into letters, which I find in my text to be four:—M-A-L-T. M, my beloved, is *moral*—A, is *allegorical*—L, is *literal*—T, is *theological*.

"1st. The moral teaches such as you drunkards good manners; therefore M, my masters—A, all of you—L, leave off—T, tippling.

"2d. The allegorical is, when one thing is spoken and another meant; the thing here spoken is Malt, the thing meant the oil of malt, which *you* rustics make M, your masters—A, your apparel—L, your liberty—T, your trusts.

"3d. The theological is according to the effects it works, which are of two kinds—the first in this world, the second in the world to come. The effects it works in this world are, *in some*, M, murder—in others, A, adultery—*in all*, L, looseness of life —and *particularly in some*, T, treason. In the world to come, the effects of it are, M, misery—A, anguish—L, lamentation —T, torment—and thus much for my text, 'Malt.'

"Infer 1st: As words of exhortation: M, my masters—A, all of you—L, leave off—T, tippling.

"2d. A word for conviction: M, my masters—A, all of you —L, look for—T, torment.

"3d. A word for caution, take this: A drunkard is the annoyance of modesty—the spoiler of civility—the destroyer of reason—the brewer's agent—the alewife's benefactor—his wife's sorrow—his children's trouble—his neighbor's scoff—a walking swill-tub—a picture of a beast—a monster of a man."

The youngsters found the truth so unpalatable, that they soon deserted their preacher, glad to get beyond the reach of his voice.

ELOQUENCE OF BASCOM.

The following passages will serve to illustrate the peculiar oratorical style of Rev. Henry B. Bascom, the distinguished Kentucky preacher:—

"Chemistry, with its fire-tongs of the galvanic battery, teaches that the starry diamond in the crown of kings, and the black carbon which the peasant treads beneath his feet, are both composed of the same identical elements; analysis also proves that a chief ingredient in limestone is carbon. Then let the burning breath of God pass over all the limestone of the earth, and bid its old mossy layers crystalize into new beauty; and lo! at the Almighty *fiat* the mountain ranges flash into living gems with a lustre that renders midnight noon, and eclipses all the stars!"

He urged the same view by another example, still better adapted to popular apprehension :—

"Look yonder," said the impassioned orator, pointing a motionless finger towards the lofty ceiling, as if it were the sky. "See that wrathful thunder-cloud—the fiery bed of the lightnings and hissing hail—the cradle of tempests and floods! —What can be more dark, more dreary, more dreadful? Say, scoffing skeptic, is it capable of any beauty? You pronounce, 'no.' Well, very well; but behold, while the sneering denial curls your proud lips, the sun with its sword of light shears through the sea of vapors in the west, and laughs in your incredulous face with his fine golden eye. Now, look again at the thunder-cloud! See! where it was blackest and fullest of gloom, the sunbeams have kissed its hideous cheek; and where the kiss fell there is now a blush, brighter than ever mantled on the brow of mortal maiden—the rich blush of crimson and gold, of purple and vermilion—a pictured blush, fit for the gaze of angels—the flower-work of pencils of fire and light, wrought at a dash by one stroke of the right hand of God! Ay, the ugly cloud hath given birth to the rainbow, that perfection and symbol of unspeakable beauty!"

THE LORD BISHOP.

The following incident is said to have occurred in the parish church of Bradford, England, during a special service, on the occasion of a visit from the bishop of the diocese :—

The clerk, before the sermon, gave out the psalm in broad Wiltshire dialect, namely :—"Let us zing to the praayze an' glawry o' God, three varsses o' the hundred and vourteen zaam —a varsion 'specially 'dapted to the 'caasion,—by meself:"—

> Why hop ye zo, ye little hills,
>   An' what var de'e skip?
> Is it 'cas you'm proud to see
>   His grace the Lard Bish*ip*?
>
> Why skip ye zo, ye little hills,
>   An' what var de'e hop?

Is it 'cas to preach to we
Is com'd the Lard Bish*op?*

Eese;—he is com'd to preach to we:
Then let us aul strick up,
An' zing a glawrious zong of praayze,
An' bless the Lard Bish*up!*

THE PREACHERS OF CROMWELL'S TIME.

Dr. Echard says of the preachers who lived in the time of Cromwell,—"Coiners of new phrases, drawers-out of long godly words, thick pourers-out of texts of Scripture, mimical squeakers and bellowers, vain-glorious admirers only of themselves, and those of their own fashioned face and gesture; such as these shall be followed, shall have their bushels of China oranges, shall be solaced with all manner of cordial essences, and shall be rubbed down with Holland of ten shillings an ell."

One of the singular fashions that prevailed among the preachers of those days was that of coughing or hemming in the middle of a sentence, as an ornament of speech; and when their sermons were printed, the place where the preacher coughed or hemmed was always noted in the margin. This practice was not confined to England, for Olivier Maillard, a Cordelier, and famous preacher, printed a sermon at Brussels in the year 1500, and marked in the margin where the preacher hemmed once or twice, or coughed.

ORIGIN OF TEXTS.

The custom of taking a text as the basis of a sermon originated with Ezra, who, we are told, accompanied by several Levites in a public congregation of men and women, ascended a pulpit, opened the book of the law, and after addressing a prayer to the Deity, to which the people said Amen, "read in the book in the law of God distinctly, and gave the sense, and caused them to understand the reading." (Nehemiah viii. 8.)

Previous to the time of Ezra, the Patriarchs delivered, in public assemblies, either prophecies or moral instructions for the edification of the people; and it was not until the return of the Jews from the Babylonish captivity, during which time they had almost lost the language in which the Pentateuch was written, that it became necessary to explain, as well as to read, the Scriptures to them. In later times, the book of Moses was thus read in the synagogues every Sabbath day. (Acts xv. 21.) To this custom our Saviour conformed: in the synagogue at Nazareth he read a passage from the prophet Isaiah, then closing the book, returned it to the priest, and preached from the text.

CLERICAL BLUNDERS.

In an old book of Sermons by a divine named Milsom, we are told that it is one among many proofs of the wisdom and benevolence of Providence that the world was not created in the midst of winter, when Adam and Eve could have found nothing to eat, but in harvest-time, when there was fruit on every tree and shrub to tempt the willing hand.

Another commentator praises Divine Goodness for always making the largest rivers flow close by the most populous towns.

St. Austin undertook to prove that the ten plagues of Egypt were punishments adapted to the breach of the ten commandments,—forgetting that the law was given to the Jews, and that the plagues were inflicted on the Egyptians, and also that the law was not given in the form of commandments until nearly three months after the plagues had been sent.

PROVING AN ALIBI.

A clergyman at Cambridge preached a sermon which one of his auditors commended. "Yes," said a gentleman to whom it was mentioned, "it was a good sermon, but he stole it." This was told to the preacher. He resented it, and called on the gentleman to retract what he had said. "I am not," replied the aggressor, "very apt to retract my words, but in this instance I will. I said, you had stolen the sermon; I find I was wrong; for on returning home, and referring to the book whence I thought it was taken, I found it there."

WHITEFIELD AND THE SAILORS.

Mr. Whitefield, whose gestures and play of features were so full of dramatic power, once preached before the seamen at New York, and, in the course of his sermon, introduced the following bold apostrophe:—

"Well, my boys, we have a clear sky, and are making fine headway over a smooth sea before a light breeze, and we shall soon lose sight of land. But what means this sudden lowering of the heavens, and that dark cloud arising from the western horizon? Hark! Don't you hear the distant thunder? Don't you see those flashes of lightning? There is a storm gathering! Every man to his duty. How the waves rise and dash against the ship! The air is dark! The tempest rages! Our masts are gone. The ship is on her beam ends! What next?" The unsuspecting tars, reminded of former perils on the deep, as if struck by the power of magic, arose and exclaimed, "Take to the long boat."

PROTESTANT EXCOMMUNICATION.

John Knox, in his Liturgy for Scotch Presbyterians, sets forth the following form for the exercise of such an attribute of ecclesiastical authority in Protestant communities as excommunication:—

"O Lord Jesus Christ, thy expressed word is our assurance, and therefore, in boldness of the same, here in thy name, and at the commandment of this thy present congregation, we cut off, seclude, and excommunicate from thy body, and from our society, N. as a pround contemner, and slanderous person, and a member for the present altogether corrupted, and pernicious to the body. And this his sin (albeit with sorrow of our hearts) by virtue of our ministry, we bind and pronounce the same to be bound in heaven and earth. We further give over, into the hands and power of the devil, the said N. to the destruction of his flesh; straitly charging all that profess the Lord Jesus, to whose knowledge this our sentence shall come, to repute and hold the said N. accursed and unworthy of the familiar society of Christians; declaring unto all men that such as hereafter (before his repentance) shall haunt, or familiarly accompany him, are partakers of his impiety, and subject to the like condemnation.

"This our sentence, O Lord Jesus, pronounced in thy name, and at thy commandment, we humbly beseech thee to ratify even according to thy promise."

Puritan Peculiarities.

BAPTISMAL NAMES.

A PURITAN maiden, who was asked for her baptismal name, replied, "'Through-much-tribulation-we-enter-the-kingdom-of-Heaven,' but for short they call me 'Tribby.'"

The following names will be found in *Lower's English Sirnames*, and in the *Lansdowne Collection*. Most of them are taken from a jury-list of Sussex County, 1658. The favorite female baptismal names among the Puritans were Mercy, Faith, Fortune, Honor, Virtue; but there were among them those who preferred such high-flown names as Alethe, Prothesa, Euphrosyne, Kezia, Keturah, Malvina, Melinda, Sabrina, Alpina, Oriana.

The-gift-of-God Stringer,
Repentant Hazel,
Zealous King,
Be-thankful Playnard,
Live-in-peace Hillary,
Obediencia Cruttenden,
Goodgift Noake,

The-work-of-God Farmer,
More-tryal Goodwin,
Faithful Long,
Joy-from-above Brown,
Be-of-good-comfort Small,
Godward Freeman,
Thunder Goldsmith.

Faint-not Hewett,
Redeemed Compton,
God-reward Smart,
Earth Adams,
Meek Brewer,
Repentance Avis,
Kill-sin Pimple,
Be-faithful Joiner,
More-fruit Flower,
Grace-ful Harding,
Seek-wisdom Wood,

Accepted Trevor,
Make-peace Heaton,
Stand-fast-on-high Stringer,
Called Lower,
Be-courteous Cole,
Search-the-scriptures Moreton.
Return Spelman,
Fly-debate Roberts,
Hope-for Bending,
Weep-not Billing,
Elected Mitchell,

Fight-the-good-fight-of-faith White, The-peace-of-God Knight.

SIMILES.

Prayer is Faith's pump, where 't works till the water come;
If 't comes not free at first, Faith puts in some.
Prayer is the sacred bellows; when these blow,
How doth that live-coal from God's altar glow!

Faithful Teate's Ter. Tria., 1658.

Walking in the streets, I met a cart that came near the wall; so I stepped aside, to avoid it, into a place where I was secure enough. *Reflection:* Lord, sin is that great evil of which thou complainest that thou art pressed as a cart is pressed: how can it then but bruise me to powder?—*Caleb Trenchfield's Chris. Chymestree.*

EARLY PUNISHMENTS IN MASSACHUSETTS.

From the early records of Massachusetts we learn that the following singular punishments were inflicted in that colony two hundred years ago:—

Sir Richard Salstonstall, fined four bushels of malt for his absence from the court.

Josias Plaistowe, for stealing four baskets of corn from the Indians, to return them eight baskets again, to be fined £5, and hereafter to be called Josias, not Mr. as he used to be.

Thomas Peter, for suspicions of slander, idleness, and stubbornness, is to be severely whipped and kept in hold.

Capt. Stone, for abusing Mr. Ludlow by calling him *justass*, fined £100, and prohibited coming within the patent.

Joyce Dradwick to give unto Alexander Becks 20s., for promising him marriage without her friends' consent, and now refusing to perform the same.

Richard Turner, for being notoriously drunk, fined £2.

Edward Palmer, for his extortion in taking 32s. 7d. for the plank and work of Boston stocks, fined £5, and sentenced to sit one hour in the stocks.

John White bound in £10 to good behavior, and not come into the company of his neighbor Thomas Bell's wife alone.

VIRGINIA PENALTIES IN THE OLDEN TIME.

From the old records in the Court House of Warwick County, Virginia, we extract some entries of decisions by the court under date of October 21, 1663. It may be worth while to remark that at that early period tobacco was not only a staple commodity but a substitute for currency.

"Mr. John Harlow, and Alice his wife, being by the grand inquest presented for absenting themselves from church, are, according to the act, fined each of them fifty pounds of tobacco; and the said Mr. John Harlow ordered forthwith to pay one hundred pounds of tobacco to the sheriff, otherwise the said sheriff to levy by way of distress."

"Jane Harde, the wife of Henry Harde, being presented for not 'tending church, is, according to act, fined fifty pounds of tobacco ; and the sheriff is ordered to collect the same from her, and, in case of non-payment, to distress."

"John Lewis, his wife this day refusing to take the oath of allegiance, being ordered her, is committed into the sheriff's custody, to remain until she take the said oath, or until further ordered to the contrary."

"John Lewis, his wife for absenting herself from church, is fined fifty pounds of tobacco, to be collected by the sheriff from her husband; and upon non-payment, the said sheriff to distress."

" George Harwood, being prosecuted for his absenting himself from church, is fined fifty pounds of tobacco, to be levied by way of distress by the sheriff upon his non-payment thereof."

" Peter White and his wife, being presented for common swearing, are fined fifty pounds of tobacco, both of them; to be collected by the sheriff from the said White, and, upon non-payment of the same, to distress."

" Richard King, being presented as a common swearer, is fined fifty pounds of tobacco, to be levied by the sheriff, by way of distress, upon his non-payment."

EXTRACTS FROM THE CONNECTICUT BLUE LAWS.

When these free states were colonies
Unto the mother nation,
And in Connecticut the good
Old Blue Laws were in fashion.

The following extracts from the laws ordained by the people of New Haven, previous to their incorporation with the Saybrook and Hartford colonies, afford an idea of the strange character of their prohibitions. As the substance only is given in the transcription, the language is necessarily modernized :—

No quaker or dissenter from the established worship of the dominion shall be allowed to give a vote for the election of magistrates, or any officer.

No food or lodging shall be afforded to a quaker, adamite, or other heretic.

If any person turns quaker, he shall be banished, and not suffered to return, but upon pain of death.

No priest shall abide in the dominion : he shall be banished, and suffer death on his return. Priests may be seized by any one without a warrant.

No man to cross a river but with an authorized ferryman.

No one shall run on the sabbath-day, or walk in his garden, or elsewhere, except reverently to and from meeting.

No one shall travel, cook victuals, make beds, sweep house, cut hair or shave, on the sabbath-day.

No woman shall kiss her child on the sabbath or fasting-day.

The sabbath shall begin at sunset on Saturday.

To pick an ear of corn growing in a neighbor's garden shall be deemed theft.

A person accused of trespass in the night shall be judged guilty, unless he clear himself by oath.

When it appears that an accused has confederates, and he refuses to discover them, he may be racked.

No one shall buy or sell lands without permission of the selectmen.

A drunkard shall have a master appointed by the selectmen, who are to debar him the liberty of buying and selling.

Whoever publishes a lie to the prejudice of his neighbor, shall sit in the stocks or be whipped fifteen stripes.

No minister shall keep a school.

Men-stealers shall suffer death.

Whoever wears clothes trimmed with gold, silver, or bone lace, above two shillings by the yard, shall be presented by the grand jurors, and the selectmen shall tax the offender at £300 estate.

A debtor in prison, swearing he has no estate, shall be let out, and sold to make satisfaction.

Whoever sets a fire in the woods, and it burns a house, shall suffer death; and persons suspected of this crime shall be imprisoned without benefit of bail.

Whoever brings cards or dice into this dominion shall pay a fine of £5.

No one shall read common-prayer, keep Christmas or saint-days, make minced pies, dance, play cards, or play on any instrument of music, except the drum, trumpet, and Jews-harp.

No gospel minister shall join people in marriage; the magistrates only shall join in marriage, as they may do it with less scandal to Christ's church.

When parents refuse their children convenient marriages, the magistrate shall determine the point.

The selectmen, on finding children ignorant, may take them

away from their parents, and put them into better hands, at the expense of their parents.

A man that strikes his wife shall pay a fine of £10; a woman that strikes her husband shall be punished as the court directs.

A wife shall be deemed good evidence against her husband.

Married persons must live together, or be imprisoned.

No man shall court a maid in person, or by letter, without first obtaining consent of her parents : £5 penalty for the first offence; £10 for the second; and for the third, imprisonment during the pleasure of the court.

Every male shall have his hair cut round according to a cap.

Paronomasia.

Hard is the job to launch the desperate pun;
A *pun-job* dangerous as the Indian one.—HOLMES.

Life and language are alike sacred. Homicide and *verbicide*—that is, violent treatment of a word with fatal results to its legitimate meaning, which is its life—are alike forbidden. *Manslaughter*, which is the meaning of the one, is the same as *man's laughter*, which is the end of the other.—IBID.

THE quaint Cardan thus defineth :—"Punning is an art of harmonious jingling upon words, which, passing in at the ears and falling upon the diaphragma, excites a titillary motion in those parts; and this, being conveyed by the animal spirits into the muscles of the face, raises the cockles of the heart."

"He who would make a pun would pick a pocket," is the stereotyped dogma fulminated by laugh-lynchers from time immemorial; or, as the *Autocrat* hath it, "To trifle with the vocabulary which is the vehicle of social intercourse is to tamper with the currency of human intelligence. He who would violate the sanctities of his mother tongue would invade the recesses of the paternal till without remorse, and repeat the banquet of Saturn without an indigestion." The "inanities of this working-day world" cannot perceive any wittiness or grace in punning; and yet, according to the comprehensive definition of wit by Dr. Barrow, the eminent divine, it occupies a very considerable portion of the realm of wit. He says, "Wit is a thing so versatile and multiform, appearing in so many shapes, so many postures, so many garbs, so variously apprehended by several eyes and judgments, that it seemeth no less hard to settle a clear and certain notion thereof, than to make a portrait of Proteus, or to define the figure of the fleeting air. Sometimes it lieth in *pat allusions to a known story*, or in *seasonable application of a trivial saying*, or in feigning an apposite tale; sometimes it *playeth in words and phrases*, taking advantage of the *ambiguity of their sense, or the affinity of their sound;* sometimes it is wrapped in a dress of humorous expression, sometimes it lurketh under *an odd similitude;* sometimes it is lodged in a sly question, in a smart answer, in a *quirkish* reason, in a shrewd intimation, in cunningly, divertingly, or cleverly retorting an objection; sometimes it is couched in a bold scheme of speech, in a tart irony, in a lusty hyperbole, in a startling metaphor, in a *plausible reconciling of contradictions,* or in *acute nonsense;* sometimes a scenic representation of persons or things, a counterfeit speech, a mimic look or gesture, passeth for it. Sometimes an affected simplicity, sometimes a presumptuous bluntness, giveth it being. Sometimes it riseth only from *a lucky hitting upon what is strange;* sometimes from *a crafty wresting of obvious matter to the purpose.* Often it consisteth of one knows not what, and springeth up one can hardly tell how. Its ways are unaccountable and inexplicable, being answerable to the numberless rovings of fancy and windings of language."

If this definition be true, there is truth as well as wit in the punster's reply to the taunt of the rhetorician that "punning is the *lowest species* of wit." "Yes," said he, "for it is the *foundation* of all wit." But, whatever may be said of the practice by those who affect to despise it, it has been much in vogue in all ages. Horne, in his *Introduction to the Critical*

Study of the Holy Scriptures, tells us that it was a very favorite figure of rhetoric among the Hebrews, and is yet common among most of the Oriental nations. Professor Stuart, in his Hebrew grammar, gives numerous examples of it in the Old Testament, and Winer and Horne point out others in the New Testament, especially in the writings of St. Paul. These cannot, of course, be equivalently expressed in English.   23

Many of the Greek authors exhibit a fondness for this rhetorical figure, and some of the most excellent puns extant are to be found in the Greek Anthologies. As a specimen, the following is given from Wesseling's Diodorus Siculus :—   24

Dioscurus, an Egyptian bishop, before he began the service, had the common custom of saying ειρηνη πασιν, (irene pasin,) *peace be to all.* It was notorious that the pious churchman had at home a favorite mistress, whose name was Irene, which incident produced the following smart epigram :—

Ειρηνη παντεσσιν επισκοπος ειπεν επελθων
Πως δυναται πασιν, ἡν μονος ενδον εχει;

(The good bishop wishes peace—Irene—to all ;
But how can he give that to all, which he keeps to himself at home ?)

A PUN-GENT CHAPTER.   25

At one time there was a general strike among the workingmen of Paris, and Theodore Hook gave the following amusing account of the affair :—" The bakers, being ambitious to extend their *do*-mains, declared that a revolution was *needed*, and, though not exactly *bred* up to arms, soon reduced their *crusty* masters to terms. The tailors called a council of the *board* to see what *measures* should be taken, and, looking upon the bakers as the *flower* of chivalry, decided to follow *suit;* the consequence of which was, that a *cereous* insurrection was *lighted up* among the candle-makers, which, however *wick*-ed it might appear in the eyes of some persons, developed traits of character not unworthy of ancient *Greece.*"

Why should no man starve on the deserts of Arabia?
Because of the *sand which is* there.
How came the sandwiches there?
The tribe of *Ham* was *bred* there, and *mustered*.

A clergyman who had united in marriage a couple whose
Christian names were Benjamin and Annie, on being asked by
a mutual friend how they appeared during the ceremony, replied that they appeared both *annie*-mated and *bene*-fitted.

Mr. Manners, who had but lately been created Earl of Rut-
land, said to Sir Thomas More, just made Lord Chancellor,—
"You are so much elated with your preferment that you
verify the old proverb,—

Honores mutant MORES.*"*

"No, my lord," said Sir Thomas: "the pun will do much
better in English :—

Honors change MANNERS."

An old writer said that when *cannons* were introduced as
negotiators, the *canons* of the church were useless; that the
world was governed first by *mitrum*, and then by *nitrum*,—first
by *St. Peter*, and then by *saltpetre*.

Colman, the dramatist, on being asked whether he knew
Theodore Hook, replied, "Oh, yes: *Hook* and *Eye* are old
associates."

Punch says, "the milk of human kindness is not to be
found in the *pail* of society." If so, we think it is time for
all hands to "*kick the bucket.*"

Judge Peters, formerly of the Philadelphia Bench, observed
to a friend, during a trial that was going on, that one of the
witnesses had a *vegetable* head. "How so?" was the inquiry.
"He has *carroty* hair, *reddish* cheeks, a *turnup* nose, and a
sage look."

Tom Hood, seeing over the shop-door of a beer-vendor,—

Bear Sold Here,

said it was spelled right, because it was his own *Bruin*.

Charles Mathews, the comedian, was served by a green-grocer, named Berry, and generally settled his bill once a quarter. At one time the account was sent in before it was due, and Mathews, laboring under an idea that his credit was doubted, said, " Here's a pretty *mull*, Berry. You have sent in your *bill*, Berry, before it is *due*, Berry. Your father, the *elder* Berry, would not have been such a *goose*, Berry; but you need not look so *black*, Berry, for I don't care a *straw*, Berry, and sha'n't pay you till *Christmas*, Berry."

Sheridan, being dunned by a tailor to pay at least the interest on his bill, answered that it was not his interest to pay the principal, nor his principle to pay the interest.

In the "Old India House" may still be seen a quarto volume of *Interest Tables*, on the fly-leaf of which is written, in Charles Lamb's round, clerkly hand,—

" A book of much interest."—*Edinburgh Review*.
" A work in which the interest never flags."—*Quarterly Review*.
" We may say of this volume, that the interest increases from the beginning to the end."—*Monthly Review*.

Turner, the painter, was at a dinner where several artists, amateurs, and literary men were convened. A poet, by way of being facetious, proposed as a toast, " *The Painters and Glaziers of England*." The toast was drunk; and Turner, after returning thanks for it, proposed "*Success to the Paper-Stainers*," and called on the poet to respond.

SHORT ROAD TO WEALTH.

I'll tell you a plan for gaining wealth,
  Better than banking, trade, or leases;
Take a bank-note and fold it across,
  And then you will find your money IN-CREASES!

This wonderful plan, without danger or loss,
  Keeps your cash in your hands, and with nothing to trouble it;
And every time that you fold it across,
  'Tis plain as the light of the day that you DOUBLE IT!

" I cannot move," the plaintive invalid cries,
" Nor sit, nor stand."—If he says true, he *lies*.

Dr. Johnson having freely expressed his aversion to punning, Boswell hinted that his illustrious friend's dislike to this species of small wit might arise from his inability to play upon words. "Sir", roared Johnson, "if I were punish-ed for every pun I shed, there would not be left a puny shed of my punnish head." Once, by accident, he made a singular pun. A person who affected to live after the Greek manner, and to anoint himself with oil, was one day mentioned to him. Johnson, in the course of conversation on the singularity of his practice, give him the denomination of *this man of Grease.*

Sydney Smith—so Lord Houghton in his *Monographs* tells us—has written depreciatingly of all playing upon words; but his rapid apprehension could not altogether exclude a kind of wit which, in its best forms, takes fast hold of the memory, besides the momentary amusement it excites. His objection to the superiority of a city feast: "I cannot wholly value a dinner by the test you do (*testudo*);"—his proposal to settle the question of the wood pavement around St. Paul's: "Let the Canons once lay their heads together and the thing will be done ;" —his pretty compliment to his friends, Mrs. Tighe and Mrs. Cuffe: "Ah ! there you are : the cuff that every one would wear, the tie that no one would loose"—may be cited as perfect in their way.

Admiral Duncan's address to the officers who came on board his ship for instructions, previous to the engagement with Admiral de Winter, was laconic and humorous : "Gentlemen, you see a severe Winter approaching; I have only to advise you to keep up a good fire."

Theodore Hook plays thus on the same name :—

> Here comes Mr. Winter, inspector of taxes;
> I advise you to give him whatever he axes;
> I advise you to give him without any flummery,
> For though his name's Winter his actions are *summary.*

Henry Erskine's toast to the mine-owners of Lancashire :—
Sink your pits, blast your mines, dam your rivers, consume your manufactures, disperse your commerce, and may your labors be in *vein.*

TOM MOORE.

When Limerick, in idle whim,
    Moore as her member lately courted,
'The boys,' for form's sake, asked of him
    To state what party he supported.

When thus his answer promptly ran,
    (Now give the wit his meed of glory :)
"I'm of no party as a man,
    But as a poet *am-a-tory*."

TOP AND BOTTOM.

The following playful colloquy in verse took place at a dinner-table, between Sir George Rose and James Smith, in allusion to Craven street, Strand, where the latter resided :—

J. S.—At the top of my street the attorneys abound,
    And down at the bottom the barges are found :
    Fly, honesty, fly to some safer retreat,
    For there's *craft* in the river, and *craft* in the street.

Sir G. R.—Why should honesty fly to some safer retreat,
    From attorneys, and barges, od-rot 'em ?
    For the lawyers are *just* at the top of the street,
    And the barges are *just* at the bottom.

OLD JOKE VERSIFIED.

Says Tom to Bill, pray tell me, sir,
    Why is it that the devil,
In spite of all his naughty ways,
    Can never be uncivil ?

Says Bill to Tom, the answer's plain
    To any mind that's bright :
Because the imp of darkness, sir,
    Can ne'er be *imp o' light*.

A PRINTER'S EPITAPH.

Here lies a *form*—place no *imposing stone*
    To mark the *head*, where weary it is lain ;
'Tis *matter dead !*—its mission being done,
    To be *distributed* to dust again.
The *body's* but the *type*, at best, of man,
    Whose *impress* is the spirit's deathless *page ;*
Worn out, the *type* is thrown to *pi* again,
    The *impression* lives through an eternal age.

STICKY.

I want to seal a letter, Dick,
  Some wax pray give to me.—
I have not got a single *stick*,
  Or *whacks* I'd give to thee.

WOMEN.

When Eve brought *woe* to all mankind,
  Old Adam called her *wo-man ;*
But when she *woo'd* with love so kind,
  He then pronounced her *woo-man.*

But now with folly and with pride,
  Their husbands' pockets trimming,
The ladies are so full of *whims,*
  The people call them *whim-men.*

BEN, THE SAILOR.

His *death,* which happened in his *berth,*
  At forty odd befell :
They went and *told* the sexton, and
  The sexton *tolled* the bell.—HOOD'S *Faithless Sally Brown.*

WHISKERS VERSUS RAZOR.

With whiskers thick upon my face
  I went my fair to see;
She told me she could never love
  A *bear-faced* chap like me.

I shaved then clean, and called again,
  And thought my troubles o'er;
She laughed outright, and said I was
  More *bare-faced* than before!

COMPLIMENT OF SHERIDAN TO MISS PAYNE.

'Tis true I am ill; but I cannot complain,
For he never knew pleasure who never knew Payne.

FROM DR. HOLMES' "MODEST REQUEST."

Thus great Achilles, who had shown his zeal
In HEALING WOUNDS, died of a WOUNDED HEEL;
Unhappy chief, who, when in childhood doused,
Had saved his BACON had his feet been SOUSED !
Accursed heel, that killed a hero stout !
Oh, had your mother known that you were out,

Death had not entered at the trifling part
That still defies the small chirurgeon's art
With corn and BUNIONS,—not the glorious JOHN
Who wrote the book we all have pondered on,—
But other BUNIONS, bound in fleecy hose,
To "PILGRIM'S PROGRESS" unrelenting foes!

PLAINT OF THE OLD PAUPER.

Some boast of their FORE-fathers—I—
    I have not ONE!
I am, I think, like Joshua,
    The son of NONE!

Heedless in youth, we little note
    How quick time passes,
For then flows ruby wine, not sand,
    In OUR glasses!

Rich friends (most pure in honor) all have fled
    Sooner or later;
Pshaw! had they India's spices, they'd not be
    A nutmeg-GRATER!

I've neither chick nor child; as I have nothing,
    Why, 'tis lucky rather;
Yet who that hears a squalling baby wishes
    Not to be FATHER?

Some few years back my spirits and my youth
    Were quite amazin';
Brisk as a pony, or a lawyer's clerk,
    Just fresh from GRAY'S INN!

What am I now? weak, old, and poor, and by
    The parish found;
Their FENCE keeps me, while many an ass
    Enjoys the parish POUND!

TO MY NOSE.

Knows he that never took a pinch,
    Nosey! the pleasure thence which flows?
Knows he the titillating joy
    Which my nose knows?

Oh, nose! I am as fond of thee
    As any mountain of its snows!
I gaze on thee, and feel that pride
    A Roman knows!

BOOK-LARCENY.

Sir Walter Scott said that some of his friends were bad *accountants*, but excellent *book-keepers*.

How hard, when those who do not wish
To lend—that's lose—their books,
Are snared by anglers—folks that fish
With literary hooks;

Who call and take some favorite tome,
But never read it through;
They thus complete their sett at home,
By making one of you.

I, of my Spenser quite bereft,
Last winter sore was shaken;
Of Lamb I've but a quarter left,
Nor could I save my Bacon.

They picked my Locke, to me far more
Than Bramah's patent worth;
And now my losses I deplore,
Without a Home on earth.

Even Glover's works I cannot put
My frozen hands upon;
Though ever since I lost my Foote,
My Bunyan has been gone.

My life is wasting fast away;
I suffer from these shocks;
And though I've fixed a lock on Gray,
There's gray upon my locks.

They still have made me slight returns,
And thus my grief divide;
For oh! they've cured me of my Burns,
And eased my Akenside.

But all I think I shall not say,
Nor let my anger burn;
For as they have not found me Gay,
They have not left me Sterne.

THE VEGETABLE GIRL.

Behind a market stall installed,
I mark it every day,
Stands at her stand the fairest girl
I've met with in the bay;

Her two lips are of cherry red,
   Her hands a pretty pair,
With such a pretty turn-up nose,
   And lovely reddish hair.

'Tis there she stands from morn till night
   Her customers to please,
And to appease their appetite
   She sells them beans and peas.
Attracted by the glances from
   The apple of her eye,
And by her Chili apples, too,
   Each passer-by will buy.

She stands upon her little feet,
   Throughout the livelong day,
And sells her celery and things,—
   A big feat, by the way.
She changes off her stock for change,
   Attending to each call;
And when she has but one beet left,
   She says, "Now that beats all."

EPITAPH ON AN OLD HORSE.

Here lies a faithful steed,
A stanch, uncompromising "silver gray;"
Who ran the race of life with sprightly speed,
   Yet never ran—away.

Wild oats he never sowed,
Yet masticated tame ones with much zest:
Cheerful he bore each light allotted load,
   As cheerfully took rest.

Bright were his eyes, yet soft,
And in the main his tail was white and flowing;
And though he never sketched a single draught,
   He showed great taste for drawing.

Lithe were his limbs, and clean,
Fitted alike for buggy or for dray,
And like Napoleon the Great, I ween,
   He had a *martial neigh.*

Oft have I watched him grace
His favorite stall, well littered, warm, and fair,
With such contentment shining from his face,
   And such a stable air!

With here and there a speck
Of roan diversifying his broad back,
And, martyr-like, a halter round his neck,
    Which bound him to the rack.

Mors omnibus! at length
The hay-day of his life was damped by death;
So, summoning all his late remaining strength,
    He drew his—final breath.

GRAND SCHEME OF EMIGRATION.

The Brewers should to *Malt-a* go,
    The Loggerheads to *Scilly,*
The Quakers to the *Friendly Isles,*
    The Furriers all to *Chili.*

The little squalling, brawling brats,
    That break our nightly rest,
Should be packed off to *Baby-lon,*
    To *Lap-land,* or to *Brest.*

From *Spit-head* Cooks go o'er to *Greece;*
    And while the Miser waits
His passage to the *Guinea* coast,
    Spendthrifts are in the *Straits.*

Spinsters should to the *Needles* go,
    Wine-bibbers to *Burgundy ;*
Gourmands should lunch at *Sandwich Isles,*
    Wags in the *Bay of Fun-dy.*

Musicians hasten to the *Sound,*
    The surpliced Priest to *Rome;*
While still the race of Hypocrites
    At *Cant-on* are at home.

Lovers should hasten to *Good Hope;*
    To some *Cape Horn* is pain ;
Debtors should go to *Oh-i-o,*
    And Sailors to the *Main-e.*

Hie, Bachelors, to the *United States!*
    Maids, to the *Isle of Man ;*
Let Gardeners go to *Botany Bay,*
    And Shoeblacks to *Japan.*

Thus, emigrants and misplaced men
    Will then no longer vex us ;
And all that a'n't provided for
    Had better go to *Texas.*

THE PERILOUS PRACTICE OF PUNNING.

Theodore Hook thus cautions young people to resist provocation to the habit of punning:—

My little dears, who learn to read, pray early learn to shun
That very silly thing indeed which people call a pun.
Read Entick's rules, and 'twill be found how simple an offence
It is to make the self-same sound afford a double sense.
For instance, *ale* may make you *ail*, your *aunt* an *ant* may kill,
You in a *vale* may buy a *vail*, and *Bill* may pay the *bill*,
Or if to France your bark you steer, at Dover it may be,
A *peer appears* upon the *pier*, who, blind, still goes to *sea*.
Thus one might say when to a treat good friends accept our greeting,
'Tis *meet* that men who *meet* to eat, should eat their *meat* when *meeting*.
Brawn on the board 's no *bore* indeed, although from *boar* prepared;
Nor can the *fowl* on which we feed *foul* feeding be declared.
Thus *one* ripe fruit may be a *pear*, and yet be *pared* again,
And still be *one*, which seemeth rare, until we do explain.
It therefore should be all your aim to speak with ample care;
For who, however fond of *game*, would choose to swallow *hair?*
A fat man's *gait* may make us smile, who has no *gate* to close;
The farmer sitting on his *stile* no *stylish* person knows;
Perfumers men of *scents* must be; some Scilly men are bright;
A *brown* man oft *deep read* we see—a *black* a wicked *wight*.
Most wealthy men good manners have, however vulgar they,
And actors still the harder *slave* the oftener they *play;*
So poets can't the *baize* obtain unless their tailors choose,
While grooms and coachmen not in vain each evening seek the *mews*.
The *dyer* who by dying *lives*, a *dire* life maintains;
The glazier, it is known, receives his *profits* from his *panes;*
By gardeners *thyme* is *tied*, 'tis true, when Spring is in its prime,
But *time* or *tide* won't wait for you, if you are *tied* for *time*.
There now you see, my little dears, the way to make a pun;
A trick which you, through coming years, should sedulously shun.
The fault admits of no defense, for wheresoe'er 'tis found,
You sacrifice the *sound* for *sense*, the *sense* is never *sound*.
So let your words and actions too, one single meaning prove,
And, just in all you say or do, you'll gain esteem and love:
In mirth and play no harm you'll know, when duty's task is done;
But parents ne'er should let you go unpunished for a *pun*.

The motto of the Pilotage Commission of the river Tyne:—

In portu salus.
In port you sail us.

SONNET

On a youth who died from a surfeit of fruit.

Currants have checked the current of my blood,
And berries brought me to be buried here;
Pears have pared off my body's hardihood,
And plums and plumbers spare not one so spare:
Fain would I feign my fall; so fair a fare
Lessens not fate, but 'tis a lesson good:
Gilt will not long hide guilt; such thin-washed ware
Wears quickly, and its rude touch soon is rued.
Grave on my grave some sentence grave and terse,
That lies not, as it lies upon my clay;
But, in a gentle strain of unstrained verse,
Prays all to pity a poor patty's prey;
Rehearses I was fruit-full to my hearse,
Tells that my days are told, and soon I'm toll'd away!

Previous to the battle of Culloden, when Marshal Wade and Generals Cope and Hawley were prevented by the severity of the weather from advancing as far into Scotland as they intended, the following lines were circulated among their opposers:—

Cope could not cope, nor Wade wade through the snow,
Nor Hawley haul his cannon to the foe.

When Mrs. Norton was called on to subscribe to a fund for the relief of Thomas Hood's widow, which had been headed by Sir Robert Peel, she sent a liberal donation with these lines:—

To cheer the widow's heart in her distress,
To make provision for the fatherless,
Is but a Christian's duty, and none should
Resist the heart-appeal of *widow-Hood.*

M. Mario's visit to this country recalls to mind the sharpest witticism of Madame Grisi, at the time his wife, and one of the best bits of repartee on record. Louis Phillippe, passing through a room where Grisi stood, holding two of her young children by the hand, said gaily: "Ah! Madame, are those, then, some of your little *Grisettes?*" "No, Sire," was the quick reply, perfect in every requirement of the pun, "No, Sire, these are my little *Marionettes.*"

A learned judge, of facetious memory, is reported to have said, in an argument in arrest of the judgment of death, "I think we had better let the subject drop."

SWIFT'S LATIN PUNS.

Among the *nugæ* of Dean Swift are his celebrated Latin puns, some of which are well known, having been frequently copied, and having never been excelled. The following selections will serve as specimens. They consist entirely of Latin words; but, by allowing for false spelling, and running the words into each other, the sentences make good sense in English:—

Mollis abuti,	(Moll is a beauty,
Has an acuti,	Has an acute eye,
No lasso finis,	No lass so fine is,
Molli divinis.	Molly divine is.
Omi de armis tres,	O my dear mistress,
Imi na dis tres,	I'm in a distress,
Cantu disco ver	Can't you discover
Meas alo ver?	Me as a lover?)

In a subsequent epistolary allusion to this, he says:—

I ritu a verse o na molli o mi ne,
Asta lassa me pole, a lædis o fine;
I ne ver neu a niso ne at in mi ni is;
A manat a glans ora sito fer diis.
De armo lis abuti hos face an hos nos is,
As fer a sal illi, as reddas aro sis;
Ac is o mi molli is almi de lite;
Illo verbi de, an illo verbi nite.

(I writ you a verse on a Molly o' mine,
As tall as a may-pole, a lady so fine;
I never knew any so neat in mine eyes;
A man, at a glance or a sight of her, dies.
Dear Molly 's a beauty, whose face and whose nose is
As fair as a lily, as red as a rose is;
A kiss o' my Molly is all my delight;
I love her by day, and I love her by night.)

Extract from the consultation of four physicians on a lord that was dying.

1*st Doctor.* Is his honor sic? Præ lætus felis pulse. It do es beat veris loto de.

2d Doctor. No notis as qui cassi e ver fel tu metri it. Inde edit is as fastas an alarum, ora fire bellat nite.

3d Doctor. It is veri hei!

4th Doctor. Noto contra dictu in my juge mentitis veri loto de. It is as orto maladi, sum callet. [Here e ver id octo reti resto a par lori na mel an coli post ure.]

1st D. It is a me gri mas I opi ne.

2d D. No docto rite quit fora quin si. Heris a plane sim tomo fit. Sorites Paracelsus. Præ re adit.

1st D. Nono, Doctor, I ne ver quo te aqua casu do.

2d D. Sum arso; mi autoris no ne.

3d D. No quare lingat præ senti de si re. His honor is sic offa colli casure as I sit here.

4th D. It is æther an atro phi ora colli casu sed: Ire membri re ad it in Doctor me ades esse, here it is.

3d D. I ne ver re ad apage in it, no re ver in tendit.

2d D. Fer ne is offa qui te di ferent noti o nas i here.

1st D. It me bea pluri si; avo metis veri pro perfor a man at his age.

1st D. Is his honor sick? Pray let us feel his pulse. It does beat very slow to-day.

2d D. No, no, 'tis as quick as ever I felt; you may try it. Indeed, it is as fast as an alarum, or a fire-bell at night.

3d D. It is very high.

4th D. Not to contradict you, in my judgment it is very slow to day. It is a sort of malady, some call it. (Here every doctor retires to a parlor in a melancholy posture.)

1st D. It is a megrim, as I opine.

2d D. No, doctor, I take it for a quinsy. Here is a plain symptom of it. So writes Paracelsus. Pray read it.

1st D. No, no, doctor, I never quote a quack as you do.

2d D. Some are so; my author is none.

3d D. No quarrelling at present, I desire. His honor is sick of a colic as sure as I sit here.

4th D. It is either an atrophy, or a colic, as you said. I remember I read it in Dr. Mead's Essay: here it is.

3d D. I never read a page in it, nor ever intend it.

2d D. Ferne is of a quite different notion, as I hear.

1st D. It may be a pleurisy; a vomit is very proper for a man at his age.

2d D. Ure par donat præsanti des ire; His dis eas is a cata ride clare it.

3d D. Atlas tume findit as tone in his quid ni es.

4th D. Itis ale pro si fora uti se. Ab lis ter me bene cessa risum de cens. Itis as ure medi in manicas es.

3d D. I findit isto late tot hinc offa reme di; fori here his honor is de ad.

2d D. His ti meis cum.

1st D. Is it trudo ut hinc?

4th D. It is veri certa in. His Paris his belli sto ringo ut foris de partu re.

3d D. Næ i fis ecce lens is de ad lætus en dum apri esto præ foris sole.

2d D. Your pardon at present I desire. His disease is a catarrh, I declare it.

3d D. At last you may find it a stone in his kidneys.

4th D. It is a leprosy for aught I see. A blister may be necessary some days hence. It is a sure remedy in many cases.

3d D. I find it is too late to think of a remedy; for I hear his honor is dead.

2d D. His time is come.

1st D. Is it true, do you think?

4th D. It is very certain. His parish bell is to ring out for his departure.

3d D. Nay, if his excellency's dead, let us send 'em a priest to pray for his soul.

UNCONSCIOUS OR UNINTENTIONAL PUNS.

Elizabeth's *sylvan dress* was therefore well suited at once to her height and to the dignity of her mein, which her conscious rank and *long habits* of authority had rendered in some degree too masculine to be seen to the best advantage in ordinary *female weeds.—Kenilworth,* iii. 9.

> I'll *gild* the faces of the grooms withal
> That it may seem their *guilt.—Macbeth.*

> While underneath the eaves
> The brooding swallows cling,
> As if to show their sunny backs
> And *twit* me with the spring.—*Song of the Shirt.*

RUSSIAN DOUBLE ENTENDRE.

The following message was sent to the Emperor Nicholas by one of his generals:—

Voliä Väschä, ä Varschävoo vsi'at nemogoo.

{ Volia is yours,
{ Your will is all-powerful, } but Warsaw I cannot take.

CLASSICAL PUNS AND MOTTOES.

Sydney Smith proposed as a motto for Bishop Burgess, brother to the well-known fish-sauce purveyor, the following Virgilian pun (Æn. iv. 1),—

Gravi jamdudum *saucia* curâ.

A London tobacconist, who had become wealthy, and determined to set up his carriage, applied to a learned gentleman for a motto. The scholar gave him the Horatian question,—

QUID RIDES ?
(Why do you laugh?—*Sat. I.* 69)—

which was accordingly adopted, and painted on the panel.

A pedantic bachelor had the following inscription on his tea-caddy :—

TU DOCES.
(Thou Tea-chest.)

Epitaph on a Cat, ascribed to Dr. Johnson (Hor. lib. i., c. 12):—
MI-CAT INTER OMNES.

Two gentlemen about to enter an unoccupied pew in a church, the foremost found it locked. His companion, not perceiving it at the moment, inquired why he retreated. "*Pudor vetat,*" said he. (Modesty forbids.)

A gentleman at dinner requested a friend to help him to a potato, which he did, saying, "I think you will find that a good mealy one." "Thank you," quoth the other: "it could not be *melior*" (better).

A student of Latin, being confined to his room by illness, was called upon by a friend. "What, John," said the visitor, "sick, eh?" "Yes," replied John, "*sic sum*" (so I am).

In King's College were two delinquents named respectively Payne and Culpepper. Payne was expelled, but Culpepper escaped punishment. Upon this, a wit wrote the following apt line —

Pœna perire potest; *Culpa* perennis est.

Andrew Borde, author of the *Breviary of Health*, called himself in Latin Andreas Perforatus. This translation of a proper name was according to the fashion of the time, but in this instance includes a pun,—perforatus, *bored* or pierced.

Joseph II., Emperor of Germany, during a visit to Rome, went to see the princess Santacroce, a young lady of singular beauty, who had an evening *conversazione*. Next morning appeared the following pasquinade. "Pasquin asks, 'What is the Emperor Joseph come to Rome for?' Marforio answers, 'Abaciar la Santa Croce'"—to kiss the Holy Cross.

On the trial of Garnett, the Superior of the Jesuits, for his participation in the Gunpowder Plot, Coke, then Attorney-General, concluded his speech thus:—*Qui cum Jesu itis, non itis cum Jesuitis.*

A few years ago, several Jesuits came into the lecture-room of an Italian professor in the University of Pisa, believing he was about to assail a favorite dogma of theirs. He commenced his lecture with the following words,—

"Quanti Gesuiti sono all' inferno!"
(How many Jesuits there are in hell!)

When remonstrated with, he said that his words were—

"Quanti—Gesu!—iti sono all' inferno!"
(How many people, O Jesus! there are in hell!)

D'Israeli says that Bossuet would not join his young companions, and flew to his solitary tasks, while the classical boys avenged themselves by a schoolboy's pun; applying to *Bossuet* Virgil's *bos suet-us aratro*—the ox daily toiling in the plough.

John Randolph of Virginia, and Mr. Dana of Connecticut, while fellow-members of Congress, belonged to different political parties. On one occasion Mr. Dana paid some handsome compliments to Mr. Randolph. When the latter spoke in reply, he quoted from Virgil (Æn. ii.):—

Timeo *Danaos* et dona ferentes.

A lady having accidentally thrown down a Cremona fiddle with her mantua, Dean Swift instantly remarked,—

> "*Mantua* væ miseræ nimium vicina *Cremonæ*."

Ah, Mantua, too near the wretched Cremona. (Virg. Ecl. ix. 28.)

To an old gentleman who had lost his spectacles one rainy evening, the Dean said, "If this rain continues all night, you will certainly recover them in the morning betimes:

> "Nocte pluit tota—redeunt *spectacula* mane." (Virgil.)

> Quid facies facies veneris si veneris ante?
> Ne pereas pereas, ne sedeas, sedeas.

(What will you do if you shall come before the face of Venus? Lest you should perish through them, do not sit down, but go away.)

Sir William Dawes, Archbishop of York, was very fond of a pun. His clergy dining with him for the first time after he had lost his wife, he told them he feared they did not find things in so good order as they used to be in the time of poor Mary; and, looking extremely sorrowful, added with a deep sigh, "she was indeed *mare pacificum*." A curate who knew pretty well what her temper had been, said, "Yes, my lord, but she was *mare mortuum* first."

> That Homer should a bankrupt be,
> Is not so very ODD D'YE SEE,
> If it be true as I'm instructed,
> So ILL HE HAD his books conducted.

PUNNING MOTTOES OF THE ENGLISH PEERAGE.

Ne vile FANO—Disgrace not the altar. Motto of the FANES.

NE VILE *velis*—Form no mean wish. The NEVILLES.

CAVENDO *tutus*—Secure by caution. The CAVENDISHES.

FORTE SCU*tum, salus ducum*—A strong shield the safety of leaders. Lord FORTESCUE.

VER NON *semper viret*—The spring is not always green. Lord VERNON.

VERO *nihil verius*—Nothing truer than truth. Lord VERE.

TEMPLA *quam delecta*—Temples how beloved. Lord TEMPLE.

JEUX-DE-MOTS.

SPIRITUAL.

A wag decides—

That whiskey is the key by which many gain an entrance into our prisons and almshouses.

That brandy brands the noses of all who cannot govern their appetites.

That wine causes many a man to take a winding way home.

That punch is the cause of many unfriendly punches.

That ale causes many ailings, while beer brings many to the bier.

That champagne is the source of many a real pain.

That gin-slings have "slewed" more than the slings of old.

That the reputation of being fond of cock-tails is not a feather in any man's cap.

That the money spent for port that is supplied by portly gents would support many a poor family.

That porter is a weak supporter for those who are weak in body.

ANAGRAMMATIC.

The following sentence is said to be taken from a volume of sermons published during the reign of James I. :—

This *dial* shows that we must *die all;* yet notwithstanding, *all houses* are turned into *ale houses;* our *cares* into *cates;* our *paradise* into a *pair o' dice; matrimony* into a *matter of money*, and *marriage* into a *merry age;* our *divines* have become *dry vines:* it was not so in the days of *Noah,—ah! no*

ITERATIVE.

A clerical gentleman of Hartford, who once attended the House of Representatives to read prayers, being politely requested to remain seated near the speaker during the debate, found himself the spectator of an *unmarrying* process, so alien to his own vocation, and so characteristic of the readiness of the Legislature of Connecticut to grant divorces, that the result was the following *impromptu:*—

> For *cut*-ting all *connect*-ions famed,
> *Connect-i-cut* is fairly named;
> I twain *connect* in one, but you
> *Cut* those whom *I connect* in two.
> Each legislator seems to say,
> What you *Connect I cut* away.

Finn, the comedian, issued the following morceau upon the announcement of his benefit at the Tremont Theatre, Boston:—

> Like a *grate full* of coals I burn,
> A *great, full* house to see;
> And if I should not *grateful* prove,
> A *great fool* I should be.

A FAIR LETTER.

The following letter was received by a young lady at the post-office of a Fair held for the benefit of a church :—

Fairest of the Fair. When such *fair* beings as you have the *fair*-ness to honor our *Fair* with your *fair* presence, it is perfectly *fair* that you should receive good *fare* from the *fair* conductors of this *Fair*, and indeed it would be very un-*fair* if you should not *fare* well, since it is the endeavor of those whose wel-*fare* depends upon the success of this *Fair*, to treat all who come *fair*-ly, but to treat with especial *fair*-ness those who are as *fair* as yourself. We are engaged in a *fair* cause, a sacred war-*fare;* that is, to speak without un-*fair*-ness, a war-*fare*, not against the *fair* sex, but against the pockets of their beaux. We therefore hope, gentle reader, " still *fair*-est found where all is *fair*," that you will use all *fair* exertions in behalf of the praiseworthy af-*fair* which we have *fair*-ly undertaken. If you take sufficient interest in our wel-*fare* to lend your *fair* aid, you will appear *fair*-er than ever in our sight; we will never treat you un-*fair*-ly, and when you withdraw the light of your *fair* countenance from our *Fair*, we will bid you a kind *Fare*-well.

The following was written on the occasion of a duel in Philadelphia, several years ago:—

> Schott and Willing did engage
>   In duel fierce and hot;
> Schott shot Willing willingly,
>   And Willing he shot Schott.
>
> The shot Schott shot made Willing quite
>   A spectacle to see;
> While Willing's willing shot went right
>   Through Schott's anatomy.

WRITE WRITTEN RIGHT.

> *Write* we know is written right,
>   When we see it written *write;*
> But when we see it written wright,
>   We know it is not written right:
> For write, to have it written right,
>   Must not be written right or wright,
>   Nor yet should it be written rite;
> But *write,* for so 'tis written right.

TURN TO THE LEFT AS THE (ENGLISH) LAW DIRECTS.

> The laws of the Road are a paradox quite;
>   For when you are travelling along,
> If you keep to the LEFT you're sure to be RIGHT,
>   If you keep to the RIGHT you'll be WRONG.

> I cannot bear to see a bear, bear down upon a hare,
> When bare of hair he strips the hare, for hare I cry, "forbear!"

ON THE DEATH OF THE EARL OF KILDARE.

> Who *killed Kildare?* Who *dared Kildare* to *kill?*

Death answers,—

> I *killed Kildare,* and *dare kill* whom I will.

A *Cat*ALECTIC MONODY.

> A *cat* I sing of famous memory,
> Though *cat*achrestical my song may be:
> In a small garden *cat*acomb she lies,
> And *cat*aclysms fill her comrades' eyes;
> Borne on the air, the *cat*acoustic song
> Swells with her virtues' *cat*alogue along;
> No *cat*aplasm could lengthen out her years,
> Though mourning friends shed *cat*aracts of tears.

Once loud and strong her *ca*techist-like voice,
It dwindled to a *ca*tcall's squeaking noise;
Most *ca*tegorical her virtues shone,
By *ca*tenation joined each one to one;—
But a vile *ca*tchpoll dog, with cruel bite,
Like *ca*tling's cut, her strength disabled quite;
Her *ca*terwauling pierced the heavy air,
As *ca*taphracts their arms through legions bear;
'Tis vain! as *ca*terpillars drag away
Their lengths, like *ca*ttle after busy day,
She lingering died, nor left in kit *kat* the
Embodiment of this *ca*tastrophe.

NOVEMBER.

(The humorous lines of Hood are only applicable to the English climate, where the closing month of autumn is synonymous with fogs, long visages, and suicides.)

No sun—no moon!
No morn—no noon—
No dawn—no dusk—no proper time of day—
No sky—no earthly view—
No distance looking blue—
No roads—no streets—no t'other side the way—
No end to any row—
No indication where the crescents go—
No tops to any steeple—
No recognition of familiar people—
No courtesies for showing 'em—
No knowing 'em—
No travellers at all—no locomotion—
No inkling of the way—no motion—
'No go' by land or ocean—
No mail—no post—
No news from any foreign coast—
No park—no ring—no afternoon gentility—
No company—no nobility—
No warmth—no cheerfulness—no healthful ease—
No comfortable feel in any member—
No shade—no shine—no butterflies—no bees—
No fruits—no flowers—no leaves—no birds—
No-vember!

The name of that monster of brutality, *Caliban*, in Shakspeare's Tempest, is supposed to be anagrammatic of *Canibal*, the old mode of spelling Cannibal.

A SWARM OF BEES.

B patient, B prayerful, B humble, B mild,
B wise as a Solon, B meek as a child;
B studious, B thoughtful, B loving, B kind;
B sure you make matter subservient to mind.
B cautious, B prudent, B trustful, B true,
B courteous to all men, B friendly with few.
B temperate in argument, pleasure, and wine,
B careful of conduct, of money, of time.
B cheerful, B grateful, B hopeful, B firm,
B peaceful, *b*enevolent, willing to learn;
B courageous, B gentle, B liberal, B just,
B aspiring, B humble, *b*ecause thou art dust;
B penitent, circumspect, sound in the faith,
B active, devoted; B faithful till death.
B honest, B holy, transparent, and pure;
B dependent, B Christ-like, and you'll B secure

THE BEES OF THE BIBLE.

Be kindly affectioned one to another.
Be sober, and watch unto prayer.
Be content with such things as ye have.
Be strong in the Lord.
Be courteous.
Be not wise in your own conceits.
Be not forgetful to entertain strangers.
Be not children in understanding.
Be followers of God, as dear children.
Be not weary in well-doing.
Be holy in all manner of conversation.
Be patient unto the coming of the Lord.
Be clothed with humility.

FRANKLIN'S "RE'S."

Dr. Franklin, in England in the year 1775, was asked by a nobleman what would satisfy the Americans. He answered that it might easily be comprised in a few "Re's," which he immediately wrote on a piece of paper, thus:—

Re-call your forces.
Re-store Castle William.
Re-pair the damage done to Boston.
Re-peal your unconstitutional acts.
Re-nounce your pretensions to taxes.
Re-fund the duties you have extorted.

After this—
> Re-quire, and
> Re-ceive payment for the destroyed tea, with the voluntary grants of the
>   Colonies; and then
> Re-joice in a happy
> Re-conciliation.

THE MISS-NOMERS.

After the manner of Horace Smith's "Surnames ever go by contraries."

Miss Brown is exceedingly fair,
  Miss White is as brown as a berry;
Miss Black has a gray head of hair,
  Miss Graves is a flirt ever merry;
Miss Lightbody weighs sixteen stone,
  Miss Rich scarce can muster a guinea;
Miss Hare wears a wig, and has none,
  And Miss Solomon is a sad ninny!

Miss Mildmay's a terrible scold,
  Miss Dove's ever cross and contrary;
Miss Young is now grown very old,
  And Miss Heavyside's light as a fairy!
Miss Short is at least five feet ten,
  Miss Noble's of humble extraction;
Miss Love has a hatred towards men,
  Whilst Miss Still is forever in action.

Miss Green is a regular *blue*,
  Miss Scarlet looks pale as a lily;
Miss Violet ne'er shrinks from our view,
  And Miss Wiseman thinks all the men silly!
Miss Goodchild's a naughty young elf,
  Miss Lyon's from terror a fool;
Miss Mee's not at all like *myself*,
  Miss Carpenter no one can rule.

Miss Sadler ne'er mounted a horse,
  While Miss Groom from the stable will run;
Miss Kilmore can't look on a corse,
  And Miss Aimwell ne'er levelled a gun;
Miss Greathead has no brains at all,
  Miss Heartwell is ever complaining;
Miss Dance has ne'er been at a ball,
  Over hearts Miss Fairweather likes *reigning!*

Miss Wright, she is constantly wrong,
  Miss Tickell, alas! is not funny;
Miss Singer ne'er warbled a song,
  And alas! poor Miss Cash has no money;

Miss Hateman would give all she's worth,
    To purchase a man to her liking;
Miss Merry is shocked at all mirth,
    Miss Boxer the men don't find *striking!*

Miss Bliss does with sorrow o'erflow,
    Miss Hope in despair seeks the tomb;
Miss Joy still anticipates wo,
    And Miss Charity's never "at home!"
Miss Hamlet resides in the city,
    The nerves of Miss Standfast are shaken;
Miss Prettyman's beau is not pretty,
    And Miss Faithful her love has forsaken!

Miss Porter despises all froth,
    Miss Scales they'll make *wait,* I am thinking;
Miss Meekly is apt to be wroth,
    Miss Lofty to meanness is sinking;
Miss Seymore's as blind as a bat,
    Miss Last at a party is first;
Miss Brindle dislikes a striped cat,
    And Miss Waters has always a thirst!

Miss Knight is now changed into Day,
    Miss Day wants to marry a Knight;
Miss Prudence has just run away,
    And Miss Steady assisted her flight;
But success to the fair,—one and all!
    No miss-apprehensions be making;—
Though wrong the dear sex to *miss-call,*
    There's no harm, I should hope, in MISS-TAKING.

CROOKED COINCIDENCES.

A pamphlet published in the year 1703 has the following strange title: "The *Deformity* of Sin cured; a Sermon preached at St. Michael's, *Crooked*-lane, before the Prince of Orange, by the Rev. J. *Crookshanks.* Sold by Matthew Denton, at the *Crooked* Billet near *Cripple*-gate, and by all other booksellers." The words of the text are, "*Every crooked path shall be made straight;*" and the prince before whom it was preached was *deformed* in person.

THE COURT-FOOL'S PUN ON ARCHBISHOP LAUD.

Great praise to God, and *little Laud* to the devil.

English Words and Forms of Expression.

DICTIONARY English is something very different not only from common colloquial English, but even from that of ordinary written composition. Instead of about forty thousand words, there is probably no single author in the language from whose works, however voluminous, so many as ten thousand words could be collected. Of the forty thousand words there are certainly many more than one-half that are only employed, if they are ever employed at all, on the rarest occasions. We should be surprised to find, if we counted them, with how small a number of words we manage to express all that we have to say, either with our lips or with the pen. Our common literary English probably hardly amounts to ten thousand words; our common spoken English hardly to five thousand.

Odd words are to be found in the dictionaries. Why they are kept there no one knows; but what man in his senses would use such words as zythepsary for a brewhouse, and zymologist for a brewer; would talk of a stormy day as procellous and himself as madefied; of his long-legged son as increasing in procerity but sadly marcid; of having met with such procacity from such a one; of a bore as a macrologist; of an aged horse as macrobiotic; of important business as moliminous, and his daughter's necklace as moniliform; of some one's talk as meracious, and lament his last night's nimiety of wine at that dapatical feast, whence he was taken by ereption? Open the dictionary at any page, and you will find a host of these words.

By a too ready adoption of foreign words into the currency of the English language, we are in danger of losing much of its radical strength and historical significance. Marsh has compared the parable of the man who built his house upon the sand, as given by Matthew and Luke. Matthew uses the plain Saxon English. The learned Evangelist, Luke, employed a Latinized dictionary. "Now," he says, "compare the two passages and say which to every English ear, is the most impressive:"

"And the rain descended, and the floods came, and the winds blew, and beat upon that house, and it fell, and great was the fall of it."—*Matthew*.

"Against which the stream did beat vehemently, and immediately it fell; and the ruin of that house was great."—*Luke*.

There can scarcely be a difference of opinion as to the relative force and beauty of the two versions, and consequently we find, that while that of Matthew has become proverbial, the narrative of Luke is seldom or never quoted.

Trench says that the Anglo-Saxon is not so much one element of the English language, as the foundation of it—the basis. All its joints, its whole *articulation*, its sinews and its ligaments, the great body of articles, pronouns, conjunctions, prepositions, numerals, auxiliary verbs, all smaller words which serve to knit together and bind the larger into sentences, these—not to speak of the grammatical structure of the language—are exclusively Saxon. The Latin may contribute its tale of bricks, yea, of goodly and polished hewn stones to the spiritual building, but the mortar, with all that holds and binds these together, and constitutes them into a house, is Saxon throughout." As proof positive of the soundness of the above affirmation, the test is submitted that—"you *can* write a sentence without Latin, but you *cannot* without Saxon." The words of the Lord's Prayer are almost all Saxon. Our good old family Bible is a capital standard of it, and has done more than any other book for the conservation of the purity of our language. Our best writers, particularly those of Queen Anne's time,—Addison, Steele, Swift, &c.,—were distinguished by their use of simple Saxon.

SOURCES OF THE LANGUAGE.

Some years ago, a gentleman, after carefully examining the folio edition of Johnson's Dictionary, formed the following table of English words derived from other languages :—

Latin............6,732	Swedish............34	Irish and Erse.........2
French..........4,812	Gothic 31	Turkish..................2
Saxon 1,665	Hebrew............16	Irish and Scottish....1
Greek...........1,148	Teutonic............ 15	Portuguese.............1
Dutch......... 691	Arabic...............13	Persian 1
Italian 211	Irish 6	Frisi 1
German............116	Runic.................4	Persic....................1
Welsh..............95	Flemish 4	Uncertain 1
Danish..............75	Erse....................4	
Spanish 56	Syriac.................3	Total......15,784
Icelandic...........50	Scottish..............3	

NOUNS OF MULTITUDE.

A foreigner looking at a picture of a number of vessels, said, " See what a flock of ships." He was told that a flock of ships was called a fleet, and that a fleet of sheep was called a flock. And it was added, for his guidance, in mastering the intricacies of our language, that a flock of girls is called a bevy, that a bevy of wolves is called a pack, and a pack of thieves is called a gang, and that a gang of angels is called a host, and that a host of porpoises is called a shoal, and a shoal of buffaloes is called a herd, and a herd of children is called a troop, and a troop of partridges is called a covey, and a covey of beauties is called a galaxy, and a galaxy of ruffians is called a horde, and a horde of rubbish is called a heap, and a heap of oxen is called a drove, and a drove of blackguards is called a mob, and a mob of whales is called a school, and a school of worshippers is called a congregation, and a congregation of engineers is called a corps, and a corps of robbers is called a band, and a band of locusts is called a swarm, and a swarm of people is called a crowd.

DISRAELIAN ENGLISH.

Mr. Disraeli gives us some queer English in his novel of *Lothair*, as may be seen in the following examples:—" He guarded over Lothair's vast inheritance;" "Lothair observed on" a lady's singing; "of simple but distinguished mien, with a countenance naturally pale, though somewhat bronzed by a life of air and exercise, and a profusion of dark, auburn hair;" "he

engaged a vehicle and ordered to be driven to Leicester Square;"
" he pointed to an individual seated in the centre of the table;"
" their mutual ancestors;" " Is there anything in the *Tenebræ*
why I ought not to be present?"; " *thoughts which made him
unconscious* how long had elapsed;" "with no companions than
the wounded near them;" " The surgeon was sitting by her
side, occasionally wiping the slight foam from her brow." We
have heard of people foaming at the mouth, but never before of
a lady foaming at the brow.

" YE " FOR " THE."

Ye is sometimes used for *the* in old books wherein *the* is
the more usual form, on account of the difficulties experienced
by the printers in " spacing out." When pressed for room they
put *ye;* when they had plenty of room they put *the.* Many
people in reading old books pronounce the abbreviation *ye.* But
the proper pronunciation is *the,* for the *y* is only a corruption
of the old *thorn-letter*, or symbol for *th.*

ITS.

His is the genitive (or as we say, possessive) of *he,* (*he's,*—
his,) and *it* or *hit,* as it was long written, is the neuter of *he,*
the final *t* being the sign of the neuter. The introduction of
its, as the neuter genitive instead of *his,* arose from a mis-
conception, similar to that which would have arisen had the
Romans introduced *illudius* as the neuter genitive of *ille,* instead
of *illius.* *Its* very rarely occurs in our authorized version of the
Bible, *his* or *her* being used instead—occurs but a few times in
all Shakspeare—was unknown to Ben Jonson—was not admitted
into his poems by Milton—and did not come into common use
until sanctioned by Dryden.

THAT.

The use of the word *That* in the following examples is
strictly in accordance with grammatical rules:—

The gentleman said, in speaking of the word *that*, *that* *that that that that* lady parsed, was not *that that that that* gentleman requested her to analyze.

> Now, *that* is a word that may often be joined,
> For *that that* may be doubled is clear to the mind;
> And *that that that* is right, is as plain to the view,
> As *that that that that* we use, is rightly used too,
> And *that that that that that* line has in it, is right—
> In accordance with grammar—is plain in our sight.

28

I SAY.

A gentleman who was in the habit of interlarding his discourse with the expression " I say," having been informed by a friend that a certain individual had made some ill-natured remarks upon this peculiarity, took the opportunity of addressing him in the following amusing style of rebuke:—" I say, sir, I hear say you say I say 'I say' at every word I say. Now, sir, although I know I say 'I say' at every word I say, still I say, sir, it is not for you to say I say 'I say' at every word I say."

PATH-OLOGY.

There once resided in Ayrshire a man who, like Leman, proposed to write an Etymological Dictionary of the English language. Being asked what he understood the word *pathology* to mean, he answered, with great readiness and confidence, " Why, the art of *road-making*, to be sure."

THE PRONUNCIATION OF OUGH.

The difficulty of applying rules to the pronunciation of our language may be illustrated in two lines, where the combination of the letters *ough* is pronounced in no less than seven different ways, viz.: as *o*, *uff*, *off*, *up*, *ow*, *oo*, and *ock* :—

29

> THOUGH the TOUGH COUGH and HICCOUGH PLOUGH me THROUGH,
> O'er life's dark LOUGH my course I still pursue.

The following attempts to show the sound of *ough*, final, are ingenious:—

> *Though* from *rough cough* or *hiccough* free,
> That man has pain *enough*
> Whose wounds *through plough*, sunk in a *slough*,
> Or *lough* begin to *slough*.

> 'Tis not an easy task to show,
> How o, u, g, h, sound; since *though*,
> An Irish *lough*, an English *slough*,
> And *cough*, and *hiccough*, all allow
> Differ as much as *tough* and *through*,
> There seems no reason why they do.

> "Husband," says Joan, "'tis plain enough
> That Roger loves our daughter;
> And Betty loves him too, although
> She treats his suit with laughter.

> "For Roger always hems and coughs,
> While on the field he's ploughing;
> Then strives to see between the boughs,
> If Betty heeds his coughing.

The following *jeu d'esprit*, entitled "A Literary Squabble on the pronunciation of Monckton Milnes's Title," is stated to have been the production of Lord Palmerston:—

> The Alphabet rejoiced to hear,
> That Monckton Milnes was made a peer;
> For in the present world of letters,
> But few, if any, were his betters.
> So an address, by acclamation,
> They voted, of congratulation.
> And O U G H T and N
> Were chosen to take up the pen,
> Possessing each an interest vital
> In the new Peer's baronial title.
> 'Twas done in language terse and telling,
> Perfect in grammar and in spelling.
> But when 'twas read aloud—oh, mercy!
> There sprung up such a controversy

About the true pronunciation
Of said baronial appellation.
The vowels O and U averred
They were entitled to be heard.
The consonants denied the claim,
Insisting that they mute became.
Johnson and Walker were applied to,
Sheridan, Bailey, Webster, tried too;
But all in vain—for each picked out
A word that left the case in doubt.
O, looking round upon them all,
Cried, "If it be correct to call
T H R O U G H *throo,*
H O U G H must be *Hoo;*
Therefore there must be no dispute on
The question, we should say Lord *Hooton.*"
U then did speak, and sought to show
He should be doubled, and not O,
For sure if *ought* and *awt,* then nought on
Earth could the title be but *Hawton.*
H, on the other hand, said he,
In *cough* and *trough,* stood next to G,
And like an F was then looked oft on,
Which made him think it should be *Hofton.*
But G corrected H, and drew
Attention other cases to:
Lough, Rough and *Chough,* more than enough
To prove O U G H spelled *uff,*
And growled out in a sort of gruff tone
They must pronounce the title *Hufton.*
N said emphatically No;
For D O U G H is *Doh,*
And though (look there again) that stuff
At sea for fun, they nickname *Duff,*
He should propose they took a vote on
The question should it not be *Hoton?*
Besides, in French 'twould have such force,
A Lord must be *haut ton,* of course.
High and more high contention rose,
From words they almost came to blows,
Till S, as yet, who had not spoke,
And dearly loved a little joke,
Put in *his* word, and said, "Look here,
Plough in this row must have a *share.*"
At this atrocious pun, each page

Of Johnson whiter grew with rage.
Bailey looked desperately cut up,
And Sheridan completely shut up.
Webster, who is no idle talker,
Made a sign signifying *Walker.*
While Walker, who had been used badly,
Shook his old dirty dog-ears sadly.
But as we find in prose or rhyme,
A joke, made happily in time,
However poor, will often tend
The hottest argument to end,
And smother anger in a laugh,
So S succeeded with his *chaff,*
Containing, as it did, some wheat,
In calming this fierce verbal heat.
Authorities were all conflicting,
And S there was no contradicting.
P L O U G H was *Plow*
Even *enough* was called *enow,*
And no one who preferred *enough*
Would dream of saying "Speed the *Pluff."*
So they considered it was wise
With S to make a compromise,
To leave no loop to hang a doubt on
By giving three cheers for Lord Houghton (*Howton*).

EXCISE.

The following curious document gives the opinion of Lord Mansfield, when Attorney-General, upon Dr. Johnson's definition of the word Excise: —

Case.

Mr. Samuel Johnson has lately published a book, entitled *A Dictionary of the English Language, in which the words are deduced from their originals, and illustrated in their different significations by examples from the best writers. To which are prefixed a history of the Language, and an English grammar.*

Under the title "Excise" are the following words:—

EXCISE, n. s. (*accijs* Dutch ; *excisum*, Latin,) a hateful lax levied upon commodities and adjudged not by the common judges of property, but *wretches* hired by those to whom *Excise* is paid.

The people should pay a ratable tax for their sheep, and an *Excise* for every thing which they should eat.—HAYWARD.

Ambitious now to take *excise*
Of a more fragrant paradise.—CLEVELAND.

EXCISE.

With hundred rows of teeth the shark exceeds,
And on all trades, like Cassowar, she feeds.—MARVEL.

Can hire large houses and oppress the poor
By farmed Excise.—DRYDEN, *Juvenal, Sat. 3.*

The author's definition being observed by the Commissioners of Excise, they desire the favor of your opinion:

Qu.—Whether it will not be considered as a libel; and, if so, whether it is not proper to proceed against the author, printers, and publishers thereof, or any and which of them, by information or how otherwise?

Opinion.

I am of opinion that it is a libel; but, under all the circumstances, I should think it better to give him an opportunity of altering his definition; and, in case he don't, threaten him with an information.

29th Nov. 1755.   W. MURRAY.

PONTIFF.

Mr. Longfellow, in his *Golden Legend,* thus refers to the derivation of this word from *pons* (a bridge) and *facere* (to make):—

Well has the name of Pontifex been given
Unto the Church's head, as the chief builder
And architect of the invisible bridge
That leads from earth to heaven.

ROUGH.

Mr. Motley, in his *History of the United Netherlands,* IV. 138, thus ascribes the use of this word to Queen Elizabeth, of England, in her last illness:—

The great queen, moody, despairing, dying, wrapt in profoundest thought, with eyes fixed upon the ground or already gazing into infinity was besought by the counsellors around her to name the man to whom she chose that the crown should devolve.

"Not to a Rough," said Elizabeth, sententiously and grimly.

These particulars are apparently given on the authority of the Italian Secretary, Scaramelli, whose language is quoted in a foot-note, and who says that the word *Rough* "in lingua inglese significa persona bassa e vile."

Charles Dickens said, "I entertain so strong an objection to the euphonious softening of *ruffian* into *rough*, which has lately become popular, that I restore the right word to the heading of this paper." (*The Ruffian, by the Uncommercial Traveler, All the Year Round.*) "Lately popular" does not mean popular for two hundred and eighty years past. A word that has escaped the notice of the Glossarists cannot have been in use early in the seventeenth century. That it should have been used in its modern sense by Queen Elizabeth, passes all bounds of belief. With all her faults she did not make silly unmeaning remarks; and it would have been extremely silly in her to say she did not wish a low ruffian to succeed her on the throne. If she uttered a word having the same sound, it might possibly have been *ruff.* The "ruff," though worn by men of the upper class, was in Queen Elizabeth's time an especially female article of dress, and the queen might have said, "I will have no ruff to succeed me," just as now-a-days one might say, "I will have no petticoat government." We want better authority than that of Scaramelli before we can believe that Elizabeth used either the word *rough* or *ruff*, when consulted as to her wishes respecting her successor.

NOT AMERICANISMS.

In Bartlett's Dictionary the term "*stocking-feet*" is given as an Americanism. But the following quotation from Thackeray's *Newcomes* (vol. i. ch. viii.) shows that this is an error:—

"Binnie found the Colonel in his sitting-room arrayed in what are called in Scotland his stocking-feet."

Professor Tyndall, at the farewell banquet given in his honor by the citizens of New York, prior to his departure, in referring to his successful lecture-course in the United States, said he had had—to quote his words—"what you Americans call '*a good time*.'"

But this expression is not an Americanism. It is used by Dean Swift in his letter to Stella, (Feb. 24, 1710–11); "I hope Mrs. Wells had a good time."

That not very elegant adjective *bully*, though found in Bartlett, and used by Washington Irving cannot be claimed as an Americanism. Friar Tuck sings, in Scott's *Ivanhoe*:—

> "Come troll the brown bowl to me, bully boy,
> Come troll the brown bowl to me."

But to go further back, we find it in the burden of an old three-part song, "We be three poor Mariners," in Ravenscroft's *Deuteromelia*, 1609:

> "Shall we go dance the round, the round,
> Shall we go dance the round;
> And he that is a bully boy,
> Come pledge me on the ground."

One of the words which the English used to class among Americanisms—ignorant that it was older and better English than their own usage—was *Fall*, used as the name of the third of the seasons. The English, corrupted by the Johnsonese of the Hanoverian reigns, call it by the Latinism, Autumn. But the other term, in general use on this side of the Atlantic, is the word by which all the old writers of the language know it. "The hole yere," says scholarly Roger Ascham in his *Toxophilus*, "is divided into iiii. partes, Spring tyme, Sommer, Faule of the leafe, & Winter, whereof the hole winter for the roughnesse of it, is cleane taken away from shoting: except it be one day amonges xx., or one yeare amonges xi."

This statement, by the way, that exceptionally mild winters were in the ratio of one to eleven, is worth noting with reference to the recent announcement of science that the spots on the sun have an eleven-year period of maximum frequency.

NO LOVE LOST BETWEEN THEM.

In the ordinary acceptation of the words, " No love was lost between the two," we are led to infer that the two were on very unfriendly terms, But in the ballad of *The Babes in the Wood*, as given in Percy's *Reliques*, occur the following lines, which convey the contrary idea:—

> No love between this two was lost,
>   Each was to other kind:
> In love they lived, in love they died,
>   And left two babes behind.

THE FORLORN HOPE.

Military and civil writers of the present day seem quite ignorant of the true meaning of the words *forlorn hope*. The adjective has nothing to do with despair, nor the substantive with the "charmer which lingers still behind;" there was no such poetical depth in the words as originally used. Every corps marching in an enemy's country had a small body of men at the head (*haupt* or *hope*) of the advanced guard; and which was termed the *forlorne hope* (*lorn* being here but a termination similar to *ward* in *forward*,) while another small body at the head of the read-guard was called the *rere-lorn hope*. A reference to Johnson's Dictionary shows that civilians were misled as early as the time of Dryden by the mere sound of a technical military phrase; and, in process of time, even military men forgot the true meaning of the words. And thus we easily trace the foundation of an error to which we are indebted for Byron's beautiful line:—

> The full of hope, misnamed *forlorn.*

QUIZ.

This word, which is only in vulgar or colloquial use, and which some of the lexicographers have attemped to trace to learned roots, originated in a joke. Daly, the manager of a Dublin play-house, wagered that a word of no meaning should be the common talk and puzzle of the city in twenty-four hours. In the course of that time the letters *q u i z* were chalked on all the walls of Dublin with an effect that won the wager.

TENNYSON'S ENGLISH.

Probably no poet ever more thoroughly comprehended the value of words in metrical composition than Mr. Tennyson, but he has issued a new coinage which is not pure. Compound epithets are modelled after the Greek or revived from the uncritical Elizabethan era. Thus, where we should naturally say "The bee is cradled in the lily," Mr. Tennyson writes, "The bee is lily-cradled." When a man's nose is broken at the bridge or a lady's turns up at the tip, the one is said to be "a nose bridge-broken," and the other (with much gallantry) to be "tip-tilted, like the petal of a flower."

The movement of the metre again is very peculiar. Discarding Milton's long and complex periods, Mr. Tennyson has restored blank verse to an apparently simple rhythm. But this simplicity is in fact the result of artifice, and, under every variety of movement, the ear detects the recurrence of a set type. One of the poet's favorite devices is to pause on a monosyllable at the beginning of a line, and this affect is repeated so often as to remind the reader of Euripides and his unhappy "oil flask" in *The Frogs*. Take the following instances:—

> And the strange sound of an adulterous race,
> Against the iron grating of her cell
> Beat.
>
>   A sound
> As of a silver horn across the hills
> Blown.
>
>   And then the music faded, and the Grail
> Passed.
>
>   His eyes became so like her own they seemed
> Hers.

"THAT MINE ADVERSARY HAD WRITTEN A BOOK."

This passage from Job xxxi. 35, is frequently misapplied, being interpreted as if it had reference to a book or writing as commonly understood. It means rather, according to Gesenius, a charge or accusation. Pierius makes it "libellum accusationis," and Grotius, "scriptam accusationem" Scott expresses this in his *Commentary*: —

"Job challenged his adversary, or accuser, to produce a libel or written indictment against him: he was confident that it would prove no disgrace to him, but an honor; as every article would be disproved, and the reverse be manifested."

Other commentators understand it as meaning a record of Job's life, or of his sufferings. Coverdale translates :—"And let him that my contrary party sue me with a lybell." In the Genevan version it is, "Though mine adversarie should write a book *against me*." In the Bishop's Bible, 1595, "Though mine adversarie write a book *against me*." The meaning seems to have become obscured in our version by retaining the English book instead of the Latin *libel*, but omitting the words in italics, "against me."

ECCENTRIC ETYMOLOGIES.

To trace the changes of form and meaning which many of the words of our language have undergone is no easy task. There are words as current with us as with our forefathers, the significance of which, as we use them, is very different from that of their primitive use. And, in many instances, they have wandered, by courses more or less tortuous, so far from their original meaning as to make it almost impossible to follow the track of divergence. Hence, it is easy to understand why it has been said that the etymologist, to be successful, must have "an instinct like the special capabilities of the pointer." But there are derivations which are only revealed by accident, or stumbled upon in unexpected ways, and which, in the regular course of patient search, would never have been elicited.   The following illustrative selections will interest the general reader.

Bombastic.—This adjective has an odd derivation.   Originally bombast (from the Latin bombax, cotton) meant nothing but cotton wadding, used for filling or stuffing.   Shakspeare employs it in this sense in *Love's Labor Lost,* v. 2.

As bombast and as living to the time.

Decker, in his *Satyromastix,* says, "You shall swear not to bombast out a new play with the old linings of jests."   And Guazzo, *Civile Conversation,* 1591,—"Studie should rather make him leane and thinne, and pull out the bombast of his corpulent doublet."

Hence, by easy transition from the falseness of padding or puffing out a figure, bombast came to signify swelling pretentiousness of speech and conduct as an adapted meaning; and gradually this became the primary and only sense.

Buxom.—This word is simply bow-some or bough-some, *i. e.*, that which readily bows, or bends, or yields like the boughs of a tree.   No longer ago than when Milton wrote *boughsome,* which as *gh* in English began to lose its guttural sound,—that of the letter *chi* in Greek,— came to be written *buxom,* meant simply yielding, and was of general application.

———"and, this once known, shall soon return,
And bring ye to the place where thou and Death
Shall dwell at ease, and up and down unseen
Wing silently the buxom air."—*Paradise Lost,* II. 840.

But aided, doubtless, as Dr. Johnson suggests, by a too liberal construction of the bride's promise in the old English marriage ceremony, to be "obedient and buxom in bed and board," it came to be applied to women who were erroneously thought likely to be thus yielding; and hence it now means plump, rosy, alluring, and is applied only to women who combine those qualities of figure, face and expression.

Cadaver.—An abbot of Cirencester, about 1216, conceived himself an etymologist, and, as a specimen of his powers, has left us the Latin word cadaver, a corpse, thus dissected:—"Ca," quoth he, is abbreviated for caro; "da" for data; "ver" for vermibus.   Hence we have "caro data vermibus," flesh given to the worms.

Yet while the reader smiles at this curious absurdity, it is worth while to note that the word *alms* is constructed upon a similar principle, being formed (according to the best authority) of letters, taken from successive syllables of the cumbrous Latinized Greek word *eleemosyna.*

Canard.—This is the French for duck, and the origin of its application to hoaxing is said to be as follows:—To ridicule a growing extravagance in story-telling a clever journalist stated that an interesting experiment had just been made, calculated to prove the extraordinary voracity of ducks.   Twenty of these animals had been placed together, and one of them having been killed and cut up into the smallest possible pieces, feathers and all, and thrown to the other nineteen, had been gluttonously gobbled up in an exceedingly brief space of time.   Another was taken from the remaining nineteen, and being chopped small like its predecessor, was served up to the eighteen, and at once devoured like the other; and so on to the last, which was thus placed in the remarkable position of having eaten his nineteen companions in a wonderfully short space of time!   All this, most pleasantly narrated, obtained a success which the writer was far from anticipating, for the story ran the rounds of all the journals in Europe.   It then became almost forgotten for about a score of years, when it came back from America, with an amplification which it did not boast of at the commencement, and with a regular certificate of the autopsy of the body of the surviving animal, whose esophagus was declared to have been seriously injured!   Since then fabrications of this character have been called *canards.*

Chum.—A schoolboy's letter, written two centuries ago, has lately revealed that chum is a contraction from "chamber-fellow." Two students dwelling together found the word unwieldly, and, led by another universal law of language, they shortened it in the most obvious way.

Dandy.—Bishop Fleetwood says that "dandy" is derived from a silver coin of small value, circulated in the reign of Henry VIII., and called a "dandy-prat."

Dunce.—This word comes to us from the celebrated Duns Scotus, chief of the Schoolmen of his time. He was "the subtle doctor by preëminence;" and it certainly is a strange perversion that a scholar of his great ability should give name to a class who hate all scholarship. When at the Reformation and revival of learning the works of the Schoolmen fell into extreme disfavor with the Reformers and the votaries of the new learning, Duns, the standard-bearer of the former, was so often referred to with scorn and contempt by the latter that his name gradually became the by-word it now is for hopeless ignorance and invincible stupidity. The errors and follies of a set were fastened upon their distinguished head. Says Tyndale, 1575,—

"Remember ye not how within this thirty years, and far less, and yet dureth unto this day, the old barking curs, *Dunce's* disciples, and like draff called Scotists, the children of darkness, raged in every pulpit against Greek, Latin and Hebrew?"

Eating humble-pie.—The phrase "eating humble-pie" is traced to the obsolete French word "*ombles*," entrails; pies for the household servants being formerly made of the entrails of animals. Hence, to take low or humble ground, to submit one's self, came familiarly to be called eating "humble" or rather "umble" pie. The word "umbles" came to us from the Norman conquest, and though now obsolete, retains its place in the lexicons of Worcester and Webster, who, however, explain the entrails to be those of the deer only.

Fiasco.—A German, one day, seeing a glassblower at his occupation, thought nothing could be easier than glassblowing, and that he could soon learn to blow as well as the workman. He accordingly commenced operations by blowing vigorously, but could only produce a sort of pear-shaped balloon or little flask (fiasco). The second attempt had a similar result, and so on, until *fiasco* after *fiasco* had been made. Hence arose the expression which we not infrequently have occasion to use when describing the result of our undertakings.

Fudge.—This is a curious word, having a positive personality underlying it. Such at least it is, if Disraeli's account thereof be authentic. He quotes from a very old pamphlet entitled *Remarks upon the Navy*, wherein the author says, " There was in our time one *Captain Fudge*, commander of a merchantman, who upon his return from a voyage, how ill fraught soever his ship was, always brought home his owners a good crop of lies; so much that now, aboard ship, the sailors when they hear a great lie told, cry out, ' You fudge it'." The ship was the Black Eagle, and the time, Charles II.; and thence the monosyllabic name of its untruthful captain comes to us for exclamation when we have reason to believe assertions ill-founded.

Gossip.—This is another of that class of words which by the system of moral decadence that Trench has so ably illustrated as influencing human language, has come to be a term of unpleasant reproach. In some parts of the country, by the " gossips" of a child are meant his god-parents, who take vows for him at his baptism. The connection between these two actual uses of the word is not so far to seek as one might suppose. Chaucer shows us that those who stood sponsors for an infant were considered " *sib*," or kin, to each other in *God:* thus the double syllables were compounded. Verstigan says:—

"Our Christian ancestors understanding a spirituall affinitie for to grow between the parents, and such as undertooke for the childe at baptisme, called each other by the name of *God-sib*, which is as much as to say as that they were *sib* together, i. e. of kin together, through God."

The Roman church forbids marriage between persons so united in a common vow, as she believes they have contracted an essential spiritual relationship. But from their affinity in the interests of the child they were brought into much converse with one another; and as much talk almost always degenerates into idle talk, and personalities concerning one's neighbors, and the like, so "gossips" finally came to signify the latter, when the former use of it was nearly forgotten. It is remarkable that the French "commérage" has passed through identically the same perversion.

Grog.—Admiral Vernon, whose ardent devotion to his profession had endeared him to the British naval service, was in the habit of walking the deck, in bad weather, in a rough *grogram* cloak, and thence had obtained the nickname of *Old Grog*. Whilst in command of the West India station, and at the height of his popularity on account of his reduction of Porto Bello with six men-of-war only, he introduced the use of rum and water among the ship's company. When served out, the new beverage proved most palatable, and speedily grew into such favor that it became as popular as the brave admiral himself, and in honor of him was surnamed by acclamation "Grog."

Hocus-pocus.—According to Tillotson, this singular expression is believed to be a corruption of the transubstantiating formula, *Hoc est corpus meum*, used by the priest on the elevation of the host. Turner, in his history of the Anglo-Saxons, traces it to Ochus Bochus, a magician and demon of the northern mythology. We should certainly prefer the latter as the source of this conjurer's catch-word, which the usage of ordinary life connects with jugglery or unfair dealing, but preponderant evidence is in favor of the former.

Malingerer.—This word, brought much into use by the exigencies of our civil war, is from the French "malin gré," and signifies a soldier who from "evil will" shirks his duty by feigning sickness, or otherwise rendering himself incapable: in plain words, a poltroon.

Mustard.—Etymologists have fought vigorously over the derivation of this word. " Multum ardet," says one, or in old French, "moult arde," it burns much. " Mustum ardens, hot must, says another, referring to the former custom of preparing French mustard for the table with the sweet must of new wine. A picturesque story about the name is thus told:—Philip the Bold, Duke of Burgundy, granted to Dijon certain armorial bearings, with the motto "Moult me tarde"—I long or wish ardently. This was sculptured over the principal gate. In the course of years, by some accident, the central word was effaced. The manufacturers of sinapi or senévé (such were the former names of mustard), wishing to label their pots of condiment with the city arms, copied the mutilated motto; and the unlearned, seeing continually the inscription of "moult-tarde," fell into the habit of calling the contents by this title.

Navvy.—Many persons have been puzzled by the application of this word, abbreviated from navigator, to laborers. Why should earth-workers be called navigators? They whose business is with an element antipodean to water, why receive a title as of seafaring men? At the period when inland navigation was the national rage, and canals were considered to involve the essentials of prosperity, as railways are now, the workmen employed on them were called "navigators," as cutting the way for navigation. And when railways superseded canals, the name of the laborers, withdrawn from one work to the other, was unchanged, and merely contracted, according to the dislike of our Anglo-Saxon tongues to use four syllables where a less number will suffice.

Neighbor.—Formerly this familiar word was employed to signify "the boor who lives nigh to us." And just here is another of those words which have been degraded from their original sense; for boor did not then represent a stupid, ignorant lout, but simply a farmer, as in Dutch now.

Poltroon.—In the olden days the Norman-French "poltroon" had a significance obsolete now: days when Strongbow was a noble surname, and the yew-trees of England were of importance as an arm of national defence; then the coward or malingerer had but to cut off the thumb ("pollice truncus" in Latin) —the thumb which drew the bow, and he was unfit for service, and must be discharged.

Porpoise.—The common creature of the sea, whose gambols have passed into a jest and a proverb, the porpoise, is so named because of his resemblance to a hog when in sportive mood. "Porc-poisson," said somebody who watched a herd of them tumbling about, for all the world like swine, except for the sharp dorsal fin; and the epithet adhered.

Scrape.—Long ago roamed through the forests the red and fallow deer, which had a habit of scraping up the earth with their fore-feet to the depth of several inches, sometimes even of half a yard. A wayfaring man through the olden woods was frequently exposed to the danger of tumbling into one of these hollows, when he might truly be said to be "in a scrape." Cambridge students in their little difficulties picked up and applied the phrase to other perplexing matters which had brought a man morally into a fix.

Sterling.—This word was originally applied to the metal rather than to a coin. The following extract from Camden points out its origin as applied to money:—

In the time of his sonne King Richard the First, monie coined in the east parts of Germanie began to be of especiall request in England for the puritie thereof, and was called *Easterling* monie, as all the inhabitants of those parts were called *Easterlings*, and shortly after some of that countrie, skilful in mint matters and alloies, were sent for into this realme to bring the coins to perfection, which, since that time, was called of them *sterling* for *Easterlings*.

Surplice.—That scholastic and ministerial badge, the surplice, is said to derive its name from the Latin "superpelliceum," because anciently worn over leathern coats made of hides of beasts; with the idea of representing how the sin of our first parents is now covered by the grace of our Lord Jesus Christ, so that we are entitled to wear the emblem of innocence.

Sycophant.—The original etymology of the word *sycophant* is curious. The word συκοφαντέω (from σῦκον, a fig, and φαίνω, to show,) in its primary signification, means to inform against or expose those who exported figs from Athens to other places without paying duty, hence it came to signify *calumnior*, to accuse falsely, to be a tale-bearer, an evil speaker of others. The word *sycophanta* means, in its first sense, no more than this. We now apply it to any flatterer, or other abject dependant, who, to serve his own purposes, slanders and detracts from others.

Tariff.—Because payment of a fixed scale of duties was demanded by the Moorish occupants of a fortress on Tarifa promontory, which overlooked the entrance to the Mediterranean, all taxes on imports came to be called a tariff.

Treacle.—A remarkable curiosity in the way of derivations is one traced by that indefatigable explorer, Archbishop Trench, which connects treacle with vipers. The syrup of molasses with the poison of snakes! Never was an odder relationship; yet it is a case of genuine fatherhood, and embodies a singular superstition. The ancients believed that the best antidote to the bite of the viper was a confection of its own flesh. The Greek word ϑηριαχή, flesh of the viper, was given first to such a sweetmeat, and then to any antidote of poison, and lastly to any syrup; and easily corrupted into our present word. Chaucer has a line—

Christ, which that is to every harm triacle.

Milton speaks of the "sovran treacle of sound doctrine." A stuff called Venice Treacle was considered antidote to all poisons. "Vipers treacle yield," says Edmund Waller, in a verse which has puzzled many a modern reader, and yet brings one close to the truth of the etymology, and shows that treacle is only a popular corruption of *theriac*.

Wig.—This word may be cited as a good example to show how interesting and profitable it is to trace words through their etymological windings to their original source. Wig is abridged from *periwig*, which comes from the Low Dutch *peruik*, which has the same meaning. When first introduced into the English language, it was written and pronounced *perwick*, the *u* being changed into *w*, as may still be seen in old English books. Afterwards the *i* was introduced for euphony, and it became *periwick;* and finally the *ck* was changed into *g*, making it *periwig*, and by contraction *wig*.

The Dutch word *peruik* was borrowed from the French *perruque*. The termination *uik* is a favorite one with that nation, and is generally substituted in borrowed words for the French *uque* and the German *auch*. The French word *perruque* comes from the Spanish *peluca*, and this last from *pelo*, hair, which is derived from the Latin *pilus*. Hence the Latin word *pilus*, hair, through successive transformations, has produced the English word *wig*.

Windfall.—Centuries ago a clause was extant in the tenure of many English estates, to the effect that the owners might not fell the trees, as the best timber was reserved for the Royal Navy; but any trees that came down without cutting were the property of the tenant. Hence was a storm a joyful and a lucrative event in proportion to its intensity, and the larger the number of forest patriarchs it laid low the richer was the lord of the land. He had received a veritable "windfall." Ours in the nineteenth century come in the shape of any unexpected profit; and those of us who own estates rather quake in sympathy with our trembling trees on windy nights.

ODD CHANGES OF SIGNIFICATION.   30

The first verse of Dean Whittingham's version of the 114th Psalm may be quoted as a curious instance of a phrase originally grave in its meaning become strangely incongruous:—

> When Israel by God's address
> From Pharaoh's land was bent,
> And Jacob's house the strangers left
> And *in the same train* went.

Since the completion of the Pacific Railway, some introductory lines in Southey's *Thalaba* require correction:—

> Who at this untimely hour
> Wander o'er the *desert sands?*
> No *station* is in view.

If the author would revisit the earth, he would find numerous "stations" on the railway route across the Great American Desert.

Among funny instances of wresting from a text a meaning to suit a particular purpose, is that of the classical scholar who undertook to prove that the word "smile" was used as a euphemism for a drink in ancient times, by quoting from Horace's *Odes:*—

> Amara lento temperat risu.

Which is rendered by Martin:—

> Meets life's *bitters* with a jest,
> And *smiles* them down.

By *lento risu*, it was argued, is clearly meant a *slow* smile, or one taken through a straw!

The meaning of the word *Wretch* is one not generally understood. It was originally, and is now, in some parts of England, used as a term of the softest and fondest tenderness. This is not the only instance in which words in their present general acceptation bear a very opposite meaning to what they did in Shakspeare's time. The word *Wench*, formerly, was not used in the low and vulgar acceptation that it is at present. *Damsel* was the appellation of young ladies of quality, and *Dame* a title of distinction. *Knave* once signified a servant; and in an early translation of the New Testament, instead of "Paul, the Servant," we read "Paul, the Knave of Jesus Christ," or, Paul, a rascal of Jesus Christ. *Varlet* was formerly used in the same sense as valet. On the other hand, the word *Companion*, instead of being the honorable synonym of Associate, occurs in the play of Othello with the same contemptuous meaning which we now affix, in its abusive sense, to the word "Fellow;" for Emilia, perceiving that some secret villain had aspersed the character of the virtuous Desdemona, thus indignantly exclaims:—

> O Heaven! that such *Companions* thou'dst unfold,
> And put in every honest hand a whip,
> To lash the rascal naked through the world.—iv. 2.

Villain formerly meant a bondman. In feudal law, according to Blackstone, the term was applied to those who held lands and tenements in *villenage*,—a tenure by base services.

Pedant formerly meant a schoolmaster. Shakspeare says in his *Twelfth Night*,—

> A pedant that keeps a school in the church.—iii. 2.

Bacon, in his *Pathway unto Prayer*, thus uses the word Imp: "Let us pray for the preservation of the King's most excellent Majesty, and for the prosperous success of his entirely beloved son Edward our Prince, that most *angelic imp*."

The word *brat* is not considered very elegant now, but a few years ago it had a different signification from its present one. An old hymn or *De profundis*, by Gascoine, contains the lines,—

> "O Israel, O household of the Lord,
> O Abraham's brats, O brood of blessed seed,
> O chosen sheep that loved the Lord indeed."

It is a somewhat noticeable fact, that the changes in the signification of words have generally been to their deterioration; that is, words that heretofore had no sinister meaning have acquired it. The word *cunning*, for example, formerly meant nothing sinister or underhanded; and in Thrope's confession in Fox's "Book of Martyrs" is the sentence, "I believe that all these three persons [in the Godhead] are even in power, and in cunning, and in might, full of grace and of all goodness." *Demure* is another of this class. It was used by earlier writers without the insinuation which is now almost latent in it, that the external shows of modesty and sobriety rest on no corresponding realities. *Explode* formerly meant to drive off the stage with loud clappings of the hands, but gradually became exaggerated into its present signification. *Facetious*, too, originally meant urbane, but now has so degenerated as to have acquired the sense of buffoonery; and Mr. Trench sees indications that it will ere long acquire the sense of indecent buffoonery.

Frippery now means trumpery and odds and ends of cheap finery; but once it meant old clothes of value, and not worthless, as the term at present implies. The word *Gossip* formerly meant only a sponsor in baptism. Sponsors were supposed to become acquainted at the baptismal font, and by their sponsorial act to establish an indefinite affinity towards each other and the child. Thus the word was applied to all who were familiar and intimate, and finally obtained the meaning which is now predominant in it.

Homely once meant secret and familiar, though in the time of Milton it had acquired the same sense as at present. *Idiot*, from the Greek, originally signified only a private man as distinguished from one in public office, and from that it has degenerated till it has come to designate a person of defective mental powers. *Incense* once meant to kindle not only anger, but good passions as well; Fuller uses it in the sense of "to incite." *Indolence* originally signified a freedom from passion or pain, but now implies a condition of languid non-exertion. *Insolent* was once only "unusual."

The derivation of *lumber* is peculiar. As the Lombards were the bankers, so they were also the pawnbrokers, of the Middle Ages. The "lumber-room" was then the place where the Lombard banker and broker stored his pledges, and *lumber* gradually came to mean the pledges themselves. As these naturally accumulated till they got out of date or became unserviceable, it is easy to trace the steps by which the word descended to its present meaning.

Obsequious implies an unmanly readiness to fall in with the will of another; but in the original obsequium, or in the English word as employed two centuries ago, there was nothing of this: it rather meant obedience and mildness. Shakspeare, speaking of a deceased person, says,—

> " How many a holy and obsequious tear
> Hath dear religious love stolen from mine eye,
> As interest of the dead."

Property and *propriety* were once synonymous, both referring to material things, as the French word *propriété* does now. Foreigners do not often catch the distinction at present made in English between the two words; and we know a French gentleman who, recently meeting with some pecuniary reverses, astonished his friends by telling them that he had lost all his " propriety."

A poet is a person who writes poetry, and, according to the good old customs, a proser was a person who wrote prose, and simply the antithesis of poet. The word has now a sadly different signification; and it would not be considered very respectable to term Addison, Irving, Bancroft, or Everett " prosers."

INFLUENCE OF NAMES.

The Romans, from the time they expelled their kings, could never endure the idea of being governed by a *king*. But they submitted to the most abject slavery under an *emperor*. And Oliver Cromwell did not venture to risk disgusting the republicans by calling himself king, though under the title of Protector he exercised regal functions.

The American colonies submitted to have their commerce and their manufactures crippled by restrictions avowedly for the benefit of the mother-country, and were thus virtually *taxed* to the amount of all that they in any instance lost by paying more for some article than it would cost to make it themselves, or to buy it of foreigners. But as soon as *a tax* was imposed *under that name*, they broke out into rebellion.

It is a marvel to many, and seems to them nearly incredible, that the Israelites should have gone after other gods; and yet the vulgar in most parts of Christendom are actually serving the gods of their heathen ancestors. But then they do not *call* them *gods*, but fairies or bogles, etc., and they do not apply the word *worship* to their veneration of them, nor *sacrifice* to their offerings. And this slight change of name keeps most people in ignorance of a fact that is before their eyes.

Others, professed Christians, are believed, both by others and by themselves, to be worshippers of the true God, though they invest him with the *attributes* of one of the evil demons worshipped by the heathen. There is hardly any professed Christian who would not be shocked at the application of the word *caprice* to the acts of the Most High. And yet his choosing to inflict suffering on his creatures "*for no cause*" (as some theologians maintain) "except that *such is his will*," is the very definition of caprice.

But when Lord Byron published his poem of "Cain," which contains substantially the *very same* doctrine, there was a great outcry among pious people, including, no doubt, many who were of the theological school which teaches the same, under other *names*.

Why and how any evil comes to exist in the universe, reason cannot explain, and revelation does not tell us. But it does show us what is *not* the cause. That it cannot be from *ill will* or *indifference,* is proved by the sufferings undergone by the *beloved* Son.

Many probably would have hesitated if it had been proposed to them to join a new *Church* under that *name,* who yet eagerly enrolled themselves in the Evangelical *Alliance,*— which is in fact a church, with meetings for worship, and *sermons* under the *name* of *speeches,* and a *creed* consisting of sundry *Articles of Faith* to be subscribed; only not called by those *names.*

Mrs. B. expressed to a friend her great dread of such a medicine as tartar-emetic. She always, she said, gave her children *antimonial* wine. He explained to her that this is tartar-emetic dissolved in wine; but she remained unchanged.

Mrs. H. did not like that her daughters should be novel-readers; and *all novels* in *prose* were indiscriminately prohibited; but *any* thing in *verse* was as indiscriminately allowed.

Probably a Quaker would be startled at any one's using the very *words* of the prophets, "Thus saith the Lord:" yet he says the same things in the words, "The Spirit moveth me to say so and so." And some, again, who would be shocked at *this,* speak of a person,—adult or *child,*—who addresses a congregation in extempore prayers and discourses, as being under the *influence of the Holy Spirit;* though in neither case is there any miraculous *proof* given. And they abhor a claim to *infallibility;* only they are *quite certain* of being under the guidance of the Spirit in whatever they say or do.

Quakers, again, and some other dissenters, object to a *hired* ministry, (in reality, an *un*hired;) but their preachers are to be *supplied* with all they need; like the father of Molière's Bourgeois, who was no *shopkeeper,* but kindly chose *goods* for his friends, which he let them have for money.

The custom of using hard compounds furnished Ben Jonson opportunities of showing his learning as well as his satire. He used to call them "words un-in-one-breath-utterable." Redi mentions an epigram against the sophists, made up of compounds "a mile long." Joseph Scaliger left a curious example in Latin, part of which may be thus rendered into English:—

> Loftybrowflourishers,
> Noseinbeardwallowers,
> Brigandbeardnourishers,
> Dishandallswallowers,
> Oldcloakinvestitors,
> Barefootlookfashioners,
> Nightprivatefeasteaters,
> Craftlucubrationers;
> Youthcheaters, Wordcatchers, Vaingloryosophers,
> Such are your seekersofvirtue philosophers.

The old naturalist Lovell published a book at Oxford, in 1661, entitled *Panzoologicomineralogia*. Rabelais proposed the following title for a book:—*Antipericatametaparhengedamphicribrationes*. The reader of Shakspeare will remember Costard's *honorificabilitudinitatibus*, in Love's Labor Lost, v. 1. There was recently in the British army a major named *Teyoninhokarawen*. In the island of Mull, Scotland, is a locality named *Drimtaidhorickhillichattan*. The original Mexican for country curates is *Notlazomahnitzteopixcatatzins*. The longest Nipmuck word in Eliot's Indian Bible is in St. Mark i. 40, *Wutteppesittukqussunnoowehtunkquoh*, and signifies "kneeling down to him."

OUR VERNACULAR IN CHAUCER'S TIME.

> But rede that boweth down for every blaste
> Ful lyghtly cesse wynde, it wol aryse
> But so nyle not an oke, when it is caste
> It nedeth me nought longe the forvyse
> Men shall reioysen of a great emprise
> Atchewed wel and stant withouten dout
> Al haue men ben the longer there about.—*Troylus,* ii.

Tall Writing.

DEFINITION OF TRANSCENDENTALISM.

THE spiritual cognoscence of psychological irrefragibility connected with concutient ademption of incolumnient spirituality and etherialized contention of subsultory concretion.

Translated by a New York lawyer, it stands thus :—

Transcendentalism is two holes in a sand-bank : a storm washes away the sand-bank without disturbing the holes.

THE DOMICILE ERECTED BY JOHN.
Translated from the Vulgate.

Behold the Mansion reared by dædal Jack.

See the malt stored in many a plethoric sack,
In the proud cirque of Ivan's bivouac.

Mark how the Rat's felonious fangs invade
The golden stores in John's pavilion laid.

Anon, with velvet foot and Tarquin strides,
Subtle Grimalkin to his quarry glides,—
Grimalkin grim, that slew the fierce *rodent*
Whose tooth insidious Johann's sackcloth rent.

Lo! now the deep-mouthed canine foe's assault,
That vexed the avenger of the stolen malt,
Stored in the hallowed precincts of that hall
That rose complete at Jack's creative call.

Here stalks the impetuous Cow with crumpled horn,
Whereon the exacerbating hound was torn,
Who bayed the feline slaughter-beast that slew
The Rat predacious, whose keen fangs ran through
The textile fibers that involved the grain
Which lay in Hans' inviolate domain.

Here walks forlorn the Damsel crowned with rue,
Lactiferous spoils from vaccine dugs, who drew,
Of that corniculate beast whose tortuous horn
Tossed to the clouds, in fierce vindictive scorn,
The harrowing hound, whose braggart bark and stir
Arched the lithe spine and reared the indignant fur

Of Puss, that with verminicidal claw
Struck the weird rat in whose insatiate maw
Lay reeking malt that erst in Juan's courts we saw,
Robed in senescent garb that seems in sooth
Too long a prey to Chronos' iron tooth.

Behold the man whose amorous lips incline,
Full with young Eros' osculative sign,
To the lorn maiden whose lact-albic hands
Drew albu-lactic wealth from lacteal glands
Of that immortal bovine, by whose horn
Distort, to realm ethereal was borne
The beast catulean, vexer of that sly
Ulysses quadrupedal, who made die
The old mordacious Rat that dared devour
Antecedaneous Ale in John's domestic bower.

Lo, here, with hirsute honors doffed, succinct
Of saponaceous locks, the Priest who linked
In Hymen's golden bands the torn unthrift,
Whose means exiguous stared from many a rift,
Even as he kissed the virgin all forlorn,
Who milked the cow with implicated horn,
Who in fine wrath the canine torturer skied,
That dared to vex the insidious muricide,
Who let auroral effluence through the pelt
Of the sly Rat that robbed the palace Jack had built.

The loud cantankerous Shanghae comes at last,
Whose shouts arouse the shorn ecclesiast,
Who sealed the vows of Hymen's sacrament,
To him who, robed in garments indigent,
Exosculates the damsel lachrymose,
The emulgator of that horned brute morose,
That tossed the dog, that worried the cat, that *kilt*
The rat, that ate the malt, that lay in the house that Jack built.

FROM THE CURIOSITIES OF ADVERTISING.

TO BE LET,

To an Oppidan, a Ruricolist, or a Cosmopolitan, and may be
entered upon immediately :

The House in STONE ROW, lately possessed by CAPT. SIREE.
To avoid Verbosity, the Proprietor with Compendiosity will
give a Perfunctory description of the Premises, in the Compa-
gination of which he has Sedulously studied the convenience of

the Occupant. It is free from Opacity, Tenebrosity, Fumidity, and Injucundity, and no building can have greater Pellucidity or Translucency—in short, its Diaphaneity even in the Crepuscle makes it like a Pharos, and without laud, for its Agglutination and Amenity, it is a most Delectable Commorance; and whoever lives in it will find that the Neighbors have none of the Truculence, the Immanity, the Torvity, the Spinosity, the Putidness, the Pugnacity, nor the Fugacity observable in other parts of the town, but their Propinquity and Consanguinity occasion Jocundity and Pudicity—from which, and the Redolence of the place (even in the dog-days), they are remarkable for Longevity. For terms and particulars apply to JAMES HUTCHINSON, opposite the MARKET-HOUSE.—*Dub. News.*

FROM THE CURIOSITIES OF THE POST-OFFICE.

The following is a genuine epistle, sent by an emigrant country schoolmaster to a friend at home :—

MR M CONNORS

With congruous gratitude and decorum I accost to you this debonnaire communication. And announce to you with amicable Complacency that we continually enjoy competent laudable good health, thanks to our omnipotent Father for it. We are endowed with the momentous prerogatives of respectable operations of a supplement concuity of having a fine brave and gallant youthful daughter the pendicity ladies age is four months at this date, we denominated her Margaret Connolly.

I have to respond to the Communication and accost and remit a Convoy revealing with your identity candor and sincerity. If your brother who had been pristinely located and stationed in England whether he has induced himself with ecstasy to be in preparation to progress with you. I am paid by the respectable potent loyal nobleman that I work for one dollar per day. Announce to us in what Concuity the crops and the products of husbandry dignify, also predict how is John Carroll and his wife and family. My brother and Myself are continually employed and occupied in similar work. Living and doing good. Dictate how John Mahony wife and family is

Don't you permit oblivion to obstruct you from inserting this. Prognosticate how Mrs Harrington is and if she accept my intelligence or any convoy from either of Her 2 progenies since their embarkation for this nation. If she has please specify with congruous and elysian gratitude with validity and veracity to my magnanimous self.

I remit my respects to my former friends and acquaintances. I remain   D. CONNOLLY.

P. S. Direct your Epistle to Pembroke, State of Maine.

Dear brother-in-law

I am determined and candidly arrive at Corolary, as I am fully resolved to transfer a sufficient portion of money to you to recompense your liabilities from thence to hence. I hope your similar operations will not impede any occurrence that might obstruct your progression on or at the specified time the 17 of March next.

SPANISH PLAY-BILL,
Exhibited at Seville, 1762.

To the Sovereign of Heaven—to the Mother of the Eternal World—to the Polar Star of Spain—to the Comforter of all Spain—to the faithful Protectress of the Spanish nation—to the Honor and Glory of the Most Holy Virgin Mary—for her benefit and for the Propagation of her Worship—the Company of Comedians will this day give a representation of the Comic Piece called—   N A N I N E.

The celebrated Italian will also dance the Fandango, and the Theatre will be respectably illuminated.

In a medical work entitled *The Breviarie of Health*, published in 1547, by Andrew Borde, a physician of that period, is a prologue addressed to physicians, beginning thus:—

Egregious doctors and masters of the eximious and arcane science of physic, of your urbanity exasperate not yourselves against me for making this little volume.

THE MAD POET.

McDonald Clarke, commonly called the *mad poet*, died a few years ago in the Lunatic Asylum on Blackwell's Island, New York. He wrote those oft-quoted lines,—

> Now twilight lets her curtain down,
> And pins it with a star.

In his wilder moments he set all rules at defiance, and mingled the startlingly sublime and the laughably ridiculous in the oddest confusion. He talks thus madly of Washington :—

> Eternity—give him elbow room;
> A spirit like his is large;
> Earth, fence with artillery his tomb,
> And fire a double charge
> To the memory of America's greatest man :
> Match him, posterity, if you can.

In the following lines, he sketches, with a few bold touches, a well-known place, sometimes called a *rum-hole* :—

> Ha ! see where the wild-blazing grogshop appears,
> As the red waves of wretchedness swell ;
> How it burns on the edge of tempestuous years,
> The horrible light-house of hell !

FOOTE'S FARRAGO.

The following droll nonsense was written by Foote, the dramatist, for the purpose of trying the memory of Macklin, who boasted that he could learn any thing by heart on hearing it once:—

So she went into the garden to cut a cabbage-leaf to make an apple-pie ; and, at the same time, a great she-bear coming up the street pops its head into the shop—What ! no soap? So he died ; and she very imprudently married the barber: and there were present the Picninnies, and the Joblilies, and the Garyulies, and the great Panjandrum himself, with the little round button at top. And they all fell to playing the game of "catch as catch can," till the gunpowder ran out of the heels of their boots !

BURLESQUE OF THE STYLE OF DR. JOHNSON.

While I was admiring the fantastical ramifications of some umbelliferous plants that hung over the margin of the Liffey, the fallacious bank, imperceptibly corroded by the moist tooth of the fluid, gave way beneath my feet, and I was suddenly submerged to some fathoms of profundity. Presence of mind, in constitutions not naturally timid, is generally in proportion to the imminence of the peril. Having never learned to move through the water in horizontal progression, had I desponded, I had perished; but, being for a moment raised above the element by my struggles, or by some felicitous casualty, I was sensible of the danger, and immediately embraced the means of extrication. A cow, at the moment of my lapse, had entered the stream, within the distance of a protruded arm; and being in the act of transverse navigation to seek the pasture of the opposite bank, I laid hold on that part of the animal which is loosely pendent behind, and is formed by the continuation of the vertebræ. In this manner I was safely conveyed to a fordable passage, not without some delectation from the sense of the progress without effort on my part, and the exhilarating approximation of more than problematical deliverance. Though in some respects I resembled the pilot of Gyas, *Jam senior madidaque fluens in veste*, yet my companions, unlike the barbarous Phrygian spectators, forbore to acerbitate the uncouthness of embarrassment by the insults of derision. Shrieks of complorance testified sorrow for my submersion, and safety was rendered more pleasant by the felicitations of sympathy. As the danger was over, I took no umbrage at a little risibility excited by the feculence of my visage, upon which the cow had discharged her gramineous digestion in a very ludicrous abundance. About this time the bell summoned us to dinner; and, as the cutaneous contact of irrigated garments is neither pleasant nor salubrious, I was easily persuaded by the ladies to divest myself of mine. Colonel Manly obligingly accommodated me with a covering of camlet. I found it commodious, and more agreeable than the many compressive ligaments of modern drapery. That there might be no violation of decorum, I took care to have the loose robe fastened before with small cylindrical wires, which the dainty fingers of the ladies easily removed from their dresses and inserted into mine, at such proper intervals as to leave no aperture that could awaken the susceptibility of temperament, or provoke the cachinnations of levity.*

NEWSPAPER EULOGY.

The following alliterative eulogy on a young lady appeared, many years ago, in a newspaper :—

If *b*oundless *b*enevolence *b*e the *b*asis of *b*eatitude, and *h*armless *h*umanity a *h*arbinger of *h*allowed *h*eart, these *C*hristian concomitants *c*omposed her *c*haracteristics, and *c*onciliated the esteem of her *c*otemporary a*c*quaintances, who *m*ean to *m*odel their *m*anners in the *m*ould of their *m*eritorious *m*onitor.

CLEAR AS MUD.

In a series of *Philosophical Essays* published many years ago, the author† gives some definitions of human knowledge, the following of which he considers "least obnoxious to comprehension :"—

A coincidence between the association of ideas, and the order or succession of events or phenomena, according to the relation of cause and effect, and in whatever is subsidiary, or necessary to realize, approximate and extend such coincidence; understanding, by the relation of cause and effect, that order or

---

* The peculiar stateliness and dignity of Johnston's style, when applied to the smaller concerns of life, makes, as will be seen from the above caricature, a very ludicrous appearance. A judicious imitation of his phraseology on trifling subjects was a favorite manner of attack among the critics. Erskine's account of the Buxton baths is one of the most amusing. When several examples of this sort were shown to Johnson, at Edinburgh, he pronounced that of Lord Dreghorn the best: "but," said he, "I could caricature my own style much better myself."

† Ogilvie.

succession, the discovery or development of which empowers an intelligent being, by means of one event or phenomenon, or by a series of given events or phenomena, to anticipate the recurrence of another event or phenomenon, or of a required series of events or phenomena, and to summon them into existence, and employ their instrumentality in the gratification of his wishes, or in the accomplishment of his purposes.

INDIGNANT LETTER.

Addressed to a Louisiana clergyman by a Virginia correspondent.

Sir:—You have behaved like an impetiginous acroyli—like those inquinate orosscrolest who envious of my moral celsitude carry their mugacity to the height of creating symposically the fecund words which my polymathic genius uses with uberity to abligate the tongues of the weightless. Sir, you have corassly parodied my own pet words, as though they were tangrams. I will not conceroate reproaches. I would obduce a veil over the atramental ingratitude which has chamiered even my undisceptible heart. I am silent on the foscillation which my coadful fancy must have given you when I offered to become your fanton and adminicle. I will not speak of the liptitude, the ablepsy you have shown in exacerbating me; one whose genius you should have approached with mental discalceation. So, I tell you, Sir, syncophically and without supervacaneous words, nothing will render ignoscible your conduct to me. I warn you that I will vellicate your nose if I thought your moral diathesis could be thereby performed. If I thought that I should not impigorate my reputation by such a degladiation. Go tagygraphic; your oness inquinate draws oblectation from the greatest poet since Milton, and draws upon your head this letter, which will drive you to Webster, and send you to sleep over it.

"Knowledge is power," and power is mercy; so I wish you ʇo rovose that it may prove an external hypnotic.

INTRAMURAL ÆSTIVATION.

In candent ire the solar splendor flames;
The foles, languescent, pend from arid rames;
His humid front the cive, anheling, wipes,
And dreams of erring on ventiferous ripes.

How dulce to vive occult to mortal eyes,
Dorm on the herb with none to supervise,
Carp the suave berries from the crescent vine,
And bibe the flow from longicaudate kine!

To me, alas! no verdurous visions come,
Save yon exiguous pool's conferva-scum;
No concave vast repeats the tender hue
That laves my milk-jug with celestial blue!

Me wretched! Let me curr to quercine shades!
Effund your albid hausts, lactiferous maids!
Oh, might I vole to some umbrageous clump,—
Depart,—be off,—excede,—evade,—erump!

               Autocrat of the Breakfast-Table.

A CHEMICAL VALENTINE.

I love thee, Mary, and thou lovest me,
Our mutual flame is like the affinity
That doth exist between two simple bodies.
I am Potassium to thy Oxygen;
'Tis little that the holy marriage vow
Shall shortly make us one.   That unity
Is, after all, but metaphysical.
Oh! would that I, my Mary, were an Acid—
A living Acid; thou an Alkali
Endowed with human sense; that, brought together,
We both might coalesce into one Salt,
One homogeneous crystal.   Oh that thou
Wert Carbon, and myself were Hydrogen!
We would unite to form olefiant gas,
Or common coal, or naphtha. Would to heaven
That I were Phosphorus, and thou wert Lime,
And we of Lime composed a Phosphuret!
I'd be content to be Sulphuric Acid,
So that thou mightst be Soda. In that case,
We should be Glauber's Salt. Wert thou Magnesia
Instead, we'd form the salt that's named from Epsom.
Couldst thou Potassa be, I Aquafortis,
Our happy union should that compound form,

Nitrate of Potash—otherwise Saltpetre.
And thus, our several natures sweetly blent.
We'd live and love together, until death
Should decompose this fleshly Tertium Quid,
Leaving our souls to all eternity
Amalgamated!   Sweet, thy name is Briggs,
And mine is Johnson. Wherefore should not we
Agree to form a Johnsonate of Briggs?
We will! the day, the happy day is nigh,
When Johnson shall with beauteous Briggs combine.

THE ANATOMIST TO HIS DULCINEA.

I list as thy heart and ascending aorta
  Their volumes of valvular harmony pour;
And my soul from that muscular music has caught a
  New life 'mid its dry anatomical lore.

Oh, rare is the sound when thy ventricles throb
  In a systolic symphony measured and slow,
When the auricles answer with rhythmical sob,
  As they murmur a melody wondrously low!

Oh, thy cornea, love, has the radiant light
  Of the sparkle that laughs in the icicle's sheen;
And thy crystalline lens, like a diamond bright,
  Through the quivering frame of thine iris is seen!

And thy retina, spreading its lustre of pearl,
  Like the far-away nebula, distantly gleams
From a vault of black cellular mirrors that hurl
  From their hexagon angles the silvery beams.

Ah! the flash of those orbs is enslaving me still,
  As they roll 'neath the palpebræ, dimly translucent,
Obeying in silence the magical will
  Of the oculo-motor—pathetic—abducent.

Oh, sweet is thy voice, as it sighingly swells
  From the daintily quivering chordæ vocales,
Or rings in clear tones through the echoing cells
  Of the antrum, the ethmoid, and sinus frontales!

ODE TO SPRING.

WRITTEN IN A LAWYER'S OFFICE.

Whereas on sundry boughs and sprays
  Now divers birds are heard to sing,
And sundry flowers their heads upraise—
  Hail to the coming on of Spring!

The birds aforesaid, happy pairs!
    Love midst the aforesaid boughs enshrines
In household nests, themselves, their heirs,
    Administrators, and assigns.

The songs of the said birds arouse
    The memory of our youthful hours.
As young and green as the said boughs,
    As fresh and fair as the said flowers.

O busiest term of Cupid's court!
    When tender plaintiffs actions bring;
Season of frolic and of sport,
    Hail, as aforesaid, coming Spring!

PRISTINE PROVERBS PREPARED FOR PRECOCIOUS PUPILS.

Observe yon plumed biped fine!
    To effect his captivation,
Deposit particles saline
    Upon his termination.

Cryptogamous concretion never grows
On mineral fragments that decline repose.

Whilst self-inspection it neglects,
    Nor its own foul condition sees,
The kettle to the pot objects
    Its sordid superficies.

Decortications of the golden grain
Are set to allure the aged fowl, in vain.

Teach not a parent's mother to extract
    The embryo juices of an egg by suction:
That good old lady can the feat enact,
    Quite irrespective of your kind instruction.

Pecuniary agencies have force
To stimulate to speed the female horse.

Bear not to yon famed city upon Tyne
The carbonaceous product of the mine.

The mendicant, once from his indigence freed,
And mounted aloft on the generous steed,
Down the precipice soon will infallibly go,
And conclude his career in the regions below.

It is permitted to the feline race
To contemplate even a regal face.

Metric Prose. 33

Quid tentabam scribere versus erat.—OVID.

COWPER'S LETTER TO NEWTON.

The following letter was written to Rev. John Newton, by William Cowper, in reference to a poem *On Charity*, by the latter:—

My very dear friend, I am going to send, what when you have read, you may scratch your head, and say I suppose, there's nobody knows, whether what I have got, be verse or not;—by the tune and the time, it ought to be rhyme; but if it be, did ever you see, of late or of yore, such a ditty before?

I have writ "Charity," not for popularity, but as well as I could, in hopes to do good; and if the "Reviewer" should say to be sure, the gentleman's muse wears Methodist shoes, you may know by her pace, and talk about grace, that she and her bard have little regard for the tastes and fashions, and ruling passions, and hoydening play, of the modern day; and though she assume a borrowed plume, and now and then wear a tittering air, 'tis only her plan, to catch if she can, the giddy and gay, as they go that way, by a production of a new construction; she has baited her trap, in the hope to snap all that may come, with a sugar-plum. His opinion in this will not be amiss; 'tis what I intend, my principal end; and if I succeed, and folks should read, till a few are brought to a serious thought, I shall think I am paid for all I have said, and all I have done, although I have run, many a time, after a rhyme, as far as from hence to the end of my sense, and by hook or by crook, write another book, if I live and am here another year.

I have heard before of a room with a floor, laid upon springs, and such-like things, with so much art in every part, that when you went in, you were forced to begin a minuet pace, with an air and a grace, swimming about, now in and now out, with a deal of a state, in a figure of eight, without pipe or string, or any such thing; and now I have writ, in a rhyming fit, what will make you dance, and, as you advance, will keep you still, though against your will, dancing away, alert and gay, till you come to an end of what I have penned, which that you may do, ere madam and you are quite worn out with jigging about, I take my leave, and here you receive a bow profound, down to the ground, from you humble me—W. C.

EXAMPLE IN IRVING'S NEW YORK.

The following remarkable instance of involuntary poetic prose occurs in Knickerbocker's humorous history of New York, near the commencement of the Sixth Book:—

The gallant warrior starts from soft repose, from golden visions and voluptuous ease; where, in the dulcet "piping time of peace," he sought sweet solace after all his toils. No more in beauty's siren lap reclined, he weaves fair garlands for his lady's brows; no more entwines with flowers his shining sword, nor through the livelong summer's day chants forth his love-sick soul in madrigals. To manhood roused, he spurns the amorous flute, doffs from his brawny back the robe of peace, and clothes his pampered limbs in panoply of steel. O'er his dark brow, where late the myrtle waved, where wanton roses breathed enervate love, he rears the beaming casque and nodding plume; grasps the bright shield and ponderous lance, or mounts with eager pride his fiery steed, and burns for deeds of glorious chivalry.

In D'Israeli's *Wondrous Tale of Alvoy*, are remarkable specimens of prose poetry. For example:—

Why am I here? are you not here? and need I urge a stronger plea? Oh, brother dear, I pray you come and mingle in our festival! Our walls are hung with flowers you love; I culled them by the fountain's side; the holy lamps are trimmed and set, and you must raise their earliest flame. Without the gate my maidens wait to offer you a robe of state. Then, brother dear, I pray you come and mingle in our festival.

NELLY'S FUNERAL.

In Horne's *New Spirit of the Age*,—a series of criticisms on eminent living authors,—we find an admirable example of prose poetry thus noticed :—

A curious circumstance is observable in a great portion of the scenes of tragic power, pathos, and tenderness contained in various parts of Mr. Dickens's works, which it is possible may have been the result of harmonious accident, and the author not even subsequently conscious of it. It is that they are written in blank verse, of irregular metre and rhythms, which Southey, and Shelley, and some other poets, have occasionally adopted. Witness the following description from *The Old Curiosity Shop*.

And now the bell—the bell
She had so often heard by night and day
And listened to with solid pleasure,
    E'en as a living voice—
Rung its remorseless toll for her,
So young, so beautiful, so good.

Decrepit age, and vigorous life,
And blooming youth, and helpless infancy,
Poured forth—on crutches, in the pride of strength
    And health, in the full blush
Of promise—the mere dawn of life—
To gather round her tomb.   Old men were there
    Whose eyes were dim
    And senses failing—
Granddames, who might have died ten years ago,
And still been old—the deaf, the blind, the lame,
    The palsied,
The living dead in many shapes and forms,
To see the closing of this early grave !
    What was the death it would shut in,
To that which still would crawl and creep above it !

Along the crowded path they bore her now ;
    Pale as the new-fallen snow
That covered it ; whose day on earth
    Had been so fleeting.

> Under that porch where she had sat when Heaven
> In mercy brought her to that peaceful spot,
> She passed again, and the old church
> Received her in its quiet shade.

Throughout the whole of the above, only two unimportant words have been omitted—*in* and *its;* "granddames" has been substituted for "grandmothers," and "e'en" for "almost." All that remains is exactly as in the original, not a single word transposed, and the punctuation the same to a comma. The brief homily that concludes the funeral is profoundly beautiful.

> Oh! it is hard to take
> The lesson that such deaths will teach,
> But let no man reject it,
> For it is one that all must learn
> And is a mighty universal Truth.
> When Death strikes down the innocent and young,
> For every fragile form from which he lets
> The parting spirit free,
> A hundred virtues rise,
> In shapes of mercy, charity, and love,
> To walk the world and bless it.
> Of every tear
> That sorrowing mortals shed on such green graves,
> Some good is born, some gentler nature comes.

Not a word of the original is changed in the above quotation, which is worthy of the best passages in Wordsworth, and thus, meeting on the common ground of a deeply truthful sentiment, the two most unlike men in the literature of the country are brought into close proximation.

The following similar passage is from the concluding paragraph of *Nicholas Nickleby :*—

> The grass was green above the dead boy's grave,
> Trodden by feet so small and light,
> That not a daisy drooped its head
> Beneath their pressure.
> Through all the spring and summer time
> Garlands of fresh flowers, wreathed by infant **hands,**
> Rested upon the stone.

NIAGARA.

The same rhythmic cadence is observable in the following passage, copied verbatim from the *American Notes*:—

I think in every quiet season now,
Still do those waters roll, and leap, and roar,
  And tumble all day long;
Still are the rainbows spanning them
  A hundred feet below.
Still when the sun is on them, do they shine
  And glow like molten gold.
Still when the day is gloomy do they fall
  Like snow, or seem to crumble away,
  Like the front of a great chalk cliff,
Or roll adown the rock like dense white smoke.

But always does this mighty stream appear
  To die as it comes down.
And always from the unfathomable grave
Arises that tremendous ghost of spray
And mist which is never laid:
  Which has haunted this place
With the same dread solemnity,
  Since darkness brooded on the deep
And that first flood before the Deluge—Light
  Came rushing on Creation at the word of God.

To any one who reads this we need not say that but three lines in it vary at all from the closest requisitions of an iambic movement. The measure is precisely of the kind which Mr. Southey so often used. For the reader's convenience, we copy from *Thalaba* his well remembered lines on Night, as an instance:—

How beautiful is Night!
  A dewy freshness fills the silent air,
No mist obscures, nor cloud, nor speck, nor stain
  Breaks the serene of heaven.
In full orbed glory yonder Moon divine
  Rolls through the dark blue depths.
  Beneath her steady ray
  The desert circle spreads,
Like the round ocean, girdled with the sky.
  How beautiful is Night!

INVOLUNTARY VERSIFICATION IN THE SCRIPTURES.

The hexametric cadence in the authorized translation of the Bible has been pointed out in another portion of this volume. It is very noticeable in such passages as these, for example, from the Second Psalm:—

> Why do the heathen rage and the people imagine a vain thing?
> Kings of the earth set themselves and the rulers take counsel together.

The anapæstic cadence prevalent in the Psalms is also very remarkable:—

> That will bring forth his fruit in due season.—v. 6
> Whatsoever he doth it shall prosper.—v. 4.
> Away from the face of the earth.—v. 5.
> Be able to stand in the judgment.—v. 6.
> The way of th' ungodly shall perish.—v. 7.

Couplets may be drawn from the same inspired source, as follows:—

> Great peace have they that love thy law:
> And nothing shall offend them.—Psalm, cxix. 165.
> Thou wilt keep him in perfect peace
> Whose mind is stayed on thee.—Isaiah, xxvi. 3.
> When his branch is yet tender, and putteth forth leaves,
> Ye know that the summer is nigh.—Matthew, xxiv. 32.

UNINTENTIONAL RHYMES OF PROSERS.

The delicate ear of Addison, who would stop the press to add a conjunction, or erase a comma, allowed this inelegant jingle to escape his detection:—

> What I am going to *mention*, will perhaps deserve your *attention*.

Dr. Whewell, when Master of Trinity College, fell into a similar trap, to the great amusement of his readers. In his work on *Mechanics*, he happened to write *literatim* and *verbatim*, though not *lineatim*, the following tetrastich:—

> There is no force, however great,
> Can stretch a cord, however fine,
> Into a horizontal line,
> Which is accurately straight.

A curious instance of involuntary rhythm occurs in President Lincoln's Second Inaugural Address:—

> Fondly do we hope,
> Fervently do we pray,
> That this mighty scourge of war
> May speedily pass away:
> Yet if be God's will
> That it continue until—"

but here the strain abruptly ceases, and the President relapses into prose.

In the course of a discussion upon the involuntary metre into which Shakspeare so frequently fell, when he intended his minor characters to speak prose, Dr. Johnson observed;

> "Such verse we make when we are writing prose;
> We make such verse in common conversation."

Kemble and Mrs. Siddons, from their habit of committing to memory and reciting dramatic blank verse, unconsciously made their most ordinary observations in that measure. Kemble, for instance, on giving a shilling to a beggar, thus answered the surprised look of his companion:—

> "It is not often that I do these things,
> But *when* I do, I do them handsomely."

And once when, in a walk with Walter Scott on the banks of the Tweed, a dangerous looking bull made his appearance, Scott took the water, Kemble exclaimed:—

> "Sheriff, I'll get me up in yonder tree."

The presence of danger usually makes a man speak naturally, if anything will. If a reciter of blank verse, then, fall unconsciously into the rhythm of it when intending to speak prose, much more may an habitual writer of it be expected to do so. Instances of the kind from the table-talk of both Kemble and his sister might be multiplied. This of Mrs. Siddons,—

> "I asked for water, boy; you've brought me beer,——"

is one of the best known.

The Humors of Versification.

THE LOVERS.

IN DIFFERENT MOODS AND TENSES.

Sally Salter, she was a young teacher who taught,
And her friend, Charley Church, was a preacher, who praught!
Though his enemies called him a screecher, who scraught.

His heart, when he saw her, kept sinking, and sunk;
And his eye, meeting hers, began winking, and wunk;
While she, in her turn, fell to thinking, and thunk.

He hastened to woo her, and sweetly he wooed,
For his love grew until to a mountain it grewed,
And what he was longing to do, then he doed.

In secret he wanted to speak, and he spoke,
To seek with his lips what his heart long had soke;
So he managed to let the truth leak, and it loke.

He asked her to ride to the church, and they rode,
They so sweetly did glide, that they both thought they glode,
And they came to the place to be tied, and were tode.

Then homeward he said let us drive, and they drove,
And soon as they wished to arrive, they arrove;
For whatever he couldn't contrive, she controve.

The kiss he was dying to steal, then he stole;
At the feet where he wanted to kneel, then he knole;
And he said, "I feel better than ever I fole."

So they to each other kept clinging, and clung,
While Time his swift circuit was winging, and wung;
And this was the thing he was bringing and brung:

The man Sally wanted to catch, and had caught—
That she wanted from others to snatch, and had snaught—
Was the one she now liked to scratch, and she scraught.

And Charley's warm love began freezing and froze,
While he took to teasing, and cruelly toze
The girl he had wished to be squeezing, and squoze.

"Wretch!" he cried, when she threatened to leave him, and left,
"How could you deceive, as you have deceft?"
And she answered, "I promised to cleave, and I've cleft."

A STAMMERING WIFE.

When deeply in love with Miss Emily Pryne,
I vowed if the lady would only be mine,
 I would always be ready to please her;
She blushed her consent, though the stuttering lass
Said never a word except "You're an ass—
 An ass—an ass—iduous teazer!"

But when we were married, I found to my ruth
The stammering lady had spoken the truth;
 For often, in obvious dudgeon,
She'd say—if I ventured to give her a jog
In the way of reproof—"You're a dog—dog—dog—
 A dog—a dog—matic curmudgeon!"

And once, when I said, "We can hardly afford
This immoderate style with our moderate board,"
 And hinted we ought to be wiser,
She looked, I assure you, exceedingly blue,
And fretfully cried, "You're a Jew—Jew—Jew—
 A very ju-dicious adviser!"

Again, when it happened that, wishing to shirk
Some rather unpleasant and arduous work,·
 I begged her to go to a neighbor,
She wanted to know why I made such a fuss,
And saucily said, "You're a cuss—cuss—cuss—
 You were always ac—cus—tomed to labor!"

Out of temper at last with the insolent dame,
And feeling the woman was greatly to blame,
 To scold me instead of caressing,
I mimicked her speech, like a churl as I am,
And angrily said, "You're a dam—dam—dam—
 A dam-age instead of a blessing."

A SONG WITH VARIATIONS.

[Scene.—Wife at the piano; brute of a husband, who has no more soul
for music than his boot, in an adjoining apartment, making his toilet.]

  Oh! do not chide me if I weep!—
   Come, wife, and sew this button on.
  Such pain as mine can never sleep!—
   Zounds! as I live, another's gone!
  For unrequited love brings grief,—
   A needle, wife, and bring your scissors.

And Pity's voice gives no relief—
    The child! good Lord! he's at my razors!
No balm to ease the troubled heart,—
    Who starched this bosom?   I declare
That writhes from hate's envenomed dart!—
    It's enough to make a parson swear!
When faith in man is given up—
    How plaguey shiftless are some women!
Then sorrow fills her bitter cup—
    I'll have to get my other linen.
And to its lees the white lips quaff—
    Smith says he's coming in to-night,
While Malice yields her mocking laugh!—
    With Mrs. S., and Jones and Wright.
Oh! could I stifle in my breast—
    And Jones will bring some prime old sherry.
This aching heart, and give it rest,—
    We'll want some eggs for Tom-and-Jerry
Could Lethe's waters o'er me roll,—
    These stockings would look better mended!
And bring oblivion to my soul,—
    When-will-you-have-that-ditty-ended?
Then haply I, in other skies,—
    We'd better have the oysters fried.
Might find the love that earth denies!
    There! now at last my dickey's tied!

THOUGHTS WHILE SHE ROCKS THE CRADLE.

What is the little one thinking about?
Very wonderful thing, no doubt,
    Unwritten history!
    Unfathomable mystery!
But he laughs and cries, and eats and drinks,
And chuckles and crows, and nods and winks,
As if his head were as full of kinks,
And curious riddles, as any sphinx!
    Warped by colic and wet by tears,
    Punctured by pins, and tortured by fears,
    Our little nephew will lose two years;
      And he'll never know
      Where the summers go:
    He need not laugh, for he'll find it so!

Who can tell what the baby thinks?
Who can follow the gossamer links

By which the manikin feels his way
Out from the shores of the great unknown,
Blind, and wailing, and alone,
    Into the light of day?
Out from the shores of the unknown sea,
Tossing in pitiful agony!
Of the unknown sea that reels and rolls,
Specked with the barks of little souls—
Barks that were launched on the other side,
And slipped from heaven on an ebbing tide!
    And what does he think of his mother's eyes?
What does he think of his mother's hair?
    What of the cradle roof that flies
Forward and backward through the air?
    What does he think of his mother's breast—
Bare and beautiful, smooth and white,
Seeking it ever with fresh delight—
    Cup of his joy and couch of his rest?
What does he think when her quick embrace
Presses his hand and buries his face
Deep where the heart-throbs sink and swell
With a tenderness she can never tell,
    Though she murmur the words
    Of all the birds—
Words she has learned to murmur well?
    Now he thinks he'll go to sleep!
    I can see the shadow creep
    Over his eyes, in soft eclipse,
    Over his brow, and over his lips,
    Out to his little finger tips,
    Softly sinking, down he goes!
    Down he goes! down he goes!
    [*Rising and carefully retreating to her seat.*]
    See! he is hushed in sweet repose!

A SERIO-COMIC ELEGY.
WHATELY ON BUCKLAND.

In his "Common-Place Book," the late Archbishop Whately
records the following Elegy on the late geologist, Dr. Buckland:

    Where shall we our great professor inter,
        That in peace may rest his bones?
    If we hew him a rocky sepulchre
        He'll rise and break the stones,
    And examine each stratum which lies around,
    For he's quite in his element underground.

If with mattock and spade his body we lay
 In the common alluvial soil,
He'll start up and snatch these tools away
 Of his own geological toil;
In a stratum so young the professor disdains
That embedded should lie his organic remains.

Then exposed to the drip of some case-hardening spring,
 His carcase let stalactite cover,
And to Oxford the petrified sage let us bring,
 When he is encrusted all over;
There, 'mid mammoths and crocodiles, high on a shelf,
Let him stand as a monument raised to himself.

A REMINISCENCE OF TROY.

FROM THE SCHOLIAST.

It was the ninth year of the Trojan war—
 A tedious pull at best:
A lot of us were sitting by the shore—
 Tydides, Phocas, Castor, and the rest—
Some whittling shingles and some stringing bows,
And cutting up our friends, and cutting up our foes.

Down from the tents above there came a man,
 Who took a camp-stool by Tydides' side.
He joined our talk, and, pointing to the pan
 Upon the embers where our pork was fried,
Said he would eat the onions and the leeks,
But that fried pork was food not fit for Greeks.

"Look at the men of Thebes," he said, "and then
 Look at those cowards in the plains below:
You see how ox-like are the ox-fed men;
 You see how sheepish mutton-eaters grow.
Stick to this vegetable food of mine:
 Men who eat pork grunt, root and sleep like swine."

Some laughed, and some grew mad, and some grew red:
 The pork was hissing; but his point was clear.
Still no one answered him, till Nestor said,
 "One inference that I would draw is here:
You vegetarians, who thus educate us,
 Thus far have turned out very small potatoes."

THE POET BRYANT AS A HUMORIST.

Those who are familiar with Mr. Lowell's *Fable for Critics*, will remember the lines:—

> There is Bryant, as quiet, as cool, and as dignified,
> As a smooth, silent iceberg, that never is ignified,
> Save when by reflection 'tis kindled 'o nights
> With a semblance of flame by the chill Northern Lights.
> He may rank (Griswold says so) first bard of your nation;
> (There's no doubt he stands in supreme ice-olation,)
> Your topmost Parnassus he may set his heel on,
> But no warm applauses come, peal following peal on—
> He's too smooth and too polished to hang any zeal on;
> Unqualified merits, I'll grant, if you choose, he has 'em,
> But he lacks the one merit of kindling enthusiasm;
> If he stir you at all, it is just, on my soul,
> Like being stirred up by the very North Pole.

The Cambridge wit has either misjudged the character of Bryant's genius, or he has sacrificed a man to an epigram, and subordinated fact to a *jeu d'esprit*. Though "quiet and dignified," Mr. Bryant possesses a rare vein of humor, but its bubbling fancies are not generally known or suspected for the reason that he unbends anonymously. Only one of the diversions of his muse appears in his published works—and that is his invocation "To a Mosquito," which begins thus:—

> Fair insect! that with thread-like legs spread out,
>   And blood-extracting bill and filmy wing,
> Dost murmur, as thou slowly sail'st about,
>   In pitiless ears full many a plaintive thing,
> And tell how little our large veins would bleed,
> Would we but yield them to thy bitter need.

One day, when Mr. Bryant discovered in a fresh number of the *Atlantic Monthly* a so-called poem, which struck him as uncommonly absurd, he sat down and produced a travesty of it, which was much more effective in its ridicule than any sharper criticism could have been made. Here are the two in conjunction:—

THE "ATLANTIC" POEM.

Bellying earth no anchor throws
Stouter than the breath that blows;
Night and sorrow cling in vain;
It must toss in day again.

Hospital and battle-field,
Myriad spots where fate is sealed,
Brinks that crumble, sins that urge,
Plunge again into the surge.

How the purple breakers throw
Round me their insatiate glow.
Sweep my deck of hideous freight,
Pour through fastening and grate.

BRYANT'S TRAVESTY.

Squint-eyed bacchanals at play,
Keep a Lybian holiday,
Leading trains of solemn apes,
Tipsy with the blood of grapes.

Forty furies—thirty more
Than old Milton had before—
Scattering sparkles from their hair,
Swing their censers in the air.

Toss the flaming goblet off,
Heed not ocean's windy scoff;
Let him dash against the shore,
Gape and grin, and sweat and roar.

Since which time nothing has been heard of the Atlantic poet! Only those who were "behind the scenes," in the office of the *Evening Post*, in the year 1863, knew the authorship of the burlesque—and the burlesque itself will never appear in the poet's "collected works."

ON RECEIPT OF A RARE PIPE.

I lifted off the lid with anxious care,
　Removed the wrappages, stripe after stripe,
And when the hidden contents were laid bare,
　My first remark was: "Mercy, what a pipe!"

A pipe of symmetry that matched its size,
    Mounted with metal bright—a sight to see—
With the rich umber hue that smokers prize,
    Attesting both its age and pedigree.

A pipe to make the Royal Friedrich jealous,
    Or the great Teufelsdröck with envy gripe!
A man should hold some rank above his fellows
    To justify his smoking such a Pipe!

What country gave it birth? What blest of cities
    Saw it first kindle at the glowing coal?
What happy artist murmured, *"Nunc dimittis,"*
    When he had fashioned this transcendent bowl?

Has it been hoarded in a monarch's treasures?
    Was it a gift of peace, or prize of war?
Did the great Khalif in his "House of Pleasures"
    Wager, and lose it to the good Zaafar?

It may have soothed mild Spenser's melancholy,
    While musing o'er traditions of the past,
Or graced the lips of brave Sir Walter Raleigh
    Ere sage King Jamie blew his *Counterblast.*

Did it, safe hidden in some secret cavern,
    Escape that monarch's pipoclastic ken?
Has Shakespeare smoked it at the Mermaid Tavern,
    Quaffing a cup of sack with rare old Ben?

Ay, Shakespeare might have watched his vast creations
    Loom through its smoke—the spectre-haunted Thane,
The Sisters at their ghastly invocations,
    The jealous Moor and melancholy Dane.

'Round its orbed haze and through its mazy ringlets
    Titania may have led her elfin rout,
Or Ariel fanned it with his gauzy winglets,
    Or Puck danced in the bowl to put it out.

Vain are all fancies—questions bring no answer;
    The smokers vanish, but the pipe remains;
He were indeed a subtle necromancer
    Could read their records in its cloudy stains.

Nor this alone: its destiny may doom it
    To outlive e'en its use and history—
Some plowman of the future may exhume it
    From soil now deep beneath the Eastern sea—

And, treasured by some antiquarian Stultus,
  It may to gaping visitors be shown,
Labeled, "The symbol of some ancient Cultus,
  Conjecturally Phallic, but unkown."

Why do I thus recall the ancient quarrel
  'Twixt Man and Time, that marks all earthly things?
Why labor to re-word the hackneyed moral,
  Ὡς φύλλων γενεή, as Homer sings?

For this: Some links we forge are never broken;
  Some feelings claim exemption from decay;
And Love, of which this pipe was but the token,
  Shall last, though pipes and smokers pass away.

THE HUMAN EAR.

A sound came booming through the air—
  "What is that sound?" quoth I.
My blue-eyed pet, with golden hair,
  Made answer presently,
"Papa, you know it very well—
That sound—it was Saint Pancras Bell."

My own Louise, put down the cat,
  And come and stand by me;
I'm sad to hear you talk like that,
  Where's your philosophy?
That sound—attend to what I tell—
That sound was *not* Saint Pancras Bell.

"Sound is the name the sage selects
  For the concluding term
Of a long series of effects,
  Of which that blow's the germ.
The following brief analysis
Shows the interpolations, Miss.

"The blow which, when the clapper slips,
  Falls on your friend the Bell,
Changes its circle to ellipse,
  (A word you'd better spell),
And then comes elasticity,
Restoring what it used to be.

"Nay, making it a little more,
  The circle shifts about.

As much as it shrunk in before
   The Bell, you see, swells out;
And so a new ellipse is made,
   (You're not attending, I'm afraid).

"This change of form disturbs the air,
   Which in its turn behaves
In like elastic fashion there,
   Creating waves on waves;
Which press each other onward, dear,
Until the outmost finds your ear.

"Within that ear the surgeons find
   A *tympanum*, or drum,
Which has a little bone behind,—
   Malleus, it's called by some;
But those not proud of Latin Grammar
Humbly translate it as the hammer.

"The wave's vibrations this transmits
   On to the *incus* bone,
(*Incus* means anvil, which it hits),
   And this transfers the tone
To the small *os orbiculare*,
The tiniest bone that people carry.

"The *stapes* next—the name recalls
   A stirrup's form, my daughter—
Joins three half-circular canals,
   Each filled with limpid water;
Their curious lining, you'll observe,
Made of the auditory nerve.

"This vibrates next—and then we find
   The mystic work is crowned;
For then my daughter's gentle Mind
   First recognizes sound.
See what a host of causes swell
To make up what you call 'the Bell.'"

Awhile she paused, my bright Louise,
   And pondered on the case;
Then, settling that he meant to teaze,
   She slapped her father's face.
"You bad old man, to sit and tell
Such gibberygosh about a Bell!"

SIR TRAY: AN ARTHURIAN IDYL.

The widowed Dame of Hubbard's ancient line
Turned to her cupboard, cornered anglewise
Betwixt this wall and that, in quest of aught
To satisfy the craving of Sir Tray,
Prick-eared companion of her solitude,
Red-spotted, dirty white, and bare of rib,
Who followed at her high and pattering heels,
Prayer in his eye, prayer in his slinking gait,
Prayer in his pendulous pulsating tail.
Wide on its creaking jaws revolved the door,
The cupboard yawned, deep-throated, thinly set
For teeth, with bottles, ancient canisters,
And plates of various pattern, blue or white;
Deep in the void she thrust her hooked nose
Peering near-sighted for the wished-for bone,
Whiles her short robe of samite, tilted high,
The thrifty darnings of her hose revealed;—
The pointed feature travelled o'er the delf
Greasing its tip, but bone or bread found none
Wherefore Sir Tray abode still dinnerless,
Licking his paws beneath the spinning-wheel,
And meditating much on savoury meats.

Meanwhile the Dame in high-backed chair reposed
Revolving many memories, for she gazed
Down from her lattice on the self-same path
Whereby Sir Lancelot 'mid the reapers rode
When Arthur held his court in Camelot,
And she was called the Lady of Shalott
And, later, where Sir Hubbard, meekest knight
Of all the Table Round, was wont to pass,
And to her casement glint the glance of love.
(For all the tale of how she floated dead
Between the city walls, and how the Court
Gazed on her corpse, was of illusion framed,
And shadows raised by Merlin's magic art,
Ere Vivien shut him up within the oak.)
There stood the wheel whereat she spun her thread;
But of the magic mirror nought remained
Save one small fragment on the mantelpiece,
Reflecting her changed features night and morn.

But now the inward yearnings of Sir Tray
Grew pressing, and in hollow rumblings spake,

As in tempestuous nights the Northern seas
Within their cavern cliffs reverberate.
This touched her: "I have marked of yore," she said,
"When on my palfry I have paced along
The streets of Camelot, while many a knight
Ranged at my rein and thronged upon my steps,
Wending in pride towards the tournament,
A wight who many kinds of bread purveyed—
Muffins, and crumpets, matutinal rolls,
And buns which buttered, soothe at evensong;
To him I'll hie me ere my purpose cool,
And swift returning, bear a loaf with me,
And (for my teeth be tender grown, and like
Celestial visits, few and far between)
The crust shall be for Tray, the crumb for me."
This spake she; from their peg reached straightway down
Her cloak of sanguine hue, and pointed hat
From the flat brim upreared like pyramid
On sands Egyptian where the Pharaohs sleep,
Her ebon-handled staff (sole palfry now)
Grasped firmly, and so issued swiftly forth;
Yet ere she closed the latch her cat Elaine,
The lily kitten reared at Astolat,
Slipped through and mewing passed to greet Sir Tray.

Returning ere the shadows eastward fell,
She placed a porringer upon the board,
And shred the crackling crusts with liberal hand,
Nor noted how Elaine did seem to wail,
Rubbing against her hose, and mourning round
Sir Tray, who lay all prone upon the hearth.
Then on the bread she poured the mellow milk—
"Sleep'st thou?" she said, and touched him with her staff;
"What, ho! thy dinner waits thee!"   But Sir Tray
Stirred not nor breathed: thereat, alarmed, she seized
And drew the hinder leg: the carcase moved
All over wooden like a piece of wood—
"Dead?" said the Dame, while louder wailed Elaine;
"I see," she said, "thy fasts were all too long,
Thy commons all too short, which shortened thus
Thy days, tho' thou mightst still have cheered mine age
Had I but timelier to the city wonned.
Thither I must again, and that right soon,
For now 'tis meet we lap thee in a shroud,

And lay thee in the vault by Astolat,
Where faithful Tray shall by Sir Hubbard lie."

Up a by-lane the Undertaker dwelt;
There day by day he plied his merry trade,
And all his undertakings undertook:
Erst knight of Arthur's Court, Sir Waldgrave hight,
A gruesome carle who hid his jests in gloom,
And schooled his lid to counterfeit a tear.
With cheerful hammer he a coffin tapt,
While hollow, hollow, hollow, rang the wood,
And, as he sawed and hammered, thus he sang:—

Wood, hammer, nails, ye build a house for him,
Nails, hammer, wood, ye build a house for me,
Paying the rent, the taxes, and the rates.

I plant a human acorn in the ground,
And therefrom straightway springs a goodly tree,
Budding for me in bread and beer and beef.

O Life, dost thou bring Death or Death bring thee?
Which of the twain is bringer, which the brought?
Since men must die that other men may live.

O Death, for me thou plump'st thine hollow cheeks,
Mak'st of thine antic grin a pleasant smile,
And prank'st full gaily in thy winding sheet.

This ditty sang he to a doleful tune
To outer ears it sounded like a dirge,
Or wind that wails across the fields of death.
'Ware of a visitor, he ceased his strain,
But still did ply his saw industrious.
With withered hand on ear, Dame Hubbard stood;
"Vex not mine ears," she grated, "with thine old
And creaking saw!" "I deemed," he said, and sighed,
"Old saws might please thee, as they should the wise."
"Know," said the Dame, "Sir Tray that with me dwelt
Lies on my lonely hearthstone stark and stiff;
Wagless the tail that waved to welcome me."—
Here Waldgrave interposed sepulchral tones,
"Oft have I noted, when the jest went round,
Sad 'twas to see the wag forget his tale—
Sadder to see the tail forget its wag."
"Wherefore," resumed she, "take of fitting stuff,
And make therewith a narrow house for him."
Quoth he, "From yonder deal I'll plane the bark,

So 'twill of Tray be emblematical;
For thou, 'tis plain, must lose a deal of bark,
Since he nor bark nor bite shall practice more."
"And take thou, too," she said, "a coffin-plate,
And be his birth and years inscribed thereon
With letters twain 'S. T.' to mark Sir Tray,
So shall the tomb be known in after time."
"This, too," quoth Waldgrave, "shall be deftly done;
Oft hath the plate been freighted with his bones,
But now his bones must lie beneath the plate."
"Jest'st thou?" Dame Hubbard said, and clutched her crutch,
For ill she brooked light parlance of the dead;
But when she saw Sir Waldgrave, how his face
Was all drawn downward, till the curving mouth
Seemed a horseshoe, while o'er the furrowed cheek
A wandering tear stole on, like rivulet
In dry ravine down mother Ida's side,
She changed her purpose, smote not, lowered the staff;—
So parted, faring homeward with her grief.

Nearing her bower, it seemed a sepulchre
Sacred to memory, and almost she thought
A dolorous cry arose, as if Elaine
Did sound a caterwauling requiem.
With hesitating hand she raised the latch,
And on the threshold with reluctant foot
Lingered, as loath to face the scene of woe,
When lo! the body lay not on the hearth,
For there Elaine her flying tail pursued,—
In the Dame's chair Sir Tray alive did sit,
A world of merry meaning in his eye,
And all his face agrin from ear to ear.

Like one who late hath lost his dearest friend,
And in his sleep doth see that friend again,
And marvels scarce to see him, putting forth
A clasping hand, and feels him warm with life,
And so takes up his friendship's broken thread—
Thus stood the Dame, thus ran she, pattering o'er
The sanded tiles, and clasped she thus Sir Tray,
Unheeding of the grief his jest had wrought
For joy he was not numbered with the dead.

Anon the Dame, her primal transports o'er,
Bethought her of the wisdom of Sir Tray,
And his fine wit, and then it shameful seemed
That he bareheaded 'neath the sky should go

While empty skulls of fools went thatched and roofed;
"A hat," she cried, "would better fit those brows
Than many a courtier's that I've wotted of;
And thou shalt have one, an' my tender toes
On which the corns do shoot, and these my knees
Wherethro' rheumatic twinges swiftly dart,
Will bear me to the city yet again,
And thou shalt wear the hat as Arthur wore
The Dragon of the great Pendragonship."
Whereat Sir Tray did seem to smile, and smote
Upon the chair-back with approving tail.

Then up she rose, and to the Hatter's went,—
"Hat me," quoth she, "your very newest hat;"
And so they hatted her, and she returned
Home through the darksome wold, and raised the latch,
And marked, full lighted by the ingle-glow,
Sir Tray, with spoon in hand, and cat on knee,
Spattering the mess about the chaps of Puss.

THE OLOGIES.

We're going to begin with an ample Apology;
You'll end, we are sure, by a hearty Doxology,
If, all undeterred by our strange Phraseology,
You chose to sit down to a dish of Tautology.

One's pestered in these days by so many 'ologies,
  We thought we would fain see the tale of our foes;
A niche of your own in the new Martyrologies
  You'd earn if you'd only go halves in our woes.

We'v counted some forty! but how many more
      there are,
  We're even now wholly unable to say;
We fear that at least the same number in store
      there are,
You'll say we have found quite enough for one day.

"So now for our Catalogue: first comes Anthology—
  A bouquet of flowers, a budget of rhymes;
That's pleasant—not so the next, called Anthropology,
  The science of man in all ages and climes.

"Then comes a most useful pursuit, Arachnology;
 They're bipeds, the spiders who weave the worst webs;
But when one is asked to go in for Astrology,
 And Zadkiel! one's courage most rapidly ebbs.

" The next on our roster is old Archæology,
 A science that's lately been much in repute;
One can't say as much for Electro-biology,
 Which now-o'-days no one seems ever to bruit.

"But none can afford to make light of Chronology,
 Tho' ladies are apt to be dark upon dates;
We most of us make rather light of Conchology
 Except when the oyster-shell gapes on our plates.

" The Devil's deposed they say, and Demonology
 Would certainly seem to have gone to the De'il;
Some savants, like Hooker, still swallow Dendrology,
 But tree-names are somewhat too tough for my meal.

" The parsons are great upon Ecclesiology,
 And prate about proper pyramidal piles;
Few travelers care to neglect Entomology,
 Their wakefulness often its study beguiles.

"'Twould take you a life-time to learn Etymology,
 And dabblers get into most marvellous scrapes;
And Huxley would tell you as much of Ethnology,—
 Who really believes we are cousins of apes?

"Dean Buckland it was who first started Geology,
 And traced the rock pedigrees, fixing their ranks;
And Frank has of late taken up Ichthyology,
 The salmon already have voted him thanks.

"Von Humboldt had fairly exhausted Kosmology,
 But Nature 's a quite inexhaustible mine;
Napoleon has fulfilled a new Martyrology,
 Imbrued with the purest blue-blood of the Rhine.

" We all of us thought we were deep in Mythology,
 Till Cox and Max Müller both deepened its well;
Our sons may learn something of Meteorology—
 The weather our prophets all fail to foretell.

" The study of life is bound up with Necrology,
 And we shall have one day to enter its lists,—
And furnish some specimens for Osteology,
 The science of bones, on which Owen exists.

"At breakfast we're seldom averse to Oology,
    Or lunch, when the plovers are pleased to lay eggs;
But then one would bar embryonic Ontology,
    Preferring fowls full-grown with breast, wings, and legs!

"For oh! we decidedly like Ornithology
    And chiefly the study of grouse on the wing;
We'd leave it to doctors to study Pathology;
    The study of pain is a troublesome thing.

"We all of us need a small dose of Philology,
    If caring to make the best use of our tongues;
A careful attention to strict Phraseology
    Involves a most notable saving of lungs.

"The study of heads has been christened Phrenology,
    Professors would call it the study of brain;
But take my advice, and avoid Pneumatology,
    For spirits are apt to treat brains with disdain.

"For much the same reason, we'd banish Psychology,—
    What savant can give an account of his soul?
And if we could only abolish Theology,
    The parsons alone would be hard to console!

"If ever you happened to study Splanchnology,
    You'd know what it is theologians lack,—
Inquisitors never complain of Tautology,
    So long as rank heretics roar on the rack.

"And now is the time to strike up your Doxology,
    For we would no longer detain you, my friend;—
On Sunday we all have a turn for Zoology,
    So here is our Catalogue come to an end."

THE VARIATION HUMBUG.

The *London Charivari* thinks that there is more humbug talked, printed, and practiced in reference to music than to anything else in the world, except politics. And of all the musical humbugs extant it occurs to Mr. Punch that the variation humbug is the greatest. This party has not even the sense to invent a tune for himself, but takes else's, and starting therefrom, as an acrobat leaps from a spring-board, jumps himself into a musical reputation on the strength of the other party's ideas.   Mr. Punch wonders what would be thought of a poet who should try to make himself renown by this kind of thing—taking a well-known poem of a predecessor and doing variations on it after this fashion:—

BUGGINS' VARIATIONS ON THE BUSY BEE.

How doth the Little Busy Bee
　　Improve each shining hour,
And gather honey all the day
　　From every opening flower,
　　From every opening flower, flower, flower,
　　That sparkles in a breezy bower,
　　And gives its sweetness to the shower,
　　Exhaling scent of gentle power,
　　That lasts on kerchief many an hour,
　　And is a lady's graceful dower,
　　Endeared alike to cot and tower,
Round which the Little Busy Bee
　　Improves each shining hour,
And gathers honey all the day
　　From every opening flower,
　　From every opening flower, flower, flower,
　　From every opening flower.

How skillfully she builds her cell,
　　How neat she spreads her wax,
And labors hard to store it well,
　　With the sweet food she makes,
　　With the sweet food she makes,
　　With the sweet food she makes, makes, makes,
　　When rising just as morning breaks,
　　The dewdrop from the leaf she shakes,
　　And oft the sleeping moth she wakes,
　　And diving through the flower she takes,
　　The honey with her fairy rakes,
　　And in her cell the same she cakes,
　　Or sports across the silver lakes,
　　Beside her children, for whose sakes
How skillfully she builds her cell,
　　How neat she spreads her wax,
And labors hard to store it well,
　　With the sweet food she makes.

> In works of labor or of skill,
> 　I would be busy too,
> For Satan finds some mischief still
> 　For idle hands to do,
> 　For idle hands to do,
> 　For idle hands to do, do, do.
> 　Things which thereafter they will rue,
> 　When Justice fiercely doth pursue,
> 　Or conscience raises cry and hue,
> 　And evil-doers look quite blue,
> 　When Peelers run with loud halloo,
> 　And magistrates put on the screw,
> 　And then the wretch exclaims, Boo-hoo,
> In works of labor or of skill
> 　I wish I'd busied too,
> For Satan's found much mischief still,
> 　For my two hands to do.

There! Would a poet get much reputation for these variations, which are much better in their way than most of those built upon tunes? Would the poetical critics come out, as the musical critics do, with "Upon Watts' marble foundation Buggins has raised a sparkling alabaster palace;" or, "The old-fashioned Watts has been brought into new honor by the *étincellant* Buggins;" or "We love the old tune, but we have room in our hearts for the fairy-like fountains of bird-song which Buggins has bid start from it?" Mr. Punch has an idea that Buggins would have no such luck; the moral to be deduced from which fact is, that a musical prig is luckier than a poetical prig.

REITERATIVE VOCAL MUSIC.

A well-known reviewer, in an article on Hymnology, says:—

Who could endure to hear and sing hymns, the meaning and force of which he really felt—set, as they frequently have been, to melodies from the Opera, and even worse, or massacred by the repetition of the end of each stanza, no matter whether or not the grammar and sense were consistent with it. Take such memorable cases of incongruity as:—

> "My poor pol—
> 　My pool pol—
> 　My poor polluted heart."

To which he might have added from Dr. Watts:—

> "And see Sal—see Sal—see Salvation nigh."

Or this to the same common metre tune, "Miles's Lane":—

> "Where my Sal—my Sal—my Salvation stands."

Or this when sung to "Job":—

> "And love thee Bet—
> And love thee better than before."

Or—

> "Stir up this stu—
> Stir up this stupid heart to pray."

Or this crowning absurdity:—

> "And more *eggs*—more *eggs*—more exalts our joys."

This to the tune of "Aaron" 7's:—

> "With thy Benny—
> With thy benediction seal."

This has recently been added in a fashionable metropolitan church:—

> "And take thy pil—
> And take thy pilgrim home."

And further havoc is made with language and sense thus:—

> "Before his throne we bow—wow—wow—ow—wow."

And—

> "I love to steal
> I love to steal—awhile away."

And—

> "O, for a man—
> O, for a mansion in the skies."

To which we may add:—

> "And we'll catch the flea—
> And we'll catch the flee—ee—eeting hour."

Two trebles sing, "And learn to kiss"; two trebles and alto, "And learn to kiss"; two trebles, alto, and tenor, "And learn to kiss"; the bass, solus, "the rod."

This is sung to a tune called "Boyce":—

> "Thou art my bull—
> Thou art my bulwark and defence."

THE CURSE OF O'KELLY.

Carmac O'Kelly, the celebrated Irish harper, went to Doneraile, in the county of Cork, where his watch was pilfered from his fob. This so roused his ire that he celebrated the people in the following unexampled "string of curses:"—

Alas! how dismal is my tale,
I lost my watch in Doneraile,
My Dublin watch, my chain and seal,
Pilfered at once in Doneraile.
May fire and brimstone never fail
To fall in showers on Doneraile;
May all the leading fiends assail
The thieving town of Doneraile.
As lightnings flash across the vale,
So down to hell with Doneraile;
The fate of Pompey at Pharsale,
Be that the curse of Doneraile.
May beef or mutton, lamb or veal,
Be never found in Doneraile,
But garlic soup and scurvy kale,
Be still the food for Doneraile,
And forward as the creeping snail,
Industry be at Doneraile.
May Heaven a chosen curse entail,
On ragged, rotten Doneraile.
May sun and moon forever fail
To beam their lights on Doneraile;
May every pestilential gale
Blast that cursed spot called Doneraile;
May no sweet cuckoo, thrush or quail
Be ever heard in Doneraile;
May patriots, kings, and commonweal
Despise and harass Doneraile;
May every post, gazette and mail,
Sad tidings bring of Doneraile;
May vengeance fall on head and tail,
From north to south of Doneraile
May profit small, and tardy sale,
Still damp the trade of Doneraile:
May fame resound a dismal tale,
Whene'er she lights on Doneraile;

May Egypt's plagues at once prevail,
To thin the knaves at Doneraile;
May frost and snow, and sleet and hail,
Benumb each joint in Doneraile;
May wolves and bloodhounds race and trail
The cursed crew of Doneraile;
May Oscar with his fiery flail
To atoms thrash all Doneraile;
May every mischief, fresh and stale,
May all from Belfast to Kinsale,
Scoff, curse and damn you, Doneraile.
May neither flour nor oatmeal,
Be found or known in Doneraile;
May want and woe each joy curtail,
That e'er was known in Doneraile;
May no one coffin want a nail,
That wraps a rogue in Doneraile;
May all the thieves who rob and steal,
The gallows meet in Doneraile;
May all the sons of Gramaweal,
Blush at the thieves of Doneraile;
May mischief big as Norway whale,
O'erwhelm the knaves of Doneraile;
May curses whole and by retail,
Pour with full force on Doneraile;
May every transport wont to sail,
A convict bring from Doneraile;
May every churn and milking-pail
Fall dry to staves in Doneraile;
May cold and hunger still congeal,
The stagnant blood of Doneraile;
May every hour new woes reveal,
That hell reserves for Doneraile;
May every chosen ill prevail
O'er all the imps of Doneraile;
May th' inquisition straight impale,
The Rapparees of Doneraile;
May curse of Sodom now prevail,
And sink to ashes Doneraile;
May Charon's boat triumphant sail,
Completely manned from Doneraile;
Oh! may my couplet never fail
To find new curse for Doneraile;
And may grim Pluto's inner jail
Forever groan with Doneraile.

Hiberniana.

MARIA EDGEWORTH, in her *Essay on Irish Bulls,* remarks that "the difficulty of selecting from the vulgar herd a bull that shall be entitled to the prize, from the united merits of pre-eminent absurdity and indisputable originality, is greater than hasty judges may imagine."

Very true; but if the prize were offered for a *batch* of Irish diamonds, we think the following copy of a letter written during the Rebellion, by S——, an Irish member of Parliament, to his friend in London, would present the strongest claim :—

"My dear Sir :—Having now a little peace and quietness, I sit down to inform you of the dreadful bustle and confusion we are in from these blood-thirsty rebels, most of whom are (thank God!) killed and dispersed. We are in a pretty mess; can get nothing to eat, nor wine to drink, except whiskey; and when we sit down to dinner, we are obliged to keep both hands armed. Whilst I write this, I hold a pistol in each hand and a sword in the other. I concluded in the beginning that this would be the end of it; and I see I was right, for it is not half over yet. At present there are such goings on, that every thing is at a stand still. I should have answered your letter a fortnight ago, but I did not receive it till this morning. Indeed, hardly a mail arrives safe without being robbed. No longer ago than yesterday the coach with the mails from Dublin was robbed near this town : the bags had been judiciously left behind for fear of accident, and by good luck there was nobody in it but two outside passengers who had nothing for thieves to take. Last Thursday notice was given that a gang of rebels were advancing here under the French standard; but they had no colors, nor any drums except bagpipes. Immediately every man in the place, including women and children, ran out to meet them. We soon found our force much too little; and we were far too near to think of retreating. Death was in every face; but to it we went, and by the time half our little party were killed we began to be all alive again. Fortunately, the rebels had no guns, except pistols, cutlasses, and pikes; and as we had plenty of guns and ammunition, we put them all to the sword. Not a soul of them escaped, except some that were drowned in an adjacent bog; and in a very short time nothing was to be heard but silence. Their uniforms were all different colors, but mostly green. After the action, we went to rummage a sort of camp which they had left behind them. All we found was a few pikes without heads, a parcel of empty bottles full of water, and a bundle of French commissions filled up with Irish names. Troops are now stationed all around the country, which exactly squares with my ideas. I have only time to add that I am in great haste.

"Yours truly, ———.

"P. S.—If you do not receive this, of course it must have miscarried : therefore I beg you will write and let me know."

Miss Edgeworth says, further, that "many bulls, reputed to be bred and born in Ireland, are of foreign extraction; and many more, supposed to be unrivalled in their kind, may be matched in all their capital points." To prove this, she cites numerous examples of well-known bulls, with their foreign prototypes, not only English and Continental, but even Oriental and ancient. Among the parallels of familiar bulls to be found nearer our American home since the skillful defender of Erin's naïveté wrote her Essay, one of the best is an economical method of erecting a new jail :—

The following resolutions were passed by the Board of Coun cilmen in Canton, Mississippi :—

1. Resolved, by this Council, that we build a new Jail.

2. Resolved, that the new Jail be built out of the materials of the old Jail.

3. Resolved, that the old Jail be used until the new Jail is finished.

It was a *Frenchman* who, in making a classified catalogue of books, placed Miss Edgeworth's Essay in the list of works on *Natural History;* and it was a *Scotchman* who, having purchased a copy of it, pronounced her " a puir silly body, to write a book on bulls, and no ane word o' horned cattle in it a', forbye the bit beastie [the vignette] at the beginning." Examples from the common walks of life and from periodical literature may readily be multiplied to show that these phraseological peculiarities are not to be exclusively attributed to Ireland. But if we adopt Coleridge's definition, which is, that " a bull consists in a mental juxtaposition of incongruous ideas, with the sensation, but without the sense, of connection," we shall find frequent instances of its occurrence among standard authors. Take the following blunders, for examples :—

> Adam, the goodliest man of men *since born*
> *His sons*—the fairest of *her daughters*, Eve.
> *Milton's Paradise Lost.*
>
> The loveliest pair
> That ever *since* in love's embraces met.—*Ib. B. iv.*

Swift, being an Irishman, of course abounds in blunders, some of them of the most ludicrous character; but we should hardly expect to find in the elegant Addison, the model of classical English, such a singular inaccuracy as the following:—

> So the *pure limpid* stream, when *foul with stains*
> Of rushing torrents and descending rains.—*Cato.*

He must have *seen* in a blaze of *blinding* light (this is "ipsis Hibernis Hibernior") the vanity and evil, the folly and madness, of the worldly or selfish, and the grandeur and truth of the disinterested and Christian life.—*Gilfillan's Bards of the Bible.*

The real and peculiar magnificence of St. Petersburgh consists *in thus sailing apparently upon the bosom of the ocean,* into a city of palaces.—*Sedgwick's Letters from the Baltic.*

The astonished Yahoo, smoking, as well as he could, a cigar, *with which he had filled all his pockets.—Warren's Ten Thousand a Year.*

The following specimens are from the works of Dr. Johnson :—

Every monumental inscription should be in Latin; for that being a *dead* language, it will always *live*.

> Nor yet perceived the vital spirit fled,
> But still fought on, *nor knew that he was dead.*

Shakspeare has not only *shown* human nature as it is, but as it would be found *in situations to which it cannot be exposed.*

> Turn from the glittering bribe your scornful eye,
> Nor sell for gold *what gold can never buy.*

These observations were made *by favor of a contrary wind.*

The next two are from Pope :—

> Eight callow *infants* filled the mossy nest,
> *Herself the ninth.*

> When first young Maro, in his noble mind,
> A work t' outlast immortal Rome designed.

Shakspeare says,—

> I will strive with things impossible,
> Yea, *get the better of them.—Julius Cæsar,* ii. 1.

> A *horrid silence* first *invades the ear.*—DRYDEN.

> Beneath a mountain's brow, the most remote
> And *inaccessible* by *shepherds trod.*—HOME : *Douglass.*

In the Irish Bank-bill passed by Parliament in June, 1808, is a clause providing that the profits shall be *equally* divided and the *residue go to the Governor.*

Sir Richard Steele, being asked why his countrymen were so addicted to making bulls, said he believed there must be something in the air of Ireland, adding, " I dare say *if an Englishman were born there* he would do the same."

Mr. Cunningham, to whom we are indebted for the interesting notes to Johnson's " Lives of the Poets," pronounces his author *the most distinguished of his cotemporaries.*

Sir Walter Scott perpetrates a curious blunder in one of his novels, in making certain of his characters behold a sunset over the waters of a seaport on the *eastern* coast of Scotland.

The following occurs in Dr. Latham's *English Language.* Speaking of the genitive or possessive case, he says,—

" In the plural number, however, it is rare; so rare, indeed, that whenever the plural ends in *s* (as it always does) there is no genitive."

Byron says,—

> I stood in Venice on the Bridge of Sighs,
> A palace and a prison *on each hand.*

(He meant a palace on one hand, and a prison on the other.)

Dr. Johnson, in his Dictionary, defines a *garret* as " a room on the highest floor in the house," and a *cock-loft* as " the room over the garret."

For the sake of comparison, we recur to the favorite pasture of the genuine thorough-bred animal :—

An Irish member of Parliament, speaking of a certain minister's well-known love of money, observed, " Let not the honorable member express a contempt for money,—for if there is any one office that glitters in the eyes of the honorable member, it is that of purse-bearer : a pension to him is a compendium of all the cardinal virtues. All his statesmanship is comprehended in the art of taxing; and for good, better, and best, in the scale of human nature, he invariably reads pence, shillings, and pounds. I verily believe," continued the orator, rising to the height of his conception, " that if the honorable gentleman were an undertaker, it would be the delight of his heart to see all mankind seized with a common mortality, that he might have the benefit of the general burial, and provide scarfs and hat-bands for *the survivors.*"

The manager of a provincial theatre, finding upon one occasion but three persons in attendance, made the following address :—" Ladies and gentlemen—as there is nobody here, I'll dismiss you all. The performances of this night will not be performed; but *they will be repeated* to-morrow evening."

A Hibernian gentleman, when told by his nephew that he had just entered college with a view to the church, said, "I hope that I may live to hear you preach my funeral sermon."

An Irishman, quarrelling with an Englishman, told him if he didn't hold his tongue, he would break his impenetrable head, and let the brains out of his empty skull.

"My dear, come in and go to bed," said the wife of a jolly son of Erin, who had just returned from the fair in a decidedly how-come-you-so state: "you must be dreadful tired, sure, with your long walk of six miles." "Arrah! get away with your nonsense," said Pat: "it wasn't the *length* of the way, at all, that fatigued me: 'twas the *breadth* of it."

A poor Irishman offered an old saucepan for sale. His children gathered around him and inquired why he parted with it. "Ah, me honeys," he answered, "I would not be afther parting with it but for a little money to buy something to put in it."

A young Irishman who had married when about nineteen years of age, complaining of the difficulties to which his early marriage subjected him, said he would never marry so young again if he lived to be as ould as Methuselah.

In an Irish provincial paper is the following notice:— Whereas Patrick O'Connor lately left his lodgings, this is to give notice that if he does not return immediately and pay for the same, he will be advertised.

"Has your sister got a son or a daughter?" asked an Irishman of a friend. "Upon my life," was the reply, "I don't know yet whether I'm an *uncle* or *aunt*."

"I was going," said an Irishman, "over Westminster Bridge the other day, and I met Pat Hewins. 'Hewins,' says I, 'how are you?' 'Pretty well,' says he, 'thank you, Donnelly.' 'Donnelly!' says I: 'that's not *my* name.' 'Faith, no more is mine Hewins,' says he. So we looked at each other again, and sure it turned out to be nayther of us; and where's the bull of *that*, now?"

"India, my boy," said an Irish officer to a friend on his arrival at Calcutta, "is the finest climate under the sun; but a lot of young fellows come out here and they drink and they eat, and they drink and they die: and then they write home to their parents a pack of lies, and say it's the climate that has killed them."

In the perusal of a very solid book on the progress of the ecclesiastical differences of Ireland, written by a native of that country, after a good deal of tedious and vexatious matter, the reader's complacency is restored by an artless statement how an eminent person "abandoned the errors of the church of Rome, and adopted those of the church of England."

Here is an American Hibernicism, which is entitled to full recognition:—Among the things that Wells & Fargo's Express is not responsible for as carriers is one couched in the following language in their regulations: "Not for any loss or damage by fire, *the acts of God*, or of Indians, *or any other public enemies of the government.*"

George Selwyn once declared in company that a lady could not write a letter without adding a *postscript*. A lady present replied, "The next letter that you receive from *me*, Mr. Selwyn, will prove that you are wrong." Accordingly he received one from her the next day, in which, after her signature was the following:—

"P. S.   Who is right, now, you or I?"

The two subjoined parliamentary utterances are worthy to have emanated from Sir Boyle Roche:—

"Mr. Speaker, I boldly answer in the affirmative—No."

"Mr. Speaker, if I have any prejudice against the honorable member, it is in his favor."

A PAIR OF BULLS.

When my lord he came wooing to Miss Ann Thrope,
　　He was then a "Childe" from school;
He paid his addresses in a trope,
　　And called her his sweet bul-bul:
But she knew not, in the modern scale,
　　That *a couple of bulls* was a *nightingale.*

Blunders.

37

SLIPS OF THE PRESS.

LORD BROUGHAM was fond of relating an instance which was no joke to the victim of it. A bishop, at one of his country visitations, found occasion to complain of the deplorable state of a certain church, the roof of which was evidently anything but water-tight; after rating those concerned for their neglect, his lordship finished by declaring emphatically that he would not visit the *damp old church* again until it was put in decent order. His horror may be imagined when he discovered himself reported in the local journal as having declared: "I shall not visit this damned old church again." The bishop lost no time in calling the editor's attention to the mistake; whereupon that worthy set himself right with his readers by stating that he willingly gave publicity to his lordship's explanation, but he had every confidence in the accuracy of his reporter. The editor of an evening paper could hardly have had similar confidence in his subordinate when the latter caused his journal to record that a prisoner had been sentenced to "four months imprisonment in the House of Commons!" In this case, we fancy the reporter must have been in the same exhilarated condition as his American brother, who ended his account of a city banquet with the frank admission: "It is not distinctly remembered by anybody present who made the last speech!"

In a poem on the "Milton Gallery," by Amos Cottle, the poet, describing the pictures of Fuseli, says:—

> "The lubber fiend outstretched the chimney near,
> Or sad Ulysses on the larboard Steer."

Ulysses steered to the larboard to shun Charybdis, but the compositor makes him get upon the back of the bullock, the left one in the drove! After all, however, he only interprets the text literally. "Steer," as a substantive, has no other meaning than bullock. The substantive of the verb "to steer" is steerage. "He that hath the steerage of my course," says Shakspeare. The compositor evidently understood that Ulysses rode an ox; he would hardly else have spelt Steer with a capital S.

The following paragraphs, intended to have been printed separately, in a Paris evening paper, were by some blunder so arranged that they read consecutively:—

Doctor X. has been appointed head physician to the Hospital de la Charite. Orders have been issued by the authorities for the immediate extension of the Cemetery of Mont Parnasse. The works are being executed with the utmost dispatch.

The old story of Dr. Mudge furnishes one of the most curious cases of typographical accident on record. The Doctor had been presented with a gold-headed cane, and the same week a patent pig-killing and sausage-making machine had been tried at a factory in the place of which he was pastor. The writer of a report of the presentation, and a description of the machine, for the local paper, is thus made to "mix things miscellaneously:"—

"The inconsiderate Caxtonian who made up the forms of the paper, got the two locals mixed up in a frightful manner; and when we went to press, something like this was the appalling result: Several of the Rev. Dr. Mudge's friends called upon him yesterday, and after a brief conversation, the unsuspicious pig was seized by the hind legs, and slid along a beam until he reached the hot water tank. His friends explained the object of their visit, and presented him with a very handsome gold-headed butcher, who grabbed him by the tail, swung him round, slit his throat from ear to ear, and in less than a minute the carcass was in the water. Thereupon he came forward, and said that there were times when the feelings overpowered one; and for that reason he would not attempt to do more than thank those around him for the manner in which such a huge animal was cut into fragments was simply astonishing. The

Doctor concluded his remarks when the machine seized him, and in less time than it takes to write it, the pig was cut into fragments and worked up into delicious sausages. The occasion will long be remembered by the Doctor's friends as one of the most delightful of their lives. The best pieces can be procured for tenpence a pound; and we are sure that those who have sat so long under his ministry will rejoice that he has been treated so handsomely."

SLIPS OF THE TELEGRAPH.

The Prior of the Dominican Monastery of Voreppe, in France, recently received the following telegram:—"Father Ligier is dead (*est mort*); we shall arrive by train to-morrow, at three.—LABOREE." The ecclesiastic, being convinced that the deceased, who was highly esteemed in the locality, had selected it for his last resting-place, made every preparation. A grave was dug, a hearse provided, and with the monks, a sorrowing crowd waited at the station for the train. It arrived, and, to the astonishment of every one, the supposed defunct alighted, well and hearty. The matter was soon explained. The reverend father, returning from a visit to Rome, where he had been accompanied by the priest Laboree, stopped to visit some monks at Saint-Jean-de-Maurienne, and requested his companion to telegraph the return to his monastery. The message sent was: " Father Ligier and I (*et moi*) will arrive," &c. The clerks inadvertently changed the *et moi* into *est mort*, with what result has already been told.

A firm in Cincinnati telegraphed to a correspondent in Cleveland, as follows:—" Cranberries rising. Send immediately one hundred barrels *per* Simmons." Mr. Simmons was the agent of the Cincinnati house. The telegraph ran the last two words together, and shortly after, the firm were astonished to find delivered at their store one hundred barrels of persimmons.

SERIAL" INCONSISTENCY.

In Mrs. Oliphant's interesting story of "Ombra," there is a curious contradiction between the end of Chapter XLV. and the beginning of Chapter XLVI. A domestic picture is given, an interior, with the characters thus disposed:—

"One evening, when Kate was at home, and, as usual, abstracted over a book in a corner; when the Berties were in full possession, one bending over Ombra at the piano, one talking earnestly to her mother, Francesca suddenly threw the door open, with a vehemence quite unusual to her, and without a word of warning—without even the announcement of his name to put them on their guard—Mr. Courtenay walked into the room."

Thus ends Chapter XLV., and thus opens Chapter XLVI.:—

"The scene which Mr. Courtenay saw when he walked in suddenly to Mrs. Anderson's drawing-room, was one so different in every way from what he had expected that he was for the first moment as much taken aback as any of the company. * * * The drawing-room, which looked out on the Lung' Arno, was not small, but it was rather low—not much more than an *entresol*. There was a bright wood-fire on the hearth, and near it, with a couple of candles on a small table by her side, sat Kate, distinctly isolated from the rest, and working diligently, scarcely raising her eyes from her needle-work. The centre-table was drawn a little aside, for Ombra had found it too warm in front of the fire; and about this the other four were grouped—Mrs. Anderson, working too, was talking to one of the young men; the other was holding silk, which Ombra was winding; a thorough English domestic party—such a family group as should have gladdened virtuous eyes to see. Mr. Courtenay looked at it with indescribable surprise."

MISTAKES OF MISAPPREHENSION.

Soon after Louis XIV. appointed Bossuet, Bishop of Meaux, he inquired how the citizens liked their new Bishop, to which they answered, doubtfully: "Pretty well." "But," asked his Majesty, "what fault do you find with him?" "To say the truth," they replied, "we should have preferred a Bishop who had finished his education; for, whenever we wait upon him, we are told that he is at his studies."

There lived in the west of England, a few years since, an enthusiastic geologist, who was presiding judge of the Quarter Sessions. A farmer, who had seen him presiding on the bench, overtook him shortly afterwards, while seated by the roadside on a heap of stones, which he was busily breaking in search of fossils. The farmer reined up his horse, gazed at him for a minute, shook his head in commiseration of the mutability of human things, then exclaimed, in mingled tones of pity and surprise: "What, your Honor! be you come to this a' ready?"

Cottle, in his *Life of Coleridge*, relates an essay at grooming on the part of that poet and Wordsworth. The servants being absent, the poets had attempted to stable their horse, and were almost successful. With the collar, however, a difficulty arose. After Wordsworth had relinquished as impracticable the effort to get it over the animal's head, Coleridge tried his hand, but showed no more grooming skill than his predecessor; for, after twisting the poor horse's neck almost to strangulation, and to the great danger of his eyes, he gave up the useless task, pronouncing that the horse's head must have grown (gout or dropsy) since the collar was put on, for he said it was downright impossibility for such a huge *os frontis* to pass through so narrow a collar! Just at this moment a servant girl came up, and turning the collar upside down, slipped it off without trouble, to the great humility and wonderment of the poets, who were each satisfied afresh that there were heights of knowledge to which they had not attained.

BLUNDERS OF TRANSLATORS.

A most entertaining volume might be made from the amusing and often absurd blunders perpetrated by translators. For instance, Miss Cooper tells us that the person who first rendered her father's novel, "The Spy," into the French tongue, among other mistakes, made the following:—Readers of the Revolutionary romance will remember that the residence of the Wharton family was called "The Locusts." The translator referred to his dictionary, and found the rendering of the word to be *Les Sauterelles*, "The Grasshoppers." But when he found one of the dragoons represented as tying his horse to one of the locusts on the lawn, it would appear as if he might have been at fault. Nothing daunted, however, but taking it for granted that American grasshoppers must be of gigantic dimensions, he gravely informs his readers that the cavalryman secured his charger by fastening the bridle to one of the grasshoppers before the door, apparently standing there for that purpose.

Much laughter has deservedly been raised at French *littérateurs* who professed to be "*doctus utriusque linguæ.*" Cibber's play of "Love's Last Shift" was translated by a Frenchman who spoke "Inglees" as "*Le Dernière Chemise de l'Amour;*" Congreve's "Mourning Bride," by another, as "*L'Epouse du Matin;*" and a French scholar recently included among his catalogue of works on natural history the essay on "Irish Bulls," by the Edgeworths. Jules Janin, the great critic, in his translation of "Macbeth," renders "Out, out, brief candle!" as "*Sortez, chandelle.*" And another, who *traduced* Shakspeare, commits an equally amusing blunder in rendering Northumberland's famous speech in "Henry IV." In the passage

> "Even such a man, so faint, so spiritless,
> So dull, so dead in look, *so woe-begone.*"

the words italicized are rendered, "*ainsi douleur! va-t'en!*"— "so grief, be off with you!" Voltaire did no better with his translations of several of Shakspeare's plays; in one of which the "myriad-minded" makes a character renounce all claim to a doubtful inheritance, with an avowed resolution to *carve* for himself a fortune with his sword. Voltaire put it in French, which, retranslated, reads, "What care I for lands? With my sword I will make a fortune cutting meat."

The late centennial celebration of Shakspeare's birthday in England called forth numerous publications relating to the works and times of the immortal dramatist. Among them was a new translation of "Hamlet," by the Chevalier de Chatelain, who also translated Halleck's "Alnwick Castle," "Burns," and "Marco Bozzaris." Our readers are, of course, familiar with the following lines:—

> "How weary, stale, flat, and unprofitable
> Seem to me all the uses of this world!
> Fie on't! Oh, fie! 'tis an unweeded garden
> That grows to seed; things rank, and gross in nature,
> Possess it merely."

The chevalier, less successful with the English than with the modern American poet, thus renders them into French:—

> "*Fi donc! fi donc! Ces jours qu'on nous montrons superbes*
> *Sont un vilain jardin rempli de folles herbes,*
> *Qui donnent de l'ivraie, et certes rien de plus*
> *Si ce n'est les engins du cholera-morbus.*"

Some of the funniest mistranslations on record have been bequeathed by Victor Hugo. Most readers will remember his rendering of a peajacket as *paletot a la purée de pois*, and of the Frith of Forth as *le cinquième de le quatrième*.

The French translator of one of Sir Walter Scott's novels, knowing nothing of that familiar name for toasted cheese, "a Welsh rabbit," rendered it literally by "*un lapin du pays de Galles*," or a rabbit of Wales, and then informed his readers in a foot-note that the lapins or rabbits of Wales have a very superior flavor, and are very tender, which cause them to be in great request in England and Scotland. A writer in the Neapolitan paper, *Il Giornale della due Sicilie*, was more ingenuous. He was translating from an English paper the account of a man who killed his wife by striking her with a poker; and at the end of his story the honest journalist, with a modesty unusual in his craft, said, "*Non sappiamo per certo se questo pokero Inglese sia uno strumento domestico o bensi chirurgico*"—"We are not quite certain whether this English poker [*pokero*] be a domestic or surgical instrument."

In the course of the famous Tichborne trial, the claimant, when asked the meaning of *laus Deo semper*, said it meant "the laws of God forever, or permanently." An answer not less ludicrous was given by a French Sir Roger, who, on being asked to translate *numero Deus impare gaudet*, unhesitatingly replied, "Le numéro deux se réjouit d'être impair."

Some of the translations of the Italian operas in the librettos, which are sold to the audience, are ludicrous enough. Take, for instance, the lines in *Roberto il diavolo*,—

> Egli era, dicessi
> Abitatore
> Del tristo Imperio.

Which some smart interpreter rendered—

> "For they say he was
> A citizen of the black emporium."

Misquotations.

In Mr Collins' account of Homer's Iliad, in Blackwood's *Ancient Classics for English Readers*, occurs the following:—

.... "The spirit horsemen who rallied the Roman line in the great fight with the Latins at Lake Regillus, the shining stars who lighted the sailors on the stormy Adriatic, and gave their names to the ship in which St. Paul was cast away."

If the reader will take the trouble to refer to the *Acts of the Apostles*, xxviii, 11, he will find, that the ship of Alexandria, "whose sign was Castor and Pollux," was not the vessel in which St. Paul was shipwrecked near Malta, but the ship in which he safely voyaged from the island of "the barbarous people" to Puteoli for Rome.

The misquotations of Sir Walter Scott have frequently attracted attention. One of the most unpardonable occurs in *The Heart of Mid-Lothian*, chapter xlvii.:—

"The least of these considerations always inclined Butler to measures of conciliation, in so far as he could accede to them, without compromising principle; and thus our simple and unpretending heroine had the merit of those peacemakers, to whom it is pronounced as a benediction, that they shall *inherit the earth*."

On turning to the gospel of Matthew, v. 9, we find that the benediction pronounced upon the *peacemakers* was that "they shall be called the children of God." It is the meek who are to "inherit the earth," (ver. 5).

Another of Scott's blunders occurs in *Ivanhoe*. The date of this story "refers to a period towards the end of the reign of Richard I." (chap. i.) Richard died in 1199. Nevertheless, Sir Walter makes the disguised Wamba style himself "a poor brother of the Order of St. Francis," although the Order was not founded until 1210, and, of course, the saintship of the founder had a still later date.

Again in *Waverley* (chap. xii.) he puts into the mouth of Baron Bradwardine the words "nor would I utterly accede to the objurgation of the *younger Plinius* in the fourteenth book of his *Historia Naturalis*." The great Roman naturalist whose thirty-seven books on Natural History were written eighteen centuries ago, was the *Elder* Pliny.

Alison, in his *History of Europe*, speaks of the Grand Duke Constantine of Russia, the Viceroy of Poland, as the son of the emperor Paul I. and the celebrated empress Catherine. This Catherine was the *mother* of Paul, and wife of Peter III., Paul's father. Constantine's mother, i.e. Paul's wife, was a princess of Würtemberg.

Another of Archibald's singular errors is his translation of *droit du timbre* (stamp duty) into "timber duties." This is about as sensible as his quoting with approbation from De Tocqueville the false and foolish assertion that the American people are "regardless of historical records or monuments," and that future historians will be obliged "to write the history of the present generation from the archives of other lands." Such ignorance of American scholarship and research and of the vigorous vitality of American Historical Societies, is unpardonable.

Disraeli thus refers to a curious blunder in Nagler's *Künstler-Lexicon*, concerning the artist Cruikshank:—

Some years ago the relative merits of George Cruikshank and his brother were contrasted in an English Review, and George was spoken of as "the real Simon Pure"—the first who had illustrated "Scenes of Life in London." Unaware of the real significance of a quotation which has become proverbial among us, the German editor begins his memoir of Cruikshank by gravely informing us that he is an English artist "whose real name is Simon Pure!" Turning to the artists under letter P. we accordingly read, "Pure (Simon), the real name of the celebrated caricaturist, George Cruikshank."

This will remind some of our readers of the index which refers to Mr Justice Best. A searcher after something or other, running his eye down the index through letter B, arrived at the reference "Best—Mr. Justice—his great mind." Desiring to be better acquainted with the particulars of this assertion, he turned to the page referred to, and there found, to his entire satisfaction, "Mr. Justice Best said he had a great mind to commit the witness for prevarication."

In the fourth canto of *Don Juan*, stanza CX., Byron says:

Oh, darkly, deeply, beautifully blue,
As some one somewhere sings about the sky.

Byron was mistaken in thinking his quotation referred to the sky. The line is in Southey's *Madoc*, canto V., and describes fish. A note intimates that dolphins are meant.

> "Though in blue ocean seen,
> Blue, darkly, deeply, beautifully blue,
> In all its rich variety of shades,
> Suffused with glowing gold."

𝔉abrications.

38

THE DESCRIPTION OF THE SAVIOUR'S PERSON.

CHALMERS charges upon Huarte (a native of French Navarre) the publication (as genuine and authentic) of the Letter of Lentulus (the Proconsul of Jerusalem) to the Roman Senate, describing the person and manners of our Lord, and for which, of course, he deservedly censures him. A copy of the letter will be found in the chapter of this volume headed I. H. S.

A CLEVER HOAX ON SIR WALTER SCOTT.

The following passage occurs in one of Sir Walter Scott's letters to Southey, written in September, 1810:—

A witty rogue, the other day, who sent me a letter subscribed "Detector," proved me guilty of stealing a passage from one of Vida's Latin poems, which I had never seen or heard of; yet there was so strong a general resemblance as fairly to authorize "Detector's" suspicion.

Lockhart remarks thereupon:—

The lines of Vida which "Detector" had enclosed to Scott, as the obvious original of the address to "Woman," in *Marmion*, closing with—

> "When pain and anguish wring the brow,
> A ministering angel thou!"

end as follows: and it must be owned that if Vida had really written them, a more extraordinary example of casual coincidence could never have been pointed out.

> "Cum dolor atque supercilio gravis imminet angor,
>   Fungeris angelico sola ministerio."

"Detector's" reference is Vida *ad Eranen*, El. ii. v. 21; but it is almost needless to add there are no such lines, and no piece bearing such a title in Vida's works.

It was afterwards ascertained that the waggish author of this hoax was a Cambridge scholar named Drury.

THE MOON HOAX.

The authorship of the "Moon Hoax," an elaborate description (which was first printed in the New York *Sun*) of men, animals, &c., purporting to have been discovered in the moon by Sir John Herschel, is now disputed. Until recently it was conceded to R. A. Locke, now dead; but in the *Budget of Paradoxes*, by Professor De Morgan, the authorship is confidently ascribed to M. Nicollet, a French savant, once well known in this country, and employed by the government in the scientific exploration of the West. He died in the government service. Professor De Morgan writes as follows:—"There is no doubt that it (the 'Moon Hoax') was produced in the United States by M. Nicollet, an astronomer of Paris, and a fugitive of some kind. About him I have heard two stories. First, that he fled to America with funds not his own, and that this book was a mere device to raise the wind. Secondly, that he was a *protegé* of Laplace, and of the Polignac party, and also an outspoken man. The moon story was written and sent to France, with the intention of entrapping M. Arago—Nicollet's especial foe—in the belief of it." It seems not to have occurred to the sage and critical professor that a man who could steal funds, would have little scruple about stealing a literary production. It is, hence, more than probable that Nicollet translated the article immediately after its appearance in the New York *Sun*, and afterwards sent it to France as his own.

A LITERARY SELL.

A story is told in literary circles in New York of an enthusiastic Carlyle Club of ladies and gentlemen of Cambridge and Boston, who meet periodically to read their chosen prophet and worship at his shrine. One of them, not imbued with sufficient reverence to teach him better, feloniously contrived to have the reader on a certain evening insert something of his own composition into the reading, as though it came from the printed page and Carlyle's hand. The interpolation was as follows:—"Word-spluttering organisms, in whatever place—not with Plutarchean comparison, apologies, nay rather, without any such apologies—but born into the world to say the thought that is in them—antiphoreal, too, in the main—butchers, bakers, and candlestick-makers; men, women, pedants. Verily, with you, too, it's now or never." This paragraph produced great applause among the devotees of Carlyle. The leader of the Club especially, a learned and metaphysical pundit, who is the great American apostle of Carlyle, said nothing Carlyle had ever written was more representative and happy. The actual author of it attempted to ask some questions about it, and elicit explanations. These were not wanting, and, where they failed, the stupidity of the questioner was the substitute presumption, delicately hinted. It reminds us of Dr. Franklin's incident in his life of Abraham, which he used to read off with great gravity, apparently from an open Bible, though actually from his own memory. This parable is probably the most perfect imitation of Scripture style extant.

MRS. HEMANS'S "FORGERIES."

A gentleman having requested Mrs. Hemans to furnish him with some authorities from the old English writers for the use of the word "barb," as applied to a steed, she very shortly supplied him with the following imitations, which she was in the habit of calling her "forgeries." The mystification succeeded completely, and was not discovered for some time afterwards:—

The warrior donn'd his well-worn garb
And proudly waved his crest;
He mounted on his jet-black *barb*
And put his lance in rest.

PERCY, Reliques.

Eftsoons the wight withouten more delay
Spurr'd his brown *barb*, and rode full swiftly on his way.

SPENSER.

Hark! was it not the trumpet's voice I heard?
The soul of battle is awake within me!
The fate of ages and of empires hangs
On this dread hour. Why am I not in arms?
Bring my good lance, caparison my steed!
Base, idle grooms! are ye in league against me?
Haste with my *barb*, or by the holy saints,
Ye shall not live to saddle him to-morrow.

MASSINGER.

No sooner had the pearl-shedding fingers of the young Aurora tremulously unlocked the oriental portals of the golden horizon, than the graceful flower of chivalry, and the bright cynosure of ladies eyes—he of the dazzling breast-plate and swanlike plume— sprang impatiently from the couch of slumber, and eagerly mounted the noble *barb* presented to him by the Emperor of Aspromontania.

SIR PHILIP SIDNEY, Arcadia.

See'st thou yon chief whose presence seems to rule
The storm of battle? Lo! where'er he moves
Death follows. Carnage sits upon his crest—
Fate on his sword is throned— and his white *barb*,
As a proud courser of Apollo's chariot,
Seems breathing fire.

POTTER, Æschylus.

Oh! bonnie looked my ain true knight,
His *barb* so proudly reining;
I watched him till my tearfu' sight
Grew amaist dim wi' straining.

Border Minstrelsy.

Why, he can heel the lavolt and wind a fiery *barb* as well as any gallant in Christendom. He's the very pink and mirror of accomplishment.

SHAKSPEARE.

Fair star of beauty's heaven! to call thee mine,
All other joy's I joyously would yield;
My knightly crest, my bounding *barb* resign
For the poor shepherd's crook and daisied field!

For courts, or camps, no wish my soul would prove,
So thou would'st live with me and be my love.

EARL OF SURREY, *Poems.*

For thy dear love my weary soul hath grown
Heedless of youthful sports : I seek no more
Or joyous dance, or music's thrilling tone,
Or joys that once could charm in minstrel lore,
Or knightly tilt where steel-clad champions meet,
Borne on impetuous *barbs* to bleed at beauty's feet !

SHAKSPEARE, *Sonnets.*

As a warrior clad
In sable arms, like chaos dull and sad,
But mounted on a *barb* as white
As the fresh new-born light,—
So the black night too soon
Came riding on the bright and silver moon
Whose radiant heavenly ark
Made all the clouds beyond her influence seem
E'en more than doubly dark,
Mourning all widowed of her glorious beam.

COWLEY.

SHERIDAN'S GREEK.

In *Anecdotes of Impudence*, we find this curious story:—

Lord Belgrave having clenched a speech in the House of Commons with a long Greek quotation, Sheridan, in reply, admitted the force of the quotation so far as it went; "but" said he, "if the noble Lord had proceeded a little farther, and completed the passage, he would have seen that it applied the other way!" Sheridan then spouted something *ore rotundo*, which had all the ais, ois, kons, and kois that give the world assurance of a Greek quotation: upon which Lord Belgrave very promptly and handsomely complimented the honorable member on his readiness of recollection, and frankly admitted that the continuation of the passage had the tendency ascribed to it by Mr. Sheridan, and that he had overlooked it at the moment when he gave his quotation. On the breaking up of the House, Fox, who piqued himself on having some Greek, went up to Sheridan, and said, "Sheridan, how came you to be so ready with that passage? It certainly is as you state, but I was not aware of it before you quoted it." It is unnecessary to observe that there was no Greek at all in Sheridan's impromptu.

BALLAD LITERATURE.

John Hill Burton, in his *Book Hunter*, after speaking of the success with which Surtus imposed upon Sir Walter Scott the spurious ballad of the *Death of Featherstonhaugh*, which has a place in the *Border Minstrelsy*, says:—

Altogether, such affairs create an unpleasant uncertainty about the paternity of that delightful department of literature—our ballad poetry. Where next are we to be disenchanted? Of the way in which ballads have come into existence, there is one sad example within my own knowledge. Some mad young wags, wishing to test the critical powers of an experienced collector, sent him a new-made ballad, which they had been enabled to secure only in a fragmentary form. To the surprise of its fabricator, it was duly printed; but what naturally raised his surprise to astonishment, and revealed to him a secret, was, that it was no longer a fragment, but a complete ballad,—the collector, in the course of his industrious inquiries among the peasantry, having been so fortunate as to recover the missing fragments! It was a case where neither could say anything to the other, though Cato might wonder, *quod non rideret haruspex, haruspicem cum vidisset*. This ballad has been printed in more than one collection, and admired as an instance of the inimitable simplicity of the genuine old versions!

Psalmanazar exceeded in powers of deception any of the great impostors of learning. His island of Formosa was an illusion eminently bold, and maintained with as much felicity as erudition; and great must have been that erudition which could form a pretended language and its grammar, and fertile the genius which could invent the history of an unknown people. The deception was only satisfactorily ascertained by his own penitential confession; he had defied and baffled the most learned.

39

FRANKLIN'S PARABLE.

Dr. Franklin frequently read for the entertainment of company, apparently from an open Bible, but actually from memory, the following chapter in favor of religious toleration, pretendedly quoted from the Book of Genesis. This story of Abraham and the idolatrous traveler was given by Franklin to Lord Kaimes as a "Jewish Parable on Persecution," and was published by Kaimes in his *Sketches of the History of Man*. It is traced, not to a Hebrew author, but to a Persian apologue. Bishop Heber, in referring to the charge of plagiarism raised against Franklin, says that while it cannot be proved that he gave it to Lord Kaimes as his own composition, it is " unfortunate for him that his correspondent evidently appears to have regarded it as his composition; that it had been published as such in all the editions of Franklin's collected works; and that, with all Franklin's abilities and amiable qualities, there was a degree of quackery in his character which, in this instance as well as that of his professional epitaph on himself, has made the imputation of such a theft more readily received against him, than it would have been against most other men of equal eminence."

1. And it came to pass after those things, that Abraham sat in the door of his tent, about the going down of the sun.

2. And behold a man, bowed with age, came from the way of the wilderness, leaning on a staff.

3. And Abraham arose, and met him, and said unto him, Turn in, I pray thee, and warm thy feet, and tarry all night, and thou shalt arise early on the morrow, and go on thy way.

4. But the man said, Nay, for I will abide under this tree.

5. And Abraham pressed him greatly; so he turned, and they went into the tent; and Abraham baked unleavened bread, and they did eat.

6. And when Abraham saw that the man blessed not God, he said unto him, Wherefore dost thou not worship the most High God, Creator of Heaven and Earth?

7. And the man answered and said, I do not worship the God thou speakest of, neither do I call upon his name; for I have made to myself a God, which abideth always in mine house, and provideth me with all things.

8. And Abraham's zeal was kindled against the man, and he arose and fell upon him, and drove him forth into the wilderness.

9. And at midnight God called unto Abraham, saying, Abraham, where is the stranger?

10. And Abraham answered and said, Lord, he would not worship Thee, neither would he call upon Thy name; therefore have I driven him out from before my face into the wilderness.

11. And God said, Have I borne with him these hundred and ninety and eight years, and nourished him and clothed him, notwithstanding his rebellion against Me; and couldst not thou, that art thyself a sinner, bear with him one night?

12. And Abraham said, Let not the anger of my Lord wax hot against His servant: Lo, I haved sinned; forgive me, I pray Thee.

13. And he arose, and went forth into the wilderness, and sought diligently for the man, and found him:

14. And returned with him to his tent; and when he had entreated him kindly, he sent him away on the morrow with gifts.

15. And God spake again unto Abraham, saying, For this thy sin shall thy seed be afflicted four hundred years in a strange land:

16. But for thy repentance will I deliver them; and they shall come forth with power, and with gladness of heart, and with much substance.

THE SHAKSPEARE FORGERIES.

In 1795–96 William Henry Ireland perpetrated the remarkable Shakspeare Forgeries which gave his name such infamous notoriety. The plays of "Vortigern" and "Henry the Second" were printed in 1799. Several litterateurs of note were deceived by them, and Sheridan produced the former at Drury Lane theatre, with John Kemble to take the leading part. The total failure of the play, conjoined with the attacks of Malone and others, eventually led to a conviction and forced confession of Ireland's dishonesty. For an authentic account of the Shakspeare Manuscripts see *The Confessions of W. H. Ireland;* Chalmers' *Apology for the Believers of the Shakspeare Papers;* Malone's *Inquiry into the Authenticity,* &c.; Wilson's *Shakspeariana; Gentleman's Magazine,* 1796–97 ;*Eclectic Magazine,* xvi. 476. One of the original manuscripts of Ireland, that of Henry the Second, has been preserved. The rascal seems to have felt but little penitence for his fraud.

Interrupted Sentences.

A JUDGE, reprimanding a criminal, called him a scoundrel. The prisoner replied: "Sir, I am not as big a scoundrel as your Honor"—here the culprit stopped, but finally added—"takes me to be." "Put your words closer together," said the Judge.

A lady in a dry goods store, while inspecting some cloths, remarked that they were "part cotton." "Madam," said the shopman, "these goods are as free from cotton as your breast is"—(the lady frowned) he added—"free from guile."

A lady was reading aloud in a circle of friends a letter just received. She read, "We are in great trouble. Poor Mary has been confined"—and there she stopped for that was the last word on the sheet, and the next sheet had dropped and fluttered away, and poor Mary, unmarried, was left really in a delicate situation until the missing sheet was found, and the next continued—"to her room for three days, with what, we fear, is suppressed scarlet fever."

To all letters soliciting his "subscription" to any object Lord Erskine had a regular form of reply, viz.:—"Sir, I feel much honored by your application to me, and beg to subscribe"—here the reader had to turn over the leaf—"myself your very obedient servant."

Much more satisfactory to the recipient was Lord Eldon's note to his friend, Dr. Fisher, of the Charter House:—"Dear Fisher—I cannot to day give you the preferment for which you ask. Your sincere friend, Eldon. (*Turn over*)—I gave it to you yesterday."

At the Virginia Springs a Western girl name Helen was familiarly known among her admirers as Little Hel. At a party given in her native city, a gentleman, somewhat the worse for his supper, approached a very dignified young lady and asked:

"Where's my little sweetheart? You know,—Little Hel?"
"Sir?" exclaimed the lady, "you certainly forgot yourself."
"Oh," said he quickly, "you interrupted me; if you had let me go on I would have said Little Helen." "I beg your pardon," answered the lady, "when you said Little Hel, I thought you had reached your final destination."

The value of an explanation is finely illustrated in the old story of a king who sent to another king, saying, "Send me a blue pig with a black tail, or else——." The other, in high dudgeon at the presumed insult, replied: "I have not got one, and if I had——." On this weighty cause they went to war for many years. After a satiety of glories and miseries, they finally bethought them that, as their armies and resources were exhausted, and their kingdoms mutually laid waste, it might be well enough to consult about the preliminaries of peace; but before this could be concluded, a diplomatic explanation was first needed of the insulting language which formed the ground of the quarrel. "What could you mean," said the second king to the first, "by saying, 'Send me a blue pig with a black tail, or else——?'" "Why," said the other, "I meant a blue pig with a black tail, or else some other color. But," retorted he, "what did you mean by saying, 'I have not got one, and if I had——?'" "Why, of course, if I had, I should have sent it." An explanation which was entirely satisfactory, and peace was concluded accordingly.

It is related of Dr. Mansel, that when an undergraduate of Trinity College, Cambridge, he chanced to call at the rooms of a brother Cantab, who was absent, but who had left on his table the opening of a poem, which was in the following lofty strain :—

> " The sun's perpendicular rays
> Illumine the depths of the sea,"

Here the flight of the poet, by some accident, stopped short, but Mansel, who never lost an occasion for fun, completed the stanza in the following facetious style :—

> "And the fishes beginning to sweat,
> Cried, 'Goodness, how hot we shall be.'"

That not very brilliant joke, "to lie—under a mistake," is sometimes indulged in by the best writers. Witness the following. Byron says:—

> If, after all, there should be some so blind
> To their own good this warning to despise,
> Led by some tortuosity of mind
> Not to believe my verse and their own eyes,
> And cry that they the moral cannot find,
> I tell him, if a clergyman, he lies;
> Should captains the remark, or critics make,
> They also lie too—under a mistake.
>
> *Don Juan,* Canto I.

Shelley, in his translation of the *Magico Prodigioso* of Calderon, makes Clarin say to Moscon:—

> You lie—under a mistake—
> For this is the most civil sort of lie
> That can be given to a man's face. I now
> Say what I think.

And De Quincey, *Milton versus Southey and Landor,* says:—

You are tempted, after walking round a line (of Milton) threescore times, to exclaim at last,—Well, if the Fiend himself should rise up before me at this very moment, in this very study of mine, and say that no screw was loose in that line, then would I reply: "Sir, with due submission, you are——." "What!" suppose the Fiend suddenly to demand in thunder, "What am I?" "Horribly wrong," you wish exceedingly to say; but, recollecting that some people are choleric in argument, you confine yourself to the polite answer—"That, with deference to his better education, you conceive him to lie"—that's a bad word to drop your voice upon in talking with a friend, and you hasten to add—"under a slight, a *very* slight mistake."

Mr. Montague Mathew, who sometimes amused the House of Commons, and alarmed the Ministers, with his *brusquerie*, set an ingenious example to those who are at once forbidden to speak, and yet resolved to express their thoughts. There was a debate upon the treatment of Ireland, and Mathew having been called to order for taking unseasonable notice of the enormities attributed to the British Government, spoke to the following effect:—"Oh, very well; I shall say nothing then about the murders—(*Order, order!*)—I shall make no mention of the massacres—(*Hear, hear! Order!*)—Oh, well; I shall sink all allusion to the infamous half-hangings—(*Order, order! Chair!*)

Lord Chatham once began a speech on West Indian affairs, in the House of Commons, with the words: "Sugar, Mr. Speaker——" and then, observing a smile to prevail in the audience, he paused, looked fiercely around, and with a loud voice, rising in its notes, and swelling into vehement anger, he is said to have pronounced again the word "Sugar!" three times; and having thus quelled the House, and extinguished every appearance of levity or laughter, turned around, and disdainfully asked, " Who will laugh at sugar now?"

Our legislative assemblies, under the most exciting circumstances, convey no notion of the phrenzied rage which sometimes agitates the French. Mirabeau interrupted once at every sentence by an insult, with " slanderer," " liar," " assassin," " rascal," rattling around him, addressed the most furious of his assailants in the softest tone he could assume, saying, " I pause, gentlemen, till these civilities are exhausted."

Mr. Marten, M. P., was a great wit. One evening he delivered a furious philippic against Sir Harry Vane, and when he had buried him beneath a load of sarcasm, he said:— " But as for young Sir Harry Vane——" and so sat down. The House was astounded. Several members exclaimed: "What have you to say against young Sir Harry?" Marten at once rose and added: " Why, if young Sir Harry lives to be old, *he* will be old Sir Harry."

Echo Verse.

ADDISON says, in No. 59 of the Spectator, " I find likewise in ancient times the conceit of making an Echo talk sensibly and give rational answers. If this could be excusable in any writer, it would be in Ovid, where he introduces the echo as a nymph, before she was worn away into nothing but a voice. (Met. iii. 379.) The learned Erasmus, though a man of wit and genius, has composed a dialogue upon this silly kind of device, and made use of an echo who seems to have been an extraordinary linguist, for she answers the person she talks with in Latin, Greek, and Hebrew, according as she found the syllables which she was to repeat in any of those learned languages. Hudibras, in ridicule of this false kind of wit, has described Bruin bewailing the loss of his bear to a solitary echo, who is of great use to the poet in several distichs, as she does not only repeat after him, but helps out his verse and furnishes him with rhymes."

Euripides in his Andromeda—a tragedy now lost—had a similar scene, which Aristophanes makes sport with in his Feast of Ceres. In the Greek Anthology (iii. 6) is an epigram of Leonidas, and in Book IV. are some lines by Guaradas, commencing—

<blockquote>
α Αχὼ φίλα μοι συγκαταίνεσόν τί.—β τί;
(Echo! I love: advise me somewhat.—What?)
</blockquote>

The French bards in the age of Marot were very fond of this conceit. Disraeli gives an ingenious specimen in his Curiosities of Literature. The lines here transcribed are by Joachim de Bellay :—

<blockquote>
Qui est l'auteur de ces maux avenus ?—Venus.
Qu'étois-je avant d'entrer en ce passage ?—Sage.
Qu'est-ce qu'aimer et se plaindre souvent ?—Vent.
Dis-moi quelle est celle pour qui j'endure ?—Dure.
Sent-elle bien la douleur qui me point ?—Point
</blockquote>

In *The Progresses of Queen Elizabeth* there is detailed a masque, which was enacted for her Majesty's pleasure, in which a dialogue was held with Echo " devised, penned, and pronounced by Master Gascoigne, and that upon a very great sudden."

Here are three of the verses:—

> Well, Echo, tell me yet,
>   How might I come to see
> This comely Queen of whom we talk?
>   Oh, were she now by thee!
>   By thee.

> By me? oh, were that true,
>   How might I see her face?
> How might I know her from the rest,
>   Or judge her by her grace?
>   Her grace.

> Well, then, if so mine eyes
>   Be such as they have been,
> Methinks I see among them all
>   This same should be the Queen.
>   The Queen.

LONDON BEFORE THE RESTORATION.

What want'st thou that thou art in this sad taking?
                                        a king.

What made him hence move his residing?
                                        siding.

Did any here deny him satisfaction?
                                        faction.

Tell me whereon this strength of faction lies?
                                        on lies.

What didst thou do when King left Parliament?
                                        lament.

What terms wouldst give to gain his company?
                                        any.

But thou wouldst serve him with thy best endeavor?
                                        ever.

What wouldst thou do if thou couldst here behold him?
                                        hold him.

But if he comes not, what becomes of London?
                                        undone.

The following song was written by Addison :—

> Echo, tell me, while I wander
> O'er this fairy plain to prove him,
> If my shepherd still grows fonder,
> Ought I in return to love him?
> > *Echo.*—Love him, love him.

> If he loves, as is the fashion,
> Should I churlishly forsake him?
> Or, in pity to his passion,
> Fondly to my bosom take him?
> > *Echo.*—Take him, take him.

> Thy advice, then, I'll adhere to,
> Since in Cupid's chains I've led him,
> And with Henry shall not fear to
> Marry, if you answer, "Wed him."
> > *Echo.*—Wed him, wed him.

PASQUINADE.

The following squib, cited by Mr. Motley in his *Dutch Republic*, from a MS. collection of pasquils, shows the prevalent opinion in the Netherlands concerning the parentage of Don John of Austria and the position of Barbara Blomberg :—

> —sed at Austriacum nostrum redeamus—*eamus*
> Hunc Cesaris filium esse satis est notum—*notum*
> Multi tamen de ejus patre dubitavere—*vere*
> Cujus ergo filium eum dicunt Itali—*Itali*
> Verum mater satis est nota in nostra republica—*publica*
> Imo hactenus egit in Brabantiâ ter voere—*hoere*
> Crimen est ne frui amplexu unius Cesaris tam generosi—*osi*
> Pluribus ergo usa in vitâ est—*ita est*
> Seu post Cesaris congressum non vere ante—*ante*
> Tace garrula ne tale quippiam loquare—*quare?*
> Nescis quâ pœna afficiendum dixerit Belgium insigne—*igne*, &c.

THE GOSPEL ECHO.

Found in a pew in a church in Scotland, written in a female hand.

> True faith producing love to God and man,
> Say, Echo, is not this the gospel plan?
> > *Echo.*—The gospel plan!

> Must I my faith in Jesus constant show,
> By doing good to all, both friend and foe?
> > *Echo.*—Both friend and foe'

When men conspire to hate and treat me ill,
Must I return them good, and love them still?
　　　　Echo.—Love them still!

If they my failings causelessly reveal,
Must I their faults as carefully conceal?
　　　　Echo.—As carefully conceal!

But if my name and character they tear,
And cruel malice too, too plain appear;
And, when I sorrow and affliction know,
They smile, and add unto my cup of woe;
Say, Echo, say, in such peculiar case,
Must I continue still to love and bless?
　　　　Echo.—Still love and bless!

Why, Echo, how is this? Thou'rt sure a dove:
Thy voice will leave me nothing else but love!
　　　　Echo.—Nothing else but love!

Amen, with all my heart, then be it so;
And now to practice I'll directly go.
　　　　Echo.—Directly go!

This path be mine; and, let who will reject,
My gracious God me surely will protect.
　　　　Echo.—Surely will protect!

Henceforth on him I'll cast my every care,
And friends and foes, embrace them all in prayer.
　　　　Echo.—Embrace them all in prayer.

ECHO AND THE LOVER.

LOVER.—Echo! mysterious nymph, declare
　　　　Of what you're made and what you are.
ECHO.—　　　　　　Air!

LOVER.—Mid airy cliffs and places high,
　　　　Sweet Echo! listening, love, you lie—
ECHO.—　　　　　　You lie!

LOVER.—Thou dost resuscitate dead sounds—
　　　　Hark! how my voice revives, resounds!
ECHO.—　　　　　　Zounds!

LOVER.—I'll question thee before I go—
　　　　Come, answer me more apropos!
ECHO.—　　　　　　Poh! poh!

LOVER.—Tell me, fair nymph, if e'er you saw
　　　　So sweet a girl as Phœbe Shaw?
ECHO.—　　　　　　Pshaw!

LOVER.—Say, what will turn that frisking coney
    Into the toils of matrimony?
ECHO.—   Money!

LOVER.—Has Phœbe not a heavenly brow?
    Is it not white as pearl—as snow?
ECHO.—   Ass! no!

LOVER.—Her eyes! Was ever such a pair?
    Are the stars brighter than they are?
ECHO.—   They are!

LOVER.—Echo, thou liest, but can't deceive me;
    Her eyes eclipse the stars, believe me—
ECHO.—   Leave me!

LOVER.—But come, thou saucy, pert romancer,
    Who is as fair as Phœbe? answer!
ECHO.—   Ann, sir.

ECHO ON WOMAN.

In the Doric manner.

These verses of Dean Swift were supposed, by the late Mr. Reed, to have been written either in imitation of Lord Stirling's *Aurora*, or of a scene of Robert Taylor's old play, entitled *The Hog has lost his Pearl.*

SHEPHERD.—Echo, I ween, will in the woods reply,
    And quaintly answer questions. Shall I try?
ECHO.—   Try.
SHEP.—What must we do our passion to express?
ECHO.—   Press.
SHEP.—How shall I please her who ne'er loved before?
ECHO.—   Be fore.
SHEP.—What most moves women when we them address?
ECHO.—   A dress.
SHEP.—Say, what can keep her chaste whom I adore?
ECHO.—   A door.
SHEP.—If music softens rocks, love tunes my lyre.
ECHO.—   Liar.
SHEP.—Then teach me, Echo, how shall I come by her?
ECHO.—   Buy her.
SHEP.—When bought, no question I shall be her dear.
ECHO.—   Her deer.
SHEP.—But deer have horns: how must I keep her under?
ECHO.—   Keep her under.

SHEP.—But what can glad me when she's laid on bier?
ECHO.—   Beer.
SHEP.—What must I do when women will be kind?
ECHO.—   Be kind.
SHEP.—What must I do when women will be cross?
ECHO.—   Be cross.
SHEP.—Lord! what is she that can so turn and wind?
ECHO.—   Wind.
SHEP.—If she be wind, what stills her when she blows?
ECHO.—   Blows.
SHEP.—But if she bang again, still should I bang her?
ECHO.—   Bang her.
SHEP.—Is there no way to moderate her anger?
ECHO.—   Hang her.
SHEP.—Thanks, gentle Echo! right thy answers tell
        What woman is, and how to guard her well.
ECHO.—   Guard her well.

BONAPARTE AND THE ECHO.

The original publication of the following exposed the publisher, Palm, of Nuremberg, to trial by court-martial. He was sentenced to be shot at Braunau in 1807,—a severe retribution for a few lines of poetry.

BONA.—Alone I am in this sequestered spot, not overheard.
ECHO.—Heard.
BONA.—'Sdeath! Who answers me? What being is there nigh?
ECHO.—I.
BONA.—Now I guess! To report my accents Echo has made her task.
ECHO.—Ask.
BONA.—Knowest thou whether London will henceforth continue to resist?
ECHO.—Resist.
BONA.—Whether Vienna and other courts will oppose me always?
ECHO.—Always.
BONA.—Oh, Heaven! what must I expect after so many reverses?
ECHO.—Reverses.
BONA.—What! should I, like coward vile, to compound be reduced?
ECHO.—Reduced.
BONA.—After so many bright exploits be forced to restitution?
ECHO.—Restitution.
BONA.—Restitution of what I've got by true heroic feats and **martial**
        address?
ECHO.—Yes.
BONA.—What will be the end of so much toil and trouble?
ECHO.—Trouble.

Bona.—What will become of my people, already too unhappy?
Echo.—Happy.
Bona.—What should I then be that I think myself immortal?
Echo.—Mortal.
Bona.—The whole world is filled with the glory of my name, you know.
Echo.—No.
Bona.—Formerly its fame struck the vast globe with terror.
Echo.—Error.
Bona.—Sad Echo, begone! I grow infuriate! I die!
Echo.—Die!*

EPIGRAM ON THE SYNOD OF DORT.

Dordrechti synodus, nodus; chorus integer, æger;
Conventus, ventus; sessio stramen. Amen!

Referring to the extravagant price demanded in London, in 1831, to see and hear the Orpheus of violinists, the Sunday Times asked,—

What are they who pay three guineas
To hear a tune of Paganini's?
Echo.—Pack o' ninnies

THE CRITIC'S EPIGRAMMATIC EXCUSE.

I'd fain praise your poem, but tell me, how is it,
When I cry out, "Exquisite," Echo cries, "Quiz it!"

ECHO ANSWERING.

What must be done to conduct a newspaper right?—Write.
What is necessary for a farmer to assist him?—System.
What would give a blind man the greatest delight?—Light.
What is the best counsel given by a justice of the peace?—Peace.
Who commit the greatest abominations?—Nations.
What cry is the greatest terrifier?—Fire.
What are some women's chief exercise?—Sighs.

---

* Napoleon himself, (*Voice from St. Helena*,) when asked about the execution of Palm, said, "All that I recollect is, that Palm was arrested by order of Davoust, and, I believe, tried, condemned, and shot, for having, while the country was in possession of the French and under military occupation, not only excited rebellion among the inhabitants and urged them to rise and massacre the soldiers, but also attempted to instigate the soldiers themselves to refuse obedience to their orders and to mutiny against their generals. I *believe* that he met with a fair trial."

REMARKABLE ECHOES.

An echo in Woodstock Park, Oxfordshire, repeats seventeen syllables by day, and twenty by night. One on the banks of the Lago del Lupo, above the fall of Terni, repeats fifteen. But the most remarkable echo known is one on the north side of Shipley Church, in Sussex, which distinctly repeats twenty-one syllables.

In the Abbey church at St. Alban's is a curious echo. The tick of a watch may be heard from one end of the church to the other. In Gloucester Cathedral, a gallery of an octagonal form conveys a whisper seventy-five feet across the nave.

The following inscription is copied from this gallery :—

> Doubt not but God, who sits on high,
> Thy inmost secret prayers can hear ;
> When a dead wall thus cunningly
> Conveys soft whispers to the ear.

In the Cathedral of Girgenti, in Sicily, the slightest whisper is borne with perfect distinctness from the great western door to the cornice behind the high altar,—a distance of two hundred and fifty feet. By a most unlucky coincidence, the precise focus of divergence at the former station was chosen for the place of the confessional. Secrets never intended for the public ear thus became known, to the dismay of the confessors, and the scandal of the people, by the resort of the curious to the opposite point, (which seems to have been discovered accidentally,) till at length, one listener having had his curiosity somewhat over-gratified by hearing his wife's avowal of her own infidelity, this tell-tale peculiarity became generally known, and the confessional was removed.

In the whispering-gallery of St. Paul's, London, the faintest sound is faithfully conveyed from one side to the other of the dome, but is not heard at any intermediate point.

In the Manfroni Palace at Venice is a square room about twenty-five feet high, with a concave roof, in which a person standing in the centre, and stamping gently with his foot on the floor, hears the sound repeated a great many times ; but as his position deviates from the centre, the reflected sounds grow

fainter, and at a short distance wholly cease. The same phenomenon occurs in the large room of the Library of the
Museum at Naples.

EXTRAORDINARY FACTS IN ACOUSTICS.

An intelligent and very respectable gentleman, named Ebenezer Snell, who is still living, at the age of eighty and upwards,
was in a corn-field with a negro on the 17th of June, 1776, in
the township of Cummington, Mass., one hundred and twenty-
nine miles west of Bunker Hill by the course of the road, and
at least one hundred by an air-line. Some time during the
day, the negro was lying on the ground, and remarked to
Ebenezer that there was war somewhere, for he could distinctly
hear the cannonading. Ebenezer put his ear to the ground,
and also heard the firing distinctly, and for a considerable time.
He remembers the fact, which made a deep impression on his
mind, as plainly as though it was yesterday.

Over water, or a surface of ice, sound is propagated with remarkable clearness and strength. Dr. Hutton relates that, on
a quiet part of the Thames near Chelsea, he could hear a person read distinctly at the distance of one hundred and forty feet,
while on the land the same could only be heard at seventy-six.
Lieut. Foster, in the third Polar expedition of Capt. Parry, found
that he could hold conversation with a man across the harbor of
Port Bowen, a distance of six thousand six hundred and ninety-
six feet, or about a mile and a quarter. This, however, falls short
of what is asserted by Derham and Dr. Young,—viz., that at
Gibraltar the human voice has been heard at the distance of
ten miles, the distance across the strait.

Dr. Hearn, a Swedish physician, relates that he heard guns
fired at Stockholm, on the occasion of the death of one of the
royal family, in 1685, at the distance of thirty Swedish or one
hundred and eighty British miles.

The cannonade of a sea-fight between the English and
Dutch, in 1672, was heard across England as far as Shrews-
bury, and even in Wales, a distance of upwards of two hundred
miles from the scene of action.

Puzzles.

THE fastidiousness of mere book-learning, or the overween·
ing importance of politicians and men of business, may be employed to cast contempt, or even odium, on the labor which is
spent in the solution of puzzles which produce no useful knowledge when disclosed; but that which agreeably amuses both
young and old should, if not entitled to regard, be at least
exempt from censure. Nor have the greatest wits of this and
other countries disdained to show their skill in these trifles.
Homer, it is said, died of chagrin at not being able to expound a
riddle propounded by a simple fisherman,—*" Leaving what's
taken, what we took not we bring."* Aristotle was amazingly
perplexed, and Philetas, the celebrated grammarian and poet of
Cos, puzzled himself to death in fruitless endeavors to solve the
sophism called by the ancients *The Liar:*—" If you say of yourself, 'I lie,' and in so saying tell the truth, you lie. If you
say, 'I lie,' and in so saying tell a lie, you tell the truth."
Dean Swift, who could so agreeably descend to the slightest
badinage, was very fond of puzzles. Many of the best riddles
in circulation may be traced to the sportive moments of men
of the greatest celebrity, who gladly seek occasional relaxation
from the graver pursuits of life, in comparative trifles.

Mrs. Barbauld says, Finding out riddles is the same kind of
exercise for the mind as running, leaping, and wrestling are for
the body. They are of no use in themselves; they are not
work, but play; but they prepare the body, and make it alert
and active for any thing it may be called upon to perform. So
loes the finding out good riddles give quickness of thought,
and facility for turning about a problem every way, and viewing
it in every possible light.

The French have excelled all other people in this species of
literary amusement. Their language is favorable to it, and
their writers have always indulged a fondness for it. As a

specimen of the ingenuity of the earlier literati, we transcribe a rebus of Jean Marot, a favorite old priest, and valet-de-chambre to Francis I. It would be inexplicable to most readers without the version in common French, which is subjoined :—

```
        riant        fus      n'agueres
         En                      pris
    t   D'une   o             affettée
    u   tile      s
        espoir                 haitée
        Que                     vent
                                 ai

        d
  Mais  fus  quand  pr  s'amour  is
                             ris
  Car  j'apper  ses  mignards
                que
     traits
  Etoient d'amour  mal   as
                         ée
                             riant
                              En

  L'œil
  Ecus  de  elle  a  pris
        moi
  manière rusée
  te  me  nant
  Et quand je veux chez elle e faire e
                que
  Me dit to y us mal appris
                      riant
                       En
```

RONDEAU.

En souriant fus n'agueres surpris
D'une subtile entrée tous affettée,
Que sous espoir ai souvent souhaitée,
Mais fus deçue, quand s'amour entrepris ;
Car j'apperçus que ses mignards souris
Etoient soustraits d'amour mal assurée
      En souriant.

Ecus soleil dessus moi elle a pris,
M'entretenant sous manière rusée ;
Et quand je veux chez elle faire entrée,
Me dit que suis entrée tous mal appris
      En souriant

BONAPARTEAN CYPHER.

The following is a key to the cypher in which Napoleon Bonaparte carried on his private correspondence :—

A	a	b	c	d	e	f	g	h	i	k	l	m
B	n	o	p	q	r	s	t	u	w	x	y	z
C	a	b	c	d	e	f	g	h	i	k	l	m
D	z	u	o	p	q	r	s	t	u	w	x	y
E	a	b	c	d	e	f	g	h	i	k	l	m
F	y	z	n	o	p	q	r	s	t	u	w	x
G	a	b	c	d	e	f	g	h	i	k	l	m
H	x	y	z	n	o	p	q	r	s	t	u	w
I	a	b	c	d	e	f	g	h	i	k	l	m
K	w	x	y	z	n	o	p	q	r	s	t	u
L	a	b	c	d	e	f	g	h	i	k	l	m
M	u	w	x	y	z	n	o	p	q	r	s	t
N	a	b	c	d	e	f	g	h	i	k	l	m
O	t	u	w	x	y	z	n	o	p	q	r	s
P	a	b	c	d	e	f	g	h	i	k	l	m
Q	s	t	u	w	x	y	z	n	o	p	q	r
R	a	b	c	d	e	f	g	h	i	k	l	m
S	r	s	t	u	w	x	y	z	n	o	p	q
T	a	b	c	d	e	f	g	h	i	k	l	m
U	q	r	s	t	u	w	x	y	z	n	o	p
W	a	b	c	d	e	f	g	h	i	k	l	m
X	p	q	r	s	t	u	w	x	y	z	n	o
Y	a	b	c	d	e	f	g	h	i	k	l	m
Z	o	p	q	r	s	t	u	w	x	y	z	n

The subjoined is a proclamation, in cypher, from Bonaparte to the French army; a copy of which was in the hands of one or more persons in almost every regiment in the service.

PROCLAMATION.

Neyiptwhklmopenclziuwicetttklmeprtgzkp
Achwhrdpkdabkfntzimepunggwymgftgq
Efdesronwxqfkzxbchqnfmysnqangopolfa
PmmfampabJarwccqznauruvzskqdknh
Hihydghbailxdfqkngtxyogwrlnlwtoy
Pbcizopbgairfgkpzawrwlqipdgacrkff
mwzfcrgpech.

The same deciphered by means of the table and key :—

"Français! votre pays étoit trahi; votre Empereur seul peut vous re-
mettre dans la position splendide que convient à la France. Donnez toute
votre confiance à celui qui vous a toujours conduit à la gloire. Ses aigles
pleniront encore en l'air et étonneront les nations."

Frenchmen! your country was betrayed; your Emperor alone can replace
you in the splendid state suitable to France. Give your entire confidence
to him who has always led you to glory. His eagles will again soar on
high and strike the nations with astonishment.

The key (which, it will be seen, may be changed at pleasure)
was in this instance " La France et ma famille," France and
my family. It is thus used :—

L being the first letter of the key, refer to that letter in the
first column of the cypher in capitals; then look for the letter f,
which is the first letter of the proclamation, and that letter
which corresponds with f being placed underneath, viz., n, is
that which is to be noted down. To decipher the proclamation, of course the order of reference must be inverted, by
looking for the corresponding letter to n in the division opposite that letter L which stands in the column.

CASE FOR THE LAWYERS.

X. Y. applies to A. B. to become a law pupil, offering to pay
him the customary fee as soon as he shall have gained his *first
suit in law.* To this A. B. formally agrees, and admits X. Y.
to the privileges of a student. Before the termination of X.
Y.'s pupilage, however, A. B. gets tired of waiting for his
money, and determines to sue X. Y. for the amount. He rea-
sons thus :—If I gain this case, X. Y. will be compelled to pay
me by the decision of the court; if I lose it, he will have to
pay me by the condition of our contract, he having won his
first law-suit. But X. Y. need not be alarmed when he learns
A. B.'s intention, for he may reason similarly. He may say,—
If I succeed, and the award of the court is in my favor, of
course I shall not have to pay the money; if the court decides
against me, I shall not have to pay it, according to the terms of
our contract, as I shall not yet have gained my first suit in law.
Vive la logique.

SIR ISAAC NEWTON'S RIDDLE.

Four persons sat down at a table to play,
They played all that night and part of next day.
It must be observed that when they were seated,
Nobody played with them, and nobody betted;
When they rose from the place, each was winner a guinea.
Now tell me this riddle, and prove you're no ninny.

42

COWPER'S RIDDLE.

I am just two and two, I am warm, I am cold,
And the parent of numbers that cannot be told;
I am lawful, unlawful,—a duty, a fault,
I am often sold dear, good for nothing when bought,
An extraordinary boon, and a matter of course,
And yielded with pleasure—when taken by force.

CANNING'S RIDDLE.

There is a word of plural number,
A foe to peace and human slumber :
Now, any word you chance to take,
By adding S, you plural make ;
But if you add an S to this,
How strange the metamorphosis !
Plural is plural then no more,
And sweet, what bitter was before.

THE PRIZE ENIGMA.

The following enigma was found in the will of Miss Anna Seward (the Swan of Lichfield), with directions to pay £50 to the person who should discover the solution. When competition for the prize was exhausted, it was discovered to be a curtailed copy of a rebus published in the *Gentleman's Magazine*, March, 1757, and at that time attributed to Lord Chesterfield.

The noblest object in the works of art,
The brightest scenes which nature can impart ;
The well-known signal in the time of peace,
The point essential in a tenant's lease ;
The farmer's comfort as he drives the plough,
A soldier's duty, and a lover's vow ;
A contract made before the nuptial tie,
A blessing riches never can supply ;

A spot that adds new charms to pretty faces,
An engine used in fundamental cases ;
A planet seen between the earth and sun,
A prize that merit never yet has won ;
A loss which prudence seldom can retrieve,
The death of Judas, and the fall of Eve ;
A part between the ankle and the knee,
A papist's toast, and a physician's fee ;
A wife's ambition, and a parson's dues,
A miser's idol, and the badge of Jews.

If now your happy genius can divine
The correspondent words in every line,
By the first letter plainly may be found
An ancient city that is much renowned.

QUINCY'S COMPARISON.

Josiah Quincy, in the course of a speech in Congress, in 1806, on the embargo, used the following language :—

They who introduced it abjured it.   They who advocated it did not wish, and scarcely knew, its use.   And now that it is said to be extended over us, no man in this nation, who values his reputation, will take his Bible oath that it is in effectual and legal operation.   There is an old riddle on a coffin, which I presume we all learned when we were boys, that is as perfect a representation of the origin, progress, and present state of this thing called non-intercourse, as it is possible to be conceived :—

There was a man bespoke a thing,
Which when the maker home did bring,
That same maker did refuse it,—
The man that spoke for it did not use it,—
And he who had it did not know
Whether he had it, yea or no.

True it is, that if this non-intercourse shall ever be, in reality, subtended over us, the similitude will fail in a material point.   The poor tenant of the coffin is ignorant of his state. But the people of the United States will be literally buried alive in non-intercourse, and realize the grave closing on themselves and on their hopes, with a full and cruel consciousness of all the horrors of their condition

SINGULAR INTERMARRIAGES.

There were married at Durham, Canada East, an old lady and gentleman, involving the following interesting connections:—

The old gentleman is married to his daughter's husband's mother-in-law, and his daughter's husband's wife's mother. And yet she is not his daughter's mother; but she is his grandchildren's grandmother, and his wife's grandchildren are his daughter's step-children. Consequently the old lady is united in the bonds of holy matrimony and conjugal affection to her daughter's brother-in-law's father-in-law, and her great-grandchildren's grandmother's step-father; so that her son-in-law may say to his children, Your grandmother is married to my father-in-law, and yet he is not your grandfather; but he is your grandmother's son-in-law's wife's father. This gentleman married his son-in-law's father-in-law's wife, and he is bound to support and protect her for life. His wife is his son-in-law's children's grandmother, and his son-in-law's grandchildren's great-grandmother.

A Mr. Harwood had two daughters by his first wife, the eldest of whom was married to John Coshick; this Coshick had a daughter by his first wife, whom old Harwood married, and by her he had a son; therefore, John Coshick's second wife could say as follows :—

My father is my son, and I'm my mother's mother;
My sister is my daughter, and I'm grandmother to my brother.

PROPHETIC DISTICH.

In the year 1531, the following couplet was found written on the wall behind the altar of the Augustinian monastery at Gotha, when the building was taken down :—

MC quadratum, LX quoque duplicatum,
ORAPS peribit et Huss Wiclefque redibit.

MC quadratum is MCCCC, i.e. 1400. LX duplicatum is LLXX, i.e. 120 = 1520. ORAPS is an abbreviation for *ora pro nobis* (pray for us). The meaning is, that in the sixteenth century praying to the saints will cease, and Huss and Wickliffe will again be recognized.

THE NUMBER OF THE BEAST.

43

VICARIVS FILII DEI.

$$5 + 1 + 100 + 1 + 5 + 1 + 50 + 1 + 1 + 500 + 1 = 666.$$

Among the curious things extant in relation to Luther is the covert attempt of an ingenious theological opponent to make him the apocalyptic beast or antichrist described in Revelation ch. xiii. The mysterious number of the beast, "six hundred threescore and six," excited the curiosity of mankind at a very early period, particularly that of Irenæus, in the second century, who indulged in a variety of shrewd conjectures on the subject. But after discovering the number in several names, he modestly says, "Yet I venture not to pronounce positively concerning the name of antichrist, for, had it been intended to be openly proclaimed to the present generation, it would have been uttered by the same person who saw the revelation." A later expositor, Fevardent, in his Notes on Irenæus, adds to the list the name of Martin Luther, which, he says, was originally written Martin Lauter. "Initio vocabatur *Martin Lauter*," says Fevardent; "cujus nominis literas si Pythagorice et ratione subducas et more Hebræorum et Græcorum alphabeti crescat numerus, primo monadum, deinde decadum, hinc centuriarum, numerus nominis Bestiæ, id est, 666, tandem perfectum comperies. hoc pacto."

M	30	L	20
A	1	A	1
R	80	U	200
T	100	T	100
I	9	E	5
N	40	R	80

Total, 666.

It is but just to Fevardent, however, to observe that he subsequently gave the preference to *Maometis*.

GALILEO'S LOGOGRAPH.

Galileo was the first to observe a peculiarity in the planet Saturn, but his telescope had not sufficient refractive power to separate the rings. It appeared to him like three bodies arranged in the same straight line, of which the middle was the largest, thus, ∘○∘ . He announced his discovery to Kepler under the veil of a logograph, which sorely puzzled his illustrious cotemporary. This is not to be wondered at, for it ran—

Smasmrmilmepoetalevmibvnienvgttaviras.

Restoring the transposed letters to their proper places, we have the following sentence :—

Altissimum planetam tergeminum observavi.

(I have observed the most distant planet to be threefold.)

PERSIAN RIDDLES.

Between a thick-set hedge of bones,
A small red dog now barks, now moans.

The answer rung,—
" A human tongue !"

A soul above it,
And a soul below,
With leather between,
And swift it doth go.

The answer is a *saddle*
On horse, with man a-straddle.

CHINESE TEA SONG.

Punch has favored the world with the following song, sung before her Britannic Majesty by a Chinese lady. It looks rather difficult at first; but if the reader studies it attentively, he will see how easy it is to read Chinese :—

Ohc ometo th ete asho pwit hme,
Andb uya po undo f thebe st,
'Twillpr oveam ostex cellentt ea,
Itsq ua lit yal lwi lla tte st.

'Tiso nlyf oursh illi ngs apo und,
Soc omet othet eama rtan dtry,
Nob etterc anel sewh erebefou nd,
Ort hata nyoth er needb uy.

DEATH AND LIFE.

	cur	f	w	d	dis	and p
A	sed	iend	rought	eath	ease	ain.
bles	fr	b	br		and	ag

THE REBUS.

Ben Jonson, in his play *The Alchemist*, takes an opportunity of ridiculing the Rebus, among the other follies of his day which he so trenchantly satirizes. When Abel Drugger, the simple tobacconist, applies to the impostor Subtle to invent for him a sign-board that will magically attract customers to his shop, the cheat says to his confederate, in presence of their admiring dupe,—

> I will have his name
> Formed in some mystic character, whose radii,
> Striking the senses of the passers-by,
> Shall, by a virtual influence, breed affections
> That may result upon the party owns it.
> As thus: He first shall have *a bell*—that's *Abel;*
> And by it standing one whose name is *Dee,*
> In a *rug* gown; there's *D* and *rug*—that's *Drug;*
> And right anenst him a dog snarling *er*—
> There's *Drugger*. ABEL DRUGGER, that's his sign,
> And here's now mystery and hieroglyphic.

A motto of the Bacon family in Somersetshire has an inge-nious rebus,—

ProBa-conScientia;

the capitals, thus placed, giving it the double reading, Proba conscientia, and Pro Bacon Scientia.

WHAT IS IT?

> A Headless man had a letter to write;
> 'Twas read by one who lost his Sight;
> The Dumb repeated it word for word,
> And he was Deaf who listened and heard.

THE BOOK OF RIDDLES.

The Book of Riddles alluded to by Shakspeare in the Merry Wives of Windsor (Act I. sc. 1) is mentioned by Laneham, 1575, and in the English Courtier, 1586; but the earliest edi-tion of this popular collection now preserved is dated 1629. It is entitled *The Booke of Merry Riddles, together with proper Questions and witty Proverbs to make pleasant pastime; no less usefull then behovefull for any yong man or child, to know if he be quick-witted or no.* The following extract from this very rare work will be found interesting.

Here beginneth the first Riddle.

Two legs sat upon three legs, and had one leg in her hand; then in came foure legs, and bare away one leg; then up start two legs, and threw three legs at foure legs, and brought again one leg.

Solution.—That is, a woman with two legs sate on a stoole with three legs, and had a leg of mutton in her hand; then came a dog that hath foure legs, and bare away the leg of mutton; then up start the woman, and threw the stoole with three legs at the dog with foure legs, and brought again the leg of mutton.

The Second Riddle.

He went to the wood and caught it,
He sate him down and sought it;
Because he could not finde it,
Home with him he brought it.

Solution.—That is a thorne: for a man went to the wood and caught a thorne in his foote, and then he sate him downe, and sought to have it pulled out, and because he could not find it out, he must needs bring it home.

The iii. Riddle.

What work is that, the faster ye worke, the longer it is ere ye have done, and the slower ye worke, the sooner ye make an end?

Solution.—That is turning of a spit; for if ye turne fast, it will be long ere the meat be rosted, but if ye turne slowly, the sooner it is rosted.

The iv. Riddle.

What is that that shineth bright all day, and at night is raked up in its own dirt?

Solution.—That is the fire, that burneth bright all the day, and at night is raked up in his ashes.

The v. Riddle.

I have a tree of great honour,
Which tree beareth both fruit and flower;

> Twelve branches this tree hath nake,
> Fifty [*sic*] nests therein he make,
> And every nest hath birds seaven;
> Thankéd be the King of Heaven;
> And every bird hath a divers name:
> How may all this together frame?

Solution.—The tree is the yeare; the twelve branches be the twelve months; the fifty-two nests be the fifty-two weekes; the seven birds be the seven days in the weeke, whereof every one hath a divers name.

BISHOP WILBERFORCE'S PUZZLE.

All pronounce me a wonderful piece of mechanism, and yet few people have numbered the strange medley of which I am composed. I have a large box and two lids, two caps, two musical instruments, a number of weathercocks, three established measures, some weapons of warfare, and a great many little articles that carpenters cannot do without; then I have about me a couple of esteemed fishes, and a great many of a smaller kind; two lofty trees, and the fruit of an indigenous plant; a handsome stag, and a great number of a smaller kind of game; two halls or places of worship, two students or rather scholars, the stairs of a hotel, and half a score of Spanish gentlemen to attend on me. I have what is the terror of the slave, also two domestic animals, and a number of negatives."

REPLY.—"Chest—eye-lids—kneecaps—drum of the ear—veins—hand, foot, nail—arms—nails—soles of the feet—muscles—palms—apple—heart (hart)—hairs (hares) temples—pupils—insteps—tendons (ten Dons)—lashes—calves—nose (no's.)"

CURIOSITIES OF CIPHER.

IN 1680, when M. de Louvois was French Minister of War, he summoned before him one day, a gentleman named Chamilly, and gave him the following instructions:—

"Start this evening for Basle, in Switzerland, which you will reach in three days; on the fourth, punctually at two o'clock, station yourself on the bridge over the Rhine, with a portfolio, ink, and a pen.　Watch all that takes place, and make a memorandum of every particular.　Continue doing so for two hours; have a carriage and post-horses await you; and at four precisely, mount and travel night and day till you reach Paris.　On the instant of your arrival, hasten to me with your notes."

De Chamilly obeyed; he reaches Basle, and on the day, and at the hour appointed, stations himself, pen in hand, on the bridge.　Presently a market-cart drives by, then an old woman with a basket of fruit passes; anon, a little urchin trundles his hoop by; next an old gentlemen in blue top-coat jogs past on his gray mare.　Three o'clock chimes from the cathedral-tower.　Just at the last stroke, a tall fellow in yellow waistcoat and breeches saunters up, goes to the middle of the bridge, lounges over, and looks at the water; then he takes a step back and strikes three hearty blows on the footway with his staff. Down goes every detail in De Chamilly's book.　At last the hour of release sounds, and he jumps into his carriage.　Shortly before midnight, after two days of ceaseless traveling, De Chamilly presented himself before the Minister, feeling rather ashamed at having such trifles to record.　M. de Louvois took the portfolio with eagerness, and glanced over the notes.　As his eye caught the mention of the yellow-breeched man, a gleam of joy flashed across his countenance.　He rushed to the king, roused him from sleep, spoke in private with him for a few moments, and then four couriers, who had been held in readiness since five on the preceding evening, were dispatched with haste. Eight days after the town of Strasbourg was entirely surrounded by French troops, and summoned to surrender; it capitulated and threw open its gates on the 30th September, 1681.　Evidently the three strokes of the stick given by the fellow in yellow costume, at an appointed hour, were the signal of the success of an intrigue concerted between M. de Louvois and the magistrates of Strasbourg, and the man who executed this mission was as ignorant of the motive as was M. de Chamilly of the motive of his errand.

Now this is a specimen of the safest of all secret communications; but it can only be resorted to on certain rare occasions. When a lengthy dispatch is required to be forwarded, and when such means as those given above are out of the question, some other method must be employed. Herodotus gives us a story to the point; it is found also, with variations, in Aulus Gellius:—

"Histiæus, when he was anxious to give Aristagoras orders to revolt, could find but one safe way, as the roads were guarded, of making his wishes known; which was by taking the trustiest of his slaves, shaving all the hair from off his head, and then pricking letters upon the skin, and waiting till the hair grew again. This accordingly he did; and as soon as ever the hair was grown, he dispatched the man to Miletus, giving him no other message than this: 'When thou art come to Miletus, bid Aristagoras shave thy head, and look thereon.' Now the marks on the head were a command to revolt."—(Bk. V. 35.)

Is this case no cipher was employed. We shall come now to the use of ciphers.

When a dispatch or communication runs great risk of falling into the hands of the enemy, it is necessary that its contents should be so veiled that the possession of the document may afford him no information whatever. Julius Cæsar and Augustus used ciphers, but they were of the utmost simplicity, as they consisted merely in placing D in the place of A; E in that of B and so on; or else in writing B for A, and C for B, &c.

Secret characters were used at the Council of Nicæa; and Rabanus Maurus, Abbot of Fulda and Archbishop of Mayence, in the Ninth Century, has left us an example of two ciphers, the key to which was discovered by the Benedictines. It is only a wonder that any one could have failed to unravel them at the first glance. This is a specimen of the first:—

.N c . p . t v : r s : . : s B : : n f : c . . : r c h . g l : : r : : s . q : . : : m :
rt . r . s

The clue to this is the suppression of the vowels and the filling of their places by dots—one for i, two for a, three for e, four for o, and five for u. In the second example, the same sentence would run—Knckpkt vfrsxs Bpnkf bckk, &c., the vowel places being filled by the consonants—b, f, k, p, x. By changing every letter in the alphabet, we make a vast improvement on this last; thus, for instance, supplying the place of a with z, b with x, c with v, and so on. This is the very system employed by an advertiser in a provincial paper, which we took up the other day in the waiting-room of a station, where it had been left by a farmer. As we had some minutes to spare, before the train was due, we spent them in deciphering the following:—

Jp Sjddjzbrza rzdd ci sijmr. Bziw rzdd xrndzt, and in ten minutes we read: "If William can call or write, Mary will be glad."

When the Chevalier de Rohan was in the Bastile his friends wanted to convey to him the intelligence that his accomplice was dead without having confessed. They did so by passing the following words into his dungeon written on a shirt: "Mg dulhxecclgu ghj yxuj; lm ct ulge alj." In vain did he puzzle over the cipher, to which he had not the clue. It was too short; for the shorter a cipher letter, the more difficult it is to make out. The light faded, and he tossed on his hard bed, sleeplessly revolving the mystic letters in his brain; but he could make nothing out of them. Day dawned, and with its first gleam he was poring over them; still in vain. He pleaded guilty, for he could not decipher "*Le prisonnier est mort; il n'a rien dit.*"

A curious instance of cipher occured at the close of the sixteenth century, when the Spaniards were endeavoring to establish relations between the scattered branches of their vast monarchy, which at that period embraced a large portion of Italy, the Low Countries, the Philippines, and enormous districts in the New World. They accordingly invented a cipher, which they varied from time to time, in order to disconcert those who might attempt to pry into the mysteries of their correspondence. The cipher, composed of fifty signs, was of great value to them through all the troubles of the "Ligue," and the wars then desolating Europe. Some of their dispatches having been intercepted, Henry IV. handed them over to a clever mathematician, Viete, with the request that he would find the clue. He did so, and was able also to follow it as it varied, and France profited for two years by his discovery. The Court of Spain, disconcerted at this, accused Viete before the Roman Court as a sorcerer and in league with the devil. This proceeding only gave rise to laughter and ridicule.

A still more remarkable instance is that of a German professor, Herman, who boasted, in 1752, that he had discovered a cryptograph absolutely incapable of being deciphered without the clue being given by him; and he defied all the savants and learned societies of Europe to discover the key. However, a French refugee, named Beguelin, managed after eight days' study to read it. The cipher—though we have the rules upon which it is formed before us—is to us perfectly unintelligible. It is grounded on some changes of numbers and symbols; the numbers vary, being at one time multiplied, at another added, and become so complicated that the letter e, which occurs nine times in the paragraph, is represented in eight different ways; n is used eight times, and has seven various signs. Indeed, the same letter is scarcely ever represented by the same figure. But this is not all; the character which appears in the place of i takes that of n shortly after; another symbol for n stands also for t. How any man could have solved the mystery of this cipher is astonishing.

All these cryptographs consist in the exchange of numbers of characters for the real letters; but there are other methods quite as intricate, which dispense with them.

The mysterious cards of the Count de Vergennes are an instance. De Vergennes was Minister of Foreign Affairs under Louis XVI., and he made use of cards of a peculiar nature in his relations with the diplomatic agents of France. These cards were used in letters of recommendation or passports, which were given to strangers about to enter France; they were intended to furnish information without the knowledge of the bearers. This was the system. The card given to a man contained only a few words, such as:—

ALPHONSE D'ANGEHA,
Recommande a Monsieur
le Comte de Vergennes, par le Marquis de Puysegur, Ambassadeur
de France a la Cour de Lisbonne.

The card told more tales than the words written on it. Its color indicated the nation of the stranger. Yellow showed him to be English; red, Spanish; white, Portuguese; green, Dutch; red and white, Italian; red and green, Swiss; green and white, Russian; &c. The person's age was expressed by the shape of the card. If it were circular, he was under 25; oval, between 25 and 30; octagonal, between 30 and 45; hexagonal, between 45 and 50; square, between 50 and 60; an oblong showed that he was over 60. Two lines placed below the name of the bearer indicated his build. If he were tall and lean, the lines were waving and parallel; tall and stout, they converged; and so on. The expression of his face was shown by a flower in the border. A rose designated an open and amiable countenance, whilst a tulip marked a pensive and aristocratic appearance. A fillet round the border, according to its length, told whether he were bachelor, married, or widower. Dots gave information as to his position and fortune. A full stop after his name showed that he was a Catholic; a semicolon, that he was a Lutheran; a comma, that he was a Calvinist; a dash, that he was a Jew; no stop indicated him an Atheist. So also his morals and character were pointed out by a pattern in the card. So, at one glance the Minister could tell all about his man, whether he were a gamester or a duelist; what was his purpose in visiting France; whether in search

of a wife or to claim a legacy; what was his profession—
that of physician, lawyer, or man of letters; whether he
were to be put under surveillance or allowed to go his way
unmolested.

We come now to a class of cipher which requires a certain
amount of literary dexterity to conceal the clue.

During the Great Rebellion, Sir John Trevanion, a distinguished cavalier, was made prisoner, and locked up in
Colchester Castle. Sir Charles Lucas and Sir George Lisle had
just been made examples of, as a warning to "malignants:"
and Trevanion had every reason for expecting a similar bloody
end. As he awaits his doom, indulging in a hearty curse
in round cavalier terms at the canting, crop-eared scoundrels
who hold him in durance vile, and muttering a wish that he
had fallen, sword in hand, facing the foe, he is startled by the
entrance of the jailor, who hands him a letter:

"May't do thee good," growls the fellow; "it has been well
looked to before it was permitted to come to thee."

Sir John takes the letter, and the jailor leaves him his lamp
by which to read it:—

WORTHIE SIR JOHN:—Hope, that is ye best comport of ye afflictyd,
cannot much, I fear me, help you now. That I wolde saye to you, is this
only: if ever I may be able to requite that I do owe you, stand not upon
asking of me. 'Tis not much I can do; but what I can do, bee verie sure
I wille. I knowe that, if dethe comes, if ordinary men fear it, it fnights
not you, accounting it for a high honour, to have such a rewarde of your
loyalty. Pray yet that you may be spared this soe bitter, cup. I fear
not that you will grudge any sufferings; only if it bie submission you
can turn them away, 'tis the part of a wise man. Tell me, an if you can,
to do for you any thinge that you would have done. The general goes
back on Wednesday. Restinge your servant to command. R. T.

Now this letter was written according to a preconcerted
cipher. Every third letter after a stop was to tell. In this
way Sir John made out—"Panel at east end of chapel slides."
On the following even, the prisoner begged to be allowed to
pass an hour of private devotion in the chapel. By means of

a bribe, this was accomplished.　Before the hour had expired, the chapel was empty—the bird had flown.

An excellent plan of indicating the telling letter or words is through the heading of the letter.　"Sir," would signify that every third letter was to be taken; "Dear Sir," that every seventh; "My dear sir," that every ninth was to be selected. A system, very early adopted, was that of having pierced cards, through the holes of which the communication was written. The card was then removed, and the blank spaces filled up.　As for example:—

MY DEAR X.—[The] lines I now send you are forwarded by the kind-ness of the [Bearer], who is a friend.　[Is not] the message delivered yet [to] my brother?　[Be] quick about it, for I have all along [trusted] that you would act with discretion and dispatch.　Yours ever,　　　Z.

Put your card over the note, and through the piercings you will read: "The Bearer is not to be trusted."

Poe, in his story of "The Gold Bug," gives some valuable hints on the interpretation of the most common cryptographs. He contends that the ingenuity of man can construct no enigma which the ingenuity of man cannot unravel.　And he actually read several very difficult ciphers which were sent to him after the publication of "The Gold Bug."

But we saw, several years ago, a method which makes the message absolutely safe from detection.　We will try to de-scribe it.

Take a square sheet of paper of convenient size, say a foot square.　Divide it by lines drawn at right angles into five hundred and seventy-six squares, twenty-six each way; in the upper horizontal row write the alphabet in its natural order, one letter in each square; in the second horizontal row write the alphabet, beginning with B.　There will then be one square left at the end of this row; into this put A.　Fill the third row by beginning with C, and writing A and B after Z at the end. So on until the whole sheet is filled.　When completed, the table, if correct, will present this appearance.　In the upper horizontal row, the alphabet in its natural order from left to right; in the left-hand vertical row, the same from top to bottom; and the diagonal, from upper right to lower left-hand corner, will be a line of Z's.

Each party must have one of the tables. A keyword must be agreed upon, which may be any word in the English language, or from any other language if it can be represented by English letters, or, indeed, it may even be a combination of letters which spells nothing.

Now, to send a message, first write the message in plain English. Over it write the key-word, letter over letter, repeating it as many times as it is necessary to cover the message. Take a simple case as an illustration. Suppose the key-word to be *Grant*, and the message *We have five days' provisions.* It should be placed thus:—

Grantgrantgrantgrantgran
Wehavefivedaysprovisions

Now find, in the upper horizontal row of the table, the first letter of the key-word, G, and in the left-hand vertical column, the first letter of the message, W. Run a line straight down from G, and one to the right from W, and in the angle where the two lines meet will be found the letter which must be written as the first letter of the cipher. With the second letter of the key-word, R, and the second letter of the message, E, find in the same way the second letter of the cipher.

The correspondent who receives the cipher goes to work to translate it thus:—He first writes over it the key-word, letter over letter, repeating it as often as necessary. Then finding in the upper row of his table the first letter of the key-word, he passes his pencil directly down until he comes to the first letter or the cipher; the letter opposite to it in the left vertical column is the first letter of the translation. Each of the succeeding letters is found in a similar way.

A third party, into whose hands such a cipher might fall,

could not read it, though he possessed a copy of the table and knew how to use it, unless he knew the key-word. The chance of his guessing this is only one in millions. And there is no such thing as interpreting it by any other method, because there are no repetitions, and hence all comparison is at fault. That is to say, in the same cipher, in one place a letter, as for instance C may stand for one letter in the translation, and in another place C may stand for quite a different letter. This is the only kind of cryptograph we have ever seen which is absolutely safe.

44　　Refractory Rhyming.

WHEN Canning was challenged to find a rhyme for *Julianna*, he immediately wrote,—

> Walking in the shady grove
> With my Julianna,
> For lozenges I gave my love
> Ipecacuanha.

Ipecacuanha lozenges, though a myth when the stanza was written, are now commonly sold by apothecaries.

Three or four wits, while dining together, discussed the difficulty of finding rhymes for certain names. General Morris challenged any of the party to find a happy rhyme for his name; and the challenge was instantly taken up by John Brougham, whose facility at extempore rhyming is proverbial:—

> All hail to thee, thou gifted son !
> The warrior-poet Morris !
> 'Tis seldom that we see in one
> A Cæsar and a Horace.

Some years ago a French speculator found himself ruined by a sudden collapse in the stock-market. He resolved to commit suicide, but, as he was a connoisseur in monumental literature, he decided first to compose his own epitaph. The first line—a very fine one—terminated with the word *triomphe*. To this, search as he might, he could find no rhyme, and he could not bring himself to sacrifice his beloved line. Time passed, finding him still in search of his rhyme, assisted by a number of benevolent friends, but all in vain. One day a promising speculation presented itself: he seized the opportunity and regained his fortune.

The rhyme so zealously sought has at length been found, and the epitaph completed. Here it is:—

> Attendre que de soi la vétusté triomphe,
> C'est absurde ! Je vais au devant de la mort.
> Mourir a plus d'attraits quand on est jeune encore:
> A quoi bon devenir un vieillard monogomphe?

Monogomphe; a brilliant Hellenism signifying " who has but a single tooth."

To get a rhyme in English for the word *month* was quite a matter of interest with curious people years ago, and somebody made it out or forced it by making a quatrain, in which a lisping little girl is described as saying:—

> ——I can get a rhyme for a month.
> I can thay it now, I thed it wunth !

Another plan was to twist the numeral *one* into an ordinal. For instance:—

Search through the works of Thackeray—you'll find a rhyme to month;
He tells us of Phil Fogarty, of the fighting onety-oneth !

A parallel lisp is as follows:—

> " You can't," says Tom to lisping Bill,
> " Find any rhyme for month."
> " A great mithtake," was Bill's reply;
> "I'll find a rhyme at *onth*."

And

> Among our numerous English rhymes,
> They say there's none to month;
> I tried and failed a hundred times,
> But succeeded the hundred and *onth*.

But these are hardly fair. The rhyme is good, but the English is bad. Christina Rosetti has done better in the admirable book of nursery rhymes which she has published under the title of *Sing-Song* :—

> How many weeks in a month?
> Four, as the swift moon runn'th—

In both of these instances, however, the rhymes are evasions of the real issue. The problem is not to make a word by compounding two, or distorting one, but to find a word ready-made, in our unabridged dictionaries that will rhyme properly to month. We believe there is none. Nor is there a fair rhyme to the word *silver*, nor to *spirit*, nor to *chimney*. Horace Smith, one of the authors of the *Rejected Addresses*, once attempted to make one for chimney on a bet, and he did it in this way :—

> Standing on roof and by chimney
> Are master and 'prentice with slim knee.

Another dissyllabic poser is *liquid*. Mr. C. A. Bristed attempts to meet it as follows :—

> After imbibing liquid,
>   A man in the South
> Duly proceeds to stick quid
> (Very likely a thick quid)
>   Into his mouth.

And "Mickey Rooney" contributes this :—

> Shure Quicquid is a thick wit,
> If he can not rhyme to liquid,
> A thing that any Mick wid
> The greatest aise can do:

Just take the herb called chick-weed,
Which they often cure the sick wid,
That's a dacent rhyme for liquid,
And from a Mickey, too.

Some one having challenged a rhyme for *carpet*, the following "lines to a pretty barmaid" were elicited in response:—

Sweet maid of the inn,
'Tis surely no sin
To toast such a beautiful bar pet;
Believe me, my dear,
Your feet would appear
At home on a nobleman's carpet.

Rhymes were thus found for *window*:—

A cruel man a beetle caught,
And to the wall him pinned, oh !
Then said the beetle to the crowd,
"Though I'm stuck up I am not proud,"
And his soul went out of the window.

Bold Robin Hood, that archer good,
Shot down fat buck and *thin* doe;
Rough storms withstood in thick greenwood,
Nor care for door or window.

This for *garden*:—

Though Afric's lion be not here
In showman's stoutly barred den,
An "Irish Lion" you may see
At large in Winter Garden.

The difficulty with porringer has thus been overcome:—

The second James a daughter had,
Too fine to lick a porringer;
He sought her out a noble lad,
And gave the Prince of Orange her.

And in this stanza:—

When nations doubt our power to fight,
We smile at every foreign jeer ;
And with untroubled appetite,
Still empty plate and porringer.

These for *orange* and *lemon:*—

> I gave my darling child a lemon,
> That lately grew its fragrant stem on;
> And next, to give her pleasure *more* range
> I offered her a juicy orange,
> And nuts—she cracked them in the door-hinge.

> And many an *ill*, grim,
> And travel-worn pilgrim,

has traveled far out of his way before succeeding with widow:—

> Who would not always as he's bid do,
> Should never think to wed a widow.

> The jury found that Pickwick did owe
> Damages to Bardell's widow.

Pickwick *loquitur:*—

> Since of this suit I now am rid, O,
> Ne'er again I'll lodge with a widow!

Among the stubborn proper names are *Tipperary and Timbuctoo.* The most successful effort to match the latter was an impromptu by a gentleman who had accompanied a lady home from church one Sunday evening, and who found her hymn-book is his pocket next morning. He returned it with these lines:—

> My dear and much respected Jenny,
> You must have thought me quite a ninny
> For carrying off your hymn-book to
> My house. Had you thoughts visionary,
> And did you dream some missionary
> Had flown with it to Timbuctoo?

Another attempt runs thus:—

> I went a hunting on the plains,
> The plains of Timbuctoo;
> I shot one buck for all my pains,
> And he was a slim buck too.

An unattainable rhyme might be sought for *Euxine*, had not Byron said—

> ———Euxine,
> The dirtiest little sea that mortal ever pukes in.

The following is from Tom Moore's *Fudge Family in Paris*:—

> Take instead of rope, pistol, or dagger, a
> Desperate dash down the Falls of Niagara.

A request for a rhyme for Mackonochie elicited numerous replies, one of which, in reference to a charitable occasion, begins thus:—

> Who, folk bestowing
> Their alms, when o'erflowing,
>   The coffer unlocks?
> Fingers upon a key
> Placing, Mackonochie
> Opens the box.

Canning's amusing little extravaganza, with which everybody is familiar, beginning:—

> Whene'er with haggard eyes I view
>   The dungeon that I'm rotting in,
> I think of the companions true
> Who studied with me at the U-
>   niversity of Gottingen,

has been parodied a hundred times; but it is itself a parody of Pindar, whose fashion of dividing words in his odes all students of the classics have abundant occasion to remember. The last stanza was appended by William Pitt,—a fact not generally known:—

> Sun, moon, and thou, vain world, adieu,
>   That kings and priests are plotting in
> Here doomed to starve on water gru-
> el, never shall I see the U-
>   niversity of Gottingen.

Of these fantastic rhymes, Richard Harris Barham, has given us the finest examples in the language, in his celebrated "Ingoldsby Legends." In the legend "Look at the Clock," we have this :—

> "Having once gained the summit, and managed to cross it, he
> Rolls down the side with uncommon velocity."

This from "The Ghost":—

> "And, being of a temper somewhat warm,
>   Would now and then seize upon small occasion,
> A stick or stool, or anything that round did lie,
> And baste her lord and master most confoundedly."

In the "Tragedy" we have one even more whimsical and comical:—

> "The poor little Page, too, himself got no quarter, but
>   Was served the same way,
>   And was found the next day
> With his heels in the air, and his head in the water-butt."

Byron has more than matched any of these in completeness of rhyme and extent, if we may call it so, of rhyming surface, and matched even himself in acidity of cynicism, in his couplet:—

> "——Ye lords of ladies intellectual,
> Come tell me, have they not hen-pecked you all."

Punch has some very funny samples of eccentric rhymes, of which the best is one that spells out the final word of a couplet, the last letter or two, making so many syllables rhyme with the ending word of the preceding line.   Thus:—

> "Me drunk! the cobbler cried, the devil trouble you,
> You want to kick up a blest r-o-w,
> I've just returned from a teetotal party,
> Twelve on us jammed in a spring c-a-r-t,
> The man as lectured now, was drunk; why bless ye,
> He's sent home in a c-h-a-i-s-e."

Twenty-five years or more ago, in Boston, Monday was the gathering time for Universalist clergymen, Tompkins' book store being the place of rendezvous.   At these unions, King, Chapin, Hosea Ballou, Whittemore, and other notabilities, were pretty sure to be present; and as it was immediately after the graver labors of the Sabbath, the parsons were apt to be in an unusually frisky condition.

Chapin, ordinarily, is of reticent habit; but when the company is congenial, and he is in exhilarant mood, his wonderful flow of language and quick perception make him a companion rarely equalled for wit and repartee. On one occasion, when King and Chapin, and a dozen other clergymen were at Tompkins's, as was their wont, Chapin began to rhyme upon the names of those present. Without a moment's hesitation, he ran off the name of each, rhyming it in verse, to the huge delight of the company. Finally, after exhausting that list, the names of absent clergymen were given to the ready poet, and there was not a single failure. At last a clergyman said:—

"I can give you a name, Brother Chapin, to which you cannot make a rhyme."

"Well, what is it?"

"Brother Brimblecomb."

Without a moment's pause, Chapin said:—

> "There was a man in our town,
>   His name—they called it Brimblecomb;
> He stole the tailor's needle and shears,
>   But couldn't make the thimble come."

Butler's facility in overcoming stubborn words is amusing. For instance:—

> There was an ancient sage philosopher,
> Who had read Alexander Ross over.

Coleridge, on the eve of his departure from Göttingen, being requested by a student of the same class in the university to write in his *Stammbuch*, or album, complied as follows:—

> We both attended the same college,
>   Where sheets of paper we did blur many;
> And now we're going to sport our knowledge,
>   In England I, and you in Germany.

Father Prout, in his polyglot praise of rum punch, says:—

> Doth love, young chiel, one's bosom ruffle?
> Would any feel ripe for a scuffle?
> The simplest plan is just to take a
> Well stiffened can of old Jamaica.

We parted by the gate in June,
   That soft and balmy month,
Beneath the sweetly beaming moon,
   And (wonth—hunth—sunth—bunth—I can't find a rhyme to month)

Years were to pass ere we should meet;
   A wide and yawning gulf
Divides me from my love so sweet,
   While (ulf—sulf—dulf—mulf—stuck again; I can't get any rhyme to
      gulf. I'm in a gulf myself).

Oh, how I dreaded in my soul
   To part from my sweet nymph,
While years should their long seasons roll
   Before (nymph—dymph—ymph—I guess I'll have to let it go at that)..

Beneath my fortune's stern decree
   My lonely spirit sunk,
For a weary soul was mine to be
   And (hunk—dunk—runk—sk—that will never do in the world).

She buried her dear, lovely face
   Within her azure scarf,
She knew I'd take the wretchedness
   As well as (parf—sarf—darf—half-and-half; that won't answer either).

O, I had loved her many years,
   I loved her for herself;
I loved her for her tender fears,
   And also for her (welf—nelf—helf—pelf; no, no; not for her pelf).

I took between my hands her head,
   How sweet her lips did pouch !
I kissed her lovingly and said:
   (Bouch—mouche—louche—ouch; not a bit of it did I say ouch!)

I sorrowfully wrung her hand.
   My tears they did escape,
My sorrow I could not command,
   And I was but a (sape —dape—fape—ape; well, perhaps I did feel like
      an ape).

I gave to her a fond adieu,
   Sweet pupil of love's school;
I told her I would e'er be true,
   And always be a (dool—sool—mool—fool; since I come to think of it, I
      was a fool, for she fell in love with another fellow before I was
      gone a month).

Hood's *Nocturnal Sketch* presents a remarkable example of *la difficulté vaincue.* Most bards find it sufficiently difficult to obtain one rhyming word at the end of a line; but Hood secures three, with an ease which is as graceful as it is surprising :—

> Even has come; and from the dark park, hark
> The signal of the setting sun—one gun !
> And six is sounding from the chime—prime time
> To go and see the Drury Lane Dane slain,
> Or hear Othello's jealous doubt spout out,
> Or Macbeth raving at that shade-made blade,
> Denying to his frantic clutch much such;
> Or else to see Ducrow, with wide tide, stride
> Four horses as no other man can span;
> Or in the small Olympic pit, sit split,
> Laughing at Liston, while you quiz his phiz.
>
> Anon night comes, and with her wings brings things
> Such as, with his poetic tongue, Young sung :
> The gas up blazes with its bright white light,
> And paralytic watchmen prowl, howl, growl,
> About the streets, and take up Pall-Mall Sal,
> Who, trusting to her nightly jobs, robs fobs.
> Now thieves do enter for your cash, smash, crash,
> Past drowsy Charley, in a deep sleep, creep,
> But, frightened by policeman B 3, flee,
> And while they're going, whisper low, "No go !"
>
> Now puss, while folks are in their beds, treads leads,
> And sleepers grumble, Drat that cat!
> Who in the gutter caterwauls, squalls, mauls
> Some feline foe, and screams in shrill ill will.
>
> Now bulls of Bashan, of a prize size, rise
> In childish dreams, and with a roar gore poor
> Georgy, or Charles, or Billy, willy nilly;
> But nurse-maid, in a night-mare rest, chest-pressed,
> Dreameth of one of her old flames, James Grœmes,
> And that she hears—what faith is man's—Ann's banns
> And his, from Reverend Mr. Rice, twice, thrice;
> White ribbons flourish, and a stout shout out,
> That upward goes, shows Rose knows those beaux' woes.

Conformity of Sense to Sound.

In the hexameter rises the fountain's silvery column;
In the pentameter aye falling in melody back.—COLERIDGE: *trans. Schiller*

ARTICULATE IMITATION OF INARTICULATE SOUNDS.

Soft is the strain when zephyr gently blows,
And the smooth stream in smoother numbers flows;
But when loud surges lash the sounding shore,
The hoarse, rough verse should like the torrent roar.
POPE: Essay on Criticism.

On a sudden open fly,
With impetuous recoil and jarring sound,
Th' infernal doors, and on their hinges grate
Harsh thunder.—MILTON: *Paradise Lost, ii.*

Grate on their scrannel pipes of wretched straw.—MILTON: *Lycidas.*

His bloody hand
Snatched two unhappy of my martial band,
And dashed like dogs against the stony floor.—POPE: *Hom. Odys.*

The Pilgrim oft
At dead of night, 'mid his orison, hears
Aghast the voice of time, disparting towers,
Tumbling all precipitous down-dashed,
Rattling around, loud thundering to the moon.
DYER: Ruins of Rome.

What! like Sir Richard, rumbling, rough, and fierce,
With arms, and George, and Brunswick, crowd the verse,
Rend with tremendous sounds your ears asunder,
With drum, gun, trumpet, blunderbuss, and thunder?
Then all your muse's softer art display:
Let Carolina smooth the tuneful lay,
Lull with Amelia's liquid name the nine,
And sweetly flow through all the royal line.—POPE: *Sat. I.*

Remarkable examples are afforded by Dryden's *Alexander's Feast*, and *The Bells* of Edgar A. Poe.

IMITATION OF TIME AND MOTION.

When the merry bells ring round,
And the jocund rebecs sound

> To many a youth and many a maid
> Dancing in the checkered shade.—MILTON: *L'Allegro.*

Up the high hill he heaves a huge round stone;
The huge round stone, resulting with a bound,
Thunders impetuous down, and smokes along the ground.
POPE: *Hom. Odys.*

Which urged, and labored, and forced up with pain,
Recoils and rolls impetuous down, and smokes along the plain.
DRYDEN: *Lucretius.*

A needless Alexandrine ends the song,
That, like a wounded snake, drags its slow length along.
POPE: *Essay on Criticism.*

Not so when swift Camilla scours the plain,
Flies o'er th' unbending corn, and skims along the main.
POPE: *Essay on Criticism.*

> Oft on a plat of rising ground
> I hear the far-off curfew sound,
> Over some wide-watered shore,
> Swinging slow with sullen roar.—MILTON: *Il Penseroso.*

The well-known hexameters of Virgil, descriptive respectively of the galloping of horses over a resounding plain, and of the heavy blows in alternately hammering the metal on the anvil, afford good examples,—the dactylic, of rapidity, the spondaic, of slowness.

Quadrupe- | dante pu- | trem soni- | tu quatit | ungula | campum,
Æneid, viii. 596.

Illi in- | ter se- | se mag- | na vi | brachia | tollunt.—*Æneid,* viii. 452.

IMITATION OF DIFFICULTY AND EASE.

When Ajax strives some rock's vast weight to throw,
The line, too, labors, and the words move slow, &c.—POPE: *Ess. on Criticism.*

He through the thickest of the throng gan threke.—CHAUCER: *Knight's Tale.*

And strains from hard-bound brains six lines a year.—POPE: *Sat. Frag.*

> Part huge of bulk,
> Wallowing, unwieldy, enormous in their gait,
> Tempest the ocean.—MILTON: *Paradise Lost,* vii.

He came, and with him Eve, more loath, though first
To offend, discountenanced both, and discomposed.
MILTON: *Paradise Lost,* x.

So he with difficulty and labor hard
Moved on, with difficulty and labor he.—MILTON: *Paradise Lost,* ii.

NOTES

BY

MARTIN GARDNER

(See page 25.) Since Bombaugh wrote his book, the most noteworthy lipogram in English is a 50,000-word novel called *Gadsby*, published as a hard-cover book in 1939 by Wetzel Publishing Company, Inc., Los Angeles. The novel is entirely without the letter E. A frontispiece photograph of the author, Ernest Vincent Wright (note the three E's in his name), shows him to be a white-haired gentleman with metal-rimmed spectacles and long white beard. The book is dedicated "To Youth," of which the novel's hero, John Gadsby, seems to be some sort of champion.

"The entire manuscript of this story," Wright opens his introduction, "was written with the E type-bar of the typewriter *tied down*; thus making it impossible for that letter to be printed. This was done so that none of that vowel might slip in, accidentally; and many *did* try to do so!" The author goes on to explain some of the difficulties he had to surmount. For example, he had to avoid such pronouns as he, she, her, they, them, and common substitutes for "said" such as replied, answered, asked, and so on. Most verbs in past tense were ruled out because they end in "ed." Numbers above six and below thirty were unavailable. Being a purist, Wright refused to use them even in numeral form. He also avoided "Mr." and "Mrs." because an E is implied when each word is read aloud. "The book may prove," Wright writes, "a valuable aid to school children in English composition."

As a novel, it could be worse. A parody of Clement Moore's familiar Christmas poem appears on page 251. It begins:

> 'Twas a night, almost Christmas,
> And all through that room
> A warm joy is stirring;
> No sign of a gloom.

And ends:

> Happy Christmas to all;
> And to all a Good Night.

Some lipograms are unintentional. Consider, for example, the following familiar nursery rhyme:

> Old Mother Hubbard
> Went to the cupboard
> To get her poor dog a bone,

> But when she got there
> The cupboard was bare
> And so her poor dog had none.

You will look in vain for the letter I in the above lines.

Mention should be made here of James Thurber's *The Wonderful O*, 1957. It is a kind of spoof on lipogramists, though it is mainly a political fable for children, telling what happened when Captain Black, a pirate who hated O, banished this letter from the island of Ooroo.

2. (See page 27.) The plot of Edgar Allan Poe's short story, "X-ing a Paragrab," hinges on an editor's fondness for the letter O and contains a lengthy paragraph (beginning, "So ho, John! How now?") in which with few exceptions, the only vowel is O. See also James Thurber's amusing article, "The Watchers of the Night," (*New Yorker*, December 26, 1959) on the wonders of the letter P.

3. (See page 27.) Four better examples, each containing all the letters of the alphabet are:

> A quick brown fox jumps over the lazy dog. (33 letters)
> Pack my box with five dozen liquor jugs. (32)
> Quick wafting zephyrs vex bold Jim. (29)
> Waltz, nymph, for quick jigs vex Bud. (28)

The famous English mathematician Augustus De Morgan, in his *A Budget of Paradoxes*, (Dover edition, 1954, Vol. 1, pages 273–74) mentions that he and his distinguished colleague William Whewell once amused themselves by trying to write sentences that used all the letters of the alphabet once and once only. The best they could achieve were sentences that left out V and J, of which the following (by De Morgan) is an example:

> I, quartz pyx, who fling muck beds.

De Morgan comments:

> I long thought that no human being could say this under any circumstances. At last I happened to be reading a religious writer —as he thought himself—who threw aspersions on his opponents thick and threefold. Heyday! came into my head, this fellow flings muck beds; he must be a quartz pyx. And then I remembered that a pyx is a sacred vessel, and quartz is a hard stone, as hard as the heart of a religious foe-curser. So that the line is the motto of the ferocious sectarian, who turns his religious vessels into

mud-holders, for the benefit of those who will not see what he sees.

I can find no circumstances for the following, which I received from another:

Fritz! quick! land! hew gypsum box.

From other quarters I have the following:

Dumpy quiz! whirl back fogs next.

This might be said in time of haze to the queer little figure in the Dutch weather-toy, which comes out or goes in with the change in the atmosphere. Again,

Export my fund! Quiz black whigs.

This Squire Western might have said, who was always afraid of the whigs sending the sinking-fund over to Hanover. But the following is the best: it is good advice to a young man, very well expressed under the circumstances:

Get nymph; quiz sad brow; fix luck.

Which in more sober English would be, Marry; be cheerful; watch your business.

As far as I know, no one has yet succeeded in producing an intelligible sentence of 26 letters, using the entire alphabet and avoiding strange words and proper names. The best 26-letter pangrams that I have seen are the following two sentences constructed by Dmitri A. Borgmann, of Oak Park, Illinois.

Cwm, fjord-bank glyphs vext quiz.
Zing! Vext cwm fly jabs Kurd qoph!

The first sentence is explained by Mr. Borgmann as follows: "A 'cwm' is a circular valley, and a 'quiz' is an eccentric person (see *Webster's* unabridged). Accordingly, the sentence means: carved figures on the bank of a fjord and in a circular valley irritated an eccentric person."

Mr. Borgman explains the second sentence like this: "Zing! An irritated valley fly jabs at the Hebrew letter 'qoph,' written by a Turkish tribesman."

There are many words that contain in proper order the six vowels a, e, i, o, u, y: *abstemiously, facetiously, arseniously, arteriously, bacteriously,* and *caesiously.* The five vowels in reverse order are found in such words as *duoliteral* and *quodlibetal*. Should you ever be asked if there is a word in the English language containing all six vowels, it has been suggested that a good answer is "*Unquestionably*!"

For other word curiosities along similar lines, I turn to the inexhaustible files of Mr. Borgmann. He supplied all the following.

The shortest words containing the five vowels are: *eunoia* (alertness of mind and will), *Euodia* (a New Testament name), and *Euboia* (a Greek island). A charming example from the French language is *oiseau* (bird).

Uncopyrightable, *dermatoglyphics*, and *misconjugatedly* are fifteen-letter words in which no letter is used more than once. If we coin a word by adding an S to uncopyrightable, we can stretch the record to sixteen letters.

Strengths is a nine-letter word containing only one vowel. *Archchronicler*, *Knightsbridge* (a street in London), *latchstring*, *lengthsman*, and *postphthisic* are words containing six consecutive consonants. Nine consecutive consonants are found in *wppwrmwste* (an old spelling of "uppermost") and *Nosmnbdsgrsutt* (the land of flying people in a 1751 novel by Robert Paltock). To these examples I add *pyrzqxgl*, the eight-letter magic word that plays such a prominent role in L. Frank Baum's *The Magic of Oz*. (Pronounce it properly and you can transform yourself or anyone else into whatever you please.)

Defenselessnesses, *strengthlessnesses*, and *self-centerednesses* are long words in which E is the only vowel. For I, an elegant example is *indivisibility*. For O, *Chrononhotonthologos*, the title and hero of a burlesque tragedy by Henry Carey, produced in 1734. Mr. Borgmann informs me that there are similarly long words for A, U, and Y. He did not think them elegant enough to pass on, with the exception of *Mynyddyslwyn*, a village in Monmouthshire, England.

Among words consisting only of vowels there are *Aeaea* (the fabled abode of Circe), *aiaiai* (the roseate spoonbill), *euouae* (a melodic formula in Gregorian music), *Oueioi* (an ancient Tuscan city in Etruria), and *aye-aye* (a Madagascan lemur). Words consisting entirely of consonants, Y also being excluded, are *crwths* (stringed musical instruments of ancient Ireland), *Llwchwr* (a city-district in Wales), and Joe *Btfsplk* (a character in the Li'l Abner comic strip). The Shakespearean word *honorificabilitudinitatibus* is interesting in that it alternates vowels and consonants. So also do *verisimilitudes* and *superacidulated*.

Lewis Carroll in one of his published letters mentions that an eight-lettered hyphenated word can be made from the first seven letters of the alphabet plus I. Carroll does not supply the word, but Mr. Borgmann tells me that it must be *big-faced*. He adds that the shortest words containing the first six letters are *boldface* and *feedback*. The shortest word using the first nine letters is *bright-faced*. The shortest word with the eight consecutive letters from N to U is *Queensport*, a town in Nova Scotia. *Absconder* is an example of a word that has the first five letters of the alphabet in serial order. Bombaugh, in his *Facts and Fancies*, records the following bit of dialogue: "It's as plain as ABC." "That may be, but I'm DEF."

The longest words using only letters from the first half of the alphabet, says Mr. Borgmann, are: *diddle-daddled*, *fiddle-faddled*, *gibblegabbled*, *ill-effaceable*, and *higglehaggled*. The second half of the alphabet yields *poppyworts*, *prosupport*, *puttyroots*, *synsporous*, *zoosporous*, and *nonsupports*. Large words with letters that do not extend either above or below the line are *overnervousnesses* and *overnumerousnesses*. Longer words, if one overlooks the dot on the I, are *overconsciousnesses* and *unceremoniousnesses*.

Long words typed by using only the top row of letters on the keyboard are *proterotype*, *rupturewort*, *proprietory*, and *prettypretty*. (Surprisingly, *typewriter* is also such a word.) On the middle row: *flagfalls*, *galagalas*, *Khalakhkha*. There are no words for the bottom row, due to the absence of vowels. Long words typed with only the left hand: *aftercataracts*, *tesseradecades*. Right hand: *niminy-piminy*, *phyllophyllin*, *johnny-jump-up*. Here is a sentence by Mr. Borgmann that can be typed entirely with the right hand: *IN JULY, OH MY KILLJOY MOLLY, I'LL LOOK IN UPON MY JUMPY POLO PONY UP IN HILLY HONOLULU.*

4. (See page 27.) The standard linotype keyboard is based on this old chart. To see if his machine is in good working order, a typesetter may run his finger down the two left-hand columns of the keyboard. This produces those two cabalistic words, *ETAOIN SHRDLU* (the first twelve letters in order of frequency), that are sometimes seen in badly proofed newspapers.

5. (See page 34). Alliterative sentences, often called "tongue twisters" because it is difficult to say them rapidly, are legion. The two best known in the United States are "Peter Piper picked a peck of pickled peppers" (on hot days, I am told, Ubangi women fan each other by reciting this), and "She sells sea shells by the seashore."

Some short examples, surprisingly difficult to say, are "Rubber baby buggy bumpers," "Bug's bad blood," and "The sinking steamer sunk." Also well known is the skunk that sat on a stump; the skunk thunk the stump stunk, but the stump thunk the skunk stunk. Some are on the blue side, such as the curious cream-colored cat that crept into the crypt, crapped, and crept out again. It is said that a famous radio actor once refused a detective role when he learned that one of his lines would be "Show me the chair Schmidt sat in when he was shot." "Whip gig, whip gig, whip gig . . ." and "troy boat, troy boat, troy boat . . ." are both exceedingly difficult to repeat many times. An amusing children's catch is to challenge someone to recite "Betty Boop, Betty Boop . . ." rapidly. After about the fifth "Betty Boop," wave your hat and shout "Heigh ho, Silver!" A good collection of tongue twisters can be found in *A Book of Prize-Winning Tongue-Twisters*, Little Blue Book No. 1261; and scattered through the pages of Clark Kinnaird's *Encyclopedia of Puzzles and Pastimes*, 1946.

Carolyn Wells, in her *Such Nonsense* anthology, includes this alliterative gem by W. E. Southwick:

THE STORY OF ESAW WOOD

Esaw Wood sawed wood.

Esaw Wood *would* saw wood!

All the wood Esaw Wood saw Esaw Wood would saw. In other words, all the wood Esaw saw to saw Esaw sought to saw.

Oh, the wood Wood would saw! And oh, the wood-saw with which Wood would saw wood.

But one day Wood's wood-saw would saw no wood, and thus the wood Wood sawed was not the wood Wood would saw if Wood's wood-saw would saw wood.

Now, Wood would saw wood with a wood-saw that would saw wood, so Esaw sought a saw that would saw wood.

One day Esaw saw a saw saw wood as no other wood-saw Wood saw would saw wood.

In fact, of all the wood-saws Wood ever saw saw wood Wood never saw a wood-saw that would saw wood as the wood-saw Wood saw saw wood would saw wood, and I never saw a wood-saw that would saw as the wood-saw Wood saw would saw until I saw Esaw Wood saw wood with the wood-saw Wood saw saw wood.

Now Wood saws wood with the wood-saw Wood saw saw wood.
Oh, the wood the wood-saw Wood saw would saw!
Oh, the wood Wood's woodshed would shed when Wood would
saw wood with the wood-saw Wood saw saw wood!
Finally, no man may ever know how much wood the wood-saw
Wood saw would saw, if the wood-saw Wood saw would saw all
the wood the wood-saw Wood saw would saw.

A classic instance of orderly alliteration is provided by the first
five lines of Coleridge's "Kubla Khan" in which words at the close
of every line have the same initials:

> In Xanadu did Kubla Khan
> A stately pleasure-dome decree:
> Where Alph, the sacred river, ran
> Through caverns measureless to man
> Down to a sunless sea.

A curious penchant for alliteration livens the style of Mrs. Amanda
McKittrick Ros (1861–1939), whose remarkable English novels are
known, Aldous Huxley has written, "only to a small and select band
of admirers." Her three published works of fiction are *Irene Iddesleigh*,
Delina Delaney, and *Donald Dudley*. A fourth novel, *Helen Huddleson*
(concerning Lord Raspberry, his sister Cherry, Peter Plum, Lily Lentil,
the Earl of Grape, and other noble characters) remains unpublished.
She claimed to be the author of two other novels, *The Lusty Lawyer*
and *Motherless Moon*, but no one has yet found evidence that they
were ever written.

Here is the final sentence of *Irene Iddesleigh:* "Life is too often
stripped of its pleasantness by the steps of false assumption, marring
the true path of life-long happiness, which should be pebbled with
principle, piety, purity and peace." Mrs. Ros saw absolutely nothing
funny about anything she wrote, including her two books of poetry:
Poems of Puncture and *Fumes of Formation*. You can learn all about
her in *O Rare Amanda!*, 1954, a biography by Jack Loudan.

For a ringing defense of the right of a writer to make conscious and
playful use of alliteration, see Gilbert Chesterton's "An Apology for
Buffoons" in *The Well and the Shallows*, 1935.

Closely related to the alliterative curiosities are the spoonerisms in
which initial letters of words get transposed. They are named after
Reverend W. A. Spooner, an Oxford clergyman who is said to have

asked his congregation to sing "Kinquering Kongs Their Titles Take" and to have made other accidental bloopers such as introducing Queen Victoria as "our queer old dean." Later he made them up on purpose and for a while they were an Oxford fad. "Is it kisstomary to cuss the bride?" and "Mardon me, padam, your pie is occupeued; may I sew you to another sheet?" have become clichés of the language. Another familiar classic is this appeal to the judge: "Now missen, lister. All I had was tee martoonis. Sough I theem under the affluence of inkahol, I'm not palf as hickled—half as packled—as thinkle peep—as theeple pink I am."

Bennett Cerf has reminded us of the man who poured pickle juice down a hill to see if dill waters run steep, the woman who selected a paperback from the trite side of the racks, and the lucky baker who found a four-loaf cleaver. Clifton Fadiman points out that combined charity drives put all their begs in one ask-it. "Will you please hush my brat?" said the visitor to the butler. "It's roaring with pain outside." Is it in one of George Kaufman's plays that a coed is said to have put her heart before the course? And have you read *Lady Loverley's Chatter*?

Of course the funniest spoonerisms are unprintable, but perhaps in the interests of word science I can get away with the story about the hunter in Africa who angrily shot the sacred Foo bird after the bird, perched on a branch above him, had befouled his pith helmet. Angry natives captured the hunter and boiled him in oil. The moral is a spoonerism on that old adage: if the shoe fits, wear it.

6. (See page 34.) E. Cobham Brewer, in *The Reader's Handbook*, page 719, prints a slightly different version of "The Siege of Belgrade." He attributes it to one H. Southgate, and calls it "the best-known alliterative poem in English." William S. Walsh in the *Handy-Book of Literary Curiosities*, page 38, credits it to Alaric A. Watts, and adds several similar poems by other authors.

7. (See page 39.) Lewis Carroll wrote scores of acrostic poems, usually to conceal the name of one of his "child-friends." The terminal poem of *Through the Looking Glass* is perhaps his best, the initial letters spelling the name of the original Alice. The prefatory poem of *Sylvie and Bruno* is an acrostic to Isa Bowman, and the prefatory poem of *The Hunting of the Snark* is an acrostic to Gertrude Chataway. The latter poem, reprinted below, is remarkable in that not only do the initial letters spell the girl's name, but also the initial *words* of each stanza very closely approximate it.

INSCRIBED TO A DEAR CHILD:
*In Memory of Golden Summer Hours
and Whispers of a Summer Sea*

Girt with a boyish garb for boyish task,
    Eager she wields her spade: yet loves as well
Rest on a friendly knee, intent to ask
    The tale he loves to tell.

Rude spirits of the seething outer strife,
    Unmeet to read her pure and simple spright,
Deem, if you list, such hours a waste of life,
    Empty of all delight!

Chat on, sweet Maid, and rescue from annoy
    Hearts that by wiser talk are unbeguiled.
Ah, happy he who owns that tenderest joy,
    The heart-love of a child!

Away, fond thoughts, and vex my soul no more!
    Work claims my wakeful nights, my busy days—
Albeit bright memories of that sunlit shore
    Yet haunt my dreaming gaze!

Newspapers that publish poetry have to be on constant guard against jokers who send in poems with concealed acrostics. (I once did this myself with a meaningless poem called "The Swan" that appeared in my high school paper in 1930. Nobody thought it was funny.) Sometimes the joker is a rival editor. In his *Cyclopedia of Puzzles*, page 209, Sam Loyd prints the following poem that first appeared he says, in a Cincinnati paper at a time when the editor was in a spirited controversy with another editor.

SPRING

The genial spring once more with chaplets crowned
Has showered her choicest blessings all around.
Each silent valley and each verdant lawn
Enriched with flowers, looks smiling at the dawn
Demure and modest hued the violet grows;
In yonder garden blooms the blushing rose;
To these the lilac adds her fragrant dower
Of perfume cherished by the sun and shower.

Reviving Flora walks the world a queen
Of kingdoms peerless as a fairy scene.
Far o'er the hills, in many a graceful line,
The rainbow blossoms of the orchard shine.
How softly mingled all their tints unite,
Embalm the air and bless the grateful sight!
Sweet voices now are heard on every tree,
The breeze, the bird, the murmur of the bee.
And down the cliff, where rocks oppose in vain,
Runs the clear stream in music of the plain.
In noisy groups, far from their southern home,
Now round the lofty spire the swallows roam;
The fearless robin builds with glossy leaves
Her fragile nest beneath the farmer's eaves;
Embowered in woods the partridge makes her bed
With silken moss o'er tender osiers spread;
Each happy bird expands his dappled wings,
Soars with his gentle mate and sweetly sings.
The sounds of early husbandry arise
In pleasing murmurs to the pale blue skies;
Shrill floats the ploughman's whistle while he speeds
Along the yielding earth his patient steeds.
Joyous the life which tills the pregnant soil,
And sweet the profits of the farmer's toil.
Content, as smiling as an angel face
Keeps peaceful vigil round his dwelling place,
And gentle Hope and Love, forever bright,
Smiling like seraphs in their bowers of light,
Salute his mornings and embalm each night.

After a few days had passed, the editor, who printed this poem with high praise for its beauty and originality, read in the rival paper that "the editor of *The Star of the West* has fully justified the acrostic contained in a beautiful poem on spring by publishing and indorsing it in his paper." Loyd does not give the name or date of the paper, so I cannot vouch for the truth of this story.

Among recent American authors, James Branch Cabell was particularly fond of acrostics. The prefatory poem of *Jurgen* is an acrostic to Burton Rascoe and the last poem of Cabell's privately printed *Sonnets from Antan*, 1929, is an acrostic that spells "This is nonsense."

Aleister Crowley, the mad occultist and poet who has been the subject of several recent lurid biographies, enjoyed composing pious Protestant hymns and sending them to unsuspecting clerics. Not until the song had been sung for several Sundays would it dawn on the horror-stricken congregation that the initial letters spelled "Go —— yourself," or something equally inappropriate. A colorful anthology of blue acrostics could be compiled from modern sources. A striking example is the poem "A Recollection," to be found on page 71 of *The Collected Poems of John Peale Bishop*, edited by Allen Tate, 1948.

Although not examples of acrostics, this seems the best place to mention a strange collection of poems entitled *Shadows in the Moonlight*, written and privately printed in Los Angeles in 1927 by T. Page Wright, a Hollywood script writer. Wright was a skillful amateur magician who wrote the poems so that the book could be used for performing a feat of mental magic. Each of the 22 poems is so constructed that the nineteenth word is "rose" and the thirty-first word is "love." The book originally sold in magic stores for five dollars, but is now extremely scarce. Considering the purpose for which the poems were written, they are surprisingly good. I particularly like this one:

AT A MELODRAMA

> The leading lady suffered, while I yawned;
> But a girl beside
> Me sat and cried—
> Her tears that rose unbidden washed away
> The timeworn tawdriness that stained the play.
> Love was the theme——the rest she looked beyond.

(See page 49.) Anagrammatic word games of various sorts are still popular, but it is no longer fashionable to spend time composing clever anagrams on the names of friends or prominent people. The mathematician De Morgan (see note 3), in Volume I of his *A Budget of Paradoxes* (Dover edition, pages 138–39), mentions that 800 anagrams on his full name, Augustus De Morgan, had been composed by a friend (another mathematician who is left nameless). Three samples:

> Great gun! Do us a sum!
> Snug as mud to argue.
> O! Gus! Tug a mean surd!

Lewis Carroll was responsible for two excellent anagrams on William Ewart Gladstone, the prime minister whose political methods the Reverend C. L. Dodgson found not to his liking. They are:

> Wilt tear down *all* images?
> Wild agitator! Means well.

Other classic name anagrams worth mentioning are:

> Horatio Nelson: *Honor est a Nilo.*
> William Shakespeare: *We all make his praise* and
>   *I ask me, has Will a peer?*

Dmitri Borgmann was kind enough to send me the following remarkable one-word anagrams from his extensive collection:

> Lawyers: *Sly ware.*
> Punishment: *Nine thumps.*
> Compassionateness: *Stamps one as so nice.*
> Conversation: *Voices rant on.*
> Desperation: *A rope ends it.*
> Endearments: *Tender names.*
> Halitosis: *Lois has it!*
> Negation: *Get a "no" in.*
> Panties: *A step-in.*
> Therapeutics: *Apt is the cure!*
> Anagrams: *Ars Magna.* (Latin for "great art.")

An antigram, Mr. Borgmann informs me, is an anagram giving a reversal of meaning. Some one-word antigrams follow:

> Infection: *Fine tonic.*
> Misfortune: *It's* more *fun.*
> Militarism: *I limit arms.*
> Evangelists: *Evil's agents.*

Sometimes an anagram of one word is another single word. Mr. Borgmann cites these examples:

> Aristotelian: *Retaliations.*
> Tournamental: *Ultramontane.*

A rare type of single-word anagram, writes Mr. Borgmann, is one in which the word is simply split into two or more appropriate words.

An island "is land," a daredevil has "dared evil," to be gentlemanly is to be "gentle, manly." and so on.

Turning to phrase anagrams, the following are among the best in a long list supplied by Mr. Borgmann:

The United States of America: *Attaineth its cause: freedom!*

The eyes: *They see.*

Washington crossing the Delaware: *He saw his ragged Continentals row.*

Is pity love?: *Positively!*

The Leaning Tower of Pisa: *What a foreign stone pile!*

The Leaning Tower of Pisa, in Tuscany, Italy: *A funny spot in a sweet city; I o'erhang it all.*

Abandon hope all ye who enter here!: *Hear Dante! Oh, beware yon open hell!*

A decimal point: *I'm a dot in place.*

An unmarried woman: *A man-admirer unwon.*

A sentence of death: *Faces one at the end.*

A shoplifter: *Has to pilfer.*

Circumstantial evidence: *Can ruin a selected victim.*

Gold and silver: *Grand old evils!*

Life's aim: *Families!*

Medical consultations: *Noted miscalculations!*

Nova Scotia and Prince Edward Island: *Two Canadian provinces: lands I dread!*

One good turn deserves another: *Do rogues endorse that? No, never!*

One hug: *Enough?*

Saint Elmo's fire: *Is lit for seamen.*

Spring, summer, autumn, winter: *"Time's running past," we murmur.*

The countryside: *No city dust here!*

The Mona Lisa: *No hat, a smile.*

The nudist colony: *No untidy clothes!*

The state of North Carolina: *Hasten on to fair Charlotte!*

The summer vacation: *A time to charm Venus.*

The following phrase antigrams from Mr. Borgmann's files are among the best:

A picture of health: *Oft pale, I ache, hurt.*
A tragedy: *Rated gay.*
The Lenten season: *None eat less then.*
Violence: *Nice love.*
Old man winter: *Warm, indolent.*
The man who laughs: *He's glum, won't ha-ha.*

A. Cyril Pearson, who edited a number of puzzle books, was fond of converting proverbs and well-known phrases into anagrammatic sentences that had some affinity to the originals. A collection of 31 of them will be found in Pearson's *The Twentieth Century Book of Puzzles.* The following example is typical:

Many a true word is spoken in jest: *Men joke and so win trusty praise.*

During the Renaissance, scientists sometimes announced their discoveries in anagrams, apparently to get the discovery on record at a time when they were still searching for confirming evidence or because political or ecclesiastical circumstances made the time unpropitious for an announcement. Galileo, for example, announced his discovery that Venus had phases like the moon by writing, "*Haec immatura a me jam frustra leguntur—oy,*" an anagram of "*Cynthiae figuras aemulatur Mater Amorum.*"

Authors often use pseudonyms that are anagrams of their real names (e.g., Balzac's *nom de plume,* R'Hoone, an anagram of his first name, Honoré, and François Rabelais' pseudonym, Alcofribas Nasier.) The best-known anagrammatic book title is probably Samuel Butler's *Erewhon,* the letters of "nowhere" nearly backward. Among prominent modern authors, James Branch Cabell tops the list in the number of anagrams strewn through his books. In *Jurgen,* for example, Vel-Tyno is the god of novelty, Ageus is the god of usage, and there are many others.

John Winkler's biography of William Randolph Hearst tells how the New York *World* once copied from Hearst's *Journal* an obituary story on one Reflipe W. Thanuz. "Thanuz" was phonetic spelling of "the news," and "Reflipe W." was "We pilfer" spelled backward. A reviewer of Winkler's book recalled that the *World* retaliated by planting the name "Lister A. Raah" in a story. After the *Journal* had printed the story, it was pointed out that the name was an anagram of "Hearst a liar."

I wonder how many readers will be able to make one word by rearranging the letters of "new door"?

(See page 54.) Here, in my own slightly modified form, is an old British doggerel. Ivel cheese, one presumes, was cheese made somewhere in the valley of the river Ivel.

> A VILE young lady on EVIL bent,
> Lowered her VEIL with sly intent.
> "LEVI," she said, "It's time to play.
> What shall we do to LIVE today?"
> "My dear," said he, "do as you please.
> *I'm* going to eat some IVEL cheese!"

(See page 55.) Word squares have been much worked on by word puzzlists in all languages. The difficulty increases, of course, with the size of the square. Here are four fine specimens of order 7 from the files of Dmitri Borgmann. The inventors of the first three are not known. Mr. Borgmann constructed the fourth.

```
N E S T L E S        P R E P A R E
E N T R A N T        R E M O D E L
S T R A N G E        E M U L A T E
T R A I T O R        P O L E M I C
L A N T E R N        A D A M A N T
E N G O R G E        R E T I N U E
S T E R N E R        E L E C T E D

M E R G E R S        S H E A V E D
E T E R N A L        H O S T I L E
R E G A T T A        E S T A T E S
G R A V I T Y        A T A X I C S
E N T I T L E        V I T I A T E
R A T T L E R        E L E C T O R
S L A Y E R S        D E S S E R T
```

The best square of order 8 ever constructed, Mr. Borgmann believes, is this one by Margaretta Strohm, a Pennsylvania expert. All the words can be found in *Webster's* unabridged.

```
A  G  A  R  I  C  U  S
G  E  N  E  R  A  N  T
A  N  A  C  O  N  D  A
R  E  C  A  N  T  E  R
I  R  O  N  W  O  R  T
C  A  N  T  O  N  A  L
U  N  D  E  R  A  G  E
S  T  A  R  T  L  E  D
```

Order 9 squares, Mr. Borgmann writes, demand less common words and names. About 900 have been constructed in English, of which the following is considered the best. It was composed in 1928 by Wayne M. Goodwin of Chicago, who died in 1940. He was one of the greatest square experts of all time.

```
F  R  A  T  E  R  I  E  S
R  E  G  I  M  E  N  A  L
A  G  I  T  A  T  I  V  E
T  I  T  A  N  I  T  E  S
E  M  A  N  A  T  I  S  T
R  E  T  I  T  R  A  T  E
I  N  I  T  I  A  T  O  R
E  A  V  E  S  T  O  N  E
S  L  E  S  T  E  R  E  D
```

"Seven of the nine words," says Mr. Borgmann, "are in *Webster's* unabridged. Retitrate means to titrate again, and is found in the two-volume supplement to the *Century Dictionary*, 1909. Eavestone is the name of a township in eastern West Riding, a division of Yorkshire, England."

Mr. Borgmann also supplied me with the following incomparable order 9 French square:

```
G R A V A T I E R
R E F I N A N C E
A F F R O N T A T
V I R O N N E R A
A N O N N A N T S
T A N N A N T E S
I N T E N T E R A
E C A R T E R A I
R E T A S S A I T
```

From top down the words mean (1) a rubbish carter, (2) I re-finance, (3) he would have confronted, (4) he will surround, (5) hemming and hawing, (6) tanning, (7) he will sue, (8) I shall separate, (9) he recompressed. The only flaw, writes Mr. Borgmann, is that *vironnera* is Old French. The modern word is *environnera*.

Order 10 squares have been constructed, but all of them are composed entirely of rare tautonymic words, such as Pango-Pango, and are not considered true word squares.

There are many other geometrical forms into which words have been arranged. Next to the square, the most popular form is the diamond, but I have space here for only one order 7 specimen from Mr. Borgmann's bottomless files:

```
                R
              R E S
            R E S T S
          S E P T A T A
        R E C L I N E R S
      R E P L U N D E R E D
    R E S T I N G P L A C E S
      S T A N D P O I N T S
        S T E E L I N G S
          A R R A N G E
            S E C T S
              D E S
                S
```

Septata is the only word not in *Webster's*. It is a scientific term that can be found in *Funk and Wagnalls* unabridged. By using less common words and names, diamonds up to order 17 have been constructed.

11. (See page 59.) Some short palindromes of later vintage:

> Too hot to hoot.
> Pa's a sap.
> Rise to vote, sir.
> A war at Tarawa.
> Step on no pets.
> Live not on evil.
> Pull up if I pull up.
> No lemons, no melon.
> Draw, O coward!
> In a regal age ran I.
> Too bad I hid a boot.
> 'Tis Ivan, on a visit.
> Poor Dan is in a droop.
> Yreka Bakery. (A bakery at 322 W. Miner Street, Yreka, California.)

Some longer ones:

> Did Hannah see bees? Hannah did!
> Repel evil as a live leper.
> Nor I nor Emma had level'd a hammer on iron.
> Live dirt up a side track carted is a putrid evil.
> Was it a bar or a bat I saw?
> Was it a rat I saw? (This can be answered palindromically with, "No miss, it is Simon.")
> Are we not drawn onward, we few, drawn onward to new era?
> "Not New York?" Roy went on.
> No, it is open on one position.
> Straw? No, too stupid a fad. I put soot on warts.
> Emil asleep, Hannah peels a lime.
> I roamed under it as a tired, nude Maori.
> Ten animals I slam in a net.
> Too far, Edna, we wander afoot!
> Egad! A base tone denotes a bad age!
> Wonders in Italy: Latin is "red" now.
> Now, Ned, I am a maiden nun; Ned, I am a maiden won.

Most of the above palindromes are from Dmitri Borgmann's monumental collection of more than 1,500. A third of this number are original. Here are some of Mr. Borgmann's best.

> "Do nine men interpret?" "Nine men," I nod.
> Marge lets Norah see Sharon's telegram.
> A new order began, a more Roman age bred Rowena.
> I maim nine men in Saginaw; wan, I gas nine men in Miami.
> Deer flee freedom in Oregon? No, Geronimo—deer feel freed.
> Norah's moods, alas, doom Sharon.
> No misses ordered roses, Simon.
> Eva, can I stab bats in a cave?
> I moan, "Live on, O evil Naomi!"
> Do not start at rats to nod.
> Did Ione take Kate? No, I did.
> Delia sailed as a sad Elias ailed.
> No mists reign at Tangier, St. Simon!
> Did I draw Della too tall, Edward? I did.
> Noel, let's egg Estelle on.
> Help Max, Enid, in example "H."

The British palindromist J. A. Lindon recently devised a remarkable pair of palindromes, one directed to the Deity, the other to Satan:

> Do, O God, no evil deed, live on, do good.
> Live, O Devil, revel ever, live, do evil.

The two following palindromes, the second of which is in my opinion the finest in the English language, are the work of Leigh Mercer of London:

> Sums are not set as a test on Erasmus.
> A man, a plan, a canal—Panama!

When Adam remarked "Madam, in Eden; I'm Adam" (a variant by Leigh Mercer of a palindrome cited by Bombaugh), it should be mentioned that Eve palindromically replied, "Eve." And once when someone recited some palindromes to an Englishman, he shook his head and commented, "Tut-tut."

Many attempts have been made to write poems that are palindromes, but the results are invariably close to gibberish. An example titled "Puma, Puma," will be found on page 141 of *Hubert Phillips's*

Hemptameron, 1945. Palindromic poems are easier to compose if the word, instead of the letter, is taken as the basic unit. Here, for example, is a grave inscription reportedly in Cornwall, England:

> Shall we all die?
> We shall die all;
> All die shall we—
> Die all we shall.

The following anonymous doggerel, from George Milburn's *A Book of Puzzles and Brain Teasers* (Little Blue Book No. 1103) becomes a different poem when the words are taken in reverse order:

> Dies slowly fading day, winds mournfully sigh,
> Brightly stars are waking;
> Flies owlet hooting, holding revel high,
> Nightly silence breaking.

J. A. Lindon, the British word expert, is, I believe, the author of these two splendid palindromes in which the words are the units:

> King, are you glad you are king?
> What! So he is hanged, is he? So what?

Mr. Lindon also takes the palm for the longest word ever worked into an intelligible palindrome. To understand the palindrome you must know that Beryl has a beatnik husband who likes to run around his back yard in the nude. Ned has just asked him if he does this to annoy his wife, and he replies:

> Named undenominationally rebel, I rile Beryl? La, No! I tan. I'm, O Ned, nude, man!

As for palindromic words, Mr. Borgmann knows of no common English words of this sort that are longer than seven letters: *deified, rotator, repaper, reviver*. Less common but longer words include: *redivider, Malayalam* (a language spoken in India), *semitimes* (half-times), *detartrated* (separated from tartaric acid), and *Wassamassaw* (a swamp in Berkeley County, South Carolina, north of Summerville). Foreign languages do better than English in this respect. Mr. Borgmann cites: *Reliefpfeiler* (German for a relief-decorated architectural column), *att ordidrotta* (Swedish, meaning to contest with words), and *saippuakauppias* (Finnish for a soap dealer). Of special interest is the English word *radar*, coined to symbolize the rebound of radar waves.

The term "semordnilap" (palindromes spelled backward) has been proposed for words that spell different words in reverse. An example pointed out by Lewis Carroll in his novel *Sylvie and Bruno* is the word *evil*, which is *live* backward. Other examples are *straw*, *stop*, *maps*, *bard*, *strap*, *reknits*, *lamina*, *deliver*, *dog* (see James Joyce's *Ulysses*, Random House edition, page 584), *dessert*, *devil*, *mood*, *repaid*. Mr. Borgmann supplies these eight-letter semordnilaps: *stressed*, *samaroid*, *rewarder*. Among trade names one thinks of *Serutan* and *Tums*. Semordnilap sentences offer a virtually unexplored field. The best example I know is the work of Mr. Borgmann:

Slain Edward's hoop saved a boot. *Too bad! Eva's "poohs" draw denials.*

Some words, when printed or written a certain way, remain unchanged when turned upside down. Here are a few examples:

Francis J. Rigney, a New York artist, called my attention to *ZOONOOZ*, the invertible title of a magazine published monthly by the Zoological Society of San Diego, California.

The following reversible signature of a Mr. W. H. Hill appeared in *The Strand Magazine* in 1908:

Other fields that lie open to investigation are words that remain the same when a mirror is held above them (HE CHECKED BOX C.O.D.), or at the side (TOT), or at the side when the word is printed vertically:

```
T          A
O          U
M          T
A          O
T          M
O          A
           T
           A
```

Some words change to other words when inverted (MOM) or viewed by a mirror in various ways. Rex Whistler, a British muralist who died in 1944, published a remarkable collection of upside-down faces (faces that become other faces when inverted) under the title OHO. The book's title remains unchanged when inverted or viewed in a mirror held either above or at the side.

When printing is looked at through a solid transparent rod (such as a clear glass or plastic swizzle stick) the letters are reversed as though reflected in a mirror placed above the printing. Thus if one views through such a rod the phrase CHOICE QUALITY on the side of a package of Camel cigarettes, the word "choice" is unaffected, but "quality" becomes reversed. This puzzles most people. It also is possible to print sentences that alter in meaning when seen through the rod. For instance:

pop KICKED bob

turns into "bob kicked pop" when read through a swizzle stick.

Finally, there are words that change to numerals when turned upside down (*hell*) and numerals that become words when reflected. The following specimens suggest the curious possibilities of the latter principle:

```
   3414            7192
   340              41
  TH813            3HT
 --------        ---------
433TH813         40077192
```

2. (See page 62.) These words are usually arranged in the form of a
word square:

```
S A T O R
A R E P O
T E N E T
O P E R A
R O T A S
```

For a full account of the history and theories of origin of this, the
most famous of all Latin word squares, see "The Origin and Date of
the 'Sator' Word Square," by Donald Atkinson, professor of
ancient history at the University of Manchester, in *The Journal of
Ecclesiastical History*, Vol. 2, No. 1, January–April, 1951, pages 1–18.
It was a popular prophylactic charm throughout the Middle Ages.
Scholars long assumed that it had an early Christian origin because
its letters can be arranged

```
            A
            P
            A
            T
            E
            R
A PATERNOSTER O
            O
            S
            T
            E
            R
            O
```

The A's and O's stand for *alpha* and *omega*, the beginning and end.
However, in 1936 the word square was found on the plaster of a
column at Pompeii. This carries it back to before the city's destruction by Vesuvius in 79, and makes its Christian origin unlikely,

though it could have been scratched on the column by Christians of a later period.

The words do not seem to form an intelligible sentence, but various rough translations have been put forth. Dmitri Borgmann prefers "The sower Arepo holds the wheels at work." "Arepo" is the only word that is not Latin, and scholars differ on how it found its way into the square. In Celtic the word means "a plough." The square appears on the seal of Cyrus McCormick, inventor of the reaping machine.

13. (See page 65.) A remarkable ambiguous love letter is featured in the third act of Nicholas Udall's famous sixteenth century play (the earliest known English comedy) *Ralph Roister Doister*. The letter is from Ralph to the widow Christian Custance, whom he is courting. Matthew Merygreek, a practical joker, reads the letter aloud to the widow, but by altering its punctuation he completely reverses the sentiment.

14. (See page 73.) One of the funniest specimens of patchwork poetry is this soliloquy of Hamlet, recited by the Duke in Mark Twain's *Huckleberry Finn*:

> To be, or not to be; that is the bare bodkin
> That makes calamity of so long life;
> For who would fardels bear, till Birnam Wood do come to Dunsinane,
> But that the fear of something after death
> Murders the innocent sleep,
> Great nature's second course,
> And makes us rather sling the arrows of outrageous fortune
> Than fly to others that we know not of.
> There's the respect must give us pause:
> Wake Duncan with thy knocking! I would thou couldst;
> For who would bear the whips and scorns of time,
> The oppressor's wrong, the proud man's contumely,
> The law's delay, and the quietus which his pangs might take,
> In the dead waste and middle of the night, when churchyards yawn
> In customary suits of solemn black,
> But that the undiscovered country from whose bourne no traveler returns,

Breathes forth contagion on the world,
And thus the native hue of resolution, like the poor cat i'
   the adage,
Is sicklied o'er with care.
And all the clouds that lowered o'er our housetops,
With this regard their currents turn awry,
And lose the name of action.
'Tis a consummation devoutly to be wished. But soft you,
   the fair Ophelia:
Ope not thy ponderous and marble jaws,
But get thee to a nunnery—go!

The most successful of modern poetry hoaxes took place in July, 1944, when *Angry Penguins*, an *avante-garde* literary review in Australia, published the work of a hitherto unknown poet named Ern Malley. Malley had died of Graves' disease at 25 and his poems had been submitted by his sister. Editor Max Harris wrote a 30-page rhapsody to explain why Malley was "one of the two giants of contemporary Australian poetry." Not until he read about it in the Sunday supplement of a Sydney newspaper did Harris realize he had been had.

Malley was the invention of Australian army Lieutenant James MacAuley and Corporal Harold Stewart. Annoyed by the decay of meaning and craft in modern poetry, they had written Malley's poems by piecing together lines taken from *The Oxford Dictionary of Quotations* and other books that happened to be handy.

A poem called "Culture and Exhibit" contained these moving lines from a U.S. report on mosquitoes:

> Swamps, marshes, barrowpits and other
> Areas of stagnant water serve
> As breeding grounds.

From another poem, these lines:

> There have been interpolations,
>   false syndromes
> Like a rivet through the hand
> Such deliberate suppressions of crisis as
> Footscray.

Footscray is a Melbourne suburb noted for the odor of its tanneries. Editor Harris reacted in the fashion of all angry penguin art and literary critics when they have been trapped into praising something worthless. He insisted that MacAuley and Stewart had unwittingly written great poetry. (References: *The New York Times*, July 3, page 6, and July 4, page 18, 1944; *Time*, July 17, 1944; *Newsweek*, July 17, 1944.)

Ten years later, Lord Dunsany, speaking at the Author's Club in London, was much applauded after he read a poem that he later revealed to be a collation of first lines from many modern poems. Modern poems are "bells of lead," Dunsany declared. "They should tinkle melodiously but usually they just klunk."

Boswell tells us that Samuel Johnson once perpetrated a similar hoax by reading aloud a poem by James Thomson. "Well, sir," said Johnson after his listener had expressed great admiration for the work, "I have omitted every other line."

15. (See page 78.) For more examples of amusing macaronic verse see Carolyn Wells' *A Nonsense Anthology* (reprinted by Dover Publications, Inc. in 1958) and *A Whimsey Anthology*, 1906, to be republished by Dover in 1961.

16. (See page 91.) Dmitri Borgmann sends me the following example of what he calls a "snowball" sentence, uttered, no doubt, by a Bombaughstic druggist. Each word has one more letter than the preceding word.

I do not know where family doctors acquired illegibly perplexing handwriting; nevertheless, extraordinary pharmaceutical intellectuality, counterbalancing indecipherability, transcendentalizes intercommunications' incomprehensibleness.

17. (See page 92.) The most familiar example in English of an emblematic poem is the mouse's tale in *Alice in Wonderland*. For other examples, by such poets as Stéphane Mallarmé, Dylan Thomas, E. E. Cummings, and Guillaume Apollinaire, consult Charles Boltenhouse's article, "Poems in the Shape of Things," *Art News Annual*, 1959. Similar to figured verse are such affectations as writing a poem about a color and printing it with ink of the same color, or writing a poem about a mirror (there is one by Christopher Morley) and printing it, like *Jabberwocky*, in reflected form.

Closely related to emblematic verse is the poem that employs special typographical effects to convey certain meanings. The following doggerel by an unknown author is an amusing example:

For a lark,
For a prank,
Ezra Shank
Walked a plank.
These bubbles mark
            O
            O
            O
            O
            O
Where Ezra sank.

18. (See page 97.) The following verse is familiar to many school children in the U.S.

YYUR
YYUB
ICUR
YY4ME

Also widely known is this bit of dialogue between customer and waitress:

FUNEX?
SVFX
FUNEM?
SVFM
OK LFMNX

And this exchange between mother and child:

ABCD goldfish?
LMNO goldfish
OSAR2 goldfish!

19. (See page 98.) Not only can a poem be made up of monosyllables, but the poem itself can be exceedingly short. In English, the record was held for many years by the following poem "On the Condition of the United States after Several Years of Prohibition":

Wet
Yet.

This was topped, however, by the New York poet Eli Siegel. His poem, "One Question," may be found in his book *Hot Afternoons*

Have Been in Montana: Poems. In a letter to the *New York Times*, November 15, 1957, Siegel says that the poem first appeared in print in the *Literary Review* of *The New York Evening Post* in the fall of 1925, and that in the early thirties he used to recite the poem at the Village Vanguard, a Manhattan night spot. I quote the lyric in full:

I.
Why?

Shorter by one letter, though inferior because it sacrifices form to political content, is this couplet titled, "Reactions to a statement by Khrushchev that the Soviet Union has no desire to meddle in the internal affairs of other nations":

O,
So?

U.S. children used to play—perhaps they still do—a game called Stinky Pinky that involves, in a way, the construction of short poems. First you state a definition, then everyone tries to answer it with two, three, or even four words that rhyme. An example of a four-word stinky pinky: What would you call a freshly shaved Beatnik holding a stuffed canary in his hand? Answer: A neat beat with a cheat tweet. Speaking in brief rhymes of this sort is said to be one of the affectations of the current (1960) Hipster.

20. (See page 119.) The close affinity of Shakespeare and the King James Bible is suggested by the following fantastic fact. The 46th word of the 46th Psalm is "shake," and the 46th word from the end of the same Psalm (ignoring the final "selah" which is not part of the Psalm) is "spear." Why 46? Because when the King James Authorized Version was completed, in 1610, Will was exactly 46 years old!

21. (See page 124.) The topic of Biblical humor is so fascinating that I battle the temptation to write here at length about it. Paul Goodman, in his wonderfully funny little play *Preface to Jonah* (in *The Facts of Life*) exploits to the full all the comic elements in the Old Testament tale of Jonah. Surely this tale is one of the funniest short-shorts ever written. It even has a punch yock in the last four words. Some verses in the King James Version acquire unintentional humor by the italicizing of certain interpolated words. Mark Twain, when he visited the Holy Land, called attention to the passage about a street in Damascus that "is *called* straight." I Kings 13:27 supplies

another example: "And he spoke to his sons saying, Saddle me the ass. And they saddled *him*." Though it has no italics, I find Proverbs 27:14 highly amusing: "He that blesseth his friend with a loud voice, rising early in the morning, it shall be counted a curse to him."

The deeper question of course is whether it is proper to say that in some sense God himself has a sense of humor. There are four references in the Old Testament to God's laughter (Psalms 2:4, 37:13, 59:8, and Proverbs 1:26), but it is a grim mirthless laughter at the fate of the wicked. We know that Jesus wept, but there is no record of his having smiled or laughed. Gilbert Chesterton's famous book of apologetics, *Orthodoxy*, closes with this startling thought:

> . . . He never restrained His anger. He flung furniture down the front steps of the Temple, and asked men how they expected to escape the damnation of Hell. Yet He restrained something. I say it with reverence; there was in that shattering personality a thread that must be called shyness. There was something that He hid from all men when He went up a mountain to pray. There was something that He covered constantly by abrupt silence or impetuous isolation. There was some one thing that was too great for God to show us when He walked upon our earth; and I have sometimes fancied that it was His mirth.

Even for the non-Christian theist, the problem remains a profound one that has been sadly neglected by most philosophers and theologians, though not by the poets. "Once I found out the secret of the universe," says a hashish eater in Lord Dunsany's *A Dreamer's Tales*. "I have forgotten what it was, but I know that the Creator does not take Creation seriously, for I remember that He sat in space with all His work in front of Him and laughed."

Some theologians feel it impious or meaningless to attribute humor to God, but nevertheless regard humor as a divine gift to mankind and one of the many avenues to faith. The following magnificent lines are from Christopher Fry's play *The Lady's Not for Burning*:

> THOMAS. . . . For God's sake, shall we laugh?
> JENNET. For what reason?
> THOMAS. For the reason of laughter, since laughter is surely
> The surest touch of genius in creation.

Would *you* ever have thought of it, I ask you,
If you had been making man, stuffing him full
Of such hopping greeds and passions that he has
To blow himself to pieces as often as he
Conveniently can manage it—would it also
Have occurred to you to make him burst himself
With such a phenomenon as cachinnation?
That same laughter, madam, is an irrelevancy
Which almost amounts to revelation.

22. (See page 156.) "For my own part," writes Boswell in his biography
of Johnson, "I think no innocent species of wit or pleasantry should
be suppressed; and that a good pun may be admitted among the
smaller excellencies of lively conversation."

Clifton Fadiman, in his essay, "Small Excellencies: A Dissertation
on Puns" (to be found in his book *Any Number Can Play*), has this
to say about the impromptu pun:

> They are the May flies of language, living for a split second,
> dying to afford a moment's small delight. Unrepeatable, they
> are less akin to literature than to the more ephemeral arts—
> pantomime, conversation, making love. They are the work, or
> rather the play, of a unique instant, and their whole effect
> flowers from the miracle of unconsciously perfect timing.

Of course the really bad puns, the outrageous ones, are (as all
admirers of early Marx brothers movies know) usually the funniest.
The laugh-provoking quality of a pun seems to be in direct proportion to its distance from the word or phrase being punned upon,
provided it is not *too* distant. *Hawaii?* I'm fine, *Honolulu*. The door's
locked; how'm I *Gunga Din?* A *Birmingham* is worth two in the
bush. *Cigarette* life if you don't weaken. Never *conscience-stricken*
before they hatch. *Shostokovitch* small by a waterfall.

An extremely rare type of multiple pun is the sentence that
perfectly echoes the sounds of another sentence, though the meanings
are different. A sterling example concerns a detective hired to locate
the missing Mr. Rhee, who had a job with *Life* magazine. When the
detective finally found Rhee in a Third Avenue bar he cried out,
"Ah, *sweet Mr. Rhee of Life*, at last I've found you!" Fadiman
attributes this to Bennett Cerf. The essay by Fadiman is a rich
source of modern puns and the best discussion of the topic I know.

23. (See page 157.) If Albert Ten Eyck Olmstead, who was a professor of Oriental history at the University of Chicago, was correct in his contention that the Gospels are Greek translations from the original Aramaic, then they may contain many excellent puns that are lost in translation. For example, the Aramaic words for gnat and camel are, respectively, *galma* and *gamla*. Christ is known to have spoken an Aramaic dialect, so there is good reason to believe that when he warned against the hypocrisy of straining out the gnat and swallowing the camel, he was intentionally playing on the words. A more familiar instance of New Testament word-play is Christ's statement to Peter that "upon this rock" (Peter meant "rock" in Greek) he would build his church.

24. (See page 157.) Excellent puns abound in the comedies of Aristophanes where they are, as in contemporary burlesque, a rich source of blue humor.

25. (See page 157.) For chapters even more pun-gent, see L. Frank Baum's *The Emerald City of Oz*, chapters 16 and 17 (in which Dorothy visits the kingdoms of Utensia and Bunnybury), and Lewis Carroll's *Alice in Wonderland*, chapters 9 and 10.

Among eminent writers, James Joyce is surely the King of Punsters. *Finnegans Wake*, as everybody knows, contains puns by the tens of thousands, in a dozen different languages including Esperanto and Eskimo. (Sample: "Nobirdy aviar soar anywing to eagle it.") The Anna Livia Plurabelle section alone is said to pun on the names of more than 500 rivers, although Max Eastman once went over this section carefully and confessed sadly that he could find no more than $3\frac{1}{2}$ rivers. "I have always been," Joyce once said in a letter, "a joyce crying in the wilderness."

Joyce's punning style has been most successfully parodied by Edmund Wilson in "The Three Limperary Cripples" (in his *Notebooks of Night*). Here is an excerpt:

> I would ravver read *This Side of Paralyzed* by F. Scotch Fitzgerald, or *Is* (¡) by hee-hee cunnings, or a transformation by Ezra Penaloosa of the lyrics of Bertran van Boren, or some delicious little art-novel de Lux about the letches of the lousure classes by the rich Mr. Joseph Hoggesheimer, with his love for the glamourous souseland and his faiblousse for lavender and old lychee, or some Lesbian bitters by Robinson Jitters, or *For Lancelot Gobbo* by Gobbineau, or I could tates a little Yeast or Prouts!

A bit less artful, in my opinion, is the parody of Joyce in chapter 17 of Peter De Vries' novel, *The Tents of Wickedness*. Two toothless crones, like the washerwomen who talk across the river in *Finnegans Wake*, converse in a public laundromat while the machines make a sound "as of all the waters washing all the shores of the weary world." A specimen follows:

> Legal Tender Is the Night. Him laying in bed drunk singing as I dropped my shift on the cold hotel room floor, Sister Carrie Me Back to old Virginibus Puerisque. It's all a welter mitty in my head, thinkin' back so fondly. For the lad it's Beth in the Afternoon. As I went walking down the street I metamorphosis.

Joyce's style has also been attempted by Jack Kerouac in some of his less sicksexfull recent efforts.

Compulsive punsters sometimes go to great lengths to set up a situation permitting them to uncork a pun. De Vries, for example, once tried (according to *Time*) to get E. B. ("Andy") White to join him and Kingsley Amis for lunch just so he could later tell his wife that he had lunch with Amis and Andy. I myself must confess that I regard as one of the highlights of my World War II Navy career, a social occasion in Madison, Wisconsin, on which I managed to introduce a seaman named Potts to Porter Butts, the head of the University of Wisconsin's student union. (After reading this in manuscript, Stephen Barr swears that a British friend of his father once invited to his home a Mr. Bottomly, Mr. Ramsbottom, Mr. Broadbeam, and Mr. Longbotham. He had the servant show them into the library where, being hostless, they had to introduce themselves.)

26. (See page 177.) Anson D. Eby, author of *Curiosities of Language* (Little Blue Book No. 1750), has written a number of pieces similar to this poem and the one which follows. I give here only the opening sentences of several that may be found in Eby's book.

> Nott met Shott. Nott shot at Shott
> and Shott shot at Nott. One was shot,
> but whether Nott shot Shott or Shott
> shot Nott could not be told. Nott should
> not have been shot. . . .

> If a knocker with a knocker
>   Knocked the knocker on the door,
> Would the knocker with the knocker
>   Knock the knocker on the floor?

> Fords ford fords with Fords, and the Ford
> Ford uses to ford fords fords fords like Fords
> Fords use to ford fords. Fords ford fords
> Ford's Fords ford, and the fords Fords ford
> are fords Fords ford, and the Ford's Fords
> ford. . . .

Because some words have identical pronunciations but variant spellings, it is possible to compose sentences that can be spoken but not written. For example: There are three ways to spell _____ —T-W-O, T-O-O, and T-O. How should the word in the blank space be written?

. (See page 184.) And a crowd of prostitutes, it has been observed (by Clifton Fadiman in his fine essay on puns, cited earlier), can be called a jam of tarts, a flourish of strumpets, an essay of Trollope's, an anthology of pro's, or a pride of loins.

. (See page 186.) It is possible to get as many as seven "thats" in succession:

> It is true for all that, that that that that that that signifies, is not the one to which I refer.

A somewhat similar sentence that, without punctuation, would be extremely difficult to understand:

> That, that is, is; that, that is not, is not; but that, that is not, is not that that is; nor is that, that is, that that is not.

Twelve "hads" can occur in a row if we assume that two type-setters, Ed and Bill, are setting the same copy. Bill interprets certain proofreading marks to mean that the words are to be printed in italics, but Ed thinks the marks mean that the words should be capitalized. Accordingly:

> Ed, where Bill had had *had had*, had had HAD HAD. *Had had* had had the editor's approval.

If we change Bill's name to Had, we can increase the "hads" to thirteen, but this seems a bit contrived.

Here is a wonderful sentence that ends with five prepositions. Junior yells downstairs to ask his father to bring up a certain book and read to him. Dad appears with the wrong book. Says Junior: "Aw, whaddya bring that thing I don't wanna be read to out of up for?"

Leigh Mercer passed on to me the following confusing sentence: How much better it is to ride in a car and think "How much better it is to ride in a car than it is to walk" than it is to walk and to think "How much better it is to ride in a car than it is to walk."

29. (See page 186.) It is nicely illustrated also by this well-known children's riddle: If you pronounced "gh" as in "tough," "o" as in "women," and "ti" as in "emotion," how would you pronounce "ghoti"? The answer is "fish." This is how James Joyce puts it in *Finnegans Wake*: "Gee each owe tea eye smells fish. That's U."

30. (See page 205.) The word "raspberry" is an excellent example of a word once available to poets for describing a girl's lips, but no longer usable because it suggests a Bronx cheer.

31. (See page 211.) Aristophanes occasionally made up long compound words for humorous effect; one in *The Ecclesiazusae*, describing the various ingredients of a dish, is 77 syllables in the original Greek. Among modern writers, James Joyce has made the most frequent use of compound words; a practice imitated by many U.S. writers, notably John Dos Passos and William Faulkner. *Finnegans Wake* contains many thousands of words compounded in subtle ways. The longest of Joyce's portmanteau words are the ten hundred-letter thunderclaps that symbolize the voice of God, the fall of man, and the fall of Finnegan.

In Hawaii, one notes with interest, there is a large fish called *ô* and a tiny one called *homomomonukunukuaguk*.

32. (See page 211.) The Welsh town of Llanfairpwllgwyngyllgogery-chwyrndrobwllllandysiliogogogoch was in the news in February, 1959, when someone stole the 20-foot long railroad station sign. The 58-letter name means "St. Mary's Church in a hollow of white hazel close to a rapid whirlpool and St. Tysilio's Church, fronting the rocky isle of Gogo." Natives call the town Llanfair unless a tourist badgers them into pronouncing the full name.

In the United States, the longest place name is *Chargoggagoggman-chauggagoggchaubunagungamaugg*, a lake in south-central Massachusetts. Dmitri Borgmann informs me that it is listed in current editions of the Rand McNally *Cosmopolitan World Atlas*. It has 45 letters.

The longest dictionary word, Mr. Borgmann says, is also 45 letters: *pneumonoultramicroscopicsilicovolcanokoniosis*. It is a lung disease caused by inhaling quartz dust, and may be found listed in the Addenda section of *Webster's* unabridged. This defeats by 11 letters the word *pseudo-antidisestablishmentarianism* which long held the record.

Chemical substances often have jaw-breaking names, as witnessed by the following limerick:

> Said the chemist: "I'll take some dimethyloxi-
> midomesoralamide
> And I'll add just a dash of dimethylamidoazoben-
> saldehyde;
> But if these won't mix,
> I'll just have to fix
> Up a big dose of trisodiumpholoroglucintricarboxy-
> cide.

3. (See page 223.) Lewis Carroll, not surprisingly, liked to write prose letters to his "child-friends" that turned out, on closer inspection, to be in rhyme. The prose prologue to his poem "Hiawatha's Photographing" (page 856 of *The Complete Works of Lewis Carroll*, a Modern Library anthology of *some* of Carroll's works) has the same tom-tom beat as the poem, though most readers fail to notice it.

James Branch Cabell amused himself by concealing poems in the prose text of his fantasies. An eccentric but skillfully constructed sonnet, with internal rhymes and each line ending in "love," appears in chapter 14 of *Jurgen*; and a lengthy poem in hexameters, on the fleeting nature of first love, is to be found in *Figures of Earth*. Here is a portion of the latter poem:

> This is the cry of all husbands that now or may
> be hereafter,—"What has become of the girl that I
> married? and how should I rightly deal with this woman
> whom somehow time has involved in my doings? Love,
> of a sort, now I have for her, but not the love that
> was yesterday's . . ."

In 1942, when I was a publicity writer for the University of Chicago, I wrote a press release about an article that had appeared in the University's *Journal of Geology*. This article explained for the first time the origin of large, oval-shaped mounds—called Mima mounds after the name of the prairie in western Washington where the mounds are particularly numerous. Evidently a bored rewrite man on *The Chicago Tribune* found the release amusing because this is how it appeared in the *Tribune* on February 11, 1942:

GOPHERS, LONG AGO, BUILT MIMA MOUNDS, YOU KNOW

Geologists, with furrowed brow, most often only ponder how the Mima mounds of Washington upon the prairies were begun. Sometimes they also wonder who would build the Mimas; leave no clue. The *Journal of Geology* explains, today, the mystery. The gophers burrowed long ago and built the mounds, new studies show. Forget the red man, and the quake, and let the the gophers credit take.

34. (See page 225.) Thomas Wolfe had the same ability to write purple passages of highly metric prose. In 1945 a volume of Wolfe selections, the lines partitioned in the form of blank verse, was edited by J. S. Barnes and published under the title, *A Stone, a Leaf, a Door*.

35. (See page 228.) This famous bit of accidental verse will be found on page 44 of the first edition (1819) of William Whewell's *An Elementary Treatise on Mechanics*. Whewell first learned of it when Professor Sedgwick, of the Cambridge geology department, recited it in an after-dinner speech. Whewell, who did not think it funny, promptly altered the lines in the next edition of his book to eliminate the poem. Ironically, Whewell published two books of serious poetry but this is the only "poem" by him that is remembered today. For the full story, see Burton Stevenson's *Famous Single Poems*, 1923, page 393.

James Thurber, in a fine article on "The Quality of Mirth" (*The New York Times*, Sunday theatrical section, February 21, 1960) unintentionally lapsed into verse in his final sentence. I seldom look for such things, but this happened to catch my ear. Here is Thurber's sentence, without a word altered:

> If they are right and we are wrong,
> I shall return to the dignity
> Of the printed page, where it may be
> That I belong.

6. (See page 230.) Bombaugh does not discuss the limerick, which since his time has become the chief vehicle for anonymously written poetic humor, especially off-color humor. Edward Lear popularized an anemic form of nonsense limerick, in which the last line more or less repeated the first line, but it was soon discovered that the form lent itself beautifully to a punch ending. Thousands of blue limericks sprang up in English-speaking countries; in many instances, little masterpieces of unprintable wit. Norman Douglas' book, *Some Limericks*, was for decades the outstanding reference on the blue limerick, but now is superseded by Gershon Legman's monumental annotated and cross-referenced scholarly study, *The Limerick*. This amazing anthology was printed in Switzerland (in English) a few years ago and can only be obtained, alas, by making a trip to Valbonne, France, and buying a copy from the legendary Legman himself.

It is worthy of note that the Reverend Patrick Brontë, father of the Brontë sisters, invented that upsetting type of limerick in which the last line fails miserably to rhyme. Gilbert Chesterton calls attention to this (in an essay on "Bad Poetry" in *All I Survey*) and quotes two examples from memory. One of them goes:

> Religion makes beauty enchanting,
> And even where beauty is wanting,
> > The temper and mind,
> > Religion-refined,
> Will shine through the veil with sweet lustre.

"If you read much of it," Chesterton comments, "you will reach a state of mind in which, even though you know the jolt is coming, you can hardly forbear to scream . . ."

The following limerick, in which none of the lines rhyme, is attributed to W. S. Gilbert:

> There was an old man of St. Bees,
> Who was stung in the arm by a wasp.
> > When asked, "Does it hurt?"
> > He replied, "No it doesn't—
> I'm so glad that it wasn't a hornet."

I have seen adults laugh themselves silly over this limerick, but its introduction must be carefully timed. After several dozen limericks have been recited, each bluer than the last, and an alcoholic air of libidinous expectancy pervades the party, you stand up, clear your throat, and deliver the above lines.

Chesterton thought that the Reverend Brontë's poetry belonged in *The Stuffed Owl*, that amazing anthology of bad verse edited by D. B. Wyndham Lewis and Charles Lee and published in 1930. The book deserves mention here because bad poetry can, if it is bad enough, be very funny indeed. The book includes some of the best efforts of Julia Moore who, more than any other native poet, had a wonderful knack of choosing just the wrong word. (Walter Blair edited a collection of her poems in 1928, titled *The Sweet Singer of Michigan*.) It also contains, however, some fine specimens by such top-caliber rhymsters as Keats, Byron, Wordsworth, Poe and Tennyson.

Back to limericks. Here are two classics that we must not fail to pass on:

> There was a young man of Japan
> Whose limericks never would scan.
> > When someone asked why
> > He replied with a sigh,
> "It's because I always try to get as many words
> > into the last line as I possibly can."

> Another young poet in China
> Had a feeling for rhythm much fina.
> > His limericks tend
> > To come to an end
> Quite suddenly.

A splendid essay on the limerick will be found in Clifton Fadiman's book *Any Number Can Play*, followed by an equally delightful piece on the clerihew. The clerihew is named after its inventor, Edmund Clerihew Bentley, best known as the author of *Trent's Last Case* and the friend to whom Chesterton dedicated his immortal fantasy, *The Man Who Was Thursday*. The clerihew has become a popular light verse form in England, second only to the limerick. I append two examples:

Bentley's best-known effort:

> Sir Christopher Wren
> Said, "I am going to dine with some men.
> If anybody calls
> Say I'm designing St. Paul's."

And a fine clerihew by Fadiman:

> Hegel
> Never ate a bagel.
> Conversely, few Hegelians
> Are to be found among Lindy's bagelians.

7. (See page 259.) So many great writers have made careless slips that one wonders if a certain amount of carelessness may not be the rule rather than the exception for literary masterpieces. Cervantes had Sancho Panza sell his ass, then later in the tale Sancho is suddenly riding him again. Defoe's Robinson Crusoe swims nude to the wreckage of a ship, finds some biscuits on the ship, and sticks them in his pockets. In *War and Peace*, Prince Andrei has a silver icon that later becomes gold, and Natasha is 17 in 1805 but four years later she is 24. Watson's memory slips are so numerous that they have provided the Baker Street Irregulars with one of their happiest occupations—devising explanations for them. For other examples, see "Mistakes of Authors" in William S. Walsh's *Handy-Book of Literary Curiosities*.

8. (See page 269.) The subject of literary hoaxes is much too vast and generally unfunny to document here with any completeness. The interested reader should consult Curtis MacDougall's book *Hoaxes*, reissued by Dover in 1958. H. L. Mencken's magnificent history of the bathtub is, I suppose, the most successful spoof in American letters (the best discussion of it is an article in, of all places, *The Saturday Evening Post*, November 13, 1943). Other notable examples of United States works purporting to be factual but actually hoaxes (or frauds, or both) are:

> *The Memoirs of Li Hung Chang*, William Mannix, 1913.
> *Trader Horn*, Etheldreda Lewis, 1927.
> *The Cradle of the Deep*, Joan Lowell, 1929.
> *Behind the Flying Saucers*, Frank Skully, 1951.
> *The Man Who Wouldn't Talk*, Quentin Reynolds, 1953.

The last book, published by Random House and condensed by *Readers Digest*, was an account of the cloak-and-dagger experiences of George DuPre, a Canadian businessman who apparently had served as an intelligence agent in France during World War II. Not until a third printing had been ordered was it discovered that DuPre had made up the whole story. DuPre was active in the

Canadian Boy Scouts and had been generously turning over his royalties to them.

A recent book hoax in the United States involves the novel, *I, Libertine*, still selling in paperbacks. Jean Shepherd, an all-night disk-jockey in Manhattan, kept talking about a non-existent historical novel called *I, Libertine* until so many people began asking for it in bookstores that Ballantine decided to publish such a book. It was written by Theodore Sturgeon, the well-known science-fiction author, under the pseudonym of Frederick R. Ewing, and published in 1956 in both hard and soft covers.

The most amusing of United States poetry hoaxes was the Spectrist school, founded in 1916 by Witter Bynner and Arthur Ficke. These two wags wrote meaningless poems under the names of Anne Knish and Emmanuel Morgan that were published in various literary magazines and finally in a book called *Spectra*, now prized by collectors of such things. Critics took the work seriously and most of them praised it. Vincent Starrett, who wrote an amusing article about the hoax in *Coronet*, February, 1939, fondly remembers this line from one of the poems: "The liquor of her laughter and the lacquer of her limbs."

Rabelais liked to refer to the books of non-existent authors, and many recent novelists have indulged in the same whimsy. One thinks first of J. K. Huysmans, Norman Douglas, and James Branch Cabell. Cabell's favorite authority, that distinguished German scholar, Gottfried Johannes Bülg, is the subject of an amusing essay by Ben Ray Redman ("Bülg the Forgotten," reprinted in *A Round-Table in Poictesme*, edited by Don Bregenzer and Samuel Loveman, 1924). *From the Hidden Way*, which purported to be a translation by Cabell of seventy-five poems by medieval French and Italian poets, hornswoggled a great many reviewers when it was published in 1916. More than one reviewer pretended to be familiar with the originals.

Six imaginary books were perceptively reviewed by Gerald Johnson in *The New York Times Book Review*, January 2, 1949. I suppose there are other instances of the imaginary book review, but these are the only ones that have come to my notice. Readers interested in the topic of phony book titles should consult the definitive reference, *Browsing Through Obfuscaland*, by Professor Kurt P. Mudd, 1953.

Biographies of non-existent persons are a bit rarer than titles of non-existent books. Some unknown practical joker sent at least 84 imaginary biographies to the editors of Appleton's *Cyclopedia of American Biography* where they appeared in the 1886 and 1888 editions. Nobody noticed it until 1919 when a bibliographer discovered fourteen of them. Seventy more were found by 1936 and there may be others still undetected. *Biographical Memoirs of Extraordinary Painters*, 1780, by William Beckford includes details about the lives of such ghost painters as Blunderbussian of Venice, Herr Sucrewasser of Vienna, Watersouchy of Amsterdam, Og of Bason and óthers.

Some amusing fake biographies have been written by Noel Coward. In his *Terribly Intimate Portraits*, published in 1922, you can read all about the lives of Julie de Poopinac, E. Maxwell Snurge, Jabez Puffwater, and other unusual personages. In 1932 Coward edited an anthology called *Spangled Unicorn* that includes, in addition to specimens of verse by ten widely unknown poets, their photographs and biographical sketches. Crispin Pither, Jane Southerby Danks, and Tao Lang Pee are among the poets here immortalized. In 1925 Coward also edited *Chelsea Buns*, a collection of poems by Hernia Whittlebot, with an introduction (in French) by Gaspard Pustontin.

Authors occasionally slip a non-existent word into what otherwise is an orthodox text. Lord Dunsany, for example, in his story "The Bird of the Difficult Eye," writes that "beasts prowling the blackness *gluttered* at Neepy Thang." (my italics). Faulkner has the same habit of making up words—e.g., *toyment, impedeless, mamalinity*—but I find most of them dull and hardly worth inventing.

Chapter 4 of Mark Twain's *A Double Barrelled Detective Story* (a satire on Sherlock Holmes) opens with the following descriptive paragraph:

> It was a crisp and spicy morning in early October. The lilacs and laburnums, lit with the glory-fires of autumn, hung burning and flashing in the upper air, a fairy bridge provided by kind Nature for the wingless wild things that have their homes in the tree-tops and would visit together; the larch and the pomegranate flung their purple and yellow flames in brilliant broad splashes along the slanting sweep of the woodland; the sensuous fragrance of innumerable deciduous flowers rose upon the swooning atmosphere; far in the empty sky a solitary oesophagus slept upon motionless wing; everywhere brooded stillness, serenity, and the peace of God.

"Oesophagus" isn't exactly a made-up word, but of course there is no bird of that name. Very few readers, Twain later recalled, noticed anything wrong with the passage.

The only dictionary of invented words that I have seen, aside from dictionaries of artificial languages, is *Burgess Unabridged: A New Dictionary of Words You Have Always Needed*, by Gelett Burgess (of purple cow fame), 1914. Among the one hundred new words defined by Burgess, only "blurb" has entered the language. The words "bromide," and "goop" (meaning respectively a cliché and an ill-behaved person) were also coined by Burgess, but they appear in other books. (Actually, a bromide, according to Burgess' original definition, is the utterer of a "bromidiom.") Burgess defines a blurb as "praise for one's self, inspired laudation," but now it has come to refer to short notes of praise on dust jackets of books and to other advertising copy. The following poem by Burgess appears in the Introduction to his *Dictionary*, but you will have to consult the book to find out what it means:

When vorianders seek to huzzlecoo,
　　When jurpid splooch or vilpous drillig bores,
When cowcats kipe, or moobles wog, or you
　　Machizzled are by yowfs or xenogores,

Remember Burgess Unabridged, and think,
　　How quisty is his culpid yod and yab!
No fidgeltick, with goigsome iobink,
　　No varmic orobaldity—his gab!

No more tintiddling slubs, like fidgelticks,
　　Rizgidgeting your speech, shall lallify;
But your jujasm, like vorgid gollohix,
　　Shall all your woxy meem golobrify!

This is perhaps the most appropriate spot for mentioning the art of double-talk which, in one of its variants, consists of inserting nonsense words into one's conversation, but so subtly that the listener thinks he failed to hear correctly or perhaps just didn't quite get the meaning of what was said. The technique reached its height in the United States during the forties (its Hollywood popularity provides an amusing scene in F. Scott Fitzgerald's *The Last Tycoon*). The burlesque of a Hitler speech by Chaplin in *The Great Dictator* was a superb example of German double-talk.

Scat singing is closely related, though here there is seldom an attempt to deceive the listener. Similar also are the neologisms of schizophrenics and the glossolalia of religious hysterics, or what in Christianity is called the Unknown Tongue. It was quite respectable in the early churches (Saint Paul could speak the "tongue of angels") but now is confined to the Pentecostal or Holiness sects and a few other fringe movements of Protestant fundamentalism. References to modern double-talk include an article by George Frazier in *Life*, July 6, 1943; a chapter in H. Allen Smith's *The Compleat Practical Joker*; and several privately printed booklets by Wallace Lee, a skillful double-talker who lives in Durham, North Carolina.

. (See page 274.) George Psalmanazar was one of the most brazen and convincing frauds of all time. Posing as a cannibal from Formosa who had been converted to Christianity, he was lionized by British society and sent to Oxford by the Bishop of London to complete his Christian education so that he could return to Formosa as a missionary. He published several books, including a *Historical and Geographical Description of Formosa* (1704) that was entirely imaginary (he had never been there). He died in 1763 and his memoirs were published a year later. To this day his real name and place and date of birth are not known. An amusing chapter on him appears in William Targ's *Carousel for Bibliographers*.

. (See page 288.) Whispering galleries are rooms with ellipsoidal ceilings. If a sound originates close to one of the two foci of the ellipsoid, all the sound waves striking the ceiling will be reflected to the other focus. In the United States the most famous whispering gallery is in the Capitol at Washington. No guided tour is complete without a demonstration. Less well-known are the echo properties of a small square-shaped area in front of the Oyster Bar on the lower level of Grand Central Station in New York. If two persons stand at diagonally opposite corners they can converse easily in whispers even though the area may be bustling and noisy.

. (See page 290.) The liar paradox wears many disguises. Here is a neat variation proposed by the English mathematician P. E. B. Jourdain (see his "Tales with Philosophical Morals," *Open Court*, Vol. 27, 1913, pages 310–15). On one side of a card print:

The sentence on the other side of this card is true.

On the card's opposite side print:

The sentence on the other side of this card is false.

Modern logicians have a clever dodge that enables them to sidestep this sort of thing. They refuse to permit a logical language to talk about the truth of its own statements. Such talk must occur in a higher language called a "metalanguage." Paradoxes in the meta-language must in turn be avoided by assuming a still higher meta-language. This hierarchy of languages is infinite, but logicians prefer being stuck with it to being stuck with the paradoxes.

Paul's Epistle to Titus, 1:12–13, reads as follows: "One of them-selves, even a prophet of their own, said, The Cretians are always liars, evil beasts, slow bellies. This witness is true." Apparently Paul was not aware of the logical paradox in what he was saying.

42. (See page 294.) This doggerel is often attributed to the American puzzlist Sam Loyd because it appears, in slightly altered form, in Loyd's famous *Cyclopedia of Puzzles*. The answer is that the men were musicians.

43. (See page 297.) A thick book could be written about the hundreds of ways that 666 has been identified with various individuals, organizations, movements, and countries, but the topic is such a dreary one, and calls to mind so much human folly, that I limit myself to one recent example. If we add up the numerical values of the six letters in *Hitler* (counting A as 100, B as 101, C as 102, and so on), by Lucifer! they total exactly 666! Readers interested in pursuing the topic further will find much beastial material in the following references: *A Budget of Paradoxes*, by Augustus De Morgan, Dover, 1954, Vol. 2, pages 218–40; *Numerology*, by Eric Temple Bell, Williams and Wilkins, 1933; and my column on "Mathematical Games" in *Scientific American*, January, 1960.

44. (See page 310.) Stephen Barr of Woodstock, N.Y., author of many a fine mystery story and science-fiction yarn, is responsible for the following rhymes:

> The wicked shades
> All go to Hades,
> But not there gone
> Is Hermione.
> She sings, we hope,
> With Calliope,
> Under a proscenium
> Resembling the Atheneum.

To read correctly Barr's second effort, you must understand that Klee is pronounced "Klay" and Kley is pronounced "Klai."

> Paul Klee and Heinrich Kley
> —neither one of them worked in clay—
> Each would say, "Will any one buy
> What I draw with glee?" But who can weigh
> The merits of different *Träumerei?*
> "Hey!" cried Kley, "Do you know what they
> Say about me?" And Klee said, "Hi!
> Just look at *my* sky! Peculiar, eh?"
>
> Envoi:
> Prints (of both) can be had today:
> Those of Klee come rather high,
> While those by Kley are slightly fey—
> Each in his way may last for aye.

In *The Adventures of Huckleberry Finn*, chapter 17, Mark Twain tells the sad story of a young girl who enjoyed composing poetic tributes whenever someone in the community died, and who herself "pined away" after failing to find a rhyme for a deceased person named Whistler. Her "Ode to Stephen Dowling Botts" (who had been drowned in a well) includes this touching stanza:

> Despised love struck not with woe
>   That head of curly knots,
> Nor stomach troubles laid him low,
>   Young Stephen Dowling Botts.

INDEX.

371

A CATALOGUE OF SELECTED DOVER BOOKS
IN ALL FIELDS OF INTEREST

A CATALOGUE OF SELECTED DOVER
BOOKS IN ALL FIELDS OF INTEREST

CONDITIONED REFLEXES, Ivan P. Pavlov. Full translation of most complete statement of Pavlov's work; cerebral damage, conditioned reflex, experiments with dogs, sleep, similar topics of great importance. 430pp. 5⅜ x 8½.   60614-7 Pa. $4.50

NOTES ON NURSING: WHAT IT IS, AND WHAT IT IS NOT, Florence Nightingale. Outspoken writings by founder of modern nursing. When first published (1860) it played an important role in much needed revolution in nursing. Still stimulating. 140pp. 5⅜ x 8½.   22340-X Pa. $3.00

HARTER'S PICTURE ARCHIVE FOR COLLAGE AND ILLUSTRATION, Jim Harter. Over 300 authentic, rare 19th-century engravings selected by noted collagist for artists, designers, decoupeurs, etc. Machines, people, animals, etc., printed one side of page. 25 scene plates for backgrounds. 6 collages by Harter, Satty, Singer, Evans. Introduction. 192pp. 8⅞ x 11¾.   23659-5 Pa. $5.00

MANUAL OF TRADITIONAL WOOD CARVING, edited by Paul N. Hasluck. Possibly the best book in English on the craft of wood carving. Practical instructions, along with 1,146 working drawings and photographic illustrations. Formerly titled *Cassell's Wood Carving*. 576pp. 6½ x 9¼.
23489-4 Pa. $7.95

THE PRINCIPLES AND PRACTICE OF HAND OR SIMPLE TURNING, John Jacob Holtzapffel. Full coverage of basic lathe techniques—history and development, special apparatus, softwood turning, hardwood turning, metal turning. Many projects—billiard ball, works formed within a sphere, egg cups, ash trays, vases, jardiniers, others—included. 1881 edition. 800 illustrations. 592pp. 6⅛ x 9¼.   23365-0 Clothbd. $15.00

THE JOY OF HANDWEAVING, Osma Tod. Only book you need for hand weaving. Fundamentals, threads, weaves, plus numerous projects for small board-loom, two-harness, tapestry, laid-in, four-harness weaving and more. Over 160 illustrations. 2nd revised edition. 352pp. 6½ x 9¼.
23458-4 Pa. $6.00

THE BOOK OF WOOD CARVING, Charles Marshall Sayers. Still finest book for beginning student in wood sculpture. Noted teacher, craftsman discusses fundamentals, technique; gives 34 designs, over 34 projects for panels, bookends, mirrors, etc. "Absolutely first-rate"—E. J. Tangerman. 33 photos. 118pp. 7¾ x 10⅝.   23654-4 Pa. $3.50

THE SENSE OF BEAUTY, George Santayana. Masterfully written discussion of nature of beauty, materials of beauty, form, expression; art, literature, social sciences all involved. 168pp. 5⅜ x 8½.   20238-0 Pa. $3.00

ON THE IMPROVEMENT OF THE UNDERSTANDING, Benedict Spinoza. Also contains *Ethics, Correspondence,* all in excellent R. Elwes translation. Basic works on entry to philosophy, pantheism, exchange of ideas with great contemporaries. 402pp. 5⅜ x 8½.   20250-X Pa. $4.50

THE TRAGIC SENSE OF LIFE, Miguel de Unamuno. Acknowledged masterpiece of existential literature, one of most important books of 20th century. Introduction by Madariaga. 367pp. 5⅜ x 8½.
20257-7 Pa. $4.50

THE GUIDE FOR THE PERPLEXED, Moses Maimonides. Great classic of medieval Judaism attempts to reconcile revealed religion (Pentateuch, commentaries) with Aristotelian philosophy. Important historically, still relevant in problems. Unabridged Friedlander translation. Total of 473pp. 5⅜ x 8½.   20351-4 Pa. $6.00

THE I CHING (THE BOOK OF CHANGES), translated by James Legge. Complete translation of basic text plus appendices by Confucius, and Chinese commentary of most penetrating divination manual ever prepared. Indispensable to study of early Oriental civilizations, to modern inquiring reader. 448pp. 5⅜ x 8½.   21062-6 Pa. $5.00

THE EGYPTIAN BOOK OF THE DEAD, E. A. Wallis Budge. Complete reproduction of Ani's papyrus, finest ever found. Full hieroglyphic text, interlinear transliteration, word for word translation, smooth translation. Basic work, for Egyptology, for modern study of psychic matters. Total of 533pp. 6½ x 9¼. (Available in U.S. only)   21866-X Pa. $5.95

THE GODS OF THE EGYPTIANS, E. A. Wallis Budge. Never excelled for richness, fullness: all gods, goddesses, demons, mythical figures of Ancient Egypt; their legends, rites, incarnations, variations, powers, etc. Many hieroglyphic texts cited. Over 225 illustrations, plus 6 color plates. Total of 988pp. 6⅛ x 9¼. (Available in U.S. only)
22055-9, 22056-7 Pa., Two-vol. set $16.00

THE STANDARD BOOK OF QUILT MAKING AND COLLECTING, Marguerite Ickis. Full information, full-sized patterns for making 46 traditional quilts, also 150 other patterns. Quilted cloths, lame, satin quilts, etc. 483 illustrations. 273pp. 6⅞ x 9⅝.   20582-7 Pa. $4.95

CORAL GARDENS AND THEIR MAGIC, Bronsilaw Malinowski. Classic study of the methods of tilling the soil and of agricultural rites in the Trobriand Islands of Melanesia. Author is one of the most important figures field of modern social anthropology. 143 illustrations. Indexes. of text. 5⅝ x 8¼. (Available in U.S. only)
23597-1

A MAYA GRAMMAR, Alfred M. Tozzer. Practical, useful English-language grammar by the Harvard anthropologist who was one of the three greatest American scholars in the area of Maya culture. Phonetics, grammatical processes, syntax, more. 301pp. 5⅜ x 8½. 23465-7 Pa. $4.00

THE JOURNAL OF HENRY D. THOREAU, edited by Bradford Torrey, F. H. Allen. Complete reprinting of 14 volumes, 1837-61, over two million words; the sourcebooks for *Walden*, etc. Definitive. All original sketches, plus 75 photographs. Introduction by Walter Harding. Total of 1804pp. 8½ x 12¼. 20312-3, 20313-1 Clothbd., Two-vol. set $70.00

CLASSIC GHOST STORIES, Charles Dickens and others. 18 wonderful stories you've wanted to reread: "The Monkey's Paw," "The House and the Brain," "The Upper Berth," "The Signalman," "Dracula's Guest," "The Tapestried Chamber," etc. Dickens, Scott, Mary Shelley, Stoker, etc. 330pp. 5⅜ x 8½. 20735-8 Pa. $4.50

SEVEN SCIENCE FICTION NOVELS, H. G. Wells. Full novels. *First Men in the Moon, Island of Dr. Moreau, War of the Worlds, Food of the Gods, Invisible Man, Time Machine, In the Days of the Comet.* A basic science-fiction library. 1015pp. 5⅜ x 8½. (Available in U.S. only) 20264-X Clothbd. $8.95

ARMADALE, Wilkie Collins. Third great mystery novel by the author of *The Woman in White* and *The Moonstone.* Ingeniously plotted narrative shows an exceptional command of character, incident and mood. Original magazine version with 40 illustrations. 597pp. 5⅜ x 8½. 23429-0 Pa. $6.00

MASTERS OF MYSTERY, H. Douglas Thomson. The first book in English (1931) devoted to history and aesthetics of detective story. Poe, Doyle, LeFanu, Dickens, many others, up to 1930. New introduction and notes by E. F. Bleiler. 288pp. 5⅜ x 8½. (Available in U.S. only) 23606-4 Pa. $4.00

FLATLAND, E. A. Abbott. Science-fiction classic explores life of 2-D being in 3-D world. Read also as introduction to thought about hyperspace. Introduction by Banesh Hoffmann. 16 illustrations. 103pp. 5⅜ x 8½. 20001-9 Pa. $2.00

THREE SUPERNATURAL NOVELS OF THE VICTORIAN PERIOD, edited, with an introduction, by E. F. Bleiler. Reprinted complete and unabridged, three great classics of the supernatural: *The Haunted Hotel* by Wilkie Collins, *The Haunted House at Latchford* by Mrs. J. H. Riddell, and *The Lost Stradivarius* by J. Meade Falkner. 325pp. 5⅜ x 8½. 22571-2 Pa. $4.00

AYESHA: THE RETURN OF "SHE," H. Rider Haggard. Virtuoso sequel featuring the great mythic creation, Ayesha, in an adventure that is fully as good as the first book, *She.* Original magazine version, with 47 original illustrations by Maurice Greiffenhagen. 189pp. 6½ x 9¼. 23649-8 Pa. $3.50

THE DEPRESSION YEARS AS PHOTOGRAPHED BY ARTHUR ROTH-STEIN, Arthur Rothstein. First collection devoted entirely to the work of outstanding 1930s photographer: famous dust storm photo, ragged children, unemployed, etc. 120 photographs. Captions. 119pp. 9¼ x 10¾.
23590-4 Pa. $5.00

CAMERA WORK: A PICTORIAL GUIDE, Alfred Stieglitz. All 559 illustrations and plates from the most important periodical in the history of art photography, Camera Work (1903-17). Presented four to a page, reduced in size but still clear, in strict chronological order, with complete captions. Three indexes. Glossary. Bibliography. 176pp. 8⅜ x 11¼.
23591-2 Pa. $6.95

ALVIN LANGDON COBURN, PHOTOGRAPHER, Alvin L. Coburn. Revealing autobiography by one of greatest photographers of 20th century gives insider's version of Photo-Secession, plus comments on his own work. 77 photographs by Coburn. Edited by Helmut and Alison Gernsheim. 160pp. 8⅛ x 11.
23685-4 Pa. $6.00

NEW YORK IN THE FORTIES, Andreas Feininger. 162 brilliant photographs by the well-known photographer, formerly with Life magazine, show commuters, shoppers, Times Square at night, Harlem nightclub, Lower East Side, etc. Introduction and full captions by John von Hartz. 181pp. 9¼ x 10¾.
23585-8 Pa. $6.95

GREAT NEWS PHOTOS AND THE STORIES BEHIND THEM, John Faber. Dramatic volume of 140 great news photos, 1855 through 1976, and revealing stories behind them, with both historical and technical information. Hindenburg disaster, shooting of Oswald, nomination of Jimmy Carter, etc. 160pp. 8¼ x 11.
23667-6 Pa. $5.00

THE ART OF THE CINEMATOGRAPHER, Leonard Maltin. Survey of American cinematography history and anecdotal interviews with 5 masters—Arthur Miller, Hal Mohr, Hal Rosson, Lucien Ballard, and Conrad Hall. Very large selection of behind-the-scenes production photos. 105 photographs. Filmographies. Index. Originally Behind the Camera. 144pp. 8¼ x 11.
23686-2 Pa. $5.00

DESIGNS FOR THE THREE-CORNERED HAT (LE TRICORNE), Pablo Picasso. 32 fabulously rare drawings—including 31 color illustrations of costumes and accessories—for 1919 production of famous ballet. Edited by Parmenia Migel, who has written new introduction. 48pp. 9⅜ x 12¼. (Available in U.S. only)
23709-5 Pa. $5.00

NOTES OF A FILM DIRECTOR, Sergei Eisenstein. Greatest Russian filmmaker explains montage, making of Alexander Nevsky, aesthetics; comments on self, associates, great rivals (Chaplin), similar material. 78 illustrations. 240pp. 5⅜ x 8½.
22392-2 Pa. $4.50

AN AUTOBIOGRAPHY, Margaret Sanger. Exciting personal account of hard-fought battle for woman's right to birth control, against prejudice, church, law. Foremost feminist document. 504pp. 5⅜ x 8½.
20470-7 Pa. $5.50

MY BONDAGE AND MY FREEDOM, Frederick Douglass. Born as a slave, Douglass became outspoken force in antislavery movement. The best of Douglass's autobiographies. Graphic description of slave life. Introduction by P. Foner. 464pp. 5⅜ x 8½. 22457-0 Pa. $5.50

LIVING MY LIFE, Emma Goldman. Candid, no holds barred account by foremost American anarchist: her own life, anarchist movement, famous contemporaries, ideas and their impact. Struggles and confrontations in America, plus deportation to U.S.S.R. Shocking inside account of persecution of anarchists under Lenin. 13 plates. Total of 944pp. 5⅜ x 8½.
22543-7, 22544-5 Pa., Two-vol. set $12.00

LETTERS AND NOTES ON THE MANNERS, CUSTOMS AND CONDITIONS OF THE NORTH AMERICAN INDIANS, George Catlin. Classic account of life among Plains Indians: ceremonies, hunt, warfare, etc. Dover edition reproduces for first time all original paintings. 312 plates. 572pp. of text. 6⅛ x 9¼. 22118-0, 22119-9 Pa.. Two-vol. set $12.00

THE MAYA AND THEIR NEIGHBORS, edited by Clarence L. Hay, others. Synoptic view of Maya civilization in broadest sense, together with Northern, Southern neighbors. Integrates much background, valuable detail not elsewhere. Prepared by greatest scholars: Kroeber, Morley, Thompson, Spinden, Vaillant, many others. Sometimes called Tozzer Memorial Volume. 60 illustrations, linguistic map. 634pp. 5⅜ x 8½.
23510-6 Pa. $10.00

HANDBOOK OF THE INDIANS OF CALIFORNIA, A. L. Kroeber. Foremost American anthropologist offers complete ethnographic study of each group. Monumental classic. 459 illustrations, maps. 995pp. 5⅜ x 8½.
23368-5 Pa. $13.00

SHAKTI AND SHAKTA, Arthur Avalon. First book to give clear, cohesive analysis of Shakta doctrine, Shakta ritual and Kundalini Shakti (yoga). Important work by one of world's foremost students of Shaktic and Tantric thought. 732pp. 5⅜ x 8½. (Available in U.S. only)
23645-5 Pa. $7.95

AN INTRODUCTION TO THE STUDY OF THE MAYA HIEROGLYPHS, Syvanus Griswold Morley. Classic study by one of the truly great figures in hieroglyph research. Still the best introduction for the student for reading Maya hieroglyphs. New introduction by J. Eric S. Thompson. 117 illustrations. 284pp. 5⅜ x 8½. 23108-9 Pa. $4.00

A STUDY OF MAYA ART, Herbert J. Spinden. Landmark classic interprets Maya symbolism, estimates styles, covers ceramics, architecture, murals, stone carvings as artforms. Still a basic book in area. New introduction by J. Eric Thompson. Over 750 illustrations. 341pp. 8⅜ x 11¼.
21235-1 Pa. $6.95

HOUSEHOLD STORIES BY THE BROTHERS GRIMM. All the great Grimm stories: "Rumpelstiltskin," "Snow White," "Hansel and Gretel," etc., with 114 illustrations by Walter Crane. 269pp. 5⅜ x 8½.
21080-4 Pa. $3.50

SLEEPING BEAUTY, illustrated by Arthur Rackham. Perhaps the fullest, most delightful version ever, told by C. S. Evans. Rackham's best work. 49 illustrations. 110pp. 7⅞ x 10¾.
22756-1 Pa. $2.50

AMERICAN FAIRY TALES, L. Frank Baum. Young cowboy lassoes Father Time; dummy in Mr. Floman's department store window comes to life; and 10 other fairy tales. 41 illustrations by N. P. Hall, Harry Kennedy, Ike Morgan, and Ralph Gardner. 209pp. 5⅜ x 8½.
23643-9 Pa. $3.00

THE WONDERFUL WIZARD OF OZ, L. Frank Baum. Facsimile in full color of America's finest children's classic. Introduction by Martin Gardner. 143 illustrations by W. W. Denslow. 267pp. 5⅜ x 8½.
20691-2 Pa. $3.50

THE TALE OF PETER RABBIT, Beatrix Potter. The inimitable Peter's terrifying adventure in Mr. McGregor's garden, with all 27 wonderful, full-color Potter illustrations. 55pp. 4¼ x 5½. (Available in U.S. only)
22827-4 Pa. $1.25

THE STORY OF KING ARTHUR AND HIS KNIGHTS, Howard Pyle. Finest children's version of life of King Arthur. 48 illustrations by Pyle. 131pp. 6⅛ x 9¼.
21445-1 Pa. $4.95

CARUSO'S CARICATURES, Enrico Caruso. Great tenor's remarkable caricatures of self, fellow musicians, composers, others. Toscanini, Puccini, Farrar, etc. Impish, cutting, insightful. 473 illustrations. Preface by M. Sisca. 217pp. 8⅜ x 11¼.
23528-9 Pa. $6.95

PERSONAL NARRATIVE OF A PILGRIMAGE TO ALMADINAH AND MECCAH, Richard Burton. Great travel classic by remarkably colorful personality. Burton, disguised as a Moroccan, visited sacred shrines of Islam, narrowly escaping death. Wonderful observations of Islamic life, customs, personalities. 47 illustrations. Total of 959pp. 5⅜ x 8½.
21217-3, 21218-1 Pa., Two-vol. set $12.00

INCIDENTS OF TRAVEL IN YUCATAN, John L. Stephens. Classic (1843) exploration of jungles of Yucatan, looking for evidences of Maya civilization. Travel adventures, Mexican and Indian culture, etc. Total of 669pp. 5⅜ x 8½.
20926-1, 20927-X Pa., Two-vol. set $7.90

AMERICAN LITERARY AUTOGRAPHS FROM WASHINGTON IRVING TO HENRY JAMES, Herbert Cahoon, et al. Letters, poems, manuscripts of Hawthorne, Thoreau, Twain, Alcott, Whitman, 67 other prominent American authors. Reproductions, full transcripts and commentary. Plus checklist of all American Literary Autographs in The Pierpont Morgan Library. Printed on exceptionally high-quality paper. 136 illustrations. 212pp. 9⅛ x 12¼.
23548-3 Pa. $12.50

HOLLYWOOD GLAMOUR PORTRAITS, edited by John Kobal. 145 photos capture the stars from 1926-49, the high point in portrait photography. Gable, Harlow, Bogart, Bacall, Hedy Lamarr, Marlene Dietrich, Robert Montgomery, Marlon Brando, Veronica Lake; 94 stars in all. Full background on photographers, technical aspects, much more. Total of 160pp. 8⅜ x 11¼.   23352-9 Pa. $6.00

THE NEW YORK STAGE: FAMOUS PRODUCTIONS IN PHOTO-GRAPHS, edited by Stanley Appelbaum. 148 photographs from Museum of City of New York show 142 plays, 1883-1939. *Peter Pan, The Front Page, Dead End, Our Town,* O'Neill, hundreds of actors and actresses, etc. Full indexes. 154pp. 9½ x 10.   23241-7 Pa. $6.00

DIALOGUES CONCERNING TWO NEW SCIENCES, Galileo Galilei. Encompassing 30 years of experiment and thought, these dialogues deal with geometric demonstrations of fracture of solid bodies, cohesion, leverage, speed of light and sound, pendulums, falling bodies, accelerated motion, etc. 300pp. 5⅜ x 8½.   60099-8 Pa. $4.00

THE GREAT OPERA STARS IN HISTORIC PHOTOGRAPHS, edited by James Camner. 343 portraits from the 1850s to the 1940s: Tamburini, Mario, Caliapin, Jeritza, Melchior, Melba, Patti, Pinza, Schipa, Caruso, Farrar, Steber, Gobbi, and many more—270 performers in all. Index. 199pp. 8⅜ x 11¼.   23575-0 Pa. $7.50

J. S. BACH, Albert Schweitzer. Great full-length study of Bach, life, background to music, music, by foremost modern scholar. Ernest Newman translation. 650 musical examples. Total of 928pp. 5⅜ x 8½. (Available in U.S. only)   21631-4, 21632-2 Pa., Two-vol. set $11.00

COMPLETE PIANO SONATAS, Ludwig van Beethoven. All sonatas in the fine Schenker edition, with fingering, analytical material. One of best modern editions. Total of 615pp. 9 x 12. (Available in U.S. only)
                                23134-8, 23135-6 Pa., Two-vol. set $15.50

KEYBOARD MUSIC, J. S. Bach. Bach-Gesellschaft edition. For harpsichord, piano, other keyboard instruments. English Suites, French Suites, Six Partitas, Goldberg Variations, Two-Part Inventions, Three-Part Sinfonias. 312pp. 8⅛ x 11. (Available in U.S. only)   22360-4 Pa. $6.95

FOUR SYMPHONIES IN FULL SCORE, Franz Schubert. Schubert's four most popular symphonies: No. 4 in C Minor ("Tragic"); No. 5 in B-flat Major; No. 8 in B Minor ("Unfinished"); No. 9 in C Major ("Great"). Breitkopf & Hartel edition. Study score. 261pp. 9⅜ x 12¼.
                                                      23681-1 Pa. $6.50

THE AUTHENTIC GILBERT & SULLIVAN SONGBOOK, W. S. Gilbert, A. S. Sullivan. Largest selection available; 92 songs, uncut, original keys, in piano rendering approved by Sullivan. Favorites and lesser-known fine numbers. Edited with plot synopses by James Spero. 3 illustrations. 399pp. 9 x 12.   23482-7 Pa. $9.95

UNCLE SILAS, J. Sheridan LeFanu. Victorian Gothic mystery novel, considered by many best of period, even better than Collins or Dickens. Wonderful psychological terror. Introduction by Frederick Shroyer. 436pp. 5⅜ x 8½. 21715-9 Pa. $6.00

JURGEN, James Branch Cabell. The great erotic fantasy of the 1920's that delighted thousands, shocked thousands more. Full final text, Lane edition with 13 plates by Frank Pape. 346pp. 5⅜ x 8½.
23507-6 Pa. $4.50

THE CLAVERINGS, Anthony Trollope. Major novel, chronicling aspects of British Victorian society, personalities. Reprint of Cornhill serialization, 16 plates by M. Edwards; first reprint of full text. Introduction by Norman Donaldson. 412pp. 5⅜ x 8½. 23464-9 Pa. $5.00

KEPT IN THE DARK, Anthony Trollope. Unusual short novel about Victorian morality and abnormal psychology by the great English author. Probably the first American publication. Frontispiece by Sir John Millais. 92pp. 6½ x 9¼. 23609-9 Pa. $2.50

RALPH THE HEIR, Anthony Trollope. Forgotten tale of illegitimacy, inheritance. Master novel of Trollope's later years. Victorian country estates, clubs, Parliament, fox hunting, world of fully realized characters. Reprint of 1871 edition. 12 illustrations by F. A. Faser. 434pp. of text. 5⅜ x 8½. 23642-0 Pa. $5.00

YEKL and THE IMPORTED BRIDEGROOM AND OTHER STORIES OF THE NEW YORK GHETTO, Abraham Cahan. Film *Hester Street* based on *Yekl* (1896). Novel, other stories among first about Jewish immigrants of N.Y.'s East Side. Highly praised by W. D. Howells—Cahan "a new star of realism." New introduction by Bernard G. Richards. 240pp. 5⅜ x 8½. 22427-9 Pa. $3.50

THE HIGH PLACE, James Branch Cabell. Great fantasy writer's enchanting comedy of disenchantment set in 18th-century France. Considered by some critics to be even better than his famous *Jurgen*. 10 illustrations and numerous vignettes by noted fantasy artist Frank C. Pape. 320pp. 5⅜ x 8½. 23670-6 Pa. $4.00

ALICE'S ADVENTURES UNDER GROUND, Lewis Carroll. Facsimile of ms. Carroll gave Alice Liddell in 1864. Different in many ways from final Alice. Handlettered, illustrated by Carroll. Introduction by Martin Gardner. 128pp. 5⅜ x 8½. 21482-6 Pa. $2.50

FAVORITE ANDREW LANG FAIRY TALE BOOKS IN MANY COLORS, Andrew Lang. The four Lang favorites in a boxed set—the complete *Red, Green, Yellow* and *Blue* Fairy Books. 164 stories; 439 illustrations by Lancelot Speed, Henry Ford and G. P. Jacomb Hood. Total of about 1500pp. 5⅜ x 8½. 23407-X Boxed set, Pa. $15.95

PRINCIPLES OF ORCHESTRATION, Nikolay Rimsky-Korsakov. Great classical orchestrator provides fundamentals of tonal resonance, progression of parts, voice and orchestra, tutti effects, much else in major document. 330pp. of musical excerpts. 489pp. 6½ x 9¼.   21266-1 Pa. $7.50

TRISTAN UND ISOLDE, Richard Wagner. Full orchestral score with complete instrumentation. Do not confuse with piano reduction. Commentary by Felix Mottl, great Wagnerian conductor and scholar. Study score. 655pp. 8⅛ x 11.   22915-7 Pa. $13.95

REQUIEM IN FULL SCORE, Giuseppe Verdi. Immensely popular with choral groups and music lovers. Republication of edition published by C. F. Peters, Leipzig, n. d. German frontmaker in English translation. Glossary. Text in Latin. Study score. 204pp. 9⅜ x 12¼.
23682-X Pa. $6.00

COMPLETE CHAMBER MUSIC FOR STRINGS, Felix Mendelssohn. All of Mendelssohn's chamber music: Octet, 2 Quintets, 6 Quartets, and Four Pieces for String Quartet. (Nothing with piano is included). Complete works edition (1874-7). Study score. 283 pp. 9⅜ x 12¼.
23679-X Pa. $7.50

POPULAR SONGS OF NINETEENTH-CENTURY AMERICA, edited by Richard Jackson. 64 most important songs: "Old Oaken Bucket," "Arkansas Traveler," "Yellow Rose of Texas," etc. Authentic original sheet music, full introduction and commentaries. 290pp. 9 x 12.   23270-0 Pa. $7.95

COLLECTED PIANO WORKS, Scott Joplin. Edited by Vera Brodsky Lawrence. Practically all of Joplin's piano works—rags, two-steps, marches, waltzes, etc., 51 works in all. Extensive introduction by Rudi Blesh. Total of 345pp. 9 x 12.   23106-2 Pa. $14.95

BASIC PRINCIPLES OF CLASSICAL BALLET, Agrippina Vaganova. Great Russian theoretician, teacher explains methods for teaching classical ballet; incorporates best from French, Italian, Russian schools. 118 illustrations. 175pp. 5⅜ x 8½.   22036-2 Pa. $2.50

CHINESE CHARACTERS, L. Wieger. Rich analysis of 2300 characters according to traditional systems into primitives. Historical-semantic analysis to phonetics (Classical Mandarin) and radicals. 820pp. 6⅛ x 9¼.
21321-8 Pa. $10.00

EGYPTIAN LANGUAGE: EASY LESSONS IN EGYPTIAN HIEROGLYPHICS, E. A. Wallis Budge. Foremost Egyptologist offers Egyptian grammar, explanation of hieroglyphics, many reading texts, dictionary of symbols. 246pp. 5 x 7½. (Available in U.S. only)
21394-3 Clothbd. $7.50

AN ETYMOLOGICAL DICTIONARY OF MODERN ENGLISH, Ernest Weekley. Richest, fullest work, by foremost British lexicographer. Detailed word histories. Inexhaustible. Do not confuse this with *Concise Etymological Dictionary,* which is abridged. Total of 856pp. 6½ x 9¼.
21873-2, 21874-0 Pa., Two-vol. set $12.00

THE AMERICAN SENATOR, Anthony Trollope. Little known, long unavailable Trollope novel on a grand scale. Here are humorous comment
on American vs. English culture, and stunning portrayal of a heroine/
villainess. Superb evocation of Victorian village life. 561pp. 5⅜ x 8½.
                                                23801-6 Pa. $6.00

WAS IT MURDER? James Hilton. The author of *Lost Horizon* and *Good-
bye, Mr. Chips* wrote one detective novel (under a pen-name) which was
quickly forgotten and virtually lost, even at the height of Hilton's fame.
This edition brings it back—a finely crafted public school puzzle resplendent with Hilton's stylish atmosphere. A thoroughly English thriller by
the creator of Shangri-la. 252pp. 5⅜ x 8. (Available in U.S. only)
                                                23774-5 Pa. $3.00

CENTRAL PARK: A PHOTOGRAPHIC GUIDE, Victor Laredo and
Henry Hope Reed. 121 superb photographs show dramatic views of
Central Park: Bethesda Fountain, Cleopatra's Needle, Sheep Meadow, the
Blockhouse, plus people engaged in many park activities: ice skating, bike
riding, etc. Captions by former Curator of Central Park, Henry Hope
Reed, provide historical view, changes, etc. Also photos of N.Y. landmarks
on park's periphery. 96pp. 8½ x 11.   23750-8 Pa. $4.50

NANTUCKET IN THE NINETEENTH CENTURY, Clay Lancaster. 180
rare photographs, stereographs, maps, drawings and floor plans recreate
unique American island society. Authentic scenes of shipwreck, light-
houses, streets, homes are arranged in geographic sequence to provide
walking-tour guide to old Nantucket existing today. Introduction, captions.
160pp. 8⅞ x 11¾.   23747-8 Pa. $6.95

STONE AND MAN: A PHOTOGRAPHIC EXPLORATION, Andreas
Feininger. 106 photographs by *Life* photographer Feininger portray man's
deep passion for stone through the ages. Stonehenge-like megaliths, fortified towns, sculpted marble and crumbling tenements show textures, beauties, fascination. 128pp. 9¼ x 10¾.   23756-7 Pa. $5.95

CIRCLES, A MATHEMATICAL VIEW, D. Pedoe. Fundamental aspects
of college geometry, non-Euclidean geometry, and other branches of mathematics: representing circle by point. Poincare model, isoperimetric property, etc. Stimulating recreational reading. 66 figures. 96pp. 5⅝ x 8¼.
                                                63698-4 Pa. $2.75

THE DISCOVERY OF NEPTUNE, Morton Grosser. Dramatic scientific
history of the investigations leading up to the actual discovery of the
eighth planet of our solar system. Lucid, well-researched book by well-
known historian of science. 172pp. 5⅜ x 8½.   23726-5 Pa. $3.50

THE DEVIL'S DICTIONARY. Ambrose Bierce. Barbed, bitter, brilliant
witticisms in the form of a dictionary. Best, most ferocious satire America
has produced. 145pp. 5⅜ x 8½.   20487-1 Pa. $2.25

ART FORMS IN NATURE, Ernst Haeckel. Multitude of strangely beautiful natural forms: Radiolaria, Foraminifera, jellyfishes, fungi, turtles, bats, etc. All 100 plates of the 19th-century evolutionist's *Kunstformen der Natur* (1904). 100pp. 9⅜ x 12¼. 22987-4 Pa. $5.00

CHILDREN: A PICTORIAL ARCHIVE FROM NINETEENTH-CENTURY SOURCES, edited by Carol Belanger Grafton. 242 rare, copyright-free wood engravings for artists and designers. Widest such selection available. All illustrations in line. 119pp. 8⅜ x 11¼. 23694-3 Pa. $4.00

WOMEN: A PICTORIAL ARCHIVE FROM NINETEENTH-CENTURY SOURCES, edited by Jim Harter. 391 copyright-free wood engravings for artists and designers selected from rare periodicals. Most extensive such collection available. All illustrations in line. 128pp. 9 x 12. 23703-6 Pa. $4.50

ARABIC ART IN COLOR, Prisse d'Avennes. From the greatest ornamentalists of all time—50 plates in color, rarely seen outside the Near East, rich in suggestion and stimulus. Includes 4 plates on covers. 46pp. 9⅜ x 12¼. 23658-7 Pa. $6.00

AUTHENTIC ALGERIAN CARPET DESIGNS AND MOTIFS, edited by June Beveridge. Algerian carpets are world famous. Dozens of geometrical motifs are charted on grids, color-coded, for weavers, needleworkers, craftsmen, designers. 53 illustrations plus 4 in color. 48pp. 8¼ x 11. (Available in U.S. only) 23650-1 Pa. $1.75

DICTIONARY OF AMERICAN PORTRAITS, edited by Hayward and Blanche Cirker. 4000 important Americans, earliest times to 1905, mostly in clear line. Politicians, writers, soldiers, scientists, inventors, industrialists, Indians, Blacks, women, outlaws, etc. Identificatory information. 756pp. 9¼ x 12¾. 21823-6 Clothbd. $40.00

HOW THE OTHER HALF LIVES, Jacob A. Riis. Journalistic record of filth, degradation, upward drive in New York immigrant slums, shops, around 1900. New edition includes 100 original Riis photos, monuments of early photography. 233pp. 10 x 7⅞. 22012-5 Pa. $7.00

NEW YORK IN THE THIRTIES, Berenice Abbott. Noted photographer's fascinating study of city shows new buildings that have become famous and old sights that have disappeared forever. Insightful commentary. 97 photographs. 97pp. 11⅜ x 10. 22967-X Pa. $5.00

MEN AT WORK, Lewis W. Hine. Famous photographic studies of construction workers, railroad men, factory workers and coal miners. New supplement of 18 photos on Empire State building construction. New introduction by Jonathan L. Doherty. Total of 69 photos. 63pp. 8 x 10¾. 23475-4 Pa. $3.00

AMERICAN ANTIQUE FURNITURE, Edgar G. Miller, Jr. The basic coverage of all American furniture before 1840: chapters per item chronologically cover all types of furniture, with more than 2100 photos. Total of 1106pp. 7⅞ x 10¾.   21599-7, 21600-4 Pa., Two-vol. set $17.90

ILLUSTRATED GUIDE TO SHAKER FURNITURE, Robert Meader. Director, Shaker Museum, Old Chatham, presents up-to-date coverage of all furniture and appurtenances, with much on local styles not available elsewhere. 235 photos. 146pp. 9 x 12.   22819-3 Pa. $6.00

ORIENTAL RUGS, ANTIQUE AND MODERN, Walter A. Hawley. Persia, Turkey, Caucasus, Central Asia, China, other traditions. Best general survey of all aspects: styles and periods, manufacture, uses, symbols and their interpretation, and identification. 96 illustrations, 11 in color. 320pp. 6⅛ x 9¼.   22366-3 Pa. $6.95

CHINESE POTTERY AND PORCELAIN, R. L. Hobson. Detailed descriptions and analyses by former Keeper of the Department of Oriental Antiquities and Ethnography at the British Museum. Covers hundreds of pieces from primitive times to 1915. Still the standard text for most periods. 136 plates, 40 in full color. Total of 750pp. 5⅜ x 8½.
23253-0 Pa. $10.00

THE WARES OF THE MING DYNASTY, R. L. Hobson. Foremost scholar examines and illustrates many varieties of Ming (1368-1644). Famous blue and white, polychrome, lesser-known styles and shapes. 117 illustrations, 9 full color, of outstanding pieces. Total of 263pp. 6⅛ x 9¼. (Available in U.S. only)   23652-8 Pa. $6.00

Prices subject to change without notice.

Available at your book dealer or write for free catalogue to Dept. GI, Dover Publications, Inc., 180 Varick St., N.Y., N.Y. 10014. Dover publishes more than 175 books each year on science, elementary and advanced mathematics, biology, music, art, literary history, social sciences and other areas.